"Reading this book is like h expert who patiently and scientific research and wisd there are other books on O with which Dr. Wagner presents information make this comprehensive resource a must-read for parents, school personnel and professionals."

The OCD Newsletter (Newsletter of the Obsessive ⌐   n)

"Dr. Aureen Wagner has compl   on treatment of OCD in children. Her p   rry *Hill* for children with OCD certainly   ans. But *What to do when your Child has OCD*   exactly what to do and what not to do when a child has OCD. Dr. Wagner has done it again! We can only hope that she will continue writing books that share her consummate experience about treating children with anxiety disorders."

John Greist, M.D., Distinguished Senior Scientist, Madison Institute of Medicine, Clinical Professor of Psychiatry, University of Wisconsin Medical School

About the author

Dr. Aureen Pinto Wagner is Director of The Anxiety Wellness Center, in Cary, NC, a member of the Scientific Advisory Board of the International OCD Foundation and Adjunct Associate Professor of Psychiatry at the University of North Carolina at Chapel Hill School of Medicine. Dr. Wagner is a clinical child psychologist whose child-friendly *Worry Hill®* approach to cognitive-behavioral therapy has gained her international recognition. She is the author of several other highly acclaimed books, including: *Worried No More: Help and Hope for Anxious Children, Up and Down the Worry Hill: A Children's Book about Obsessive-Compulsive Disorder and its Treatment* and *Treatment of OCD in Children and Adolescents: Professional's Kit.* The latter two resources and this one comprise the *only* integrated set of resources for children with OCD, their parents, and their therapists.

Dr. Wagner received her education at St. Agnes College, the University of Iowa, Yale University Child Study Center and Brown University. She is a sought-after international speaker and presents workshops for parents, school professionals and clinicians.

Aureen Pinto Wagner, Ph.D.

What to do when your Child has Obsessive-Compulsive Disorder

Strategies and Solutions

A Lighthouse Press book

The information and techniques offered in this book should not be used as a replacement for guidance, consultation, assessment or treatment by a qualified mental health professional.

No part of this book may be reproduced by any process whatsoever without the written permission of the copyright owner.

WORRY HILL is a registered trademark of Lighthouse Press, Inc.

Library of Congress Control Number
00091278
Published by Lighthouse Press, Inc.
Toll free USA 1-888-749-8768
www.Lighthouse-Press.com

Publisher's Cataloging-in-Publication
Wagner, Aureen Pinto.
           What to do when your child has obsessive-compulsive
    disorder : strategies and solutions / by Aureen Pinto
    Wagner
       p. cm.
       ISBN-10: 0-9677347-1-1
       ISBN-13: 978-096773471-2

       1.Obsessive-compulsive disorder in children.
    I.Title.
    RJ506.O25W34 2000   618.92'85227
                                  QBI00-717
Tenth Printing
Printed in the United States of America

Acknowledgements

It is only due to the sharing, caring and wisdom of my patients and their parents, my family and colleagues that this book has traveled the road from fantasy to reality. I am deeply grateful to the many children and families with whom I have worked over the past dozen years. In allowing me to help them help themselves, they shared with me their anguish and their triumphs, their deepest insights and personal moments on the journey to recovery from OCD. The strategies and solutions I describe in this book grew out of our work together.

I owe thanks to all those gifted psychiatrists and psychologists from whose pioneering work my knowledge of OCD and Cognitive-Behavioral Therapy is derived, including Drs. Lee Baer, David Barlow, Aaron Beck, Edna Foa, John Greist, Henrietta Leonard, Michael Jenike, Philip Kendall, John March, Judith Rapoport, Jeffrey Schwartz, Susan Swedo and others. Many teachers and mentors over the years, including Greta Francis, Sr. Marie Evelyn, Sr. John Francis, Lilly Kamath, Olga Noronha, Jacob Sines, Mewa Singh, Sara Sparrow and Elsie Tharien inspired in me the thirst for knowledge and the quest for the best.

My friends and colleagues including Laurence Guttmacher, M.D., Emily Richardson, Ph.D. and Martha Spital, MSW, generously gave of their time and expertise to provide invaluable criticism and suggestions for making this book scientifically sound yet accessible to parents and families. Thomas Williams, M.D., Ph.D., shared his dual expertise as a child psychiatrist and psychopharmacologist in reviewing the chapter on medications.

I have been blessed with a wonderful family without whose love, support and guidance none of this would have been possible. My parents, Baptist and Winifred Pinto, believed in me enough to let me travel half way around the world to pursue my dreams. My sister Merlyn lent her sharp eyes and skills to this manuscript as she perused it for accuracy and presentation. My siblings Adrian, Jean and Kevin have provided support and encouragement.

And there are three others who make all the time and sacrifices this book involved worthwhile. My husband and soul mate Scott has been behind me through the ups and downs of this project with his unwavering confidence, love and support. This book evolved, grew and came together with the countless hours he gave to being a critic, proofreader and consultant. Our children, Catherine and Ethan, are the best gifts I have been given. I am indebted to them for the time they gave up with me during the long days and months of writing. The joy and love they give me is unconditional, free and so forgiving. They light up the days gone by and those to come. As this book comes to completion, I look forward eagerly to giving back the time I borrowed from them.

To Scott, Catherine and Ethan

The joy of my life

Also by the author

Up and Down the Worry Hill: A Children's Book about Obsessive-Compulsive Disorder and its Treatment

Companion book to:
What to do when your Child has Obsessive-Compulsive Disorder.
See the back of this book for ordering information.

Worried No More: Help and Hope for Anxious Children

For parents, school personnel and healthcare professionals.
See the back of this book for ordering information.

For more information and reviews of Dr. Wagner's books, please visit www.Lighthouse-Press.com

Table of Contents

List of Tables

List of Figures

Introduction

As a parent, you have a vision for your child when you bring him or her into the world. A childhood of carefree frolic and laughter, a perfect world to live in, dreams to chase after and every opportunity to succeed. That vision doesn't include Obsessive-Compulsive Disorder (OCD). No parent is prepared for OCD. You are alarmed and helpless as you witness your child's metamorphosis through a peculiar illness that torments his mind. He is caught in a tailspin of absurd and frightening fears and rituals. OCD steals the pleasures of childhood from him. It places the burden of Atlas on his shoulders and destroys the innocence of his youth. It robs you of your dreams for him. It's not what you hoped for or expected.

Tried and true parenting skills don't seem to help now. You learn that when your child is plagued by doubt, common sense and reasoning do not assuage her fears. When she is begging for reassurance, guarantees do not help. When she is scrubbing and disinfecting, having a floor that's clean enough to eat off doesn't meet the standard. You are often in despair, not knowing how to break through the vicious grip of OCD on your child. When you have a chance to be alone with your thoughts, worry and fear pervade. What is this crazy illness? Is there an end to this ordeal? Will my child be "normal" again? Can she ever regain control of her mind? What can we do? What did I do wrong? Why does my child have to suffer this pain? Why us? What does the future hold? Can anybody help us?

Parents have looked to doctors and therapists to help their child overcome OCD. Sad to say, the history of OCD is fraught with blame and shame; the professionals they trusted to help were not able to deliver on their promises. But this is an era of hope born of new awareness. Rapid and astounding developments in understanding OCD and its treatment, both in adults and children, have sprung highly effective treatments. Cognitive-Behavioral Therapy (CBT) and medications now offer children and their families highly powerful ways to bring OCD under control. Now is a time for great hope and optimism.

For many years, parents have been delegated the role of passive onlookers in their child's recovery from OCD. Their potential as "natural" resources most easily available and accessible to the child has been overlooked. They have been left to their own devices to figure out how to get their child from one day to the next, from home to school, from homework to bed. The tide is turning. Professionals are beginning to recognize that parents have a wealth of expertise about their child that is second to none. What better way to help children learn to overcome OCD than to garner the help of their parents in their recovery? You know your child better than anyone else. You may be the first one to know when things don't seem so right with your child. You may even be the first to suggest that it might be OCD. You have raised, guided and carried your child through many challenges in life thus far. You can get him through this one too.

This book offers you the blueprint to be an active helper in your child's journey back from the land of OCD. You will learn how to work collaboratively with your child's therapist to help your child help himself. This book is both for neophytes and "veterans" dealing with OCD, for parents and for the professionals who work with children.

When I set out to write this book, there were several crucial messages I wanted to convey loud and clear to parents: You and your child are not alone. Your child is one of millions of children with OCD. There are many parents who walk in your shoes. OCD is not a bunch of childish worries and silly habits your child engages in deliberately. It is a legitimate illness. Your child is not crazy. He is still a rational human being, sometimes tyrannized by an irrational illness. You did not cause your child's OCD. Nor did he or she. No one is to blame. There is no reason to be ashamed of having OCD in your family. Early diagnosis and treatment may save your child a future of anguish and torment. With the right help, your child can learn to overcome OCD and regain a "normal" life again. You and your child have the power of choice. Your child can choose to overcome OCD by his thoughts and actions. You play a very crucial role in your child's recovery. You will make mistakes along the way. It's okay to make mistakes. You must have hope. You must give your child hope.

I have imparted these messages to the parents of my patients and they have appreciated hearing them so directly. One parent found it helpful to remind herself of these messages often. She wrote them on an index card that she carried in her purse. When she wavered, doubted and despaired, she reached for the card to ground herself in the facts, not the feelings.

With this book, I hope to arm you with a practical approach to helping your child recover from OCD. The book is organized into two parts. Part I (Chapters 1 to 6) covers the essential facts about OCD, its diagnosis, causes and treatments. Knowing the facts is the first step to mastery of OCD. In Part I, I discuss the various ways in which OCD can invade your child's thoughts and behaviors and how to tell OCD apart from normal fears or habits and other conditions. You will learn about the *Vicious Cycle of Avoidance* that fuels OCD and about treatment with Exposure and Ritual Prevention (ERP). ERP helps break your child free of the cycle of avoidance. You will learn about the medication options available today for OCD and when it may be appropriate to consider them for your child.

Part II (Chapters 7-14) lays out the master plan and a child-friendly approach to helping your child overcome OCD. Recovery is a process, not an event. I present a series of steps that will help you systematically tackle that process to work in your favor. You will be provided with the map and the instructions to make this journey. You will learn how to take charge of your lives, take back control from OCD and take care of yourself so that you can take better care of your child. You will also find strategies for the unique parenting challenges that OCD brings and an approach to helping your child through schooling issues. Each chapter ends with answers to parents' *Frequently-Asked Questions*.

The material in this book comes from the scientific literature on OCD as well as my experience of the past dozen years in treating children with OCD and their families. When I look back on how it all started, I recall that I wanted to become a child psychologist when I was fifteen years old. Of course, I knew next to nothing about the profession at the time, but I had always been fond of children and the idea of helping children appealed to me. Perhaps I thought that I could continue to play with children while having a respectable occupation to claim. I could play while the sign on the door said, "At work." Perhaps I imagined myself as a fairy godmother who could wave away the troubles of childhood with a magic wand.

In the years since then, I have learned that I could not have chosen a better profession. It turned out to be a little different than I had imagined. The long and arduous years of training to become a child psychologist didn't seem like play at all. I learned that I couldn't wave the children's problems away like a fairy godmother. What I did learn was that I could help children find the magic and the power within them to help themselves. And the children have risen to the occasion. They have taught me that they have far more courage, forgiveness and resilience than I ever imagined. They just need help unlocking the vitality that is within them. They are immensely relieved when they feel understood and accepted. They are eager, enthusiastic and creative learners. In many ways, I have learned more from them than they have learned from me.

Along the way, I became a parent myself. With the sublime joy of being a mother came a deep sense of humility about exactly how little I knew about the charge one is given as a parent. I had a new appreciation and respect for the challenges that parents of children with OCD or any other illness have to face. I have been deeply moved by the numerous personal tragedies and victories that these children and their parents encounter daily. Things that most families take for granted are an enormity for them. I am in awe of the courage, persistence and hope that they retain in spite of it all. Seeing them rise above their darkest hours has been incredibly inspiring and gratifying.

It was my little patients who inspired within me the idea of the *Worry Hill*. I was searching for a "universal" way to talk to my patients, young and not-so-young, about OCD and Exposure therapy. It was a pleasant summer and it seemed like all the children who walked through my doors one week were eager to tell me about their exploits on their bicycles. One child was recounting his heroic ride up a hill near his home. It came to me then. I talked about OCD looming in front of them like a big hill—a Worry Hill. I talked about what it would be like to get to the other side of that hill and to have OCD behind them. It would mean having to ride up that hill and all the way to the top before they could coast down the other side. Facing their fears would be like riding their bicycles up that Worry Hill. It would be tough going, but only if they stuck it out would they get to the top of that hill. Then, they could revel in the thrill of coasting down the other side of the hill. When they faced their fears, they could get past them—they could coast down the Worry Hill.

My patients liked it. Their parents liked it. It made perfect sense to them. They urged me to write it in a book for children with OCD. Thus was born *Up and Down the Worry Hill: A Children's Book about OCD and its Treatment*. This book followed. It is based on the metaphor of the Worry Hill and is the companion guide to the children's book. In this book, I discuss how your child can RIDE up the Worry Hill while you RALLY for him. Your therapist will be your guide during this journey. Read this book in conjunction with *Up and Down the Worry Hill*. As you read these books, you will learn a language of metaphors with which to talk to your child about OCD and treatment.

With this book, I hope to reach many more parents than I can possibly hope to have in my office. I wish to convey the messages and the strategies that have helped my patients and their parents and the many others who have benefited from the same principles from which I derived my approach. You will come across many people in your lives who do not understand OCD. They may be people you know and trust, like close friends and family members. They may be your child's doctor, teacher or school counselor. Although the dark ages of OCD are behind us, we have not disseminated the word as widely and well as we should. That is part of the goal of this book—to spread the word about OCD, set the record straight and take back the stigma of an illness that is no one's fault.

The pages of this book reflect my understanding and application of the current scientific literature on OCD in children and adolescents. I have attempted to provide accurate information and to be as complete and relevant as possible, although it is not possible to anticipate or address every issue that families with OCD face. The strategies described in this book are guidelines, not absolutes. Each child and family is different. Your situation and your child's situation, while similar to those described in this book, will be unique to you. A therapist's help is necessary to apply the treatment strategies described in this book to your situation. The information here does not replace the help of a qualified mental health professional, which is strongly recommended for children with OCD.

The stories of OCD described here are true, but the names of the children and parents have been changed to protect their identity. I am grateful to the children and their parents who bravely agreed to allow others a glimpse into deeply personal moments of their lives—to help other children and parents. "He" and "she" are used interchangeably in the text to refer to children and are not meant to suggest a specific gender.

I hope that as you read this book and put it into action, you will experience relief, affirmation and a tremendous sense of hope. I hope that you will have a new found understanding of your child's illness and a deep compassion for him and the other millions of children of today and yesterday who have suffered quietly, without the help and hope that is now available; that you will become a messenger of hope to other children with OCD by sharing this message with your child's school, doctors, family and friends; that you will accept and use the power of choice to help your child recover the joys of childhood; that your child will be able to live life to the fullest *in spite of* OCD. Your vision for your child is not lost. It is just a little different than you imagined.

Part I:

The Essential Facts

about

Obsessive-Compulsive Disorder

in children and adolescents

Chapter 1

The Prison Of The Mind

Back almost three years ago, I started doing these strange rituals. I constantly had fears that I would get someone sick by not washing my hands enough. These fears came to my mind after I heard on the news that hepatitis is spread by not washing your hands properly before handling foods. At first, I washed a few extra times so I would feel more secure. Then, before I knew it, I was washing my hands for 30 minutes. I never really knew why I had to wash for so long, but I couldn't stop. Then I began to have fears that I was not washing enough in the shower. My showers became 45 minutes long. My life began to revolve around the bathroom. And let me remind you, my mother had to help me wipe, shower and wash or I'd never stop. I was very depressed...

Maria, age 12

I used to be so scared all the time. Scared that if I didn't do certain things, something bad would happen. My parents kept asking me what was the bad thing that I was afraid of, but I couldn't say. I didn't even know. Something told me that if I spit on my hands and rubbed it on my eyes, it would make the bad thing go away. So I was spitting and wiping all the time, till my mouth was dry and my eyes were red and stinging. I had to drink water all the time and I started getting sores on my mouth. I couldn't do my school work because I was spitting and wiping like every couple of minutes. The other kids called me "cry baby" because my eyes were red and wet. Then, I had to arrange the silverware on the table so that each fork was the same distance from the next one, and I couldn't eat anything until I had cut it up into tiny pieces to see if there was any glass in it. I don't even know why I thought there would be glass in it. No one else was weird like me.

Paul, age 15

When I was in kindergarten, I had a counting problem. I had to count even when I was talking. Back when my counting problem began, I couldn't stand it any longer. I had to count the stairs and people and things on TV. I had to count almost everywhere I went. My biggest problem started near the end of kindergarten. When I wore underwear, it felt like they would fall down, so I had to keep pulling them up every minute, like 80 times a day. I had to wear bathing suits to school under my clothes because I couldn't wear underwear. The same thing happened with my socks, so I stopped wearing socks. These problems made me frustrated and upset.

Alyssa, age 7

Maria, Paul and Alyssa have Obsessive-Compulsive Disorder (OCD), an extraordinary illness that affects children, adolescents and adults from all walks of life. They were going about the business of being "regular" children in "regular" families when strange worries and habits invaded their minds and their actions. Although they seemed to choose to do these bizarre rituals, they didn't really have a choice. They knew that something was terribly wrong but could neither understand nor explain it. There were no words in their vocabularies to describe the torment of obsessions or the stranglehold of compulsions. They were prisoners of their minds.

OCD can happen to children who are otherwise as normal as normal can be. If you were not privy to the fact that Maria, Paul and Alyssa had OCD, you would never know from seeing them at school, at play, or at the store. You would not have any inkling that their minds were paralyzed with bizarre and frightening thoughts. OCD is more common than you may know. Between one and three in every one hundred children is afflicted with this strange illness of the mind. That amounts to about three to five children in an average-sized elementary school and about 20 children in a large high school.

This chapter will help you understand the nature of OCD and the many ways, obvious and obscure, in which it can permeate the minds, behaviors and feelings of children. If you are not sure your child's behaviors are OCD, Chapter 2 will help you tell normal worries and habits apart from OCD. If you believe your child may have OCD, Chapter 3 will walk you through the steps in the diagnosis of OCD.

WHAT IS OCD?

Like Maria, Paul and Alyssa, children and adults with OCD are subjected to unwarranted and unwelcome obsessions and compulsions. *Obssions* are unfounded and upsetting *thoughts, images* or *urges* that are unrelenting, uncontrollable and unstoppable. They are like a broken record that replays endlessly. Maria's obsession was the fear of contracting hepatitis and Alyssa had the uncomfortable feeling that her clothing would fall down. Paul was haunted by the possibility of undefined "bad luck." Frantic efforts to stop obsessions are often in vain because stopping obsessions is not merely a matter of desire, will power or strength.

Compulsions, also known as *rituals*, are deliberate physical or mental *actions* that are propelled by obsessions; they are geared towards relieving the worry and discomfort created by the obsessions. They appear to be senseless habits that are excessive and unreasonable. Maria washed her hands and cleaned herself copiously; Alyssa counted until she was out of breath and pulled up underwear diligently. Paul spent his day going *spit, wipe, spit, wipe, spit again, wipe again.* Ironically, although compulsions are far from pleasant, they are repeated with intensity because they relieve anxiety at the moment. Your child may be miserable and crying, yet she cannot stop the rituals. She *must* do them or else... For a little while, rituals make her world right again.

The sad fact is that although OCD can be successfully treated, many children still suffer unnecessarily because they remain undiagnosed, misdiagnosed or untreated. Not enough parents and not even enough healthcare providers know about the effective treatments that are now available. This book will help you understand the right treatments and arm you with the tools to give your child the best chance at recovery.

The shadow of doubt

Why are rituals repeated? Why does Maria need to wash for hours? Doesn't she feel clean after one good wash? Can't Alyssa *see* that her socks aren't slipping down? Yes, but...Doubt is the underlying driver of rituals. It is the hallmark of OCD.

As far back as 1875, the French referred to OCD as the *folie du doute— the doubting disease*. Living with OCD is like living in the shadow of doubt; doubt that follows your child around everywhere, all day. Worse yet, unlike real shadows, the shadows of OCD stay with him even after the sun has set. They torment him at bedtime, perhaps more than during the day. Relentless, nagging doubt about anything from the mundane and trivial to the critical and life threatening is a key ingredient of OCD. There is an insatiable need to be certain; a need that is unyielding to logic or common sense. It is sheer torture to live one's life pursuing certitude in a world that is full of uncertainty. In John F. Kennedy's words, "The one unchangeable certainty is that nothing is certain or unchangeable." We cannot even be sure there will be a tomorrow; we must learn to live with this ambiguity.

If you don't have OCD, washing your hands is hardly an ordeal. A quick rinse of your hands and you feel clean enough. Most likely, you've given it as much thought or effort as you do to breathing. But if you have OCD, the feelings of being clean or being "okay" are perpetually elusive. You are plagued by doubt—"*Is it really?*" "*But what if?*" "*It just could happen.*" The exhausting process of verifying, checking, and assuaging these doubts can consume hours or days on end, derailing the ability to do much of anything else. Maria's hands never felt *clean enough* and Alyssa's underwear never *tight enough*. For Paul, it was *not good enough*. For the OCD sufferer, *it is never enough*.

Sixteen-year-old Thomas finally got his driver's license! He had been eagerly awaiting his freedom and was looking forward to driving to his job, to visiting friends and simply to "cruising" around town. But it wasn't going to be that way. He was driving to school the next day, carefully following all the signs, when he drove over a bump in the road. He didn't like the feel of that bump and couldn't stop thinking about it. It must have been a pothole that he didn't see. It felt bigger than a pothole, almost a thud. Perhaps he had hit something lying on the road. What if he had run over and killed a small animal? Worse yet, what if it was a person? Could it have been a child that he didn't see? He knew that didn't make sense. But the doubt kept nagging him. Perhaps the child had been hidden by the bush on the corner and had crossed the road out of his view.

Now he was really worried that he had run over the child. He had to go back and check to be sure. That would make him feel better. He turned around and drove back over his path. No bodies, no dead animals. He breathed a sigh of relief. He was on his way when that doubt crept in again. Just one more time, he thought. If I just go back this time, I'll know for sure. Then I won't have to worry about it anymore. Thomas drove the route again, slowly and deliberately. His heart was in his mouth, not quite prepared to encounter the mangled body he was quite sure he would find. No body. "Phew, okay, I've got to get out of here," he thought. Frantically, he stepped on the gas. He was going to speed out of this trap. The car lurched forward, bumping back and forth. Thomas drove away. I'm done, he thought. I did it. He almost made it home, when that creeping voice was back…"The cops are knocking at your door, looking for the hit-and-run driver." Thomas collapsed on the couch in tears, defeated by his own thoughts.

An anxiety disorder

Although OCD seems to involve faulty thinking, it is not a *thought* disorder. It is an anxiety disorder. It involves the fear of uncertainty and of catastrophe. OCD is all about *feeling* unsure, despite every assurance to the contrary. OCD sufferers are as capable of lucid thinking as anyone else is. OCD expert Dr. Judith Rapoport likens this incongruity to having "a foreign body in their otherwise quite sensible minds." Yet, they can be simultaneously logical and irrational in ways that baffle parents and family members. If your child is sometimes full of common sense, and at other times completely absurd, you are not alone. If you have had the sneaking doubt in the back of your mind, "*Does she have control over this? Can she turn it on and off?*" you are in good company. Even children with OCD are usually painfully aware that their minds have become irrational. They may continue to function at home, school and the playground, silently enduring the torment and pain.

The OCD paradox

Ironically, although rituals seem to bring immediate relief from the anxiety caused by obsessions, rituals eventually result in *more*, not less anxiety and fear. When rituals reduce anxiety, your child begins to believe that the rituals actually prevented the obsessive fear from coming true. *"I stepped to the left and then to the right three times, so now my mom won't die in a plane crash."* Next, she begins to believe that rituals are the only way to get rid of obsessions. Therefore, if she doesn't do the rituals, her fears will come true. Is she willing to take the chance that you will die if she doesn't do her little hop-skip-dance? Unlikely. So she continues to believe her obsessions and appeases them with rituals. Unfortunately, when she's caught up in her fears, she's only focused on relief *now*. She's hardly thinking about long-term implications. Before long, your child is trapped in a vicious cycle of obsessions and compulsions. Chapter 4 describes the *Vicious Cycle of OCD* in more detail and Chapter 5 offers an effective approach to break the cycle.

Avoidance strengthens fear

If you avoid something that makes you afraid, would that not take care of the problem? On the contrary, avoidance fuels obsessions in much the same way as compulsions do. When you avoid something, you do not give yourself the chance to verify if your fear is justifiable or exaggerated. And yet, at the moment, avoiding the fear is just a lot easier. Paul merely stopped eating when dissecting his food got to be too cumbersome. Alyssa stopped wearing underwear and socks altogether because it was easier than having to pull them up all day. She averted the problem of underwear by wearing a one-piece swimsuit that could not slip off her waist. Did she overcome her fear? No, she merely avoided it.

THE MANY FACES OF OCD IN CHILDREN

One of the many perplexing things about OCD is that it isn't always easy to recognize. Most people have heard about the classic hand washing or the sensational story of a man trapped in his house full of hoarded newspapers. It may surprise you to know that there are a myriad of different manifestations of OCD. Perhaps your daughter is deeply religious and prays for hours on end; you may be shocked when the doctor tells you she has OCD. Although each child's obsessions and compulsions have a personal slant to them, there are some broad categories into which most symptoms fall. The common unifying thread is that of uncontrollable urges and repeated rituals woven with endless doubt. Most children with OCD have multiple obsessions accompanied by many rituals. Common childhood obsessions and compulsions are described below; Table 1 provides specific examples.

Common obsessions

Many obsessions are simply gross exaggerations of concerns that occupy all of us, such as germs, disease and harm to loved ones. On the other hand, others appear to be unrealistic, illogical and incredible, such as urges to confess or to have things be "just right." Older children and adolescents tend to have more specific fears such as getting ill with the flu or AIDS. In young children, obsessions may be vague and difficult to gauge.

❖ *Fear of germs, contamination and disease*

Concern about germs, contamination, dirt, disease or death is probably the most universal of OCD fears. Fears may pertain to specific illnesses such as rabies or hepatitis, contaminants, chemicals, cleaning substances, poisons or environmental toxins. Fears of diseases that receive coverage in the media, such as AIDS, cancer, rabies or hepatitis are common. Whereas some children fear harm to themselves, many are more fearful of contaminating others such as parents, classmates or pets. It is not uncommon to have a fear of vomiting in school, the school bus or in public places. Preoccupations about being unclean or soiled after using the bathroom are also common. Sometimes, children may be unable to name a specific fear but describe it only as a strong sense of uneasiness.

❖ Fear of "bad things" happening

Children with this type of obsession experience an ominous sense of impending doom, calamity and tragedy. Sometimes, the fears are specific and graphic, such as a parent dying of a heart attack or in a car accident, a fire that destroys the house or intruders breaking in. More often than not, it is a vague sense of uneasiness, e.g., "*Something bad will happen.*" There may also be a displaced and unfounded sense of personal responsibility for failing to prevent harm or injury to others. "*If I don't tap three times, it will be my fault if my Mom gets sick.*" Children may also be terrified by the urge, deliberately or unwittingly, to hurt themselves or an unsuspecting victim for no apparent reason. They cannot trust themselves around sharp or heavy objects such as knives, forks or rocks and avoid them with abject fear. Lest you are concerned, there is usually no basis in reality for these fears—OCD sufferers are terrified they will act on their impulses, but almost never do. (See *Frequently Asked Questions* at the end of this chapter for more information on urges to hurt others).

❖ Need for symmetry, precision and closure

Children often describe this urge as an inexplicable need to feel "*just so.*" There is an overpowering internal sense that the balance, order, place, frequency or position of something is disturbed and must be corrected. Something that was said, read, written or touched was not "just right," "even" or complete. The touch, feel, texture, sound or smell of something is intensely disturbing until it is "fixed." You may watch your child in disbelief as he agonizes over these strange and idiosyncratic rules that don't make any sense to you. The compulsions that generate closure include repeating the activity, touching, counting or arranging, described in the next section, *Common Compulsions*.

❖ Urge to tell, confess, ask, or know with certainty

Some children with OCD experience the urge to tell someone, usually a parent, the intimate details of what they are thinking, ranging from the trivial to the bizarre. This may extend to the need to "confess" minor transgressions that they perceive as major and unforgivable. A passing unkind thought about another person or the fear that they have insulted someone by their thoughts or actions may create great angst. Frequently, children with OCD feel the urge to know nonessential matters with certainty. They cannot rest easy until they know every detail of the schedule, some factual detail, what is being served for dinner, or every nuance of a conversation.

❖ *Saving and hoarding*

A child with hoarding obsessions may be mortally afraid of losing or throwing away things that may be needed sometime or somehow in the indefinite future. Some children are not even able to explain why they hoard. Don't be alarmed if your child won't part with his thread-bare baby blanket, a well thumbed-through book or a broken wind-up toy. That's not OCD; that's normal sentimental behavior. If your child has hoarding OCD, he will be holding on to what most of us would consider fit for the trash such as candy wrappers, stones, old shoelaces, or scraps of paper.

❖ *Moral dilemmas and religious preoccupations*

Also known as *scrupulosity*, this form of obsession involves fears of offending higher powers, committing unforgivable sins, having blasphemous "evil" thoughts and blurting out obscenities or unkind words. Children may ruminate over imperceptible distinctions between "right" and "wrong" for seemingly trivial matters. They adhere strictly to rules that are interpreted in all-or-none terms. They become quite upset when unsuspecting friends or family callously disregard "the rules." For isntance, some children may watch the speed guage of the car like a hawk, in nervous anticipation of the parent exceeding the speed limit by two or three miles her hour. They are so burdened by worrying about, "Is it the *right* thing to do?" that they are unable to derive pleasure from normal childhood pastimes. Older children and adolescents may be plagued with existential concerns: "*Am I real? Do I have a soul? Do I have faith?*"

Table 1: Common Obsessions and Compulsions in Children

Obsessions	Compulsions (Rituals)
Fear of germs/contamination/disease: Louis is afraid that he will contract rabies from animals.	Louis washes his hands copiously, changes his clothes and disinfects his shoes after stepping outdoors, even if it is only to the car, with no any contact with an animal. If he sees an animal, he cleanes all over again. He insists that family members do likewise. Louis refuses to go into the back yard and repeatedly asks if he has rabies.
Fear of harm/danger: Lisa worries that her father will die, but she is not sure how it will happen.	Lisa checks on her father's whereabouts, asks for reassurance regarding his safety, says a series of prayers every hour, touches the walls three times and refuses to say goodbye.
Urge for symmetry, precision and closure: Scott feels an intense internal discomfort that he can't quite describe because things don't appear to be even or balanced.	Scott must repeat his actions until things are "right." He touches objects, goes through doorways and gets in and out of bed over and over again. He brushes his hair with 24 even strokes, steps on the carpet with his left foot first, and climbs the stairs sideways.
Urge to tell, ask, confess or know: Dante must know every detail of the day's schedule.	Dante starts his day by asking his mother, "What are we doing today?" If she leaves out a minute detail, he insists that she start from the beginning. It doesn't matter that he already knows the schedule and that it's the same everyday.
Saving/hoarding: Hannah is very upset when she can't find something because she is afraid it is lost or was thrown away. She is afraid she won't have it when she needs it.	Hannah saves pages of homework, school projects, artwork, letters, receipts, candy wrappers and broken furniture. She refuses to give away outgrown clothing and shoes, and checks the garbage twice a day to make sure nothing got away. She is tearful on garbage collection day.

Table 1: Common Obsessions and Compulsions in Children

Moral/religious preoccupations: Emily fears she will be responsible for "bad things"happening if she doesn't follow the rules.	Emily "confesses" each and every thought she has to her mother, asks if it was right or wrong and apologizes numerous times for trivial things.
Sexual or forbidden thoughts: Nicole has uncontrollable images of God as "evil" and a "wish" that someone will die.	Nicole prays several times a day, asking for forgiveness, confesses all her thoughts, and has to immediately think a "good" thought to replace and "fix" the bad thought.
Obsessive slowness: Brian believes he must be methodical and systematic when he gets ready for school.	Getting dressed takes Brian an hour each morning. He lays his shirt and shorts out and smoothes out the creases. If they don't smooth the right way, he must put them back in the drawer and start all over again. Every step involves careful deliberation.
Magical thinking: Nancy believes that she will become "fat"or a "bad person" if she wears a blue sweater.	Nancy spends hours choosing clothing that doesn't have blue in it; she checks repeatedly for blue specks or threads. She walks through doorways and touches walls a "right" number of times.

❖ *Sexual and "forbidden" thoughts*

Older children and adolescents may experience this form of OCD, which is not to be confused with commonplace adolescent fantasies. A common theme is the fear of being homosexual, which may be triggered by events as innocuous as looking at a picture of a same sex person in a magazine or making eye contact with one. The ugly thoughts that send shivers down the spine are then followed by endless doubt, with no basis in reality, about whether he might have been aroused, sought out the arousal, or even acted upon homosexual urges. Other sexual themes may include constant images of genitals or "perverted" sexual acts. These OCD thoughts are extremely distasteful and disgusting to the person; there is no pleasure or enjoyment derived from them. Sexual obsessions are almost never acted upon, although the sufferer is petrified of doing so.

❖ *Obsessive slowness*

All obsessions and compulsions slow down the person, but for some, slowness itself is the problem. Obsessive slowness involves approaching routine activities with protracted deliberation. Simple daily routines take hours to complete, as they must be executed very precisely. If disturbed, the activity is resumed and the patterns are repeated. Other rituals are usually not involved. Obsessive slowness may be related to indecisiveness, "just right" feelings or *mental rituals* (see *Common Compulsions*).

❖ *Magical thinking*

Children may become preoccupied with lucky or unlucky numbers, colors, words, actions, sayings or superstitions, and link them to catastrophe or amorphos "bad things" happening. The child truly believes and lives by these rules and consequences. Some children believe that the mere act of thinking results in the realization of a feared event. Peter feared that merely thinking of a "bad" person such as an unlikable classmate would make him like that classmate. Robert was afraid he would get sick if he wore clothes in which he had previously been sick, even though the clothes had since been washed.

Common compulsions

Obsessions are typically accompanied by the compulsions that are listed below but there is no one-to-one correspondence between specific obsessions and compulsions. Many obsessions may be expressed through a variety of compulsions and vice versa.

❖ *Washing, cleaning and grooming*

If your child has obsessions about germs, contamination or disease, you will most likely encounter him engaged in excessive washing and disinfecting of hands, body or possessions. Other rituals may include showering, brushing teeth, toilet routines such as repeated wiping or fastidious cleaning of personal objects and household items. In severe cases, physical injury such as bleeding or chapped hands may be incurred from excessive washing and cleaning, chafed or torn skin from excessive wiping or drying and bleeding gums from vigorous brushing. In addition to rituals, there may be strong avoidance of triggers such as doorknobs, sick people, cleaning supplies or other possible contaminants.

❖ *Repeating, retracing and redoing*

Routine activities take on new meaning if your child has these rituals. The urge to feel "just right" drives children to correct actions, events or thoughts that were not completed properly. A child may repeatedly walk through doorways, go up and down stairs, get dressed, turn pages in a book, read words or sentences, erase or re-write until it is "correct," and the accompanying uneasiness is relieved. Adam drank a sip of water from five different glasses each night before he went to bed to prevent bad luck.

❖ *Touching or tapping*

Younger children, especially young males, commonly display the ritual of touching or tapping doors, walls, objects, furniture etc. It is usually related to the need for evenness, "just so" feelings or averting bad luck.

❖ *Checking*

Checking rituals are geared towards preventing irrecoverable errors that may lead to calamity. Children may check to see if they have everything they might need in their lockers, backpacks and desks, if the doors and windows are locked, and if items are in the same location or position as they were left. When there is a fear of disease, children may physically check or feel various body parts for growths, rashes or tenderness. They may ask their parents to check them or ask to see the doctor frequently.

❖ *Counting*

Counting is associated both with the need to avert danger or harm, as well as with the urge for symmetry, closure or evenness. Children may count objects or words in a book, use specific numbers, or count in specific sequences or multiples of numbers. Lucky, unlucky or "magical" numbers are also commonly used to avert danger and harm.

❖   *Ordering/arranging*

Ordering rituals are usually related to the need for symmetry, sequence or evenness. Children may arrange items in specific patterns that may not make intuitive or logical sense to others. Your child may insist that the bed covers are folded at a specific distance from the pillow or that the stuffed animals must be arranged in a specific sequence. She may have to arrange food on the plate so that different foods do not touch each other, eat foods in a certain order or alternate a specific number of bites or sips.

❖   *Reassurance seeking*

It is normal and natural for any child to seek comfort and reassurance when afraid or to ask numerous questions when curious. Curiosity is a good thing and fear is normal. But children with OCD take questioning to a different plane altogether because they are filled with doubt and uncertainty. OCD questions often pertain to safety or health. *"Promise me I'll be okay. I won't die tonight, will I?" "Are sea creatures going to come through the shower spigot?" "How can you be sure there are no chemicals in the soup?" "At what time will you be home today?" "What time is it?" "Did I do something wrong?" "Are you sure I didn't say something mean to you?"* When you are exasperated after answering the same questions repeatedly, you realize that the facts are not what your child is after.

❖   *Confessing and apologizing*

A close cousin of reassurance seeking is the compulsion to confess and apologize—profusely and continuously—for just about everything or nothing at all. Typically, this ritual is driven by scrupulosity and the anxiety of having sinned or erred, when, in reality, the child has not violated any moral or social rules. *"I had an angry thought about Jamie," "I'm sorry, just in case I did it," "Forgive me for touching you,"* and *"Did I just say a mean word?"* are the familiar echoes of this compulsion. The discomfort of the obsession is not quieted until atonement has been done.

❖   *Hoarding*

Hoarding is a particularly challenging compulsion, because it violates so many social norms. Fortunately, it is less common in children than it is among adults. Children may collect items such as outgrown clothing, worn sneakers, rocks, leaves or gift-wrap. They become very upset if others try to throw out or disturb their collection.

❖ *Mental rituals*

Compulsions are generally noticeable habits and actions but can also be "invisible" or hidden. Known as mental rituals, these compulsions include thoughts, prayers, counting, or reciting words and phrases silently. Jimmy has violent thoughts about a friend being stabbed to death, so he says an elaborate set of specific prayers to keep his friends safe from harm. The prayers are the mental rituals that reduce his anxiety. Mental rituals often go unrecognized, and can be confusing because they may be difficult to tell apart from obsessions. The difference is that obsessions are the *bad thoughts* and mental rituals are designed to *correct* the bad thoughts. Whereas obsessions are involuntary, uncontrollable and increase anxiety, mental rituals are purposeful and decrease anxiety.

SHIFTING SANDS: THE COURSE OF OCD

OCD can either begin suddenly and abruptly, or gradually over a period of weeks, months or years. For some children, OCD appears to be sparked by stress or transitions such as a death in the family, moving to a new place or school, beginning of the school year, loss of friends, or even an exciting celebration like a birthday. For a few children, an unlikely culprit such as a strep infection may set off OCD (see Chapter 4 for more details). For many children, OCD appears without any apparent trigger.

You may be dismayed to learn that OCD is a lifelong illness. Although few children are completely freed of OCD symptoms, about 5% can live with minimal symptoms, and unfortunately, 15% progress to significant debilitation. The rest are somewhere in between. For many, life with OCD is full of unpleasant surprises, thanks to its "waxing and waning" course. Symptoms sometimes flare up and sometimes lie quiet, for no obvious reason. They often worsen during times of stress (see Chapter 4 for more about stress and OCD). They may even disappear completely for a few months or years, leading you to hope that it was, perhaps, nothing more than a phase, or that your child has recovered. To make it more confusing, OCD symptoms can also "morph" or change in character quite frequently. Existing symptoms may disappear and new fears and rituals may pop up in their place. One week your child must have her clothes and hair "just so" and the next she is counting, counting, counting and couldn't seem to care less about her disheveled appearance. Pretty soon, you could be riding a roller coaster of confusion. Chapter 7, *The Battle Plan against OCD*, helps you prepare yourself and your child for what to expect and how to manage the tempestuous nature of OCD.

Yet, there is encouraging news: With the new treatments described in Chapters 5 and 6, your child can be among the 80% of children with OCD who can expect to have good control over OCD and live relatively normal lives. It is definitely an era of hope and optimism. Maria, Paul and Alyssa are among those that have conquered OCD. Instead of spending countless hours washing hands, spitting and wiping or pulling up underwear, they are now spending their time doing what most children their age do. Maria's mother recounted with pride how her daughter had bravely ventured on a school trip to the nation's capital—and had a wonderful time! Perhaps not a spectacular achievement for most children, it was a feat for Maria, because it would have been impossible for her to do when she was in the grip of OCD. How could a child who spent 45 minutes in the shower and on the toilet while needing her mother's constant assistance ever get through a day of sharing bathrooms with a roomful of classmates? Paul is entering his senior year in high school and will be applying to colleges. Alyssa is now thriving with piano and ballet. Wearing leotards, pants or socks was unthinkable when she was in the throes of OCD.

THE EMOTIONAL CAGES OF OCD

When OCD is untreated, your child may lose out on the three most important assignments of childhood: learning, making friends and having fun. Unchecked OCD can rob children of the chance to be who they really are. Emotionally, children with OCD can become trapped in CAGES of *Confusion, Anger, Guilt, Embarrassment* and *Sadness*.

Figure 1: The Emotional CAGES of OCD

The Emotional **CAGES** of OCD
Confusion
Anger
Guilt
Embarrassment
Sadness

Confusion and fear are perhaps the primary emotions experienced by children with OCD. OCD is such a baffling illness for adults-it is hard to imagine what it must be like for children because they don't have the level of understanding, experience, or coping skills of adults to assimilate these logical incongruties. Particularly poignant is the fact that most children do not know how to understand or explain the terrifying experience of having their minds commandeered. It is not surprising that children with OCD are often perplexed and seem to be unable to make even simple decisions. They are afraid that dire consequences await them if they do not bow to the dictates of OCD. They may fear that they are "crazy." They are burdened with the fear of discovery by others and may go to elaborate lengths to conceal their symptoms. The children in Alyssa's kindergarten class often asked her why she was wearing a swimsuit under her dress. How is a five-year old to explain the absurdity of OCD to her classmates? Fortunately, they merely puzzled over Alyssa's strange attire—they were yet too young and innocent to tease and taunt her.

Anger and irritation commonly accompany OCD. In fact, it is frequently one of the first signs that parents have that something is wrong. The time and energy devoured by OCD makes children ill tempered, moody, defiant, easily frustrated and "stressed out." The barrage of intrusive and unwelcome obsessions is a continuous irritant to the child. Parents, siblings or teachers may meet with rage when they unwittingly or purposefully thwart the child's rituals. Sometimes, they appear to be on a hair-trigger and have unexpected meltdowns and panic-stricken episodes when they are at their wits' end. Angry and frustrated children can be perceived as spoiled brats when they behave in unexpectedly immature ways, because no one understands the torment they endure. They are unable to explain OCD to parents. Often, their attempts to describe their thoughts may be brushed off by disbelieving parents or teachers.

Guilt often stems from obsessions pertaining to harm and injury. Plagued by OCD's threats, the child may believe that he has failed to prevent "bad" things from happening, because he has been unable to do enough to appease OCD. Children with OCD also quickly find themselves in the role of the troublemaker and the "bad" kid; the one who creates problems for the family with OCD's rules and demands.

Embarrassment and shame sneak in when the weight of "ugly" thoughts and impulses sinks in. Children struggle to conceal all this "madness" from the world of friends, school and family for fear of discovery. They become skilled at keeping up facades. But all the time and energy spent in keeping up the charade leaves little time for socializing, having fun and meeting other age-appropriate expectations. They may be immensely sleep-deprived, haunted by the nightly rituals and ruminations that don't turn off with the lights. Schoolwork begins to decline, grades drop drastically and classes are missed. They may be unable to accept or reciprocate social invitations. Older adolescents may be unable to have dating relationships or to learn how to drive.

Sadness is often the result of the sinking feeling of being defeated and powerless. Children with OCD suffer never-ending pain and sadness—a hurt that someone who has not suffered OCD cannot have experienced. To add insult to injury, they are easily misunderstood by parents, teachers, siblings and friends, who may believe that the silly rituals, senseless fears, secrecy, decline in performance, rigid demands and temper tantrums are merely a reflection of laziness or willful lack of cooperation. Where does all this eventually lead children with OCD? For many, it leads to bruised and battered self-esteem, hopelessness and passive surrender to OCD. They become isolated, preoccupied, and consumed by the world of OCD. They cannot realize their full potential. In the worst cases, a child may not be able to leave the house or to get more than three hours of sleep or rest in a day. Suicidal thoughts may surface when escape from OCD seems impossible, although children with OCD don't typically act on these thoughts. Although many children with OCD may start out feeling trapped, there is no need for them to remain ensnared. Part II of this book shows you the many ways in which you can liberate your child from the emotional CAGES of OCD.

If your child has OCD, you are painfully aware that OCD leaves a trail of other little known victims in its wake—parents, siblings and families. The repercussions of OCD ripple through the family because parents and siblings become ensnared in the child's fears and rituals. These ripples can quickly become tidal waves that shake the foundations of families once comfortable in their stability. Chapters 8 and 14 are dedicated to understanding and taking care of the aftermath of OCD for you and your family.

FREQUENTLY-ASKED QUESTIONS

At what age does OCD begin?'

OCD usually appears between the ages of seven and 12, and most commonly around age 10. It can begin as early as ages three to five for children with a strong family history of OCD. About half of the adults who have OCD say their symptoms began before age 15. Most people with OCD develop it before the age of 25. Only 15% develop it after the age of 35. Boys with OCD tend to develop it earlier than girls, typically before the age of 12. Girls' symptoms are likely to start during early adolescence.

It can be difficult to recognize OCD or differentiate it from normal fears and rituals in very young children. Parents may not be aware of OCD symptoms for months or years. In fact, they often say that, in retrospect, their child had definite symptoms of OCD as early as the toddler years or even infancy, but they did not know it at the time. Sometimes, children are the first to bring their symptoms to their parents' attention.

I never heard of kids having OCD until now. Is it increasing in occurrence?

It is unlikely that OCD is actually increasing in occurrence in recent years. What is more likely to explain the apparent trend is the growing awareness that OCD is a legitimate disorder. As recently as 10-15 years ago, there were few professionals who knew how to recognize or appropriately treat OCD in adults, let alone children. Surveys found that only one fourth of the children with OCD were receiving treatment. However, most of these children were not diagnosed as having OCD, nor were they receiving treatment for OCD. For many children, OCD symptoms were treated as "bad habits" that had to be broken. When OCD was correctly recognized, there was often no access to the right treatment. Many adults with OCD say that their symptoms began in childhood. Although they may have realized at the time that their behaviors were unusual, they either dismissed them as quirks, or hid them because they were silly or bizarre. The shame and secrecy then kept them away from professionals and added to OCD becoming a badly misunderstood disorder.

Fortunately, the tide is turning and there are now good treatments that are far more effective. More adults and children are now seeking help for symptoms that would have gone untreated in the past. Of course, the increased awareness can also lead to the danger of over-diagnosing OCD, although this is arguably the lesser of the two evils. For more information on how to recognize what's OCD and what's not, see Chapter 2.

Is OCD different in boys and girls?

OCD is generally similar in boys and girls with a few differences. Among children, there are more boys with OCD than girls. In adolescents and adults with OCD, the sex ratio is about equal. With regard to types of symptoms, young boys are more likely to have urges for symmetry and closure (the "just right" feelings) and touching rituals. They are also more likely to have accompanying tics and Attention-Deficit/Hyperactivity Disorder (ADHD; see Chapter 2). Girls tend to have more concerns regarding germs and contamination, and have more washing and cleaning rituals. Girls are also more likely to be depressed, fearful and anxious.

Is OCD in children similar to that in adults?

In general, the obsessive themes and rituals of children and adults are quite similar. For instance, both adults and children can have fears pertaining to germs, death and danger and rituals of cleaning, washing and repeating. The differences are really mostly due to age, conceptual and language development and maturity. Children may not be able to recognize, label or articulate their fears. They may say, "*I just have to do it*" or "*It won't feel right,*" or "*It just does.*" The obsessions and rituals of adults are usually logically connected, as in washing hands to remove germs. In contrast, there may not be any obvious logical connection between the rituals and corresponding worries of children. For example, Mary is convinced that stepping on all the floortiles will prevent her dog from getting lost.

Most adults with OCD recognize that their symptoms are senseless and excessive. Although older children and adolescents usually have good insight, shame and defensiveness may lead them to be secretive or deny their symptoms. Young children are usually less secretive because they may not realize that they have anything to hide. Children are also more likely than adults to passively give in to the dictates of OCD. They are less aware of their ability to resist and less able to tolerate the anxiety that resistance generates. Finally, as you might have learned the hard way, family members of children are more frequently dragged into participating in the child's OCD in order to keep the peace. Children are more reactive and may resort to tantrums if they are not obliged.

How much control does my child have over OCD? Sometimes, her fears and rituals appear to be "put on" to get our attention or get out of doing her work. The teacher says she has no OCD at school—how can that be?

This is a very sensitive issue for many families. You may often be skeptical about the "I can't help it, it's my OCD" protests you hear from your child, particularly when the symptoms appear at times that are highly convenient for him. The amount of control over symptoms may vary among children and from one situation to the next for the same child.

When your child is truly in the throes of an OCD episode, he may have little control over his symptoms and behaviors. However, most children have at least partial control and can hold back their symptoms to some degree in situations where the social price is high, e.g., at school or at a friend's house. This partial control does not necessarily imply that the child is doing it willfully. In most cases, the child has to muster a tremendous amount of energy to "keep it together" at school or at a party. Outwardly, he may look like he's doing just fine, but he is struggling with internal chaos. By the time he gets home, this pressure-cooker of tension is ready to blow its top off and you are the privileged recipient of its fury.

On the other hand, children with OCD may be no different than any other children with regard to testing limits, working situations to their advantage or turning a deaf ear to your injunctions. There are certainly some children who, in some situations, may use OCD as a crutch, to gain sympathy or special treatment and to avoid responsibility. If this is clear to you, you need to handle it just as you would if your child did not have OCD. However, that is easier said than done. In most cases, it is deeply intertwined with OCD and difficult to sort out. You may need to give your child the benefit of the doubt when it's not as plain as day. Sometimes, trying to figure out whether your child is being manipulative can distract you from more important issues. See Chapter 12 for more suggestions.

My child has obsessive thoughts of harming people. He is not an aggressive or violent child. Should I be concerned that he will hurt someone?

Adults and children with OCD are mortally afraid of their impulses to harm others but are not known to actually carry out these urges. Remember that obsessions are involuntary and very disturbing and frightening for your child. They are not something he chooses to have. In fact, your son is probably tormented by his thoughts, finds them horrifying, is plagued by guilt and remorse and is desperate to get rid of the urges. If your son's thoughts are truly obsessions, it is highly improbable that he will actually carry them out.

It is best to have your child evaluated by a mental health professional (see Chapter 3) to determine if your son's urges are indeed obsessions or represent other issues. Although OCD itself does not spur sufferers to carrying out urges to harm, a child with OCD may have other reasons to consider harming another person. Children who are impulsive by nature, intensely angry, highly frustrated, looking for revenge or psychotic may be more likely to hurt someone. In contrast to children with obsessions, they are more likely to indulge in violent thoughts, not feel particularly put off by them, and not feel remorseful or guilty. See Chapter 11 for more on impulses to harm.

Chapter 2

Setting the Record Straight: What's OCD, What's Not?

After Danny was diagnosed with OCD at age four, it was easy to look back and see why he did some of the things he did when he was very young. I remember that when we put him to bed, all his animals and covers had to be in just the right position. He also had a rigid routine as to who would say goodnight last, and exactly what words had to be said. We now know that we could never do it right. Needless to say, bedtime was often a disaster. The same was true at his daycare. Once, the director called on the phone and asked me to talk to him. Danny was hysterical because the goodbye routine wasn't followed. He was three at the time.

One incident that really stands out is when he began pointing to the side of his temple with his forefinger. We had no idea what was going on, but it was constant and frequent. We found out that a teacher in preschool had told him to stop and think and had pointed to her head to emphasize her words. She said she did it once, but he did it non-stop for six months! All it took with him was one word of caution or warning and it would get locked into his brain. Once, when he and Grandpa went for a walk, his Grandpa said, "Check your feet before you walk in the house to see if they are wet." For the next six months, he checked his feet, lifting one foot and then the other, every step he took in the house. We were afraid he would fall down the stairs. Then, when he was four, he spent a week unable to stop washing his hands. I think his teacher had stressed cleanliness. It was obvious this was very serious. We had to get help.

Teresa, grandmother of Danny, 6

You might nod with familiarity as you recognize the goodbye routines and bedtime rituals that your child had when he was younger. You begin to wonder about OCD when you wouldn't have given it a second thought before. Seven-year-old Tommy is adamant about having his cars arranged just so, and gets very upset when his sister goes within a foot of them—does he have OCD? Dante, 11, has been worried about "catching AIDS" ever since he heard about it at a school presentation—is this normal?

Not every unusual fear or ritual is OCD. It is both very common and entirely normal for all children to have some repetitive behaviors. Although the differences are often obvious, it is sometimes not so easy to tell them apart if you don't know what to look for. Part of the reason parents are sometimes unsure is that the terms "obsessive" and "compulsive" are sometimes used quite loosely. This chapter lays out the differences between benign childhood fears, rituals and OCD and provides guidelines for telling them apart. It will help you pick up telltale signs of OCD sooner rather than later. Other behavioral and emotional conditions associated with OCD in children are described at the end of the chapter.

NORMAL RITUALS

"Step on a crack, break your mother's back...step on a crack..." You watch your daughter and her friends playing on the sidewalk and smile as you recall reciting the same chant when you were a child. Walking around ladders, keeping fingers crossed, knocking on wood and avoiding black cats--we've all indulged in common superstitions at some time or another. These are benign childhood beliefs, routines and rituals that are universal. If you did not consider these OCD, you are right--they are not.

Don't we all have rituals and habits? We may go through our toilet and grooming routines in the same invariant sequence every day. We may turn off all the lights and check all the doors and windows at night. We've all had the nagging doubt that the headlights of the car were left on in the parking lot. And of course, the tune that you heard on the radio this morning may still be "stuck" in your head. You chuckle as you casually call yourself "obsessive" or "compulsive."

Why do we have these seemingly inconsequential routines? How are they different from the repetitions of OCD? These habits actually have a very important part to play in our lives. Routines and schedules make us more productive, organized and efficient. We become so familiar with routines that we can do them automatically with little effort. That frees our attention and energy to attend to more important demands in our lives. Normal rituals help us thrive, succeed and gain mastery over our day-to-day environment. They are building blocks rather than obstacles to our progress and development. In fact, many highly accomplished scientists and professionals are successful because they are "compulsive" in their work habits. Checking, repetition and perfectionism make them methodical, thorough and accurate in their work.

Like adults children also have many ritualistic habits, rules and routines that are entirely normal in nature. About two-thirds of young children may insist on sameness in the daily routine and are vociferous in their objections when the "rules" are changed. Jenny must have her "favorite" blue cup at breakfast and will only allow her mother to spread the jam on her toast from the bottom to the top. Three-year-old Catherine, who is being dressed in haste protests, "But Mommy, we always put my pants on *before* we put on my shirt." Why are youngsters so particular about such trivial matters? Because the routine is familar, comfortable and predictable and makes their day a lot easier than having to encounter new ways of doing things each day.

How many times have you read the same book or played the same game with your child? You have no doubt answered the same question numerous times for your child. All children, particularly toddlers and pre-school-aged children, seek repetition because it helps them learn faster. It is also normal for children to ask for reassurance from their parents and it is natural for parents to comfort and reassure. For children, rituals and routines play an even greater role in development than they do for adults. They provide security, soothing and comfort. They allow the child to cope with change, uncertainty and fears, to develop mastery and control in learning new tasks and to sort through an often overwhelming world.

As children grow into adolescence, they automatically phase out of these early rituals. As they get older, they are more interested in collecting things such as stamps or sports cards, or knowing every detail of a specific topic such as dinosaurs, airplanes or fiction characters. These habits and hobbies are not merely enjoyable and satisfying; they also allow youngsters to gather a large amount of knowledge about the world around them.

NORMAL FEARS

Fears are just as normal a part of our existence as are rituals and routines. Almost every one of us experiences fears or worries about germs, illness, harm, death and day-to-day dilemmas. What is the purpose of fear in our lives? Fear is an essential emotion for our survival because it prepares us to respond to everyday threats and dangers. It primes us to be alert, vigilant, and cautious and to protect ourselves from harm by "fight or flight." We also teach our children to have fear and caution—with good reason. If we did not teach them to be afraid of strangers, oncoming traffic and fire, they would not survive the dangers of the world.

Fears are so common a part of growing up that almost half of the children between the ages of six and 12 have seven or more fears. Girls tend to report more fears than boys do at most ages. But not all fears are a part of normal development, and not all of them are outgrown without assistance. Knowing the normal course of childhood fears will help you gauge if your child is in a phase that he will outgrow or if you should indeed be concerned. The following is a summary of fears across the lifespan. *Worried No More: Help and Hope for Anxious Children* (see *Resources*) provides an in-depth discussion of anxieties in children.

❖ Infants begin to fear strangers around the age of seven months and outgrow this fear naturally around the second year of life.

❖ Toddlers fear separation from their parents. They may be afraid of loud or sudden noises and new, large or potentially dangerous things.

❖ Preschoolers shy away from new, unfamiliar and overwhelming environments. They may fear potentially harmful or dangerous things such as large dogs, snakes, the dark, bad dreams or imaginary characters such as monsters.

❖ Elementary school children become aware of the real dangers of the world such as strangers, diseases, accidents, disasters and death.

❖ During middle childhood, the focus of fears is on school-related events, particularly those involving academic performance and friendships. Natural phenomena such as thunderstorms, earthquakes and floods are also worrisome. Older children may worry about their parents getting hurt or dying.

❖ Adolescent fears shift into the more abstract realm including the future, rejection in social relationships, moral issues, dating compe tence, independence and career choices.

❖ Adults worry about the challenges of supporting themselves and the family financially, job satisfaction and stability, marital or dating rela tionships, children and parenting.

❖ Fears pertaining to illness, pain, death, medical and dental procedures, doctor visits, natural disasters, wars and traumatic events can occur among both children and adults.

School-aged children may also take to heart newly learned information pertaining to danger and safety. As a parent, you may have encountered your youngster's alarm and excessive vigilance after learning about the dangers of salmonella at school. Suddenly, your previously "grubby" child became the epitome of hygiene, meticulously washing his hands and monitoring the entire family's health habits. Your initial delight in your child's metamorphosis soon turned to dismay, as his constant queries and admonitions about cleanliness began to fray your nerves. However, in most cases, there is a novelty effect present and the intensity of the preoccupation wears off in due time.

NORMAL VS. OCD: WHAT'S THE DIFFERENCE?

Carl and Elaine, the parents of Maria, the 12 year-old you met in Chapter 1, recalled their early experiences with OCD:

The first clues we got that something was wrong were in the summer before the start of the 6th grade for Maria. Our beautiful, bright talkative girl had begun washing her hands over and over again. Going to the bathroom had become a 20-minute affair. She was very nervous about germs and cleanliness. Was this normal? Although concerned, we blamed it on the pressure of starting middle school and on the news about a local hepatitis outbreak. We figured she'd outgrow it.

Like Maria's parents, you might spend time debating between, "*Something's not right here,*" and sighing with resignation, "*Maybe it's just a passing phase.*" On the other hand, if you have already been sensitized to OCD, you might start questioning every habit you child has. Conceptually, normal and OCD behaviors are different in many ways, as described below:

❖ *Phase*

Normal rituals occur at specific stages in life and are outgrown in due time. OCD rituals are usually mismatched with the phase in which they appear, i.e., they either appear at a point in the child's life when they should have been outgrown or persist beyond the stage in which they are appropriate. You need not be unduly concerned if your five-year-old child has an elaborate bedtime routine of recitations and repetitions. After she says her prayers, she whispers, "*Sleep tight, sweet dreams all night,*" insists that you repeat it back to her twice, and arranges her pillows just so. On the other hand, it would be unusual if your 12-year old did the same.

❖ *Themes*

Normal fears are not particularly bizarre. Although OCD preoccupations can be about normal topics such as germs or death, they are often unrealistic and implausible such as fears of catching AIDS from having merely said the word.

❖ *Excessiveness*

In contrast to normal fears or rituals, OCD worries are unreasonable and disproportionate to the context. Common cautions are taken to extremes. After Robert read about Lyme Disease in the newspaper, he confined himself to the house and would not set foot in the backyard or playground. If required to go outside, he would go through an elaborate sequence of checking and disinfecting to ensure that he was tick-free.

❖ *Interference*

Normal fears and rituals don't affect everyday life and sometimes actually help the child become more motivated, organized and productive. In contrast, OCD gets in the way of completing day-to-day tasks that are clearly within the child's capability, such as getting bathed and dressed, doing schoolwork, learning normally and having friends. Repetitive rituals such as checking, re-reading, erasing or counting may render a child "stuck" and unable to proceed. Sometimes, OCD ruminations consume so much of the child's mental and physical energy and time that she simply does not have any left for necessary activities. In extreme cases, a child may be unable to leave the home due to inability to extricate from rituals.

❖ *Distress*

Usually, normal rituals are calming and often result in enjoyment and satisfaction. Although there may be passing protest if interrupted, the child is rarely distraught if she cannot complete normal rituals. With OCD, the child does not enjoy rituals; yet, there might be cascades of tears or temper outbursts if a ritual is knowingly or unwittingly interrupted.

❖ *Logic and control*

Normal fears and rituals are amenable to reason and logic. Fears born out of OCD are particularly impervious to common sense, logic, factual information, reassurance, explanations or distraction. Children can also stop normal rituals with ease and of their choosing. In contrast, the child's efforts to control, resist or stop OCD worries are typically unsuccessful.

❖ *Duration*

Normal rituals take up a negligible amount of time in a child's day. In contrast, OCD rituals and obsessions are time-consuming and cannot be easily terminated. In mild cases, OCD symptoms may consume an hour or more per day; in severe cases, it may devour eight or more hours each day.

❖ *Insight*

Children usually know the difference between normal and OCD behaviors. Most children are aware that their OCD fears and rituals are extreme and irrational, although younger children may be less likely to perceive their symptoms as irrational.

❖ *Wasted effort*

Normal "perfectionism," meticulousness, checking, redoing or ordering make us efficient and proficient. In contrast, the energy and time invested in OCD are wasted. There is absolutely nothing accomplished from OCD worries or rituals; nothing to show for all that time spent agonizing.

Table 2: Normal vs. OCD Behaviors Checklist

Check the box on the right of each statement if your answer is YES			
Normal		**OCD**	
The habit or fear is:			
Commonly seen or typical		Bizarre or unusual	
At a nuisance level		Extreme or exaggerated	
Pleasing, satisfying, relaxing or soothing for child		Upsetting, tormenting or bothersome to child	
Not detrimental; may even help with normal activities		Gets in the way of normal activities	
One that child feels he chooses to do		One that child feels forced to do	
One that child could easily stop if he chose to		One that child feels he cannot stop even if he wants to	
Interrupted without difficulty		Creates distress if interrupted	

❖ *The "contagion effect"*

Normal rituals are usually limited to specific areas or items. OCD symptoms can "spread" continuously. Over time, fears and rituals seem to expand into more and more areas. Although specific fears and rituals may come and go, the threshold for danger seems to decrease over time.

The checklist in Table 2 can help you gauge if your child's behaviors are suggestive of OCD. If you check any items in the "OCD" column, it would be wise to seek an evaluation from a qualified professional (see Chapter 3).

TELLTALE SIGNS OF OCD

In addition to knowing the conceptual differences between normal behaviors and OCD, it is helpful if you can spot specific behaviors that may be clues to OCD. None of the behaviors described below imply a definite diagnosis of OCD in and of themselves, as many other factors have to be taken into consideration. They are merely indicators to be investigated further. Neither are these signs exclusive markers of OCD. They may also be clues to other problems for which your child may benefit from intervention. It is important that you seek consultation with a qualified professional (see Chapter 3) if you see the following signs for over a month:

❖ *Out-of-character behaviors*

If you find yourself thinking that your child is "not acting his age," "not like himself," or if you wonder "what on earth has gotten into him," you should probably pay closer attention. Dramatic and unusual changes in mood, compliance, eating habits or preferences, hygiene, ordering, or separation fears are often red flags for OCD. A generally amiable child who is suddenly stubborn or demanding, insists that others follow unusual rules or refuses to complete routine activities also merits closer observation.

❖ *Depression or withdrawal*

Unhappiness, depression or withdrawal is often the initial reason that parents seek help for their children. Children are often secretive and try to hide their OCD and may present as depressed and preoccupied because they suffer in silence. They may also have problems sleeping, nightmares, sadness, tension, and loss of appetite. In addition, it is common to have irritability, frustration and temper outbursts when interrupted in rituals.

❖ *Unwarranted cleanliness*

Washing one's hands before every meal and after using the toilet is perfectly normal. Spending several minutes lathering, scrubbing and rinsing, washing frequently or complaining about feeling dirty is not normal.

❖ *Slowness and tardiness*

If your child is habitually late, it might be worth your while to find out what is holding her up. If she spends an inordinately long time in the bathroom, getting dressed, doing homework or gets to school or bed late, she may have obsessions and compulsions.

❖ *Reluctance or refusal to go to school*

School refusal may reflect fears and rituals centered on school-related issues such as writing, reading, or contracting germs from classmates.

❖ *Perfectionism*

When the tendency to be meticulous or thorough becomes a hindrance, your child may be dealing with OCD or anxiety. Children with OCD often repeat tasks endlessly, getting frustrated that they are not perfect, even long after others have indicated satisfaction with the quality of their work.

❖ *Frequent physical complaints*

Nausea, vomiting, feeling on edge, or many aches and pains for which no medical cause can be found may point to underlying anxiety.

❖ *Unexplained physical changes*

If your trips to the dermatologist, expensive hand creams and ointments have been futile for your son's sore, chapped, red hands, he may be doing some elaborate hand washing in secret. If he has become untidy and slovenly, wears strange attire or the same clothes repeatedly, he may have obsessions about clothing being contaminated or unlucky. Bleeding gums may be a sign of copious brushing of teeth to get them clean enough. The rash or scabs on his legs and arms may be indicators of skin picking. Frequent urinary urges for which no medical problem can be found may be obsessive urges to "clean out" the bladder.

❖   *Changes in concentration, attention and organization*

Children with OCD are often misdiagnosed as having ADHD because they are distracted and preoccupied by obsessions. They are not day-dreaming willfully but are at the mercy of their meandering minds.

❖   *Reassurance seeking*

If your child has OCD, you will find that no amount of answering satisfies him. "Am I going to be OK, do I have a brain tumor, am I going to throw up?" "Can you feel my forehead and see if I have a fever?"

❖   *Need for certainty*

Repeated questions about seemingly trivial issues such as, "What time does the mail come?" "What's for dinner tonight?" "Is the TV show on yet?" "Was the garage door shut properly?" may be signs of OCD.

❖   *Apologizing and confessing*

Confessing to inconsequential "misdeeds," asking for forgiveness repeatedly for trivial actions or praying often may be clues to OCD.

❖   *Sleep problems*

Sleep difficulties can be the result of staying up late, absorbed in rituals or obsessions. It is common for children to lie awake waiting for their fears to quiet down, or to be caught up in interminable rituals into the wee hours. They are unable to wake up on time in the morning and are exhausted and drowsy all day at school.

❖   *Circuitous paths*

OCD may induce a child to take elaborate pains to circumvent or avoid triggers. She may take the laborious route to a place or item when the easy one is obvious and accessible. Opening doors, lockers, desks, or books with elbows or with tissue in hand, holding hands in the air to avoid physical contact, refusal to shake hands or share supplies with others may also be instances of avoidance of OCD triggers.

❖   *Avoidance*

Sudden avoidance or reluctance to encounter foods, people, activities or objects, especially those that were formerly not an issue can also be a sign of OCD. Fears of contamination, death or harm may coerce children into avoiding all kinds of potential triggers of these fears. The triggers are not always intuitive or logically related to the fear.

❖   *Unusual patterns and rules*

Odd behaviors such as walking in specific patterns through doorways, counting tiles or syllables, touching or tapping in symmetry or sitting and standing repeatedly may be "just right" rituals. Frequent checking of the backpack or under the desk and chair may be checking rituals. Opening and shutting lockers, lining up or arranging items are other signs of rituals. Unusual rules or preferences around food may also be clues to OCD.

❖   *Secretiveness*

Clandestine behaviors, attempts at concealment, or lengthy unexplained "disappearances" into the bathroom or bedroom may also be clues to OCD. Adolescents with OCD are commonly very secretive, because they are embarrassed and ashamed to disclose their senseless rituals. They are old enough to realize how absurd their behavior is, but young enough that they do not trust that anyone will understand or be able to help. If confronted, they may often hide, minimize or deny difficulty and resist help. Parents may assume it's just an adolescent phase, or mistakenly assume they are hiding the use of drugs.

❖   *Magical thinking*

Children with OCD may be highly superstitious with regard to lucky and unlucky things, good luck and bad luck. They are very serious about these beliefs, and are not able to take them lightly or joke about them.

DISORDERS ASSOCIATED WITH OCD

As discussed in Chapter 1, OCD is an anxiety disorder. The symptoms of OCD can often be confused with those of other conditions, as there are several disorders that resemble and overlap with OCD. To make matters more complicated, children with OCD can often be diagnosed with more than one condition. For instance, more than half the children with OCD suffer from another anxiety disorder or depression. Conversely, children with other psychiatric disorders may also show some obsessive and compulsive behaviors, although they may not have OCD.

Diagnosis is a complex task that requires training, experience and astute clinical judgment. It should only be made by a qualified mental health professional after a thorough evaluation. This section is intended to help you become informed and aware of the range of disorders that might be associated with OCD in children and adolescents, to aid in early detection and referral. Chapter 3 covers the process of evaluation and diagnosis of OCD and related conditions.

OCD and Anxiety Disorders

OCD is one of several Anxiety Disorders in the current system of diagnosis, the *Diagnostic and Statistical Manual of Mental Disorders, Fourth Edition* (DSM-IV) of the American Psychiatric Association. By definition, there are some similarities in symptoms among the different disorders that are grouped into the family of anxiety disorders. The following anxiety disorders may overlap or occur in conjunction with OCD. Similarities and differences of each disorder with OCD are discussed. *Worried No More: Help and Hope for Anxious Children* (see *Resources*) describes all the anxiety disorders and their treatment in children and adolescents.

Separation Anxiety Disorder (SAD)

An eight-year-old that panics and cries hysterically when her mother makes a trip to the grocery store may have SAD, the most common anxiety disorder among children. Separation fears are normal in children from around seven months of age to the preschool years. Your child's first few days at daycare, preschool or kindergarten may be etched in your mind as days of crying, clinging and seemingly inconsolable grief when you left her at the door. However, the teachers told you it was all over soon after you had left, and after a few days, the partings became less and less traumatic for both of you. Before you knew it, your child was enjoying her time with other children so much that she didn't want to leave when you arrived to pick her up!

Signs and Symptoms of Separation Anxiety Disorder

- ☐ Extreme, disproportionate distress over separation from loved ones
- ☐ Unwillingness to leave home, attend school, or go on outings
- ☐ Unrealistic worry about harm to self or loved ones
- ☐ Frequent reassurance seeking about safety of self or loved ones
- ☐ Crying, clinging, nausea or tantrums in anticipation of separation
- ☐ Reluctance to be alone, especially at night
- ☐ Nightmares about harm and danger
- ☐ Symptoms for at least four weeks

Unfortunately for some children, time and age do not "settle" this fear. The separation never seems to get easier, and may in fact, get worse. For others, who made the early transitions to preschool and kindergarten relatively uneventfully, separation fears emerge when they are older and well past the age for normal separation fears. Children with SAD beg for reassurance when a parent is away even briefly, cower from any opportunity to be separated, hover around their parents, and may even follow them from room to room. Parents who "abandon" them to go to the next room without their knowledge and consent may be met with hysterical admonitions. In school, there may be stomach aches, nausea and frequent trips to the nurse's office. The child asks to call the parent in order to "check in" and be reassured that all is well.

Although SAD and OCD share common features with regard to fears of harm coming to loved-ones and ritualistic reassurance seeking, the anxiety in SAD is limited to separation from loved ones, and there are no compulsions to avert or prevent harm.

Generalized Anxiety Disorder (GAD)

GAD involves uncontrollable worry or rumination over day-to-day events, both trivial and major, with disproportionate fears of catastrophic consequences. This is the "What if...?" disorder. Children with GAD are the "worry worts" who carry the weight of the world on their shoulders. Past conversations, things that have been said or done, family matters, friendships, school performance, finances and "global" concerns such as nuclear war, the end of the world and universal peace saturate the minds of these children. GAD is the most common anxiety disorder among adolescents. Perfectionism is very common in GAD, and is a symptom that overlaps with OCD. In contrast to OCD, the themes of GAD worries are usually everyday concerns, and are typically not bizarre or unusual in nature. In addition, there are no compulsions associated with GAD, with the exception of seeking reassurance, or the repetitious behaviors associated with perfectionism.

Signs and Symptoms of Generalized Anxiety Disorder

☐ Unrealistic fears over many routine events

☐ Uncontrollable, unstoppable worry

☐ Irritability, tension, nausea, aches and pains, poor concentration

☐ Difficulty sleeping, fatigue

☐ Perfectionism

☐ Frequent reassurance and approval seeking

☐ Significant interference with daily life activities

Post-Traumatic Stress Disorder

Post-Traumatic Stress Disorder (PTSD) is an anxiety reaction that occurs in response to exposure to a catastrophe of great magnitude. Unfortunately, children today have been exposed to many tragic events such as the terrorist attacks on the World Trade Center and the Pentagon that took place on September 11, 2001. These and other tragic events such as the school shootings at Columbine High School have had a direct impact on children, parents and school personnel because they have come close to home. PTSD can also occur among children who have endured physical, sexual or emotional abuse.

Persons exposed to a disastrous or tragic event can have a range of reactions that is influenced by the proximity of exposure, the direct impact of the trauma, previous exposure to trauma, age and temperament. Although most people have reactions to tragedies, the reactions of most fade with time. For some, PTSD reactions may develop. Initial reactions may include shock, disbelief, helplessness, and a sense of the surreal. As reality sinks in, a multitude of tumultuous emotions may surface. There may be intense, overwhelming grief, panic, confusion and feelings of unreality. Dreams, nightmares, tension and vigilance are also common PTSD symptoms. If the event was manmade, deliberate or preventable, there may be anger, outrage and urges for justice or vengeance.

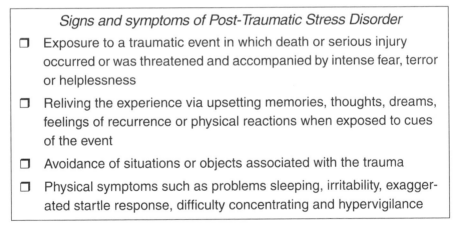

Signs and symptoms of Post-Traumatic Stress Disorder

❐ Exposure to a traumatic event in which death or serious injury occurred or was threatened and accompanied by intense fear, terror or helplessness

❐ Reliving the experience via upsetting memories, thoughts, dreams, feelings of recurrence or physical reactions when exposed to cues of the event

❐ Avoidance of situations or objects associated with the trauma

❐ Physical symptoms such as problems sleeping, irritability, exaggerated startle response, difficulty concentrating and hypervigilance

Children may also have a range of responses to trauma. Some do not fully appreciate the nature of the event and may have limited interest or passing curiosity. At the other end of the spectrum, some children may develop intense fear, a sense of horror and confusion. Reactions may evolve over a period of time and not happen in a predictable sequence. Children who are prone to anxiety or who have previously experienced trauma may have more severe reactions, even if they are not directly impacted. They may question their safety and lose trust in adults who were unable to keep them safe. They may express fear that the event will reoccur or will happen directly to them. Separation fears may emerge, as children may worry that they or their parents will be killed or hurt if the event recurs. They may be confused over the difference between real and imagined events, particularly those in movies and TV shows.

Some children may become easily upset and revert to immature and regressed behaviors such as thumb sucking, bedwetting, clinging or tantrums. Bedtime fears and nightmares may resurface or increase; some may insist on having parents stay with them at night. Older children and adolescents grasp the larger implications of a tragic event or disaster, and may question the possible reasons for the event. They may experience confusion, sadness, anger and a need to seek justice or vengeance. Sometimes, teenagers may appear callous by joking about the events. Although humor is a normal way of coping, some may carry it to insensitive levels.

The duration of PTSD reactions also varies. For most, the impact fades with time and with support and they are able to move on with their lives. For others, the emotional trauma may persist and resurface over time. Over the long term, there may be increased emotional "numbness," detachment, and an inability to feel or express feelings. There may also be strong avoidance of situations related to the trauma and its aftermath.

Specific Phobias

Phobias involve intense fear of one or more specific events or objects such as animals, insects, storms, heights, etc. Although the object of the phobia may be one that poses some threat for most people, the phobic reaction is at the level of panic. For instance, whereas the threat of a bee sting may make most people cautious around bees, a child who has a phobia of bees may have an overly dramatic reaction to the mention of bees, even when none are within sight. She may refuse to go outdoors even when no bees are present. Unlike other types of anxiety, phobias are very specific and are usually accompanied by strong avoidance of the feared object. Children do not generally display any anxiety if they can avoid the feared stimulus. They do not have undue anxiety in other situations.

Signs and Symptoms of Specific Phobias

☐ Unreasonable, persistent fear of objects or situations such as animals, insects, the dark, medical procedures, thunderstorms

☐ Anticipation of or exposure to the feared object triggers fear

☐ Strong avoidance or distressed endurance of the feared object

☐ Exposure elicits panic, freezing, crying, clinging

Social Phobia

Social Phobia, which may be better recognized by many as excessive shyness, involves intense and paralyzing concern about appearing foolish or doing something to embarrass or humiliate oneself. Children with Social Phobia are very self-conscious in social and performance situations, and generally try to avoid them. School, family gatherings, church and public places may elicit fears about being evaluated and ridiculed. The child with social phobia is often misunderstood as willfully avoidant and not trying hard enough to deal with shyness. Whereas OCD fears can also extend to social concerns, social phobia is limited to social fears, and does not involve rituals.

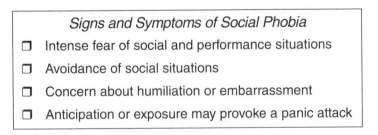

Signs and Symptoms of Social Phobia

☐ Intense fear of social and performance situations

☐ Avoidance of social situations

☐ Concern about humiliation or embarrassment

☐ Anticipation or exposure may provoke a panic attack

Panic Disorder

Panic *attacks* occur when anxiety peaks abruptly and is intolerable to the sufferer. A myriad of symptoms such as pounding heart, trembling, faintness, dizziness, chest pain, choking sensations, fears of dying, going crazy or being "detached" may occur within a few seconds or minutes.

People with OCD can also have panic attacks when they are exposed to something that triggers an intense OCD fear. Even though your child may have one of these attacks, it does not mean that he has panic disorder. To have panic *disorder*, which is rare in children, the child must have repeated, *unexpected* panic attacks that are unrelated to fears stemming from OCD, separation, or generalized anxiety. There is persistent anxiety about an impending panic attack.

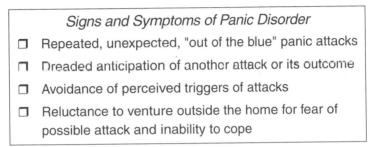

Signs and Symptoms of Panic Disorder
- ❏ Repeated, unexpected, "out of the blue" panic attacks
- ❏ Dreaded anticipation of another attack or its outcome
- ❏ Avoidance of perceived triggers of attacks
- ❏ Reluctance to venture outside the home for fear of possible attack and inability to cope

Tourette Syndrome (TS)

As many as 30% of the children diagnosed with OCD have a tic disorder such as Tourette Syndrome (TS), which consists of multiple involuntary motor and vocal tics (e.g., jerking motions, eye blinks, grunts and sniffs). Conversely, as many as 60% of the children who are diagnosed with TS also have OCD. TS is thought to originate in the same part of the brain as OCD but it not clear how exactly they are related (see Chapter 4). Children who have both OCD and TS are also more likely to have difficulties with attention, learning and oppositional behavior than children who have OCD alone. It is quite common for children to have tics and "nervous mannerisms" that come and go over time, with no harm done. Tics may sometimes be caused by medications.

It is important to differentiate between TS and OCD, because the treatments for the two disorders are quite different. Often, tics may well disappear without intervention. Tics are only treated with medication if they are severe enough to cause disruption in the child's life, or are very distressing for the child. Telling OCD and TS apart can be difficult because they can look quite similar. Tics can resemble OCD rituals and tics and compulsions can co-occur. Rituals may be difficult to differentiate from complex tics, which may involve a sequence of movements or vocalizations.

Signs and Symptoms of Tourette Syndrome

☐ Sudden, brief and frequent abnormal movements (motor tics) of the body such as eye blinks, facial grimaces, neck jerks, jumping, stamping, smelling

☐ Sudden, brief and frequent unnecessary noises (vocal tics) such as grunts, sniffs, coughs, throat clearing, barking, repeating words out of context

---

In order to differentiate tics from OCD compulsions, it is necessary to pay attention to the actual behaviors and the context and triggers to which they are related. Tics are usually sudden, rapid, involuntary and purpose-less movements and sounds. They happen more randomly, occur in a wide variety of situations and are not designed to defuse anxiety or obsessions. In contrast, compulsions are always purposeful, deliberate actions that are designed to counteract anxiety. Children also appear to be more con-sciously aware of engaging in compulsions than tics. Compulsions are usually more elaborate, follow rigid rules and occur in specific situations. For instance, if a child taps three times before getting into his bed at night, and not at any other time, it is likely to be a compulsion. If it were a tic, it would occur erratically and not necessarily in the same situation each day.

The most telling clues to the difference are evident when children can articulate the thoughts behind the action. James, an insightful nine-year-old, helped me understand how he knew could tell apart his rituals from his tics. "*My brain makes me want to touch things again and again, but when my eyes blink, they just do that on their own.*" He was aware that the touching was a more purposeful urge and was a compulsion that he felt driven to perform, whereas the eye blink happened automatically and was a tic.

Attention Deficit Hyperactivity Disorder (ADD/ADHD)

You are probably familiar with ADHD, given the extent of attention it has received in the schools and in the press in recent years. Inattention, distractibility, impulsivity and high levels of motor activity are the hallmarks of ADHD. Children with OCD are often mistakenly thought to have ADHD, because they appear inattentive and distracted and have difficulty with concentration at school. In reality, children with OCD have poor attention and concentration because obsessions and ruminations preoccupy them, not because they have a deficit in the ability to attend. Rebecca, who had to fend off fears of death each time she came across an unlucky number in math class was thought to be disinterested and unmotivated in math class. Rituals or attempts to disguise rituals can be mistaken for hyperactivity. Jason, who opened and shut his desk and backpack several times each day was seen as fidgety and hyperactive.

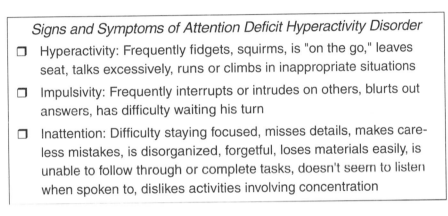

Signs and Symptoms of Attention Deficit Hyperactivity Disorder

☐ Hyperactivity: Frequently fidgets, squirms, is "on the go," leaves seat, talks excessively, runs or climbs in inappropriate situations

☐ Impulsivity: Frequently interrupts or intrudes on others, blurts out answers, has difficulty waiting his turn

☐ Inattention: Difficulty staying focused, misses details, makes careless mistakes, is disorganized, forgetful, loses materials easily, is unable to follow through or complete tasks, doesn't seem to listen when spoken to, dislikes activities involving concentration

Some children may have both OCD and ADHD, but the quality of the inattention in OCD is different from that in ADHD. Children with OCD are more likely to appear distant and preoccupied, as they are dealing with obsessions that perimeate their minds against their will. They may appear deep in thought, serious or distressed in countenance and unaware of their surroundings. In contrast, the attention of children with ADHD is more likely to shift from one activity to the next in rapid succession, with no particular distress involved.

Depression

Depression and anxiety share some common symptoms that can make it harder to discern one from the other. These include despondency, withdrawal, sleep problems, nightmares, tension, poor concentration, fatigue, guilt and loss of appetite. Children with OCD can be prone to demoralization, discouragement and hopelessness. For some children, this can reach the severity of a depressive episode. Children with depression are down in the dumps and are more sad than anxious. Depressed children are also prone to rumination, but the focus of their preoccupations is typically their negative self-worth, which is consistent with their mood. OCD may be much harder to treat when it is complicated by depression.

Signs and Symptoms of Depression

Most of the time, nearly every day:

☐ Noticeably sad or irritable

☐ Lack of interest or pleasure in almost all activities

☐ Unable to think, concentrate or make simple decisions

☐ Sleeping poorly at night or too much in the day

☐ Noticeable decrease or increase in appetite or weight

☐ Restless or lethargic and slowed down

☐ Tired, with no energy for no good reason

☐ Feels hopeless, helpless, worthless or guilty

☐ Thoughts of own death (not just fear of dying)

Autism and Asperger's Syndrome

Autism and Asperger's Syndrome are Pervasive Developmental Disorders (PDD), a spectrum of disorders involving deficits in developmental tasks such as socialization and communication. Classic autism, which may involve complete lack of language and social interaction, is at the severe end of the spectrum, whereas Asperger's Syndrome (AS) is somewhere on the continuum between autism and normal development. Children with AS have deficits primarily in social interaction. Although they develop functional language skills, their conversations are stilted, and they do not appreciate the emotional or reciprocal aspects of social dialogue. They often appear awkward, odd or different.

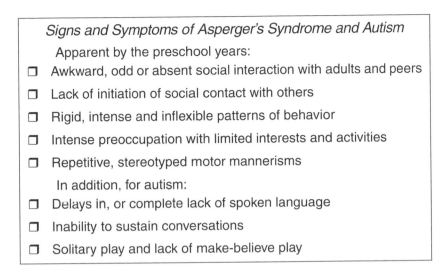

Signs and Symptoms of Asperger's Syndrome and Autism

Apparent by the preschool years:

☐ Awkward, odd or absent social interaction with adults and peers

☐ Lack of initiation of social contact with others

☐ Rigid, intense and inflexible patterns of behavior

☐ Intense preoccupation with limited interests and activities

☐ Repetitive, stereotyped motor mannerisms

In addition, for autism:

☐ Delays in, or complete lack of spoken language

☐ Inability to sustain conversations

☐ Solitary play and lack of make-believe play

Children with PDD also experience tremendous anxiety when faced with unfamiliar people or surroundings, abstract tasks, unclear expectations, physical and social contact, transitions and changes in routine. They may lack flexibility and the ability to shift gears in response to change. There are many children who fall in the shades of gray of the PDD spectrum, displaying milder versions of PDD behaviors. To make matters more complex, these children may sometimes have OCD in addition to PDD.

Extreme sensory sensitivity is a prominent feature of PDD. Children with PDD are often highly sensitive and over-reactive to sensory inputs like noise, touch or light that are barely noticed by most other children. Many children with OCD, TS and other developmental disorders also have this form of sensitivity, which you may have heard described as Sensory Integration Dysfunction (SID). Sensory sensitivity is a symptom, not a psychiatric disorder. Children with this problem have dramatic reactions to sensations that do not even register in most people's awareness. For instance, a child will revel in horseplay, but "flip out" if he is tapped lightly on the shoulder. Others are very bothered by sudden noises, but far exceed the average startle response. Many experience intense and intolerable discomfort at the feeling of clothing, labels and tags, textures, weights of fabrics, waistbands and seams on socks. They may be very selective in the few items they will wear or absolutely refuse to wear certain items of clothing. Some are very sensitive to food textures and smells and others to sticky substances; they may therefore be very picky eaters with a highly restricted range of acceptable foods.

Trichotillomania (TTM)

TTM or impulsive hair plucking is often associated with an increasing sense of tension prior to plucking, but followed by pleasure, gratification or relief afterwards. Adults and adolescents with TTM often feel upset and guilty later when they think about the social and medical consequences of pulling out their hair. Younger children have a harder time appreciating any consequences that are in the future, because they generally think only about the here and now. Hair pulling often tends to occur during times of stress and anxiety, but can also occur when the person is relaxed, distracted or bored. Although TTM and OCD have some similarities, one clear difference between the two is that there is no pleasure, gratification or desire associated with OCD rituals. In addition, hair plucking in TTM is not associated with obsessions or fears.

Body Dysmorphic Disorder (BDD)

The hallmark of Body Dysmorphic Disorder (BDD) is an intense preoccupation with a minor real or imagined flaw in appearance, which is perceived as a deformity and magnified to mountainous proportions. It is usually a very specific and restricted part of the body that is the offender, such as a wrinkle, scar, hair, the size or shape of the nose, eyebrow or fingernails. The sufferer is tormented because the flaw is perceived as hideous and unsightly. Her life revolves around checking, comparing, concealing and fixing this defect in appearance. Unlike OCD, BDD preoccupations are restricted to appearance, and there are no compulsions associated with it other than checking and seeking reassurance.

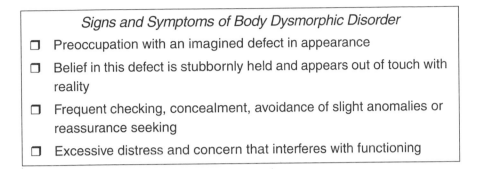

Signs and Symptoms of Body Dysmorphic Disorder

☐ Preoccupation with an imagined defect in appearance

☐ Belief in this defect is stubbornly held and appears out of touch with reality

☐ Frequent checking, concealment, avoidance of slight anomalies or reassurance seeking

☐ Excessive distress and concern that interferes with functioning

Eating Disorders

Eating disorders such as anorexia nervosa and bulimia have received considerable media attention in recent years. They typically develop during the teenage years and most commonly affect girls. The sufferer is irrationally preoccupied with being thin, and has a morbid fear of becoming fat. Although there are many ritualistic and rule-bound behaviors that are geared towards losing weight, the obsessive thinking is limited to a fear of becoming fat. There are no other obsessions, and restricted food intake is not due to fear of germs or contamination.

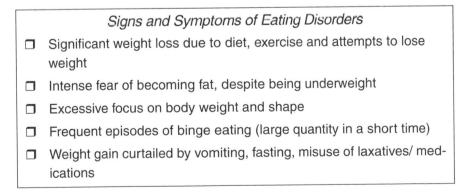

Signs and Symptoms of Eating Disorders

☐ Significant weight loss due to diet, exercise and attempts to lose weight

☐ Intense fear of becoming fat, despite being underweight

☐ Excessive focus on body weight and shape

☐ Frequent episodes of binge eating (large quantity in a short time)

☐ Weight gain curtailed by vomiting, fasting, misuse of laxatives/ medications

Children with OCD may also have significant problems with eating, although of a different quality. The food-related rituals and fears of OCD are not about getting fat but about contamination, or with the need for order, sequence and symmetry. Children with OCD may have unusual food preferences, not eat selected foods, inspect food meticulously before eating, arrange food on the plate in specific patterns, or have rigid and bizarre rules about the manner or sequence in which food is eaten. In some instances, the fear of gaining weight can also become an OCD obsession, as Nancy's experience indicates. Yet, Nancy's fear was clearly an OCD fear, not an eating disorder:

Every morning, every night, it was a struggle. What to wear, what way to go down the stairs, everything was a game. Nobody knew. How could I tell anyone that I couldn't wear my blue sweater because I might become fat? Nobody at school could tell, and I wanted to keep it that way. Eventually, it got unbearable. Everyday was another set of head games—if I didn't touch the doorframe, I would gain 10 pounds. If I didn't wear the 'right' socks, people wouldn't like me.

The reason Nancy's fear of "becoming fat" was not an eating disorder was that she did not restrict her food intake or actively try to keep her weight down. In fact, her rituals seemed so unconnected to the fear-the irrationality of touching the doorframe or wearing the right sweater to protect her from gaining weight were clear indicators of OCD thinking.

Obsessive-Compulsive Personality Disorder (OCPD)

OCPD, which is usually diagnosed in adulthood, not during child-hood, involves a personality style of rigid, inflexible fixation with order, cleanliness, rules and control. Having a diagnosis of OCD does not mean that your child has or will have OCPD when he grows up. OCD is easy to confuse with OCPD. The best way to differentiate OCD from OCPD is that persons with OCPD consider their rules and routines necessary, appropriate and desirable. As a matter of fact, they might attempt to impose them on family members or coworkers, who find them excessive and oppressive. Aunt Linda, who is fastidiously clean, insists that her husband, children and even visitors to her home follow her rules about washing from the elbows down when they enter the house and leave their shoes, coats, gloves and bags outside the door rather than inside. She becomes annoyed when her family members deviate from the pattern, and reprimands them for their noncompliance. Woe to the careless visitor who spills a crumb of food-Aunt Linda immediately evacuates everyone to another room while she sweeps and swabs until the floor is restored to its pristine state. The reason that Aunt Linda's fastidiousness is not OCD is that she doesn't see anything untoward about her behavior. She *likes* having things immaculately clean all the time.

Delusions, hallucinations and psychosis

Delusions and hallucinations are the cardinal symptoms of *psychosis*, which is usually accompanied by disorganization, confusion and deterioration in functioning. Delusions are strongly adhered-to beliefs with no basis in reality and hallucinations are sensory experiences such as hearing voices, visions and tactile sensations that have no basis in reality. When a person has delusions or hallucinations, he or she is convinced of their reality, and does not usually view them as unusual, distorted or upsetting. The other telltale signs of a psychotic disorder—disorganization, confusion, incoherence, tangential speech and disorientation, are fairly easy for a clinician to detect.

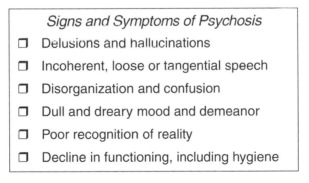

> ### Signs and Symptoms of Psychosis
> ❑ Delusions and hallucinations
> ❑ Incoherent, loose or tangential speech
> ❑ Disorganization and confusion
> ❑ Dull and dreary mood and demeanor
> ❑ Poor recognition of reality
> ❑ Decline in functioning, including hygiene

The bizarre beliefs of OCD may sometimes be mistaken for psychosis. But there are clear differences between the two. The "voices" of OCD are typically quite distinct from the voices of psychosis. The former are experienced against the will and are intrusive and upsetting. When a child is obviously upset by the "commands" and injunctions she hears, they are most likely to be OCD thoughts. In addition, she will usually know that they do not make sense, because her reality testing is good. OCD is usually accompanied by "insight," which means that sufferers know that the thoughts are bizarre or unreal. However, this insight occurs on a continuum and children, especially young ones, may not always be able to distinguish OCD thoughts from reality (or communicate this in ways we understand). Although children often play imaginary games that appear delusional, they own up to imaginary fantasies when queried properly.

That much said, it could sometimes be truly difficult to sort out the two. Beliefs in OCD thoughts can sometimes reach delusional proportions—referred to as *overvalued ideation*—which can occur both in children and in adults. A child may sometimes not be quite sure whether or not OCD thoughts are "real," or she may hold on tenaciously to the belief that they are. On occasion, children and adults with OCD may also have both OCD *and* psychosis. When children have developmental or language delays, they aren't able to communicate well and may appear to have delusions. This is when diagnosis becomes complicated, and even an experienced clinician may have to take a "time will tell" or "medications will tell" approach. Psychotic symptoms do not respond to the treatments that are effective for OCD.

It is best to seek a complete evaluation by a competent mental health professional if you are concerned about your child having delusions or hallucinations. The context of the "voices," the manner in which they manifest, the content, frequency, impact on functioning, interference, distress will help a professional put together a more accurate picture than diagnosing voices in a vacuum. See Chapter 3 for evaluation and diagnosis.

FREQUENTLY-ASKED QUESTIONS

I think my child has some early signs of OCD. I don't want to jump to conclusions, but I don't want to ignore a genuine problem. What can I do?

Trust your instincts. If the behaviors are not getting in the way, watch and wait, without drawing undue attention to them. Stay alert, and track your child's behaviors over a period of time. Let your child's pediatrician know what you are observing. If the behaviors become more severe, more frequent or start to get in the way of your child's functioning, seek an evaluation by an expert in childhood OCD. Chapter 3 covers evaluation and diagnosis of OCD.

My child asks the same questions over and over, even after I answer her. She doesn't have any other rituals or fears of which I am aware. I can't figure out if she is just trying to get my attention, having trouble understanding, or if this might be OCD?

It is important to know the context and the content of your child's questions. If your daughter is merely trying to get your attention, her questions are more likely to arise when you are otherwise occupied, perhaps with siblings or activities that absorb your time. If she is having trouble comprehending, she might look puzzled or act in ways that clearly reflect lack of understanding of the information. Natural curiosity and learning will raise questions that elicit information and more detailed knowledge. OCD questions are usually focused on issues that generate anxiety such as illness, germs, disasters and calamities, or about uncertainty in schedules and activities e.g., the agenda for the day, the menu for dinner and how much time before an anticipated event.

My kid's a pack rat. He won't throw away any of his old toys and gets very upset if we try to clean his room or if his brother touches his things. I'm concerned that it's a bit too much.

Collecting, hobbies, possessiveness about belongings and saving things are normal at certain ages. Usually, these items are treasured for sentimental value, or bring pleasure and enjoyment. With OCD, saving and hoarding is not associated with sentimental value. These are not memoirs or childhood blankets that are saved. They are items of limited value, which may qualify as appropriate for the trash can. They are often odd, unusual or bizarre items. Again, distress and interference are key elements. For instance, if your child becomes hysterical about the fact that you vacuumed and tidied his room, thereby tossing his collection of Q-tips, then OCD is a definite consideration.

Do kids with OCD continue to develop normally? My daughter was diagnosed with OCD at four. Now, at six, she seems to label all her fears and worries as OCD, even though they appear normal to me.

Learning how to discern, label and differentiate normal from excessive worry is a developmental process that takes time, maturation and experience. Even as adults, we struggle with this process. It is easy for someone with OCD to become overly sensitized to anxiety cues and cognitions-their radar thresholds are very low, and they lose touch with what's normal. Because your daughter was sensitized to OCD so young, her experience of normal fears and worries was interrupted. Now it is more confusing for her to figure out what's normal and what's OCD. Yes, she can certainly get back on track; however, she may find it more challenging to discern the difference between normal and OCD because there aren't any absolute rules to follow to tell them apart. You can help her sort this out by giving her examples of normal fears and how common they are, when the need arises. We often intuitively know the difference between normal and OCD worries, but it can be tricky to convey that to a child.

My son counts everything over and over, but says he does not have any worries or fears. Should I be concerned?

Does your son seem relaxed when he is counting? Can he stop counting if he chooses to? If so, he has probably created an enjoyable pastime for himself. If your son feels compelled to count, with great intensity, even when it is not appropriate, your son may have "just so" or "just right" obsessions and compulsions that are not associated with any fear of harm, danger or catastrophe. This is a common symptom in boys. They have an internal sense of intense discomfort that is relieved by doing certain rituals until they get that "just right" feeling—sometimes it is symmetry, sometimes just a nebulous "feeling"—the rules for this feeling cannot usually be appreciated by anyone else.

My seven-year-old pesters me non-stop after I've already said "No." She seems obsessed with some toy she wants or place she wants to go and won't let it go for days. Sometimes, I give in because I can't take the badgering anymore. Is this OCD?

The very fact that she cannot let go of "some toy she wants" is a clue that it is not OCD. What your child seems obsessed about is something that she desires and can potentially bring her pleasure. OCD obsessions are neither pleasurable nor desirable to the child. She is trying to wear you down into conceding with dogged persistence and stubborn noncompliance. The more you give in to her demands, the more likely she will repeat the behavior. For strategies to handle parenting challenges, see Chapter 12.

My son is "obsessed" with the computer and video games. He simply cannot stop, no matter what else is going on. Is this OCD?

Your son is absorbed in an activity that gives him intense fun and pleasure. He willfully seeks it out because he likes it. Once again, if the object of the "obsession" is an enjoyable, soothing or desirable situation, it is not an obsession in the psychiatric sense. True obsessions and compulsions are distressing and highly undesirable.

It seems like my daughter can't get her mind off food, overeats constantly and still complains that she is hungry. Will she outgrow this?

Although this is unlikely to be OCD, it is worth discussing your child's food habits with her pediatrician. Early eating habits can remain entrenched, leading to many weight-related health problems later. It may also be important to rule out if your daughter has a metabolic malfunction or other condition that is generating her insatiable appetite. If not, your daughter may have learned to derive pleasure and satisfaction from food and needs help learning healthier ways to meet those cravings. Your pediatrician may be able to recommend a nutritional expert or psychologist who can help her with such issues

Is spitting a tic or a compulsion?

It depends on the context. If the spitting occurs randomly, with little awareness, is not directed at a specific target, and appears automatic, it is likely to be a tic. If it is in response to things that make your child anxious, and is geared towards reducing anxiety, it is possibly an OCD ritual. If your child spits at someone because she is angry and wants to punish them, it is neither a tic nor a compulsion. It is your child's way of expressing hostility and should be managed accordingly (see Chapter 12).

My son "flips out" even at the mere mention of a cold or flu. Once, when I turned on the TV, he saw a commercial for cold medicine and had a full-blown panic attack--hyperventilating, heart pounding, feeling faint, sweating, crying hysterically. He said he thought he would catch a cold and die. Is this panic disorder or OCD?

Panic attacks can occur in the context of many different anxiety disorders including OCD. Panic Disorder consists of unexpected, repeated panic attacks that occur unpredictably and "out of the blue," without any specific trigger other than fear of the panic attack itself. The fact that your son's panic appeared to be triggered by a commercial that reminded him about colds and death suggests that he might have some OCD-related fears of disease and death. To be certain, it is best to consult with an expert on childhood anxiety disorders, as the presence of panic should be addressed in treatment.

My daughter seems to be obsessed with me. She wants to look like me and dress like me. If I'm happy, she acts happy; if I am sad, she acts sad. I think she has OCD, but no one will listen to me.

Your daughter's preoccupation with you appears to make you uncomfortable to say the least. It would be best to seek an evaluation. Your daughter's age and maturity level will help shed some light on her behavior. It would be far less concerning if she were five years old than if she were 15. There may be many different reasons for your daughter's behavior. Although it could well be an indicator of OCD, it could also be separation anxiety, a strong need for attachment, a way to keep you engaged and attentive to her, or an intense fixation that is typical of her style.

My son has been diagnosed with OCD. He used to be a pretty easy-going kid, but recently, he has been having many rage attacks, is verbally abusive to us, and manages to keep his younger sister in terror. Is this OCD?

Rage often accompanies OCD, even though temper outbursts and aggression are not part of the diagnosis of OCD. Many children with OCD do not have episodes of rage. Rage can be the result of being frustrated or thwarted in completing rituals. Children also become exhausted by the unrelenting demands of OCD, and may therefore be on a hair-trigger. They have little patience left to give to routine matters. Children with OCD could also be prone to being oppositional, defiant or noncompliant apart from OCD. Although the rage and verbal abuse are understandable, that does not make them acceptable. Children must learn to live with the norms of society for their own good. For suggestions on helping your child overcome rage, see Chapter 12.

Chapter 3

Evaluation and Diagnosis

I started washing my hands when I was eight. My brothers teased me and called me a "clean freak" and my parents just thought I was a little particular about being clean. They didn't see any harm in that, because my three older brothers were slobs and my mom complained about their messiness all the time. Pretty soon, I knew something was wrong with me, because I couldn't stop washing. My hands were raw and bleeding, and I would apply soap to the wounds, to make sure no germs got in the cuts. I would cry from the burning. Meanwhile, I was in the bathroom for hours and my brothers began banging down the door and calling me names. How could I tell my family I really was crazy? So I tried to hide my hands so no one would find out. Well, my mom finally found out when I was 10. She took me to a doctor who told her to set some rules so that everyone got equal time in the bathroom…After four more years, another doctor finally diagnosed me with OCD.

Maya, age 17

Maya's story is a sad but true reminder that, even as recently as the past decade, parents, teachers and even doctors often misunderstood OCD as bad habits, purposeful misbehavior or weakness of character. Instead of proper treatment, the prescription was tighter discipline and "better" parenting. Countless adults whose OCD began in childhood have suffered the same fate as Maya. For many, it has been an anguishing process of muddling through doctors, systems and diagnoses, until OCD has been stumbled upon. It has only been in the last 10-15 years that there has been a notable rise in the accurate and timely diagnosis of OCD, a phenomenon OCD expert Dr. Michael Jenike has called the "hidden epidemic." Fortunately, thanks to increased awareness and media exposure, the children of today and tomorrow are less likely to share Maya's experience.

A correct diagnosis is necessary for the right treatment. Yet, more often than not, the diagnosis of OCD can be elusive, especially for children. In this chapter, I will cover the importance of a proper evaluation, obstacles to getting a good diagnosis, what you can do to get your child the best evaluation possible and what to expect as you steer your way through the process. As you will learn in Chapters 5 and 6 on the treatment of OCD, your child's chances of living a good life are greatly increased if OCD is diagnosed and treated both promptly and properly.

HURDLES IN THE EVALUATION PROCESS

For the many reasons described below, diagnosing children with OCD can be far more challenging than diagnosing adults. Children and adolescents typically do not seek diagnosis or treatment for themselves. Consequently, they must rely on caregivers to seek help in their behalf.

❖   *Parental awareness*

OCD is not something that you come across in your average parenting magazine, or in your day-to-day life, so you cannot be expected to recognize early signs, unless you have some good reason to be informed about them. It can be very easy to miss early signs of OCD in children because, like many other parents, you don't have any benchmark with which to compare your child's behaviors. Even if you think something is amiss, you may brush it off as a passing phase. You may well be right, because children do have a myriad of rituals and beliefs that are entirely normal, as described in Chapter 2.

❖   *Parental anxiety and reluctance*

Let's say you do have the creeping realization that your child's recent peculiarities are not just a phase anymore. You may be reluctant to get a diagnosis for fear of the repercussions of "labeling" your child so young, especially with the wrong stamp. Labels do tend to follow children just like tags do on shirts. Accepting that your child has a "mental" condition may be a tough pill to swallow. These thoughts can be so difficult to digest that you may find it easier to deny, avoid, or minimize your child's now glaringly obvious symptoms. You may hope that they will just go away or disappear one day. The stigma of mental illness lingers because it is too often incorrectly attributed to a character flaw or bad upbringing. Unfortunately, many parents don't know how that OCD is very treatable.

❖ *Gatekeeper awareness*

Pediatricians, teachers and school counselors are often the gatekeepers for timely recognition and proper treatment of OCD in children. Many gatekeepers do not have an established or routine procedure to screen and detect anxiety or OCD in children. When you've finally summoned up the nerve to tackle the problem, your doctor may say, "Oh, you're worrying too much. He'll grow out of it. Just give it some time." You waited a long time to persuade yourself there was a problem, and now you have to spend even more time convincing everyone else that something is wrong. Your child's pediatrician, who is typically the channel of access to other specialists, may also miss the early warning signs that are described in Chapter 2. Your child's bleeding gums, chafed hands, stomach ailments and nausea which could be OCD-related may merit referral to a dentist, dermatologist or GI specialist. These specialists generally do not look for OCD, because it is such an uncommon complaint in their practices.

❖ *Shortage of experts*

Unfortunately, there is still a dearth of experts in childhood OCD. As you read in Chapters 1 and 2, OCD can be so varied in expression and have so many subtleties that it can be hidden behind the façade of depression, ADHD or oppositional behavior. Although classic forms of OCD are easily recognized, many mental health professionals are not well versed in the nuances of OCD. Children are frequently first brought to professional attention for such problems as tantrums, declining school performance, distractibility, withdrawal, depression, food restrictions, dermatitis, or constipation, but not often for obsessions and compulsions. These complaints become distracters that can easily sidetrack those who are not familiar with the intricacies of OCD. The repercussions of the wrong diagnosis can be devastating for your child. (See the next section in this chapter as well as Chapter 7 for how to find the right professionals to diagnose and treat your child).

❖ *Inexact diagnostic methods*

Having a definitive test to diagnose OCD would certainly eliminate uncertainty and confusion. Unfortunately, as of this writing, OCD can neither be confirmed nor denied by any laboratory test, X-ray or CAT scan. The diagnosis of OCD, like any other mental illness, relies both on established guidelines and on the clinical judgment of a professional. The behavior and emotions of each person are so unique that any Yes/No test would not capture the true essence of the condition. This can be frustrating, especially if you are a creature of certainty and like to have definite answers and hard data.

❖ *"Reading the minds" of children*

A large part of diagnosing OCD relies on the child's descriptions of fears, thoughts and rituals. Children, especially young ones, are not always able to communicate with us in ways we understand. They are not always able to articulate thoughts, feelings and cause-effect relationships effectively enough to help us appreciate what they are experiencing. Some children are not even aware or insightful of these processes. Older children and adolescents who are aware that they are behaving in untoward fashion may be secretive because they are confused and ashamed. All this leaves parents and clinicians with the mind-reading game, which is a dubious endeavor to begin with. It takes astuteness, time and experience to discern OCD in many cases.

❖ *Complexity of symptoms*

Diagnosis can sometimes be challenging even for experts, because OCD can come in a variety of shapes and sizes. The high rate of overlap of symptoms with other disorders (see Chapter 2) can muddy the diagnostic waters, making it difficult to diagnose OCD with certainty. It may take months or years for patterns to emerge, in which case your child may be given a "probable" diagnosis. Often, OCD may not be the primary disorder, requiring the clinician to prioritize and treat one condition at a time.

❖ *Imperfect diagnostic system*

The current system for diagnosis of OCD is the *Diagnostic and Statistical Manual of Mental Disorders, Fourth Edition* (DSM-IV) of the American Psychiatric Association. A diagnosis is made when a certain number or configuration of symptoms for a specific disorder is met. However, we don't come neatly packaged into categories, so making a diagnosis is not as simple as sorting apples from oranges. We are complex human beings; while we have many similarities that allow us to fall into categories, we also have unique attributes that do not fit into boxes. Many children with obsessions and compulsions don't neatly fit the diagnosis of OCD; others may fit more than one category. A given diagnosis therefore may not capture all aspects of a child's emotions and behaviors. In fact, there is general frustration among clinicians that many children with problematic symptoms are not adequately described by the diagnostic system. Although the DSM-IV is not sensitive enough to all aspects of a child's functioning, there is no better system yet.

FINDING CLINICIANS TO EVALUATE YOUR CHILD

It would be to your advantage to take your child to an OCD child expert as soon as you have the inkling that he may have OCD. The right expert is one who uses a *biopsychosocial* approach (see next section) to diagnosing and treating OCD in *children*, and who is familiar with Cognitive-Behavioral Therapy (CBT) and/or medications (see Chapters 5 and 6). Keep in mind that there are far more professionals who can competently *diagnose* OCD than those who can provide the *right treatment* for your child. If you have a choice at all, you would save yourself the redundancy, of two evaluations by taking your child to an OCD expert who can also treat your child. Chapter 7 discusses how to find the right clinician.

Experts in childhood OCD may be found in individual practices, small clinics or large hospitals. Sometimes, their practice location may make no difference, but if you have many experts to choose from, their location might be of interest to you. There may be differences in operation between private practices, clinics and hospitals. These may include the wait time for your first appointment, the number of procedural steps involved, the length of the evaluation, access to related services, distance and fees.

It is best to seek an expert who has access to a team of other relevant professionals. If you choose to go to a professional in a private practice, make sure he or she can access other specialists easily if your child needs them. If your child has more complex diagnostic issues such as symptoms of other disorders (see Chapter 2), you may be better off with a multidisciplinary team that includes a child psychiatrist, a psychologist, a social worker, education specialist, speech therapist etc. If your child has symptoms of TS, ADHD, Asperger's Syndrome or other such disorders, it may be to your advantage to have coordinated care at one location.

How can you locate experts in childhood OCD? Ask for referrals from your child's pediatrician, school psychologist, family and friends (see Chapter 7 for more information). Advocacy organizations such as the Obsessive Compulsive Foundation (OCF), Anxiety Disorders Association of America (ADAA) and Association for the Advancement of Behavior Therapy (AABT; see *Resources*) often maintain databases of professionals across the country. The people with the most first-hand experience in finding experts are parents like you who have children with OCD. Internet groups such as ocdandparenting (see *Resources*) may lead you to parents in your area who know a local OCD expert.

Depending on your needs, you may have to travel some distance to access the service that's right for you. Be prepared to miss work and school—you have to decide your priorities. Call for an appointment as soon as possible, even if things are going reasonably well. If you wait until symptoms become serious, you may encounter difficulty getting an appointment at short notice. It is wise to have a back-up clinician in case your first choice has a long waiting time. If you perceive the clinician to be lacking in empathy, detached, blaming you, vague or reluctant to answer questions, you would be wise to reconsider your choice.

A BIOPSYCHOSOCIAL FRAMEWORK

Dr. George Engel, a physician at the University of Rochester School of Medicine, understood that people are part of a larger context and that illnesses do not exist in a vacuum. He emphasized that a patient's diagnosis, treatment and recovery would be more effective if they attended not just to the medical, but also to psychological and social facets of the patient's life. Dr. Engel's *biopsychosocial* approach to healthcare is so critical because your child is a person, not a diagnosis. OCD is just one aspect of your child's life. Your child is unique and adapts to his world in his own distinctive way. Your child's recovery will be hastened when he is understood and treated as a *whole* person.

Biopsychosocial Assessment of OCD

❖ Past and present OCD symptoms
❖ Past and present non-OCD symptoms
❖ Past and present medical history and recent physical exam
❖ Onset of symptoms, with possible triggers and precipitants
❖ Specific details of OCD symptoms, severity, distress, interference
❖ Impact of OCD on home, school and social functioning.
❖ Developmental history: Milestones, delays, difficulties, early signs
❖ Psychological processes such as temperament, cognitive style, coping skills, insight, attitude and motivation
❖ Social relations, peer relations and interactional style
❖ Academic and school functioning
❖ Talents, abilities, skills, recreational and leisure activities
❖ Stressors, life events and transitions for the child and family
❖ Family history of OCD and other psychiatric conditions
❖ Family relationships, interactional and communication styles
❖ Impact of OCD on the family

A biopsychosocial assessment focuses on a complete and sensitive understanding of OCD in the context of the child's personal attributes, family, friends and school. Rather than merely assess OCD, it is geared towards the larger issue of the child's overall health, personality, functioning, strengths and talents, adaptation to school, family and social life. With such a complete understanding, the treatment plan for the child can be tailored to the child's unique needs and resources. Such a customized treatment approach can prevent treatment failures. Overlooking or ignoring other influences on the child's OCD and narrowly focusing on symptoms alone is unlikely to lead to recovery from OCD.

As you might expect, a biopsychosocial evaluation is a collaborative process between doctor, parent, child, school and other relevant players. The clinician must be able to obtain information from as many sources as possible using a variety of methods to bring together the big picture.

WHAT TO EXPECT DURING THE EVALUATION

Outlined below are the steps that are involved in assessing a child who may have OCD. You will find that many child OCD experts use a similar sequence of steps, although there are differences in styles and process of evaluation among experts. The length of the evaluation may range from two to four office visits of 50-90 minutes each, depending on the complexity of the child's condition and other biopsychosocial factors. The next section offers tips on what you can do to get the most out of an evaluation.

Initial telephone screening

The first phone contact is an information-gathering and screening phase. Clinicians in private practice may do their own screenings. At a large clinic or hospital, a receptionist or staff member will likely screen you before you encounter a clinician. The screener will ask about your specific concerns, needs and expectations, in order to ascertain whether he or she is the appropriate person to help you. If she is not the appropriate clinician, she should refer you to others who may be better able to help you. When I screen potential patients, I describe the steps in the assessment, the length of time it will take, the type of participation expected of parent and child and office policies regarding cancellations and fees. Following the telephone screening, I mail out a letter to parents that summarizes my assessment and treatment procedures, office and fee policies, and a handful of forms, as described below.

Pre-evaluation forms

You may be asked to complete developmental and behavioral history forms and rating scales of your child's behaviors before or during your first appointment. The information you provide on these forms gives the clinician a very important "preview" of your child's background, needs and functioning. They allow her to focus quickly on relevant matters, saving time and redundancy during the actual face-to-face visit.

Review of records

You may be asked to provide or arrange for all pertinent records to be sent to your clinician. These will include records from your child's pediatrician (physicals, immunizations, illnesses and treatments, medications), the school (grades, IQ, achievement or other school-based testing, counselor's notes) and any prior evaluations or treatments for behavioral or emotional problems. The exchange of information between your therapist and your child's school, pediatrician or previous clinicians can only take place with your explicit written permission known as a *Release of Information*. Let the clinician know if you are hesitant to sign such a release.

Interview with parent(s)

The clinician may meet with you with or without your child present at the first appointment. This should be clarified at the telephone screening. I initially meet with the parent(s) without the child present, to allow parents the chance to talk candidly and to save the child the discomfort of being the subject of discussion. Subsequently, I meet with parent(s) and the child jointly in order to build rapport with the child while he is in the company of his parents. When the child is comfortable, I meet with the child alone to allow the child to engage with me independent of his parents. With adolescents, I usually meet separately from the start.

Parents are essential and invaluable to the assessment because they can give a better chronology of events, give details more accurately and discuss family history and relationships at greater depth. Children may not always disclose sufficient information because they may be embarrassed, uncomfortable, secretive or perhaps even unaware of what is going on. They may not necessarily view their symptoms as excessive.

During the interview, your clinician will ask many questions in order to get detailed information about current and past fears and habits, behaviors and functioning at home and at school, medical, developmental and family history. You should be asked about the things that may trigger your child's fears or rituals, events surrounding the onset of his symptoms, how often they occur and in what situations, how much they bother him and how much they get in the way of his ability to function. You may be asked about many other types of behaviors and emotions such as compliance, oppositional behavior, hyperactivity, attention, anger, sadness, anxiety and other compulsive habits such as hair pulling, nail biting or scab picking. As part of a biopsychosocial assessment, the clinician will be interested in your child's personality, strengths, talents and positive qualities, school, family and social adjustment. In addition, you may be asked about life at home, how your child's symptoms have affected you, the child's siblings and your marital relationship. There will also be focus on your family history of obsessions, compulsions, anxiety, panic, tics and other emotional and behavioral disturbances. A family tree or "genogram" may be drawn to capture your family history.

Interview with your child

Although the child may not be the best historian, no one but the child can give the clinician insight into his thoughts, feelings and experiences. It is important for the clinician to understand and gauge your child's insight and experience of symptoms, how much they bother him, how eager he is to get rid of them and how willing he is to learn ways to do that. Talking to your child will help the clinician obtain answers to many other questions: Does the child perform rituals to relieve obsessions or prevent bad outcomes? How is each fear connected with each ritual? What would happen if he did not do a ritual? How does the child know when he's done enough? What does he do to relieve anxiety? What makes him feel better and what makes the thoughts go away? How does your child feel about having these behaviors and fears? Does he believe he can overcome them?

Is he hopeful and optimistic? Or does he feel defeated and dispirited? How does he feel about himself as a person?

Mental status examination

During the process of interviewing your child, the clinician will assess his mental status, which includes mood, speech and activity level, thought process, perception, insight, judgment, memory, intelligence and any unusual behaviors. The clinician will also attempt to rule out hallucinations, delusions (see Chapter 2) or other possible reasons for your child's thoughts, fears or rituals.

Medical history, physical examination and laboratory tests

A detailed medical and developmental history will help the clinician evaluate medical events such as serious head injury, brain infections or immune system illnesses as potential causes for the onset of OCD. A recent physical examination and clean bill of health are important in a biopsychosocial evaluation. If your child has not had a recent one, he should either receive one or be referred to his pediatrician for one. If your child has had an acute onset of OCD symptoms or tics, the clinician should examine his history of upper respiratory infections to evaluate the possibility of *Pediatric Autoimmune Neuropsychiatric Disorders Associated with Streptococcal Infections* (PANDAS; see Chapter 4). Additional referrals to other medical specialists for related conditions such as TS or PDD (see Chapter 2) may be made at this time.

Rating scales and self-report questionnaires

There are many different rating scales and questionnaires that help the clinician further understand the nature of your child's symptoms. The most prominent one for OCD is the *Children's Yale-Brown Obsessive-Compulsive Scale* (C-YBOCS), which is an interview with you and your child and takes about 30 minutes to complete. The C-YBOCS allows the clinician to examine obsessions and compulsions separately with regard to the time they consume in your child's day, how upsetting they are, how much they interfere with his everyday life, how much he tries to fight them off and how much control he feels he has over them. After the interview, the clinician will calculate your child's total score on the C-YBOCS. The score helps determine if your child's OCD is mild, moderate, severe or extreme. Having a "baseline" or starting C-YBOCS score is very important because it can be compared with scores obtained periodically during and after treatment to gauge improvement. Another measure is the *Leyton Obsessional Inventory-Child Version* (LOI-CV) which is completed by the child.

After completing the interviews and looking at your child's records, the clinician will decide what other scales and tests may be useful in providing additional information about your child. Questionnaires pertaining to depression, anxiety and self-concept are often given to children who are old enough to read and comprehend them. IQ and neuropsychological testing are not essential to proper diagnosis or treatment of OCD. They should only be conducted if it is suspected that IQ or learning difficulties may be affecting the child's functioning and potential response to treatment. Treatment choices may need to be modified considerably for children with lower IQ or neuropsychological difficulties. IQ testing is both time consuming and expensive, so it should be used judiciously.

Feedback and treatment planning

At the end of the evaluation, the clinician will pull all the information together and integrate it into a cohesive picture. He or she should share this cohesive biopsychosocial picture with you and give you clinical impressions. If your child has OCD, the clinician should describe what OCD is, dispel any myths and misconceptions about it and discuss all the potential treatment options for your child. Treatment options should include CBT (see Chapter 5), medication (see Chapter 6) and possibly academic interventions, family therapy and other supportive treatments as pertinent to your child and family's needs. You should be given enough information about the benefits and drawbacks of each treatment option to help you make an informed decision.

HOW YOU CAN PREPARE FOR AN EVALUATION

You and your child will get the most out of an evaluation if you prepare for it in advance and plan on being actively involved. You need to share your expertise as your child's parent with the clinician, so that he or she develops a more thorough understanding of your child and his needs. Below are some suggestions that will help you achieve this goal.

❖ *Start right away*

Get the ball rolling by seeking a consultation with the "gatekeeper" for your child's treatment, most likely the pediatrician. Write down your child's behaviors, when and how often they occur in a notebook. Recall past instances during earlier years when similar symptoms were present. Take your notes with you to your doctor, so you don't have to rely on memory during the appointment. Having specific examples will help your doctor recognize the need for a referral to an expert.

❖ *Inquire about payment policies and insurance coverage*

Obtain any necessary pre-authorizations from insurance companies to save yourself unpleasant surprises and delays. Don't assume that your insurance coverage to see a mental health professional is the same as it may be for a visit to the pediatrician. Your out-of-pocket expense to see a mental health professional may be higher than what you pay to see the pediatrician or other medical specialist.

❖ *Follow up on referrals to experts immediately*

If your doctor refers your child to an OCD specialist, call for an appointment sooner rather than later. Wait times for appointments can be as long as six to eight weeks. If you cannot get an appointment right away, ask if you can be placed on a "cancellation list" that might allow you get an earlier appointment if someone cancels.

❖ *Be an educated consumer*

Read Chapters 5 and 6 on the treatment of OCD *before* your child's evaluation is completed. This information will allow you to be more informed about the treatment options the doctor may suggest.

❖ *Ask questions*

Questions allow you to understand the clinician's diagnostic and treatment approach (see Table 10 in Chapter 7). Don't hesitate to ask about fees, insurance and payment policies. It is best if you resolve all these issues before you begin evaluation or treatment to avoid any surprises that would detract from your focus during the assessment.

❖ *Complete all forms and paperwork in a timely manner*

If you don't, you will be wasting time and the opportunity to share your expertise and knowledge of your child with the clinician. In addition, failure to complete forms might be viewed as a reflection of lack of commitment on your part.

❖ *Keep written notes of your child's symptoms*

Take a few minutes to jot down your child's past and present behaviors that have been of concern to you. See Figure 2 for an example.

Figure 2: History of Behaviors

History of Behaviors		
Child's Name: Bob	*Age: 11*	*Date: Nov 2*
Picked up after himself, without being told.	1 year old	7 years old
Wanted to save nail clippings, very upset if thrown away.	18 months	3 years later
Vacation with Grandpa, starts making lists of toys, books, missing things	7 years old, first grade	3 months later
Wants me to list everything on shelves in grocery store.	7 years old; 1 month later	3 months later
Says, "I can't stand the pain. Why go on living like this? It's too hard."	7 years, 5 months	Still says, on and off

❖ *Keep a Daily Diary of your child's behavior*

A daily diary (see Figure 3) for a week prior to your appointment will give the clinician an insider's look into a "typical week." As you well know, your child won't reveal his obsessions, compulsions and true behaviors in the space of an hour or two on the unfamiliar turf of the doctor's office. Again, you wouldn't have to rely on your memory as much if you keep track of things as they happen rather than try to recount them in the short space of an appointment. This diary will come in just as handy when your child is in treatment (see Chapter 10).

Figure 3: Daily Diary of My Child's Behaviors and Feelings

Daily Diary of My Child's Behaviors and Feelings			
Name: Laurie		Age: 12	
Date/ time	What's happening	My child's behavior in the circumstances	My child's feelings
June 12, 7 a.m.	I wake her up for school.	She starts crying because her leg is "stuck" to the sheets and she needs me to "unstick" it. I have to rotate it a certain way, then she can get out. No matter how much I try, she won't do it herself, and gets mad at me if I don't do it for her.	She's scared, mad at me, yells a lot
8 a.m.	Leaving the house.	Checks her book bag about 6 times, counts the pencils over and over.	Upset when I tell her the bus is here.
3 p.m.	Home from school	Cheerful and calm. Says she had a good day. Tells me about a friend's new puppy. Wishes she had a dog.	Happy, calm, talkative.

❖ *Compile an extended family history*

When you start asking family members for history, you may be surprised to learn that Aunt Lucille always wore elbow length gloves around the house and cousin Larry only walked up the stairs backwards.

❖ *Be on time for your appointment*

Mental health appointments are often time-bound. If you are late, you are unlikely to get an extension of time, as you would intrude into the next person's appointment. Give yourself an extra 15 minutes for traffic, construction delays and parking or if the location is unfamiliar to you.

❖ *Consolidate all relevant materials in one place*

Keep a notebook or binder in which you save and file everything from start to finish of the evaluation and treatment. This serves as your sequential record of telephone conversations, authorizations, excerpts of relevant articles and books, notes from each appointment, and other relevant material that is best consolidated under one cover. When the need arises, you will not be scrambling to piece together scraps of paper.

FREQUENTLY-ASKED QUESTIONS

I'd like to get a second opinion before accepting diagnosis of OCD for my child. What's the next step?

You should seek a second opinion by all means. Check with your insurance company for their policy on second opinions. Be sure that the doctor you see for a second opinion is at least as familiar with diagnosing OCD as the doctor who first made the diagnosis.

I have been telling my doctor about my son's fears and worries, but he says he doesn't think it's anything serious. What should I do?

Ask your doctor why she doesn't think your child's fears are serious. Ask if she has seen fears and worries such as your child's, what happens to children who have such fears, and how they get over them. Ask if she has seen children with OCD in her practice and how they are different from your child. Ask for suggestions on helping your child overcome the fears.

If you are still concerned, keep a Daily Diary (see Figure 3) and take it back to your doctor after four to six weeks. If your child's school is concerned about his fears or worries, ask them to share their concerns with your doctor. If you believe that your doctor is not responding to legitimate concerns, you should seek a second opinion.

I have an appointment scheduled but I haven't told my child yet, because I'm afraid she won't want to go. How do I tell my child about it?

Above all, don't trick your child into a doctor's appointment. It destroys your child's trust in you and sets up an instant negative start with the doctor. Your child will believe that going to the doctor must be unpleasant enough for you to want to deceive her. She will hardly want to cooperate when she's been "duped." Instead, find a quiet, uninterrupted time to spend with your child. After a good warm-up time, let your child know you have noticed she seems to be having some trouble or is doing unusual things. Ask if they are bothering her and mention that they appear to be. Tell your child that you would like to get help for her. If your child appears sensitive or defensive, let her know that it doesn't change the person she is, her good qualities or how you feel about her. If your child still seems reluctant, speak to the doctor and ask for suggestions on how to handle the situation in your circumstances.

Should I take my child to the first session? I'd like to speak to the doctor privately.

Call the doctor who will be evaluating your child and express your reservations about bringing your child to the first session. Unless there is some reason to insist that your child be present, the doctor should respect your wish to meet alone.

I've been told that my daughter has symptoms of OCD and other "alphabet soup" such as TS, ADHD and Asperger's Syndrome. She also has diabetes. Where do I find someone who knows enough about all these different disorders?

Large medical centers have many different specialists and services under one roof. Some even have education specialists who can help you work with your child's school to develop specific school-based interventions. It may be easier to find all the specialists you need and to move back and forth among doctors who are in the same facility. But don't take it for granted; it doesn't always work like it's supposed to. Further, you will still need to have one doctor to coordinate the overall care of your child, because too many doctors can be like the proverbial "too many cooks."

I'm concerned about labeling my child. I don't want her to have to carry the label as she goes through life and face the stigma that comes with it.

Ironically, the label of OCD might actually be more helpful to your child than you realize. If your child does have OCD, having a label could be a big relief to him. It makes his symptoms legitimate, not just a creation of his own mind. Knowing there's a name to it and that he's not the only one who has it absolves him from blame and lifts the burden of guilt. He may even be able to find support from other children who have OCD.

More importantly, a label is more likely to get your child the right treatment in a timely manner. It could be more harmful to your child to *not* have a label, because he may not receive treatment, which could have life-altering consequences. Yes, the stigma attached to mental illness is a regrettable fact; but you may be able to contribute to lessening that stigma by educating family, friends and school personnel about OCD. If you are concerned about the label following your child to college or the workplace, it is against the law for professionals to disclose your child's condition to anyone without written permission from you and/or your child.

Will my insurance pay for the evaluation and treatment of OCD?

Insurance plans vary tremendously. Learn all you can about what and how much your insurance covers. In most cases, OCD is considered a "mental health" disorder for reimbursement purposes, and it does not receive the same coverage as a medical disorder. Efforts towards parity for mental health services have recently gained some victories, but there is still a long way to go before it translates into real value for the consumer.

You should know that you do have recourse if your insurance company denies payment. Don't just accept a denial of benefits without seeking justification. Ask to speak to the medical director of mental health at your insurance carrier and ask for the reason for denial. Inquire about the credentials of the person who recommended the denial and ask about the process used to arrive at the denial. Request to speak to the manager of claims so that you can learn how to access the appeals process, both within and outside the insurance company. Appeal the denial in writing, and pursue the process with regularity and persistence. Make your complaints and queries written rather than verbal, so that you have documentation of all your interactions. Keep copies for yourself in your folder. When you do need to use the telephone, keep a log of all telephone calls, the person with whom you spoke, and the content of your conversation. Fax a copy of your log to your insurance company after the call. Be systematic and don't give up too easily. Your resolve will make the insurance company very careful about denying your claim without ample justification.

Inquire about any potential supplementary sources of coverage for your child's treatment. Learn if your child qualifies for any state or federally funded children's health dollars such as the Children's Health Insurance Plan, which may be known by different names in different states. Inquire about eligibility criteria for social security and Medicaid benefits. Typically, your child must have specific diagnoses, with a given duration and level of impairment to be considered eligible. Prepare yourself to encounter lots of paperwork and lengthy procedures. You must be systematic, thorough and persistent, because you are your child's best advocate.

Chapter 4

How Does OCD Develop?

To be surprised, to wonder, is to begin to understand.

Jose Ortega y Gasset

One day, about halfway through the 6th grade school year, we received a call from Maria's school counselor regarding suspicions of OCD. We scheduled an appointment with her pediatrician. When we heard that Maria probably had OCD, and that we were in for a long road of treatments and recovery, we were shocked. How could this have happened? What had gone wrong? Was it genetic? There were so many questions and so few answers.

Carl and Elaine, parents of Maria

For many parents, the first encounter with a diagnosis of OCD is a shock. Like Maria's parents, *why* and *how* are among the foremost questions in their minds. It can be difficult for parents to hear that there are no definite answers to these questions because the exact cause of OCD is unknown. Until fairly recently, OCD was considered to be the result of bad upbringing and an unhappy childhood. At least two things are now clear: First, bad parenting does not cause OCD and good parenting does not prevent it. Second, OCD is not the handiwork of deliberate misbehavior, character weakness or poor self-control.

Many *risk factors* such as brain chemistry, biology, genetics, stress and learning may play a role in the development of OCD. Some of these risk factors are fixed and unalterable; others are dynamic in their ability to *fuel* OCD. How all these risk factors come together for your child may remain a mystery. It can be incredibly frustrating to accept this when you are trying to cope with the implications of OCD for your child. Life is full of uncertainties and this is one of those uncertainties with which many parents have to learn to live. The good news is that your child can benefit from effective treatments regardless of the cause (see Chapters 5 and 6).

The various pieces of the jigsaw puzzle of OCD are discussed in this chapter. It is a far more complex puzzle than you might imagine. Although recent research has indicated some culprits in the OCD equation, we don't know how they all come together to sum up to OCD. Think of it this way: There are many different ways to add up to 10. Five plus five adds up to 10, so do three, three and four or two, two and six. You can arrive at the same end result with a variety of combinations. Likewise, each person ends up with OCD in his own unique way. The difference between this analogy and OCD is that we know all the parts of the equation that add up to 10, whereas we don't know all the terms of the OCD equation. It is actually a compliment to our complexity as humans and our uniqueness as individuals that the precise answers continue to elude us.

A few words of caution as you read through this chapter: Despite the temptation, it is important to be careful about drawing hasty conclusions about specific risk factors that seem to "fit" for your child. None of the known risk factors described here may definitely or completely explain the cause of OCD for any given child or adult.

MISFIRING CIRCUITS IN THE BRAIN

The brain is bombarded with countless signals each day to which it must attend. It must sift through the volley of messages, assign them priorities and decide what manner of response they merit. The primary areas of the brain involved in receiving, filtering, selecting, routing and acting on incoming signals are the *basal ganglia, caudate nuclei, thalamus, orbital frontal cortex* and *orbital gyri*. These areas of the brain do their jobs seamlessly without our awareness for the most part. For people with OCD, an apparent glitch in the circuitry of these areas seems to trigger a series of events that result in obsessive-compulsive behavior.

The basal ganglia, seated deep within the brain, are responsible for regulating sensations and thoughts, the ability to shift from one activity to another, carrying out "automatic" tasks and routines and behaviors such as grooming and checking. The caudate nuclei, a substructure of the basal ganglia, act as a filter for the huge amount of information that the brain receives. They are responsible for sorting the relevant from the irrelevant, and passing on only those messages that require action. The thalamus receives the messages screened by the caudate nuclei and relays them to the frontal cortex, signaling it to respond to them. The frontal cortex and orbital gyri, located in front of the brain, just above the eyes, are involved in planning, organizing, controlling, and regulating "proper" behavior. Excessive activity in these frontal areas is associated with being fastidious, meticulous, inflexible and extremely particular about rules.

Normally, only a minute fraction of the messages that the brain receives are filtered through the gates; the rest are discarded. We attend to the important messages that get through and ignore the rest. When the message has been adequately acted upon, the brain signals that the task is done and gives us the green signal to move on. For instance, many people don't even really think about the fact that they check all the doors before they leave the home. One quick check and they can leave without any further thought of it. It all happens automatically and they are generally not even aware of this routine. On the other hand, for a person with OCD, this seemingly simple and automatic process seems to go very wrong.

It is believed that, for a person with OCD, the caudate nuclei receive too many fear and danger messages, fail to filter them adequately and let them flow through to the thalamus, similar to the effect of a leaky faucet. When the shut-off valve malfunctions, the leak seeps through the brain with a cascading effect. The thalamus receives all these messages and relays them to the frontal cortex. The frontal cortex is deluged with high priority danger messages and feels compelled to take action with great urgency. Every message calls for immediate protective action. The frontal cortex then dispatches messages to set in motion parts of the brain involved in anxiety, fear, dread, doubting, checking and repetition. Because these fear messages are not normally experienced, they can be disturbing and the person may feel uneasy and unsettled. The person must make a conscious effort to quiet these troubling signals by attending to them—washing, checking or repeating over again. The "okay" signal fails to arrive; the person repeats the sequence. When efforts to trip the green signal are futile, anxiety and distress begin to skyrocket.

Imagine feeling a great sense of urgency about every single fear message because your brain's screening system is malfunctioning. Imagine trying to get through a whole day of not getting okay signals from your brain for every little automatic thought or action. It could be likened to single-handedly trying to attend to and quiet two dozen infants who are all clamoring to be fed, changed and held at the same time—all day. Or consider sitting in a noisy bar and trying to carry on a normal conversation intelligently. We've all experienced that at some time or another, but what if you could never leave the noise behind? What if the noisy bar went with you wherever you went, all day, everyday? Your brain would be in overdrive, and you would be exhausted.

In fact, Drs. Jeffrey Schwartz and Lewis Baxter at UCLA found that the brains of OCD patients *are* in overdrive and use a tremendous amount of energy trying to handle the continuous commotion of obsessions and compulsions. Positron Emission Tomography (PET) scans showed higher rates of glucose consumption in the basal ganglia, caudate nucleus and the orbital frontal areas of the brain for OCD patients compared with depressed and normal adults. Glucose consumption is reflective of the high rate of metabolic activity involved in managing the information overload. Even more fascinating and exciting, Drs. Schwartz and Baxter found that proper treatment can decrease the rate of glucose metabolism in OCD patients (see Chapter 5).

Why does a "glitch" in brain functioning occur for persons with OCD? The most widely accepted theory is that it is due to disturbances in the activity of the neurotransmitter *serotonin* in brain cells, as described below.

SEROTONIN: THE CHEMICAL LINK

The neurotransmitter serotonin (5-hydroxytryptamine; 5-HT) may lie at the core of OCD. Neurotransmitters are the chemical messengers in the brain that help the brain cells communicate with each other. These cells, known as neurons, have gaps between them known as synaptic clefts. When the neuron is stimulated by an electrical impulse, the impulse must be able to cross the synaptic cleft in order to reach the next neuron, and thereby reach all the parts of the brain to which the message is directed. The neuron therefore releases neurotransmitters that act as a bridge, allowing the electrical impulse to cross the gap. After the impulse is transmitted, the neurotransmitter is either retrieved into the cell, a process known as "reuptake," or metabolized into inactive substances. It is believed that in OCD, there is a premature reuptake of serotonin, which disrupts the proper transmission of messages to the next cell.

In the 1960's, adults with OCD who were being treated for depression with *clomipramine* (Anafranil), a *serotonin reuptake inhibitor* (SRI), found that their OCD symptoms coincidentally improved. Since then, other drugs that block serotonin reuptake have also been found to reduce OCD symptoms (see Chapter 6). In contrast, antidepressants that primarily affect other neurotransmitters do not appear to improve OCD symptoms.

Unfortunately, there is no "serotonin test" to diagnose or predict OCD. Because serotonin interacts with other neurotransmitters that play a role in thoughts, feelings and behaviors, it has been difficult to isolate serotonin as the only neurotransmitter involved in OCD. Further, although serotonin is involved in OCD, there is no real evidence that it causes OCD. It could well be that OCD causes changes in serotonin functioning.

PANDAS (Pediatric Autoimmune Neuropsychiatric Disorders Associated with Streptococcal Infections)

Perhaps the most dramatic discovery regarding potential causes in the last decade was that strep throat infections could activate OCD in some children. Drs. Swedo, Rapoport, Leonard and their colleagues at the National Institute of Mental Health (NIMH) found that a misdirected immune system reaction to strep infections might result in the abrupt development or worsening of OCD for *some, but not all* children. The antibodies generated by the immune system to combat the strep infection begin to mistake other body tissues for the strep bacteria. Sometimes, the antibodies attack the child's heart or joints and cause rheumatic heart disease or arthritis. At other times, the antibodies attack the basal ganglia in the brain, causing obsessive-compulsive symptoms, tics or Sydenham's chorea. They named this form of OCD *Pediatric Autoimmune Neuropsychiatric Disorders Associated with Streptococcal Infections* or *PANDAS* for short.

A word of caution again: Strep throat is quite common among school-aged children. Not every child who gets frequent strep infections is at risk for OCD; nor is every child's OCD caused by strep infections. It is believed that children who have a genetic predisposition to OCD (see next section) are more susceptible to the strep-OCD connection; the strep infection may be the stressor that triggers OCD.

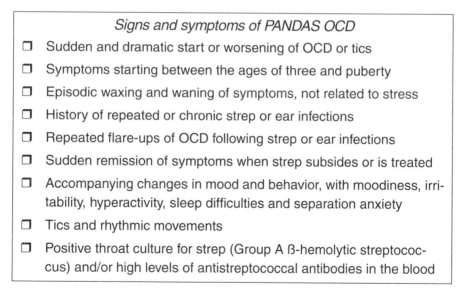

Signs and symptoms of PANDAS OCD

☐ Sudden and dramatic start or worsening of OCD or tics

☐ Symptoms starting between the ages of three and puberty

☐ Episodic waxing and waning of symptoms, not related to stress

☐ History of repeated or chronic strep or ear infections

☐ Repeated flare-ups of OCD following strep or ear infections

☐ Sudden remission of symptoms when strep subsides or is treated

☐ Accompanying changes in mood and behavior, with moodiness, irritability, hyperactivity, sleep difficulties and separation anxiety

☐ Tics and rhythmic movements

☐ Positive throat culture for strep (Group A ß-hemolytic streptococcus) and/or high levels of antistreptococcal antibodies in the blood

How do you know if your child has PANDAS OCD? First of all, your child must have a complete evaluation and receive an official diagnosis of OCD. The symptoms must have started before the onset of puberty. Then, the clinician will look for a particular pattern in the way the symptoms of OCD developed. The *onset* and *course* of PANDAS-triggered OCD is distinct from that of non-PANDAS OCD, although the actual symptoms are similar. The onset of PANDAS OCD is sudden and dramatic. Parents can often pinpoint the exact day the child's symptoms began. The symptoms also subside dramatically when the strep infection is resolved. Recurrences also occur as abruptly following a strep infection. Further, the symptoms tend to be severe rather than mild. There are also likely to be other personality changes, irritability, moodiness and separation anxiety. In non-PANDAS OCD, the onset and course are typically more gradual and insidious, with severity increasing over a period of time, not abruptly. Symptoms tend to be prolonged rather than short-lived and do not remit as quickly or completely.

In *some* cases, identifying the infection with a throat culture and treating it with a full course of antibiotics can alleviate the OCD symptoms. In addition, prophylactic antibiotic treatment may be given to prevent further strep infections in children who are prone to repeated infections and resultant OCD flare-ups. Children with PANDAS may not need therapy or anti-OCD medications if the strep infection responds well to an antibiotic and OCD symptoms subside. Prolonged use of antibiotics can compromise the body's ability to fight more serious infections in the future, as the bacteria may become resistant to frequently used antibiotics. In addition, antibiotics also destroy the "good" bacteria in the system that facilitate digestion and fend off other intruders such as yeast infections.

Researchers at the NIMH are studying some experimental treatments for very severe cases of PANDAS. One method is *plasmapharesis*, which is a filtering of the child's blood to remove strep antibodies. It is an invasive, arduous inpatient procedure requiring a few days hospital stay. The other treatment is intravenous injection of *immunoglobulin*, which is a blood product and may carry risks of viral transmission. The NIMH has issued a bulletin cautioning against the use of these treatments in clinical settings, due to their invasiveness and potential risks.

OF GENETICS AND FAMILY TREES

If you've been intrigued by Aunt Lucille's fastidious rules about cleanliness and Grandpa Warren's elaborate lists of everything, you are on to the fact that OCD and other forms of anxiety may run in some families. There are several pieces of evidence to suggest that genes and inheritance may be another piece of the OCD puzzle. Studies have shown that if one member of a twin pair has OCD, the other member of the twin pair is twice as likely to have OCD if the twins are identical rather than fraternal. Childhood OCD is more likely to be associated with a family history of OCD than OCD that begins in adulthood. Between 21% and 25% of the children of parents with OCD may develop OCD. In other words, if a parent has OCD, there may be up to a one in four chance that the child of that parent will have OCD, and a three in four chance that the child will not. Children are more likely to develop OCD if they have a parent who developed OCD during childhood or if they have other family members with OCD, other anxiety disorders or Tourette Syndrome (see Chapter 2). Among children diagnosed with OCD, about 25% have a first-degree (immediate family) relative with OCD.

Genetics is clearly not the whole story, because the majority of those who appear to have strong genetic links to OCD do not ever develop OCD; conversely, some persons without any family history also develop OCD. The good news in this is that having a family history of OCD does not doom your child to OCD. What the studies indicate is that some children may come into this world with a *predisposition* or propensity to develop OCD. It is not the actual OCD itself or even specific symptoms that they inherit; it is the *susceptibility* towards OCD. Stress, environmental, biological or unknown factors then work on that susceptibility to result in OCD for some but not all predisposed children.

At this time, there is no specific gene that has been identified for OCD, there is no genetic test for OCD and no way to predict whether a particular child will develop OCD. The underlying genetic mechanism by which OCD is passed on in families is not understood. It is believed that multiple genes working in combination most likely cause OCD, and that there may be more than one combination for different types of OCD.

STRESS

When Robert was 10, three close relatives died over a span of three months. Soon after, we started noticing a lot of ritual behavior—not using third fingers of the hand, touching spots, repetitive behavior for fear of "bad things" happening.

Sharon, mother of Robert, age 14

Like Robert's mother, many parents of children with OCD recall that their child's symptoms started at a time when some life-changing event happened—losses or transitions such as the beginning of the school year, changing schools, breaking up with friends, death or divorce in the family. Many adult OCD sufferers also connect the onset of OCD to a specific event or time in their lives. This is particularly true for those with a sudden or noticeable start of symptoms, compared to those with a gradual onset. Whether these are true triggers or pure coincidence is unclear because they are often recalled after the fact. It is an automatic and natural tendency to search for meaning in experiences that do not seem to make sense. We also tend to remember the details of major events far better than we do the specifics of uneventful days. In reality, there may have been mild symptoms that went unnoticed earlier and became conspicuous after the stress occurred.

Stress is neither necessary nor sufficient for the development of OCD. Clearly, stress does not *cause* OCD because there are many OCD sufferers who do not identify a specific stressor or trigger that set off their illness. Moreover, although no one is exempt from stress, the overwhelming majority of people do *not* develop OCD in response to major or minor stress. Whereas stress does not cause OCD, it may be a trigger for those who are already susceptible to OCD (as discussed earlier in this chapter). Like most other physical or psychological conditions, OCD is stress-sensitive. Stress may trip the switch for OCD, worsen existing symptoms or trigger relapses. Ironically, OCD itself creates a high level of stress for the sufferer, so stress and OCD can actually fuel each other.

For some children, even the everyday danger messages that come from parents, teachers or the media can become the triggers for OCD. Laurie, a kindergartner, stopped talking altogether after she and her classmates were cautioned not to talk to strangers. Her classmates didn't seem to take the warning to heart like she did. Maria started washing copiously after the news report on hepatitis in a local store. Although these danger messages might make any child uneasy and even frightened, the concerns fade with time. For children with a tendency to develop OCD, these messages are taken very literally and are of overwhelming magnitude. There begins the endless cycle of fear and rituals.

PARENTING DOES NOT CAUSE OCD

It is a fact of parenthood that we suffer when our children suffer. No matter how little or big, we agonize about what we should or shouldn't have done to prevent our child's pain. Among the many unanswered questions that race through your mind during the early days of diagnosis and treatment are: *"Why didn't I see it earlier? If only I'd known...maybe I've been too demanding...pushed him too hard. Have I been too critical? The arguments and fights we have in front of the children? Maybe it's my anger and frustration? Was it the fall down the stairs when he was a toddler, when I left the gate open? Perhaps I wasn't around enough with my job and all? Maybe I should have been a stay home mom. I wish I had spent more time with him when he was younger. I wonder about the immunizations and medicines he had as a baby... "*

If some of these questions have plagued you, you are like every other parent of a child with OCD. Rest assured, there is no evidence to show that anything you did or didn't do caused your child's OCD. No amount of "bad" parenting can cause OCD; nor can good parenting prevent it. Why is it then that parents are often blamed for a child's OCD?

For most of the last century, the prevailing influence on the understanding of OCD was that of Sigmund Freud, the father of psychoanalysis. Freud proposed that OCD symptoms were symbolic of suppressed aggressive instincts or unresolved sexual conflicts that originated in childhood, courtesy of harsh and punitive parents. This theory seemed to make intuitive sense because the content of OCD often centered on themes of harm, death, dirt, feces, sexual matter and blasphemy, which are congruent with aggressive, punitive and sexual themes. Not surprisingly, this theory became widely accepted. For most of the past century, diagnosis and treatment of OCD focused on interpreting the symbolic meaning of the sufferer's symptoms and uncovering unresolved psychological conflicts. Although this formulation was a stimulating intellectual exercise, it lacked scientific backing. There is no evidence to prove that OCD is caused by unconscious sexual or aggressive drives or by harsh parenting. Ironically, many decades of psychoanalytic treatments were ineffective in treating OCD. Rather than use this failure to question the misdirected theory, it was seen as "proof" that OCD was an untreatable disorder.

Psychoanalytic theory did a disservice to OCD sufferers and their families. Not only did it cast negative aspersions on them, it resulted in many wasted years pointing fingers in the wrong direction, while sufferers lived tormented lives receiving the wrong treatment. Many OCD sufferers have had a perfectly happy childhood and have close, positive relationships with their parents. Conversely, many who have had an unhappy childhood and harsh, rejecting parents do not ever develop OCD.

Although parenting does not *cause* OCD, it can certainly affect your child's ability to cope with and overcome OCD. How you react and respond to your child's OCD can make his symptoms and his potential for recovery better or worse. When you are supportive, understanding, trusting and calm, your child may be more open in disclosing his fears and asking for help. When your child trusts that you have his well being at heart, he may be more willing to accept help without being defensive. You may be able to get your child through the day-to-day struggles with OCD. Your child may also be more receptive and responsive to treatment because he is more likely to trust a therapist to help him.

On the other hand, although you don't deliberately or knowingly *intend* to make your child's OCD worse, you may unwittingly do just that. When you get angry with your child for senseless rituals, blame, criticize or humiliate him, he will withdraw and hide his OCD from you. Secrecy or denial may put him at greater risk for chronic OCD because it will prevent him from engaging in treatment. If you are overly protective and clear his path of all triggers, he will not develop the independence that he needs to help himself overcome OCD. If you are rigid, perfectionistic or demanding, your child may push himself beyond his limits to meet your expectations at all costs. As you know, stress can worsen OCD. If your household is full of fighting, yelling, tension or chaos, your child will have little energy left to cope with OCD. Things will get worse, not better.

In all fairness, OCD can bring out the worst in both children and parents. Parenting a child with OCD can be very, very trying. It can wear down the most patient and tolerant of parents and families, and even put them over the edge. The once easygoing, comfortable, "normal" family is transported into a war zone. Rigid, irrational and tenacious OCD beliefs and rituals can tax the most calm and understanding of parents. Especially exasperating can be the child's apparent immunity to logic and reason. Many parents can perceive this as willful noncompliance and lose sympathy very readily, resorting to a "just quit it" approach. It soon becomes a vicious cycle. Children and parents influence each other continuously in a downward negative spiral.

There are no perfect parents and every parent has engaged in these behaviors at some time in their lives. Perhaps this information is an eye-opener for you. Awareness is a good thing if it leads to change, but guilt and self-flagellation are of no use to you or your child because they will not help you move forward. You can use what you now know to help your child out of the mess of OCD. Chapters 10, 11 and 12 are devoted to parenting issues and suggestions for handling your child's OCD.

CAN OCD BE LEARNED BY IMITATION?

Could a child learn OCD from watching other family members with OCD? Is it learned by imitation? Could it be copycat behavior? Although it may seem plausible, it is unlikely that OCD can simply be learned by observation or imitation. If it is, all the children of a parent who cleans and disinfects should do the same. But that's not usually the case. In reality, all, some, or none of the children will develop OCD. Even if they do, their symptoms might be completely *different*. The children of a parent who washes may have touching or stepping rituals and vice versa.

What's quite fascinating is that a child may have the *same* OCD rituals or fears that his parents had when they were children, even though the child could never have witnessed or heard about the parent's rituals. That's what led Gregory, a longtime OCD sufferer, to bring his seven-year-old son Nicholas in for an evaluation. "It was like déjà vu," he said, shaking his head in disbelief. "Nicky was watching TV and I saw him lick the back of his hand several times. I asked him why he was doing that and he said it made the bad luck go away. That's *exactly* what I used to do when I was his age. I know Nicholas has never seen me do that and I've never mentioned it to anyone. Then I saw him rubbing his foot on the edge of the carpet and touching the staircase repeatedly—I used to do those things too. It just blew me away." Gregory's story illustrates that even when a child's symptoms are similar to his parents' symptoms, they are not simply learned by observation.

Even though OCD is not directly imitated, children do learn to navigate through the demands and challenges of everyday life from us. As parents, one of the most important roles we play is to shield our children from harm. We are vigilant and alert to threat, and we react immediately to keep our children safe. As they grow older, we teach them how to take care of themselves. We teach them to be cautious, recognize and avoid danger, and find ways to protect themselves. If we are excessively vigilant for danger, react with alarm or avoid risks at all costs, we consciously or unwittingly set an example for our children. They pick up our verbal and nonverbal cues as signals that they should take seriously. In other words, even though they do not learn OCD or anxiety from parents, they may learn an anxious coping style.

THE VICIOUS CYCLE OF AVOIDANCE

Avoidance and escape may be the most powerful of the factors that perpetuate OCD. They fuel OCD through a process known as *negative reinforcement*. Negative reinforcement is often confused with punishment, but is actually the opposite because negative reinforcement is a *reward*. It is called negative reinforcement because the behavior (avoidance or escape from the fear) is rewarded by the evasion of a negative consequence (the discomfort of the obsessions). We learn faster when we are rewarded.

This process is portrayed in Figure 4 *The Vicious Cycle of Avoidance*. When the person is faced with an anxiety trigger such as a dirty sink, his anxiety about germs begins to rise. When the anxiety from this exposure to germs becomes unbearable, the person engages in rituals. Rituals are a form of avoidance or escape, because they give the person immediate relief and allow him to flee from dealing with the unpleasantness of the obsessions. This relief is immensely gratifying. This escape would be all well and good except for the fact that the person never waits long enough to find out if the situation is really as frightening and insurmountable as he thinks it is. The person begins to believe that compulsions are the only way to get rid of obsessions, because he does not attempt any other ways to overcome obsessions. This belief is reinforced and strengthened with each successful escape. As a result, he engages in rituals more frequently and quickly. However, the relief is short-lived, because when obsessions return, the person has no other way to cope. Maria washes her hands as soon as she feels uncomfortable. She feels better and believes that washing her hands is the only way to appease her fear of germs. She does not take the time to learn that if she merely waited, her fears would not materialize. The next time the obsession strikes, she makes a beeline for the sink, thereby repeating the vicious cycle.

Figure 4: The Vicious Cycle of Avoidance

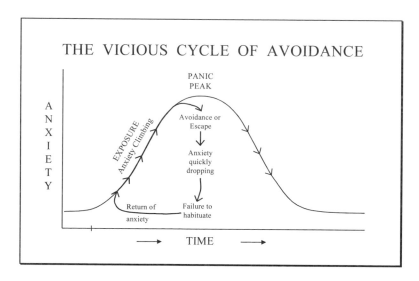

You might wonder how compulsions could be rewarding; didn't you just read that people with OCD don't enjoy their compulsions? Although rituals are not pleasant, they are rewarding because they provide instant relief from the anxiety of obsessions. What about the long-term negative consequences of compulsions? The OCD sufferer who is caught in the heat of the moment is hardly thinking about the distant future. The immediate relief in the midst of a crisis easily overshadows the price that might have to be paid in the future.

THINKING STYLES

In addition to behaviors such as avoidance and escape, thinking styles can also feed the fires of OCD. I use the *Noise at the Window* analogy to portray the powerful connection between thoughts and feelings. Let's say you heard a noise at your bedroom window at night. If you thought it was a burglar trying to break in, you would be afraid. If you thought it was just a tree branch blowing in the wind, you might find it soothing and relaxing as you drift off to sleep. If you thought it was a rusty hinge, you might be annoyed at yet another thing that needed fixing. Perhaps the thought of a squirrel at the window would be irritating. If you weren't sure, your curiosity might be aroused. If you just lay in bed and didn't get up to go see what was creating the tap, you would never know what it really was. Your *feelings* would depend on your *beliefs* about what was happening.

The Noise at the Window	
Thought	Feeling
It's a burglar	Afraid
It's a branch in the breeze	Relaxed
It's a broken hinge	Annoyed
It's a squirrel	Irritated

Yet, if you didn't confirm the source of the noise, your belief about the sound would merely be an *assumption*; your feelings then would be based on that assumption. As a result, a mistaken belief would put you through unnecessary bad feelings.

We hear the tap at the window everyday, metaphorically speaking. It is what we *think* and *say* to ourselves about the tap at the window that determines how we feel and react, not the actual tap. All of us make mistakes about the noise at the window. All of us have tendencies to be illogical, afraid and unrealistic some or all of the time. It's normal, natural and generally so automatic and subtle that we are often unaware of it. The more mistaken beliefs we have, the more likely we are to feel bad and upset about things. In order to have accurate beliefs, we would have to change our behaviors. Rather than assume things, we would need to test our beliefs-go to the window and find out what's making the noise. We can make our lives easier or more difficult by the beliefs and feelings we choose to have. It might seem hard to accept, but we do choose our feelings. Children and adults alike are surprised to learn what they think and say to themselves when they reflect on it.

People with OCD and other types of anxiety tend to be more likely to think that the noise at the window is a burglar rather than a squirrel. They see and hear more danger around them, react with alarm, imagine the worst-case scenario, feel overly responsible and guilty, and feel helpless and unable to cope. Whereas most people may assume something is safe until proven dangerous, those with anxiety are more likely to assume that something is dangerous until proven safe. They are very uncomfortable with ambiguity and seek guarantees, even where there are none. The anxious thoughts lead to a downward spiral of self-talk that increases anxiety, lowers self-confidence and makes them feel helpless and unable to take charge. *"I can't do it. It's too risky. How do I know for sure? What if it happens? What will I do? I won't be able to deal with it. It will be absolutely terrible."*

All said and done, trying to figure out the cause of OCD for your child is a guessing game at best. Your time, effort and resources are therefore best spent finding the right treatment rather than the right cause. Chapters 5 and 6 describe current treatments for OCD.

FREQUENTLY-ASKED QUESTIONS

My mother and I have OCD, and my daughter has just been diagnosed with OCD. Should she avoid having children so that we don't keep passing this on?

Even though there are genetic connections, there simply isn't any way to predict if OCD will be passed on to offspring. Although your child has a strong family history of OCD, her chances of *not* having a child with OCD are still greater than the chances of having a child with OCD. Remember that if one out of four children of an OCD parent can inherit the predisposition, three out of four children will not! If your child has a 25% chance of inheriting OCD, she also has a 75% chance of not inheriting it.

OCD is not a life threatening or terminal illness. For most people, it is not such a debilitating disorder that it easily justifies a decision to not have children. In fact, with current successful treatments, most children today can expect to have a chance at a relatively normal, healthy, happy and fulfilling life despite OCD. Treatments for OCD may also become more successful in the future. There is a lot more to life than OCD and a lot more to having children than just the risk of OCD. This is an intensely personal decision and should be weighed carefully by the person who is making it.

My daughter says she has horrible thoughts about perverse sexual acts, and washes her hands constantly to get rid of them. Could she have been sexually abused?

OCD thoughts with sexual or violent content can be both alarming and troubling. It is natural to wonder where they might come from. Nonetheless, sexual abuse is not known to cause OCD, despite the fact that your child's symptoms have sexual content. However, a person with OCD may have suffered abuse, regardless of OCD. If you are concerned about abuse, it is best to consult with your child's doctor or mental health clinician.

Can OCD be triggered by environmental factors such as toxins, leads, allergens, construction materials and such? I know at least five children with OCD in my neighborhood of about 50 families.

About two in 100 children have OCD, so that number may be well within the expected range if there are about 100 children in your neighborhood. If there are less than 100 children, it might be something to think about. It may also be no more than a coincidence if the families that live there have family histories of anxiety disorders, and just happened to move there. There is no known scientific evidence that confirms the role of environmental toxins and other such factors in OCD.

My son, who used to be the epitome of the messy kid, now spends hours in the bathroom washing and brushing. I don't understand this change.

Almost any of us can own up to the fact that we like to toilet, shower, or get dressed in much the same sequence every day. Bathroom routines include grooming, automatic behaviors or routines and social norms, all of which are regulated by the brain areas implicated in OCD. The basal ganglia are responsible for carrying out "automatic" tasks or routines, shifting from one activity to another, and grooming and checking behavior. The frontal cortex and the orbital gyri regulate "proper" social behavior. Is it any wonder that the bathroom is a stronghold of OCD, which is the prime location for all our grooming, fixed routines, social norms and taboos?

Despite our strong preference for routines and automatic sequences, we can move to the next step easily. If interrupted, we are somewhat annoyed and feel the need to repeat the step, but can generally proceed without being paralyzed. When someone has OCD, they get stuck someplace in this routine, and aren't able to move to the next step in the sequence because their brain did not send them the signal that it is okay to move on. In fact, Dr. Judith Rapoport, OCD expert, aptly refers to this form of OCD as a "grooming behavior gone awry."

My older daughter has OCD. Now my younger daughter seems to follow me around constantly. She doesn't want me to leave her and will not go on the bus without her sister. She's okay as long as she has someone with her, but won't do anything alone, like go to a friend's house. I hope she's not going to have OCD.

Since one of your daughters has OCD, her sister may have a different "strain" of anxiety such as separation anxiety. I would not assume that she would necessarily progress to OCD. Although many kids with OCD may have separation anxiety in their pasts, many kids with separation anxiety do not end up with OCD. Again, time will tell. It is best to keep brief notes, and share them with your doctor.

Chapter 5

Treatment of OCD:
Up and Down the Worry Hill

We have to start teaching ourselves not to be afraid.

William Faulkner

Every morning before school, I would end up sobbing in my room, because I could not beat my own thoughts. Forgetting all of my pride, I finally told my mom. It was the smartest decision I ever made. Soon I was headed to a therapist, but I did not feel comfortable with her. I tried to stick it out and we tried dozens of methods, but nothing worked. Meanwhile, I was falling apart inside. I needed a strategy, some plan of action that would help me control my life again. Then my Mom found a new therapist who knew the right treatment for OCD, and I saw immediate results. A few weeks later, I walked right across a spot on the rug I used to have to run my foot over. Ten minutes later, I realized what I had done, and I couldn't stop laughing. It was so incredibly wonderful. I didn't have to obey my thoughts anymore. It was spring when I was completely free of my OCD. It's been two years now, and I've never been happier.

Nancy, age 14

Nancy was free of OCD after receiving *Cognitive-Behavioral Therapy* (CBT; also known as *Behavior Therapy*), the only psychological therapy that is scientifically proven to be effective for treating OCD. CBT teaches people to break the vicious cycle of avoidance, escape and unrealistic thinking patterns that feed the fires of OCD.

There is no *cure* for OCD at this time, but after decades of being deemed nearly impossible to remedy, it is safe to say that with the right treatment, most children with OCD can expect to live relatively normal lives in spite of OCD. Children with OCD and their parents can look to the future with hope and optimism, rather than with despair and resignation. When a child's OCD is under control, parents and families find relief from stress, worry and conflict and begin to regain control of their lives. Why is it then that so many children and adolescents, even today, are struggling with uncontrolled OCD? Chances are, just like Nancy's initial experience with therapy, they are receiving a treatment that is ineffective for OCD. OCD has not been shown to respond to traditional "talk therapy" which focuses on uncovering psychological "causes."

In this chapter, I will describe the workings of CBT using the metaphor of riding a bicycle *Up and Down the Worry Hill*. I will present the *RIDE* acronym, a sequence of CBT steps I developed for children with OCD. I will discuss what to expect when your child receives CBT, the benefits and drawbacks of CBT and what makes for success in CBT. I will also give an overview of other therapies and their usefulness for OCD. Medication treatment for OCD is discussed in Chapter 6. Part II (Chapters 7 onwards) of this book is dedicated to practical applications of CBT, guidelines for finding the right clinicians to treat your child, and what you can do to help your child overcome OCD successfully.

COGNITIVE-BEHAVIORAL THERAPY (CBT): THE TREATMENT OF CHOICE

Experts agree that CBT should be the *first line of treatment* for all children with OCD. For adolescents, CBT is recommended as the first treatment for mild to moderate OCD, and CBT along with an anti-OCD medication for severe OCD. OCD experts do not endorse either the initial use of medication or the use of medication alone for children (*Expert Consensus Treatment Guidelines for Obsessive-Compulsive Disorder*, 1997). However, treating a child with CBT or medication is not an either-or decision, as they are not mutually exclusive treatments. For some children, a combination of CBT and medications is necessary for maximum relief.

In the forty odd years since the advent of CBT for adults with OCD, it has become clear that about 80% of adults become better and stay better after CBT. Pioneers in CBT for children have shown that children and adolescents can be just as successful in overcoming OCD as adults. Studies by Dr. John March at Duke University, Dr. John Piacentini at UCLA and others have found that about 80% of children can conquer OCD after CBT.

Not only does CBT improve obsessions and compulsions; it may actually reshuffle brain chemistry. As mentioned in Chapter 4, Drs. Jeffrey Schwartz and Lewis Baxter at UCLA found that PET scans showed higher rates of glucose metabolism in certain brain areas for OCD patients compared to adults without OCD. Even more fascinating is their finding that the glucose consumption decreased at a similar rate for OCD patients who improved after *either* CBT or medication. The implication of this finding is that brain chemistry can be changed, not just by medication, but *also by CBT!* Given genetic and neurobiological links to OCD (see Chapter 4), it may surprise you that OCD can be treated successfully merely by changing behavior and thinking. That's because while you may not be able to stop the thoughts that enter your mind, you *can* choose how to respond to them. In other words, OCD can be "unlearned," regardless of whether it has genetic or learned roots.

BT, CT, CBT & ERP:
WHAT DO ALL THE INITIALS MEAN?

There are many initials and acronyms used to describe the treatment of OCD. Before I proceed, let me clarify the various treatment terms and their relationship to each other. *Behavior Therapy* (BT) focuses on changing negative feelings by changing *behaviors* such as avoidance that perpetuate those feelings. *Cognitive Therapy* (CT), on the other hand, focuses on changing negative feelings by challenging *beliefs* to become more realistic and rational. *Cognitive-Behavioral Therapy* (CBT) is a blending of BT and CT and recognizes the importance of changing both behaviors *and* thinking patterns to change feelings. There are a variety of CBT techniques, all of which are very specific and goal-directed; of these, *Exposure and Ritual Prevention* (ERP; also known as *Response Prevention*), described in this chapter, are vital to the treatment of OCD. BT and CBT are often used interchangeably to refer to techniques used for OCD. It really does not matter which term is used, as long as the treatment involves Exposure and Ritual Prevention.

THE PREMISE OF CBT

CBT worked like a miracle for my son. He worked hard and it wasn't easy, but it was so rewarding so quickly that it motivated him to keep up the hard work. It also gave him the tools to work on new problems once they came up, talk with me about how to strategize, and so importantly, it really helped us all as a family talk about the OCD and share feelings and ideas. Bob is so much more open now about his disorder than ever before, and that is wonderful. CBT gave him a feeling of control and power over OCD that no medication had ever been able to do for him before.

Nina, mother of Bob, age 11

OCD makes people lose control of their thoughts and actions. CBT teaches them to take back the control. The essence of the treatment is to teach the person to change the way he thinks and behaves in response to obsessive thoughts. CBT is intensely practical, logical and active. Like bicycling, swimming or playing the violin, it can only be learned by performance and practice. Remember the *Noise at the Window* discussed in Chapter 4? CBT helps sufferers understand and see how thoughts, feelings and behaviors are closely connected and influence each other. It helps them summon up the courage to find out what the Noise at the Window is about before they waste their energy getting upset. It teaches them to think realistically, confront fears and survive doubt and uncertainty. The skills learned in CBT are valuable for a lifetime.

> Take control of OCD or let it take control of you

EXPOSURE & RITUAL PREVENTION

Exposure and Ritual Prevention (ERP) is the key CBT strategy for overcoming obsessions and compulsions. ERP is focused on changing *behavior*. Strategies to change thinking patterns are discussed later in this chapter.

Exposure refers to being exposed to or facing the situations or objects that trigger obsessive fears. It involves purposeful and conscious confrontation of fears to test their reality. Very simply said, *to overcome your fear, you must face your fear*. *Ritual Prevention* involves refraining from the rituals that relieve the anxiety of obsessions.

> To overcome your fear, you must face your fear

I find it important to distinguish between *facing* fears and *fighting* fears. Fighting implies combat and resistance. Children are confused when they are told to "fight" OCD because it suggests that they should *resist* it with all their might. Exposure is not about resisting; it's about *facing*, which refers to a purposeful and conscious acceptance of the fear. Fighting and resisting increase distress, and the emotional energy involved may actually intensify the obsessions. In a paradoxical way, one has to stop struggling with OCD to make it go away. OCD must be confronted, not resisted.

For ERP to be successful, the person must simultaneously *confront and remain in the feared situation* and *not perform any rituals* until the anxiety decreases and goes away. ERP allows the person to realize that his fears do not come true, even when he does *not* engage in rituals. The realization that the fears are false alarms reduces the potency of the obsessions. No matter how much you may have tried to convince your child of these facts, he needs to face his fears for himself to learn that they are unwarranted.

Maria was afraid of contaminating others with her dirty hands. To prevent this from happening, she washed her hands copiously. ERP for Maria involved touching others—her parents, me, a friend—with *unwashed* hands (exposure) and refraining from asking the persons she touched to wash their hands or from asking if they were going to be okay (ritual prevention). For Paul, who fended off bad luck with spitting and wiping, exposure involved thinking of specific things that were bad luck and refraining from spitting (ritual prevention). Alyssa was constantly preoccupied with the thought of her pants and underwear slipping down. For her, exposure involved deliberately selecting and wearing a loose pair of pants or underwear that slipped down to her hips, and resisting the urge to pull them up (ritual prevention).

ERP is not anywhere near as daunting as it may sound, and even children can do it remarkably well. Although it may seem counter-intuitive at first, it is actually based on straightforward principles. To understand why and how ERP works, it is essential to understand habituation, as described below. Once you understand habituation, you will see that ERP makes perfect logical sense. I will present an effective way to help children understand exposure and habituation in this chapter and in Chapter 9.

Habituation: Natural and Automatic

ERP has a lot in common with jumping into a cold swimming pool, turning off the lights at night or walking into a noisy train station. Sounds a bit far-fetched? Not really, because what these experiences have in common with ERP is a process known as *habituation*, which is the body's way of adapting to new sensations. We all know and experience habituation everyday, although we are often unaware of it and it's not a word we use in our day-to-day vocabulary. Our sensory systems—vision, sound, touch, smell and taste—are designed to accommodate to the many new experiences we have each day. After you've been in the cold pool for a few minutes, the water begins to feel warmer. When you turn off the lights at night, your eyes adapt and you begin to see silhouettes. Before you realize it, you have tuned out the rumbles and screeches of the trains at the station. The initial blast of sensation becomes almost imperceptible with time. Habituation happens automatically with little conscious effort on our part.

It might come as a surprise to you to know that *our bodies can habituate to anxiety* in much the same way as they do to smell, light, heat, cold or noise. We can get used to anxiety until it fades from our awareness. The beauty of habituation is that it is a natural phenomenon that takes place automatically. It is a physiological process that is designed to return our bodies to equilibrium. The brain is programmed to attend more actively to novel sensations, while relegating ongoing sensations to the background. We are not required to put any conscious effort into habituation, nor are we often aware of it.

How does habituation come about? Briefly stated, the *sympathetic* nervous system is delegated the task of preparing the body to react to threat and danger, and the *parasympathetic* system is entrusted with the complementary function of restoring the body to its original resting state. When threat or danger is perceived, the brain signals the sympathetic nervous system to prepare itself to protect you by either "fight or flight." In order to do so, this system releases two chemicals, *adrenaline* and *noradrenaline*, that act as dispatchers to energize the body for action. Some of the activities triggered by these chemicals are increases in heart rate, blood flow and breathing, and decreases in salivation and digestion. It is these changes in the body's metabolism that produce the all-too-familiar sensations we experience when we meet with danger or threat: heart racing, rapid breathing, head pounding, dizziness, queasiness, butterflies in the tummy, sweating or feeling flushed. Although these sensations can be quite intense, startling and anxiety provoking of themselves, they are natural, normal and harmless. The body's activation to be on alert for danger consumes a lot of energy; that explains the exhaustion you might feel after you gear up to deal with threat.

Two things happen when danger has passed: First, the parasympathetic system is activated automatically to restore the body to its resting state and to replenish depleted energy. Second, the body eventually uses up the adrenaline and noradrenaline that were released earlier in response to the threat. As a result of these two automatic events, *anxiety simply cannot continue forever*. However, it may take a while for anxiety to subside, even after the danger has passed. This delay occurs because the chemical messengers may take some time to be completely destroyed. It allows the body to reactivate rapidly if the threat should resume. It is important for the system not to get too complacent, as danger has a way of resurfacing.

Think about it for a minute: If we did not have a built-in mechanism for resetting to equilibrium, how could we possibly handle the thousands of new threats we encounter over time? Our bodies generally cannot maintain intense anxiety for more than 90 minutes at a stretch, and most of us cannot remain anxious for more than 45 minutes. During ERP, anxiety generally habituates in a much shorter time. Children average between 10 and 20 minutes to habituate to anxiety during exposure exercises.

For people with OCD, anxiety seems to be endless because the danger messages are so intense and so frequent that the sympathetic system is in an almost steady state of activation. In other words, the cycle is repeated so rapidly that anxiety seems constant and unrelenting. They feel that they have to respond to each of these messages with urgency. By doing so, they don't allow themselves to find out that the parasympathetic system will do its job, if it is only given the opportunity, and that the anxiety will disappear on its own.

Figure 5: Up and Down the Worry Hill:
Exposure and Habituation

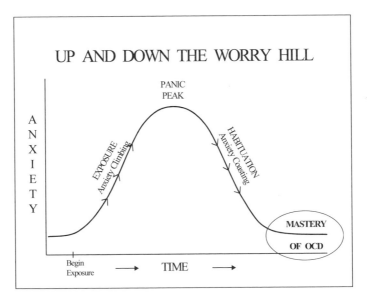

Figure 5 depicts the relationship between exposure and habituation. I call this exposure-habituation curve the "Worry Hill." The left side of the curve shows how anxiety rises when exposure to a feared situation takes place. Anxiety climbs steadily as exposure continues and eventually reaches a peak. If the person persists in confronting the fear until he reaches the peak of the Worry Hill, habituation sets in and anxiety automatically begins to decline. Exposure is the grinding trudge up the Worry Hill, and habituation is the downhill coast. For instance, Maria is afraid of germs and washes her hands frequently. When she confronts her fear of germs by eating breakfast without washing her hands, her anxiety begins to increase. She finds the increasing anxiety intolerable. Yet, if she persists and stays in the situation, habituation will occur in a matter of time.

The critical element in habituation is exposure. It is not possible to habituate to a sensation to which you have not been exposed. You must encounter your fear in order to habituate to it. You have to *allow* yourself to purposefully think about and face fears until your anxiety dissipates. When you continue to avoid or escape them via rituals, you interrupt the process of habituation. You really have to do the *opposite* of what seems intuitive in order to habituate to anxiety.

Facts about exposure and habituation

❖ Anxiety is not fatal and can be lived through
❖ Anxiety is transient and passes away
❖ Avoidance strengthens fear
❖ Exposure weakens fear
❖ Habituation is natural and automatic
❖ Exposure is necessary for habituation
❖ Anxiety in anticipation of exposure may be higher than anxiety during actual exposure

---

Unfortunately, most people do not realize that habituation of anxiety takes place naturally if they just stick it out a little longer. It is this lack of awareness and inability to tolerate increasing anxiety that leads people to give in to rituals to escape the anxiety. As described in Chapter 4 (Figure 4), escape results in the vicious cycle of OCD. The problem is that when anxiety strikes, escaping the present is far more attractive than thinking about the future. For habituation to set in, the person must continue with exposure and remain in the feared situation until anxiety peaks and begins to decline. Habituation will happen if it is allowed to happen. The person merely has to wait and let it happen. Most people, especially children, are surprised to find that the anxiety they feel during exposure is far less than they expected. For many, *anticipatory anxiety*, or the anxiety *prior* to exposure, is much greater than the anxiety experienced during exposure.

Coasting down the Worry Hill: Mastery of OCD

Figure 6 shows how exposure leads to mastery of OCD. During ERP, people confront their fears and refrain from rituals. When exposure is repeated several times, the peak of anxiety begins to diminish. Habituation sets in faster. The Worry Hill becomes smaller and smaller. Frequent practice results in decreasing anxiety and eventually to conquest of OCD.

Types of Exposure Therapy

Exposure can be conducted in several different ways. *In vivo* exposure is real-life exposure that involves confronting feared situations in their actuality. Chloe confronts her fear of vomiting on the bus by riding the bus everyday. *Imaginal exposure* refers to confronting fears or worries in imagination rather than in real life. It is used when OCD fears are difficult, unrealistic or unwise to confront in actuality. For instance, it would not be prudent to have Robert pat a wild raccoon to conquer his fear of rabies. Nor is it sensible to have Nicole repeat a grade, just to expose her to that fear. Instead, Robert and Nicole can confront these fears imaginally. Imaginal exposure is only effective when the anxiety that it generates matches the level of anxiety experienced in real life. Robert and his CBT therapist create imaginary scenes in which he sees a raccoon in his backyard, approaches it and pats it. Nicole and her CBT therapist create an imaginary scene in which Nicole receives her report card and sees that she has failed the test. She imagines her teacher's, parents' and her own reactions to her failure. The imaginal scene should resemble the real-life situation as closely as possible in its details, and must arouse anxiety in order for habituation to occur. Robert and Nicole practice imaginal exposure to these scenes repeatedly until their anxiety habituates.

Figure 6: Results of Exposure Therapy

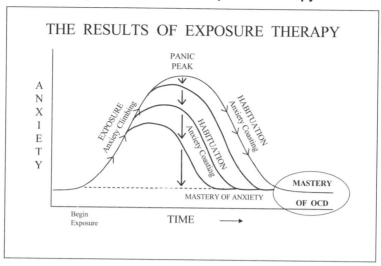

Gradual exposure, which can be applied to both in-vivo and imaginal situations, involves gradually moving in small sequential steps (see Table 3) from the least feared situations to the most anxiety-provoking situations. It is the most suitable form of exposure for children and adolescents. Starting with low anxiety situations allows the child to try out exposure with manageable distress and experience success fairly easily. Quick feedback is necessary because most children need immediate results as they have little ability to defer feedback to the future. Success early in the process helps them see that exposure can be effective and helps build confidence.

Table 3: Steps in Gradual Exposure

1. Identify fears
2. Rate the severity of each fear using the Fearmometer
3. Rank order fears on a hierarchy from least to most severe
4. Select the fear lowest on the hierarchy
5. Begin exposure to the selected fear
6. Prevent avoidance or escape
7. Wait until habituation occurs
8. Select the next lowest fear and repeat steps 5 to 7

The "Fearmometer"

Before starting gradual exposure, the therapist and the child together list all the possible situations that are fearful for the child. They then place them in order according to severity using a numerical scale such as the "*Fearmometer*" (see Figure 7). The Fearmometer, also known as a Fear Thermometer or Feeling Thermometer, is a concrete tool used to teach children how to differentiate and quantify levels of threat and anxiety. It allows children to rate their fears or "*Fear Temperature*" on a graduated scale from one to 10, where one is "No anxiety" and 10 is "Out of Control," and to communicate these ratings with the therapist or parents.

Figure 7: The "Fearmometer"

The Fearmometer

10. Out of Control! Ballistic!
9. Can't Handle It.
8. Really Tough.
7. Pretty Tough.
6. Getting Tough.
5. Not too Good.
4. Starting to Bother.
3. Just a Little Uneasy.
2. A Little Twinge.
1. Piece of Cake!

Aureen P. Wagner Ph.D. Copyright 2001

The Fearmometer allows children to develop a hierarchy of fears for gradual exposure exercises. It allows them to rank order exposure targets from least to most difficult, so that they can begin with those that are least daunting and gradually progress to those that are most unapproachable. For example, Nicole rates her fear of repeating a grade as a 10 on the Fearmometer. A gradual exposure hierarchy involving less intense fears of the same nature is developed. The lowest item on Nicole's hierarchy, with a rating of two, is missing a word on the spelling test. Getting a B on the test is a five, failing the test is a seven and failing a series of tests is an eight.

Using gradual exposure, Nicole first confronts her lowest fear, which is to spell two words incorrectly on the spelling test. She then progresses to tackling her fear of getting a B before handling her worst fear, which is repeating the grade. The Fearmometer allows Nicole to track the level of anxiety she experiences before and during exposure tasks, and to identify when habituation has taken place. It also gives her a tangible index of progress over time—"*Oh, look! I started out at eight and now I'm at three and it only took a few minutes. That's pretty decent!*"

Ritual prevention can also be implemented either completely or gradually. With complete ritual prevention, the child does not engage in any rituals. For instance, Casey would not wash his hands at all after tying his shoelaces. For children who cannot tolerate the abrupt termination of rituals, procedures involving delaying, shortening, slowing or changing the rituals are designed. For instance, Casey waits for five minutes after tying his shoelaces before washing his hands (delaying), washes for only five minutes instead of 10 (shortening), washes each part of his hands slowly and carefully (slowing) or washes parts of the hand in a different sequence (changing). By altering the rituals in this way, Casey breaks free of the OCD "rules" that he has been compelled to follow.

ERP gives the body an opportunity to experience habituation. However, the OCD sufferer must also be able to go beyond this physiological process. For long-term success, changes must take place in the belief system-habituation must also become a cognitive process. Cognitive strategies, discussed below, help modify the belief system in OCD.

COGNITIVE THERAPY STRATEGIES FOR OCD

ERP focuses on changing the *behaviors* of OCD. Cognitive Therapy (CT) is directed at changing the *thinking* patterns that perpetuate OCD (see Chapter 4). Although exposure is considered necessary for overcoming OCD, CT strategies can be a very helpful addition to ERP. They can enhance treatment readiness, help prevent relapse and improve the chances of staying well. Although it is too early to say if CT alone can help children overcome OCD, it holds promise for the future.

Most children and adults with OCD are generally logical and know that their fears are irrational. Yet, they lose sight of that fact in the heat of an OCD episode. They may get so caught up in their obsessions that they begin to lose perspective. They are unable to separate themselves from the warped logic of OCD. In addition, OCD may leave children feeling defeated, hopeless and helpless. Feelings of powerlessness may detract from the ability to focus or participate in the challenges of exposure.

CT helps adults and children learn to recognize and change OCD-style thinking. It helps them to think differently about themselves and OCD. It decreases overall anxiety, which makes them more confident and willing to take on exposure tasks. It makes their expectations more realistic and less catastrophic. CT can also help build self-esteem, self-acceptance, coping and problem solving skills. It promotes a way of thinking and an outlook on life that is conducive to overcoming fear. Your child may be fortunate to learn CT skills early in life before fearful beliefs become cemented and difficult to undo.

There are many different CT techniques for OCD. *Reframing* and *distancing* techniques teach the person to recognize and separate one's own logical thoughts from the illogical thoughts of OCD. Dr. Jeffrey Schwartz, in his book *Brain Lock*, popularized the notion of reframing and distancing. Dr. John March applies the concept of "externalizing" OCD, a reframing technique, in his CBT program for children with OCD. *Realistic thinking* teaches children how to estimate risk more accurately, accept and take risks as part of normal life, to put things into perspective and to accept and live with uncertainty. Children are taught to catch themselves in the downward spiral of negative self-talk and replace it with helpful self-talk.

CBT therapists guide their patients to arrive at logical, rational and realistic ways of thinking via *Socratic questions*, instead of merely telling them how to think. The great Greek teacher Socrates did not impart his wisdom by just expounding on it. Instead, he posed a series of questions to his pupils that challenged them to think through the problem and come to the right conclusion on their own. The wisdom they gained as a result came from within. Children respond surprisingly well to the use of Socratic questioning by a skilled therapist. The learning and change in thinking patterns is more powerful and enduring when it is internally driven. A skilled therapist will select CT strategies that are suitable for your child and weave them into the treatment protocol as required.

CBT STEPS FOR CHILDREN: RIDE UP AND DOWN THE WORRY HILL

Understanding and accepting the vital concepts of exposure, habituation and anticipatory anxiety can be half the battle against OCD. A child's chances for success in treatment might hinge on this understanding. Yet, these are not intuitive concepts. It was with this realization in mind that I developed the metaphor of riding a bicycle *Up and Down the Worry Hill* and the *RIDE* acronym to explain these complex, yet key ideas to children and adolescents. In *Up and Down the Worry Hill: A Children's book about OCD and its Treatment* (see *Resources*), Dr. Greene explains ERP to Casey.

"Casey, learning how to stop OCD is a lot like riding your bicycle up and down a hill. In the beginning, stopping your rituals feels like riding up a big "Worry Hill," because it's hard. If you keep going and don't give up, you get to the top of the Worry Hill. Once you get to the top, it's easy to come down the hill. You can only coast down the hill if you first get to the top."

In this section, I describe the RIDE, a set of CBT steps that include both exposure and cognitive strategies to treat children and adolescents with OCD. These steps are just as relevant for adults with OCD as they are for the children for whom I developed them. Chapter 9 offers more details on explaining CBT to children.

The 4-step RIDE acronym (*Rename, Insist, Defy, Enjoy*) empowers children to ride Up and Down the Worry Hill to overcome OCD. Using the focused self-talk and active steps described in the *RIDE*, children and adolescents can train themselves to conquer OCD. The RIDE, as applied to Casey's fear of contamination and illness, is described below.

Figure 8: The Worry Hill Memory Card

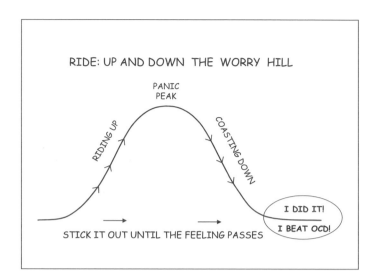

Rename the thought. "It's simply OCD, not me."
Insist that YOU are in charge! "I'm in charge, not OCD."
Defy OCD, do the OPPOSITE of what it wants.
 "I will ride up the Worry Hill and stick it out."
Enjoy your success, reward yourself. "I did it.
I can do it again."

❖ *Insist that YOU are in charge!*

In the next step, Casey awakens to the power of choice. His attitude towards OCD shifts from passive acquiescence to active assertion. Instead of complying with OCD's commands, he decides to take active control over his thoughts and actions. Statements like, *"Am I going to let OCD control me? I am in charge, not OCD,"* exemplify this step.

❖ *Defy OCD, do the OPPOSITE of what it wants.*

Now, a change in behavior must follow the change in beliefs that takes place in steps 1 and 2. It is time to face those fears. Casey understands the metaphor of *The Worry Hill*. He knows and accepts that exposure and habituation must take place in order for OCD to be overcome. He realizes that the more he confronts OCD, the easier it will be to overcome it. Casey is ready to defy OCD.

The exposure in Casey's case is eating breakfast with unwashed (contaminated) hands. Ritual prevention is refraining from washing his hands until well after he is done eating.When Casey puts the food in his mouth, his anxiety initially increases and continues to build. He finds the increasing anxiety intolerable. As he continues to eat, his anxiety peaks and then automatically begins to decline, because habituation sets in. Casey talks himself through ERP with statements like, *"I'm going to ride up the Worry Hill now. It's going to be tough going up the hill, but if I stick it out, I'll get to the top of the hill. Once I'm at the top, it will be easy to coast down the hill. I won't quit until the bad feeling passes. I won't give in to the rituals."* Casey rides to the top of the Worry Hill; then he enjoys coasting down the other side.

❖ *Enjoy your success, reward yourself.*

The final step allows the child to review his performance and to take due credit for his effort and courage. Casey learns to give himself positive feedback. *"I did it! I can do it again. Now I deserve to be good to myself."* Casey and his therapist chart his progress on a graph, so that Casey can have frequent visual reminders of how far he has come from the beginning.

As Casey undergoes the RIDE, he realizes that exposure isn't half as scary as he thought it might be. Once he has actually eaten food with unwashed hands, he doesn't feel quite as worried about getting sick. He is surprised and proud of his accomplishment. The next time around, he finds it a lot easier to eat without washing his hands. His anxiety habituates faster. As Casey continues his ERP exercises, his obsession about germs begins to fade into oblivion.

In essence, the RIDE teaches children how to stop, think and respond assertively to OCD, rather than default to an automatic reflexive compliance with the fears and rituals. Children are given the Worry Hill Memory Card (Figure 8) as a handy visual prompter. The easy acronym, logical steps and visual appeal of the Worry Hill and the RIDE acronym make it simple to grasp, remember and recall, even in the midst of anxiety. It becomes an integral part of the child's response to OCD. Maria, Paul,

Nancy and Alyssa are among scores of children and adolescents who have successfully used the RIDE to overcome OCD. Their stories and those of others who have used the RIDE are presented in Chapter 11.

TYPICAL STEPS IN CBT FOR CHILDREN: WHAT TO EXPECT

CBT is by no means a "quick fix." A typical CBT program extends over 10-15 weeks and has four separate but overlapping phases. A good rule of thumb is to expect to see the beginnings of change within four weeks and significant change after at least 10 weeks. It can be frustrating to hear this when you are impatient for relief, but rushing through treatment haphazardly can end up costing you and your child more time and unnecessary grief. Knowing what to expect can save you disappointment.

The following is an overview of the steps I use in treating children and adolescents with OCD. Most CBT therapists use similar steps. You can expect some variation among therapists, but the general process should essentially be the same.

Phase I: Assessment and treatment planning:

Phase I is the essential foundation for successful treatment. A systematic and thoughtful assessment and treatment plan are more likely to increase your child's success in treatment.

❖ *Initial Evaluation and Diagnosis*

First and foremost, it is important to establish a diagnosis of OCD (see Chapter 4 for more details on diagnosis). A thorough evaluation should identify your child's specific symptoms, needs and strengths. Medical history, family history, social relationships, school functioning and other factors that may affect your child's response to treatment must be evaluated.

❖ *OCD symptom analysis*

For a good CBT treatment plan, the therapist will need to know as many minute details as possible about your child's fears and rituals. These include when and how often obsessions and compulsions occur, how severe they are, how much they get in the way, what seems to trigger them, how much your child tries to resist or control them, if and how you assist your child and how your child eventually gets through them. The Children's Yale-Brown Obsessive-Compulsive Scale (C-YBOCS; see Chapter 4) is often the starting point for this information.

❖ *Biopsychosocial treatment plan*

There is more to a child with OCD than just obsessions and compulsions. As discussed in Chapter 4, biopsychosocial treatment addresses the well being of the whole child in his context. The therapist must use the information from the assessment to develop a treatment plan that is designed to improve the well being of your child, not just his obsessions and compulsions. Treatment is not "one size fits all" and should be tailored to your child's specific needs and strengths. Your child may need additional treatments to help her rebuild lost time and lost skills, improve self-esteem and family relationships, and to get back on track at home, in school and in the peer group. Realistically speaking, these things cannot be tackled all at once. OCD symptoms should generally be treated first, unless other issues interfere with the treatment. For example, severe depression may need to be treated or family conflict may need to be resolved before a child can engage in CBT. It is important to be focused but flexible in the treatment plan.

Phase II: Building treatment readiness:

Phase II involves gearing up for treatment. This phase of treatment is critical but often overlooked, thereby gravely jeopardizing the chances of success in treatment. Exposure can appear overwhelming, foreboding and even unthinkable to many children, until they are properly prepared and ready for treatment. I spend between one and three sessions cultivating treatment readiness in the child and parent.

❖ *Feedback and education*

If your child has OCD, the therapist must describe OCD, give you and your child accurate information about the disorder and attempt to dispel myths and misconceptions that are stumbling blocks to treatment. The therapist should offer you all viable treatment options including CBT, medication or a combination of both, discuss the pros and cons of each option, and assist you in making the best choices for your child. The therapist should be clear about what the treatment will involve, the number of weeks it may take, when you may expect to see results, and the focus and commitment that will be required of you and your child. If you opt for medication, the therapist should refer you to a child psychiatrist.

❖ Communication and persuasion

Perhaps the most critical part of treatment readiness is helping the child understand the concepts of exposure, habituation and anticipatory anxiety. This is where the metaphor of the Worry Hill and the RIDE acronym come in. The language of the child must become the language in which ERP is explained. An experienced therapist builds the child's trust and confidence steadily, not hastily. Persuasion involves getting the child to believe in the RIDE for himself. The therapist must persuade the child to participate in treatment of his own free will. The child must learn to rely on the therapists' word that facing his fears will indeed work. There must be no coercion and no surprises, in order to honor the child's trust. Chapter 9 provides a detailed discussion of building readiness for treatment.

❖ Defining roles and participation

Research and clinical experience shows that children respond better to treatment when their parents are actively involved in a planned and systematic way. The child, parent and therapist have different but complementary roles to play in the child's treatment. It is necessary for the therapist to outline these roles and their boundaries, in order to foster collaboration and preempt the conflict and frustration that can ensue from misunderstanding. As described at length in Chapter 10, the therapist's role is to guide the child's treatment, the child's role is to RIDE and the parent's role is to RALLY for the child. The child is more likely to be invested in his recovery when he perceives that he has control.

Phase III: The RIDE Up and Down the Worry Hill

Phase III is the RIDE. This is the critical part of the treatment and involves both cognitive and behavioral strategies.

❖ Cognitive strategies

The first two steps of the RIDE (Rename and Insist) are aimed at preparing the child's belief system in anticipation of exposure. They include perspective taking, reframing and distancing from OCD and empowerment to take back control. The process of changing the belief system has already begun in Phases I and II. This stage continues that process. The therapist may introduce cognitive techniques as needed for each child.

❖ Exposure and Ritual Prevention

The *Defy* step of the RIDE signals the beginning of ERP. A gradual exposure hierarchy must be constructed. Often, the therapist will model the procedure by doing it first, and then ask the child to follow suit. For instance, I would eat a snack without washing my hands, so that the child sees that I am willing to take the same risk that I am asking of him. The child selects exposure exercises and sets the pace of ERP with the therapists' guidance and input. Although the hierarchy proceeds from least to most difficult, children may sometimes choose to start ERP with a difficult task because it bothers them much more. The child must never be tricked or forced into exposure because it destroys the foundation of trust that is imperative for treatment. ERP can be a fairly intense experience and it is wise to give it full focus by clearing your child's schedule of as many things as possible and keeping his responsibilities to the minimum. (See Chapter 11 for the application of the RIDE to various OCD themes).

❖ Rewards

Rewards are important to help children maintain motivation. The child must be rewarded for *effort* rather than for success because his effort towards the goal is more important than his actual progress. Praise and attention are often more effective than material rewards. Younger children may need tangible rewards. Chapter 12 discusses rewards in detail.

❖ *Practice, practice, practice!*

Learning the RIDE is a new skill for most children. Frequent and diligent practice is crucial for mastery. It is like learning how to ride a bicycle
or swim. It is not enough to do it once a week for an hour in the therapists'
office. To be good at it, your child must practice often. The therapist
assigns daily "homework" in writing after each session. Written assignments reduce the chances that homework is forgotten or misunderstood.

Incomplete homework does not bode well for success in treatment. It is
usually a sign that there is some obstacle to the child's participation. Success in CBT will be severely limited until all barriers to full participation
are removed. Sometimes, the child is willing and enthusiastic in the therapists' office, but gets cold feet when he gets home. Perhaps things at home
are too busy to allow the child to focus on getting his ERP homework
done. Exercises may not be working as expected because the child quits
the RIDE prematurely before habituation has taken place, or replaces out-
ward rituals with silent mental rituals. To preempt these problems, I maintain daily phone contact with my patients during the early stages of the
RIDE. I ask parents and children to leave a message on my voice mail
every day, letting me know how the homework is going. This not only
increases accountability but also allows me to intervene quickly if things
are not going right.

Phase IV: After the RIDE:

❖ *Slip recovery*

As discussed in Chapter 1, OCD "slips" or relapses can happen either
unexpectedly or at times of stress and transition. When you and your child
are prepared for this sobering reality, you will not be caught off guard.
When you are taken by surprise, you are less likely to have an organized
and productive response. Your child may also become demoralized and
reluctant to take back control from OCD.

> Slips are not a sign of failure. They are merely reality.

A relapse is merely a bump in the road. You and your child should be able to get through it if you have realistic expectations, keep things in perspective, stay calm and focus on the steps to recovery. Slip recovery involves recognizing the early signs of slips and intervening immediately. When a slip occurs, OCD should be confronted head on by doing ERP exercises even more vigorously. When you fall off your bicycle, you pick yourself up. If you sat on the ground and made no attempt to get up, you wouldn't get anywhere. If you want to move on, you get up, dust yourself off, survey the damage, attend to it, and get right back on that bicycle. It is important not to fall into the trap of avoiding the feared situation. Specific Slip Recovery steps are described in Chapter 14.

❖ *Treatment completion and booster sessions*

Each child proceeds through the RIDE at her own pace, so it's important not to compare your child with Hannah or Henry. There is no fixed pattern for progress in treatment. For some children, improvement can be slow initially and then proceed rapidly. Others show progress in leaps and bounds from the start. Some ERP tasks may be completed in one session, whereas others may take several weeks to accomplish. There is no magic with the RIDE. Persistence and hard work are what yield the best results. Further discussion of the pace of treatment is available in Chapter 7.

There must be significant recognition and acknowledgment of the child's efforts and success when treatment is completed. Periodic "booster" sessions after treatment can work like bike tune-ups to keep the RIDE smooth. They help children stay well for longer. Booster sessions can be planned or scheduled as needed when your child feels vulnerable during times of stress or challenge.

PLUSSES AND MINUSES OF CBT

CBT is a real-life, pragmatic, logical and action-oriented form of learning. Above all, it involves moving forward to change the future, without dwelling in the past. It is a safe and effective treatment that teaches children the skills to take control over their thoughts and behaviors. Even though it is a collaborative treatment, the child must eventually be the one to face his fear—no one else can do it for him. The fact that it is tangible, practical and comprehensible makes it appealing to children and adolescents, who are more receptive to experiential learning. If learned early, CBT skills offer the child a set of coping tools that can be applied to dealing with everyday life.

There are no side effects to CBT other than the potential for distress during exposure exercises. Most children are relieved to find that the actual anxiety that occurs during exposure is far less than what they anticipate before the procedure—almost an anticlimax. In other words, the anxiety of confronting fears is generally overestimated. Of course, poorly administered CBT by an untrained or over-enthusiastic therapist can result in undue anxiety for the child. However, this is a clinician problem, not a problem with CBT itself. Therefore, it is important to choose your child's therapist carefully. See Chapter 7 for information on finding the right therapist for your child.

Facts about CBT

- ❖ CBT is not a quick fix; it may take up to six weeks to see results
- ❖ CBT requires active participation, effort and practice
- ❖ Improvements may be dramatic or gradual, large or small
- ❖ Treatment must be followed as prescribed for about 10-16 weeks for maximum benefit
- ❖ Symptoms may not be completely eliminated
- ❖ The benefits of CBT continue well after treatment is completed
- ❖ Periodic booster sessions help people stay well for longer periods
- ❖ There are no adverse side effects from CBT
- ❖ Approximately 20-25% of children do not benefit from CBT

Although CBT should be the first consideration when it comes to treating OCD in children, this safe, effective and long-lasting treatment option is often not offered to children and their families. Unfortunately, not enough professionals know about CBT, especially those whom you may first approach with concerns about your child. As a result, many desperate families have unwittingly taken the wrong path of treatment, resulting in much unnecessary suffering, loss of time and expense, only to end up back at square one. To make matters worse, even if CBT is offered as an option for treatment, there are not enough therapists who know how to provide proper CBT to children. Armed with an understanding of CBT, you now know what to look for; this knowledge can greatly increase your chances of finding a CBT therapist for your child.

Despite its efficacy and relatively benign nature, CBT is not for everyone. Its primary drawbacks are that it requires hard work, commitment and perseverance. It is not for those who are passive or helpless. It calls for a certain amount of self-reliance, initiative and risk-taking to confront fears. Above all, it is not a quick fix for anything.

SUCCESS IN CBT: WHO HAS THE BEST CHANCES?

Though CBT may work wonders for some, it is clearly not the solution for everyone. It is considered very effective for OCD, with an 80% success rate. That leaves about 20% who do not benefit. Naturally, you would like to know if your child will be among the 80% for whom CBT works or the 20% who have to continue to struggle with OCD. There is no way to predict whether CBT will work for any given individual ahead of time, but there are several clues that can point to treatment success vs. failure.

As a rule, CBT is most effective for children with mild to moderately severe OCD who display readiness to change, motivation, and compliance with the treatment. This does not imply that children with severe OCD cannot do well—in fact, a large number of my patients who are successful started with severe OCD. As I have discussed earlier in this chapter, good comprehension of the concepts of exposure and habituation, and willingness to take the risks of exposure are vital to treatment success. Children must be ready to believe in CBT and have hope for success. Those who are more self-reliant and independent, and who have a good alliance with their parents are more likely to participate in exposure. Chapter 9 discusses ways to maximize your child's readiness and motivation.

I remember getting the call from 11 year-old Bob's parents, who had just learned about CBT. I was five weeks away from going on maternity leave at the time. CBT had not been offered to Bob when he was diagnosed two years earlier, but he had been on medication and done well. Recently, the medica-

tion had lost its effectiveness, and Bob's OCD had returned with full force. He did not seem to be responding to medication increases, and he was suffering tremendously. I let Bob's parents know that due to my impending maternity leave, I was not accepting new patients. Their disappointment was tangible. They had finally found CBT and now it was out of reach. Hearing the plea in their voices, I offered them an option. I said five weeks was a very short time, given the severity of Bob's OCD, but that I could offer some strategies, if they believed that something was better than nothing. I emphasized the importance of motivation, commitment and practice to get the most out of CBT. They snatched the opportunity.

We started a "crash course" of CBT. I talked about the Worry Hill and Bob "got it" almost instantly. Bob and his parents were remarkable in their commitment and diligence. They were active and enthusiastic, completing all the exercises and more. Within one week, Bob was dramatically improved. He stopped checking the faucets, shortened his bathroom routines, and began to get to bed at a decent hour. At the end of five weeks, Bob and his parents rated his improvement as 90%. His OCD had dropped from the severe range to mild, as evident on the Children's Yale-Brown Obsessive Compulsive Scale. It was a testimony to the power of readiness and parent-child collaboration.

What factors reduce a child's chances of success in CBT? The most common are incorrectly conducted exposures and failure to practice. Some children may bail out before habituation has taken place; others may go through the motions but not really allow themselves to confront the fear in their minds. In other words, they may be desperately trying to think of something else to distract themselves from the reality of the fear, or may be doing silent mental rituals in place of typical rituals. Severe distress can interfere with a child's willingness to take the risks of CBT.

Children with severe depression, anxiety or tics may not respond well to CBT until these conditions are well controlled. Accompanying conditions must often be treated first if they interfere with the child's ability to focus on exposure. Children with attention difficulties, oppositional or defiant behavior may be more prone to externalize their difficulties and less willing to take on the responsibility of fixing them. If children aren't able to focus, organize, follow directions or delay gratification, they are less likely to benefit from CBT. Rage attacks or mood swings can be emotionally and physically draining for both the child and the parents, thereby detracting from the energy and focus required for exposure. CBT may be challenging for children who suffer from mental retardation, autism or Asperger's Syndrome. Not only may it be difficult to adapt the protocol to their specific needs, it may sometimes be hard to sort out which behaviors are OCD and which are perseverations (see Chapter 2).

If children are cautious, skeptical, suspicious or unwilling to risk changing the "comfort" of their existing state, they are not likely to get much better. Children who focus on denial, anger, unfairness and victimization are less likely to want to take active control over their OCD. Low patience and tolerance for frustration are also not good candidates for CBT. Children who rely excessively on others—therapist, parents, doctors— to make them well are not likely to do well because no one else can do CBT for them. Some children may be prone to seeing the glass half empty rather than half full. They may have unrealistic expectations for recovery and are not willing to see small gains. Some children hold on rigidly to the belief that their symptoms are legitimate and valid. Sometimes, children may get some secondary gain or extra mileage from their symptoms, such as tremendous attention or relief from responsibilities, making them more reluctant to give up the bonuses of being "sick." Some children who enter CBT really need medication (see Chapter 6) but either don't get it or don't want to take it. CBT is more challenging with immature children, because they may have difficulty describing their symptoms and understanding treatment, or lack the focus to go through with it.

A child whose family is up in arms all the time is not likely to do well in CBT. High levels of family conflict, criticism and stress may interfere with the alliances, trust and confidence that are favorable to CBT success. Families must be able to get past conflict and crisis, and come together in the child's best interest. Parents who are highly anxious themselves are often more skeptical about CBT than the child is and may inadvertently undermine the treatment. Some families need family therapy or marital therapy before their child can engage in CBT.

Finally, it is important to remember that there are no guarantees. If your child does not seem to benefit from properly conducted CBT, isn't ready for it, or if CBT is not available where you live, don't lose hope. Today, there are several medications that are also effective options for managing OCD. Chapter 6 covers the use of medications for OCD.

OTHER THERAPY APPROACHES

Whereas CBT is the only therapy with scientific backing for treating OCD, children with OCD often struggle with the same peer pressures, academic challenges, self-esteem issues and family conflicts that other children face. As part of a biopsychosocial treatment plan, it is important not just to decrease your child's obsessions and compulsions, but also to improve interpersonal, family and school functioning. Several other treatment approaches may be helpful in such a treatment plan.

Relaxation

Relaxation has no direct effect on obsessions and compulsions, but may help children with high levels of physical anxiety to complete ERP tasks successfully. Some children, but not all, benefit from deep breathing and muscle relaxation exercises, the use of pleasant imagery to achieve a feeling of calm and prescribed and structured leisure time to relax.

Psychotherapy

Traditional psychotherapy has not been shown to reduce OCD symptoms. However, psychotherapy may be useful to help children develop increased self-awareness, self-acceptance, coping skills, increase a sense of mastery and help improve peer and family relationships.

Play therapy

Play therapy is based on the assumption that children communicate and learn better through play rather than through talking. Although it is not directly helpful with OCD, it may be a vehicle for CBT with young children. It may have value with children for whom the verbal and reasoning skills that ERP calls for are beyond their level of maturity. Using toys, puppets and enactment, play therapy can be used to build rapport, increase comfort and confidence and demonstrate the workings of ERP to prepare children for treatment.

Rewards and punishments

Neither rewarding nor punishing a child will make OCD go away. Rewards are best used only as incentives to help children stay committed to a challenging task. Punishment is best not used at all for a child's OCD. Yet, children with OCD are no different from other children with respect to their need for expectations, limits and consequences. Sometimes, they may take out their frustration by lashing out in anger or aggression toward the family. Whereas it is important not to become distracted from the focus of ERP, it is sometimes necessary to address the issue of acceptable ways of expressing frustration. See Chapter 12 for ways to handle aggression.

Family therapy

Family therapy does not directly reduce OCD symptoms, nor does it "undo the cause" of OCD. Families of children with OCD are often just as victimized by the disorder as are the children who are afflicted. There is often turmoil and conflict between parent and child with OCD over the need for compulsions and resentment among siblings for the dominance of the child with OCD. These issues may be magnified among divorced parents who don't get along well. Turbulence in the family can have a detrimental effect on the child's readiness to engage in ERP and subsequent compliance. Families may be reluctant to disclose difficulties because they believe they will be blamed and misunderstood. They become engulfed in shame and secrecy. As a result, they may be more treatment resistant.

Even though parents are not to blame for a child's OCD, they may still benefit from help in managing and surviving the trials and tribulations of OCD. When your child's OCD frustrates and aggravates you, you may respond in ways that are probably not helpful. It takes inordinate skill and "super-parenting" to keep the family together. Rather than focus on past mistakes, family therapy should help families steer forward. It is important to realize that there is no use dwelling in the past. Family therapy can help you strengthen alliances, build coping skills and improve communication, understanding and support of each other. It can help you take care of your own needs, nurture your marital relationship and hasten the healing process. It can help with parenting skills, particularly when parents disagree on how best to parent the child with OCD. Your openness to family therapy reflects your commitment to do whatever it takes to help your child. It may mean that you have to be willing to take a hard, honest and often painful look at your coping styles, parenting, communication, and marital relationship.

Hospitalization

Inpatient treatment is often not necessary for OCD. It may be the only option in cases where no outpatient treatment is available or if a child is unable to function at home or at school, is housebound, too depressed, has no support system or no energy to engage in treatment. Hospitalization offers removal from OCD triggers at home and school as well as 24-hour observation and monitoring in a controlled environment. It is ideal when close medication management is required. It allows total immersion into treatment and is useful when rapid change is imperative or when outpatient treatment is insufficient.

On the down side, hospitalization is usually very disruptive for the entire family, as it is intense and requires concentrated time and effort from all. It can be a traumatic separation for children and parents. Children are absent from school, requiring them to deal with explaining the absence to peers, and parents have to miss work or juggle schedules.

There are very few inpatient treatment centers dedicated to treating OCD or anxiety disorders in children and adolescents (contact the Obsessive Compulsive Foundation for information on those in your area). Whereas your child really needs intense and focused ERP, non-specialized inpatient units do not provide what your child needs most. The staff approach, by necessity, has to be uniform in catering to all the children on the unit, who are there for diverse reasons. Generally, strict adherence to schedules and rules is expected. Failure to comply typically results in loss of privilege or negative consequences. This approach can often be contraindicated for children with OCD, because one of the main reasons that they are in the hospital may be their inability to keep schedules and meet expectations, not intentionally, but due to the interference of obsessions and rituals. Children with OCD are anxious to begin with, and these experiences can reinforce notions of being "bad" or crazy and the stigma of being on a "psych ward." Being in the hospital also fosters a false sense of safety and security. The abrupt change when discharged makes it easier to relapse when returned to the reality of the home or school environment. Further, inpatient stays average one to four weeks, which may be too short a time to confront OCD fears thoroughly.

Outpatient treatment is closer to the reality of daily life, allows more time for exercises between weekly appointments and is not as stressful. In my opinion, inpatient treatment should be considered only when a break from the natural environment is deemed imperative to break the vicious cycle of OCD, medication management is not possible on an outpatient basis, or when the child and family need a temporary separation to get treatment back on track.

Alternative treatments

There is no known evidence for the efficacy of alternative treatments such as homeopathy, herbs, ayurveda, or   for OCD. Some individuals report that they find such remedies helpful in reducing anxiety, stress and depression. It is critical to be very cautious about taking herbs and supplements—natural does not mean harmless. Some of these remedies may actually have potentially damaging effects if taken randomly or without professional monitoring. Some herbs interact with drugs in harmful ways or neutralize their effects. It is particularly important not to take St. John's Wort in combination with an anti-OCD medication, as it may precipitate a dangerous interaction known as serotonin syndrome (see Chapter 6). If you are on medication for OCD, it is critical to seek your doctor's permission to use any other medication or natural remedy.

FREQUENTLY-ASKED QUESTIONS

Is treatment always necessary? What will happen if my child does not receive treatment?

Although there is little research on this topic, it is widely understood that earlier diagnosis and treatment results in a better future outcome. Several adults with OCD might have been functioning fairly well, had they been diagnosed and treated earlier. When a child has mild symptoms of OCD, treatment may not be necessary. You might be able to wait and see if the symptoms get worse or disappear on their own. The problem with waiting is that it is hard to predict if and when OCD will become problematic. Treatment may be more challenging to implement at that time. If you were to go by Grandma's saying, "A stitch in time saves nine," starting sooner rather than later would be wise. Why take on the possibility of added suffering for your child, when you know that things could be a lot better if you acted now? It would be best to consult with an OCD expert and use the expert's guidance to determine if your child needs treatment now or later. The expert might be able to offer you parenting strategies to help your child get through his current mild symptoms.

My child is only five. We've been told that he's too young to understand and participate in CBT. Should we wait until he's older?

Many clinicians believe that young children cannot engage in CBT; however, children as young as four years of age can participate successfully in CBT. It may be far more challenging to adapt CBT for young children because it calls for a specific skill on the part of the therapist. CBT must be adapted to be more interesting and appealing to their age, maturity level and natural interests. Rewards and incentives add to the allure. Parents must be more actively involved, because young children are dependent on parents to help them get through the day. Parents must learn how to wean reassurance seeking, participation, assistance and avoidance and to allow the child to be exposed to fears. Young children are quite willing to go along with the fact that "nothing bad happened" when they face their fears without doing rituals.

My child's therapist wants to use "flooding" to treat my child. Does this work for OCD?

Professionals sometimes use the words 'flooding' and 'exposure' interchangeably to mean the same thing. The former is not used as much in the context of OCD as it is in the treatment of phobias. Usually, flooding refers to ungraded exposure, i.e., exposure that is conducted without generating a hierarchy of gradual steps. Ungraded exposure is usually not suitable for children, except in a few circumstances and if the child chooses to do it. Ask your therapist what exactly flooding will involve.

My daughter is afraid of germs but comes across them everyday. Why is it that she does not habituate when she is "exposed" to germs all the time?

If your daughter is not habituating to the daily exposure to germs, it is most likely that her exposure is not true exposure. By that I mean that even though she encounters germs daily, she probably does not allow herself to face her fears of them, most likely by rituals or by avoidance. In doing so, she escapes her fears; escape strengthens fears.

How often do we need to meet and how many CBT sessions are necessary?

Typically, CBT visits occur once a week for about 45 minutes to an hour. These visits may be more frequent during the early stages of treatment and less frequent during the later stages. Children whose treatment is more complicated or challenging may have more frequent visits. On average, CBT may take from 12 to 20 weeks to be completed. For some children, six to 10 sessions may be sufficient, and for a few, more than 20 may be necessary. Much depends on the severity of OCD, the child and family's understanding of the process, ability to complete exercises, and even the therapists' expertise. Your therapist should review your child's progress at each session and increase or decrease the number of sessions accordingly.

I don't want my child to have to miss a lot of school and me to miss a lot of work. Is there any way around this?

This is a common concern for parents. No one wants their child to miss school and deal with making up lost time. Appointments at non-school hours are highly coveted because every other parent is competing for the same times. However, if your child's OCD is severe enough to warrant treatment, chances are he is "missing" school already, although he may be physically present. Treatment offers the promise of getting your child back on track. After all, if your child does not get treatment, he will end up missing a lot more school than he will for treatment. You will have to step back, take perspective and decide where your priorities lie. If your child had a medical problem, would you not make treatment the first priority?

What if my child refuses to do CBT or get help of any kind?

You cannot force your child to do CBT. Scolding, blaming, nagging or power struggles will only alienate your child further. Instead, use the approach described in Chapter 9 to increase your child's readiness and reduce reluctance.

Does my child need professional help or can we do this on our own? What about the family doctor or school counselor? Can we conduct ERP with our child at home? What about at school?

Chapter 7 addresses the issue of the right therapist for ERP. Doing ERP with your child on your own is like becoming your own auto mechanic—you probably don't want to take that on, unless you have the proper training and expertise. The last thing you want is for the car to be worse off than when you first touched it! Likewise, you don't want to take your car to anyone but the best mechanics you can find. Close collaboration with school personnel may be necessary if the child has symptoms in school, but school staff are not generally trained or experienced in treating OCD.

Does hypnosis work for OCD? I am interested in alternative approaches.

There is little scientific research to support the effectiveness of hypnosis for OCD. This merely means that there are no published peer-reviewed studies. It's not to say that hypnosis may not have the potential to be effective in individual cases. If you are interested in alternative approaches, you should certainly explore them. Before you proceed, try what is known and proven to be effective, such as CBT or medications. If you have given it a good try and it's not helping, then you may want to consider less established approaches. If you decide to do that, there are three things to keep in mind:

1. Look before you leap: Learn all you can about the treatment from reliable sources.

2. Make an informed choice: Weigh the risks and benefits carefully, so that you won't be putting your child in harm's way (as is the case with some natural remedies).

3. Have realistic expectations: Don't get your hopes too high, and make sure that if it doesn't work, it doesn't discourage your child from trying something else.

Chapter 6

Medications for Childhood OCD

Medicine can cure only curable diseases.

Chinese proverb

Although medications do not *cure* OCD, they have been a blessing to many who had no respite prior to their recent advent. Today, the good fortune of having the choice of medication has given hope and a new chance for relief to millions. Yet, many parents are reluctant to consider medication for their children. You may be among those parents who are uneasy at the prospect of placing your child on medication so early in life. What about the side effects, now and in the long-term? How will they affect your child's growth, schoolwork and friendships? Will he be addicted to medications and not be able to function without? Will they make him a "zombie," change his personality, or "wipe out" his brain?

In this chapter, I will present a broad overview of the medications used to treat OCD, suggest guidelines to consider in your decision about using medication and attempt to address common concerns about safety and long-term implications. Additional information about medications may be found in Dr. Johnston's *OCD in Children and Adolescents: A Guide* or in Dr. Wilen's *Straight Talk about Psychiatric Medications for Kids*, listed in the Resources. This chapter provides the information to get you started. Medication decisions must be made in consultation with a qualified physician.

MEDICATION CHOICES FOR OCD

The main medications used to treat OCD are antidepressants that were initially developed as treatments for depression. Athough they are relatively new, early findings suggest that medication can be as effective as CBT in treating OCD in children and that a combination of CBT and medication may work best for some. Not only do medications help soften the symptoms of OCD, they also ease the fear, anxiety and depression that often come with the territory. Your child may gain relief not just from the assault of obsessions and compulsions, but may find herself more cheerful and energetic, and less withdrawn, irritable or depressed. As a parent, you may notice that there are fewer and less intense OCD "episodes," mood swings and hair-trigger meltdowns.

Among the many antidepressant drugs, only those that selectively affect the neurotransmitter serotonin are useful for OCD. As discussed in Chapter 4, *The Causes of OCD*, certain nerve cells or neurons in the brain release serotonin to allow them to pass messages back and forth to other neurons. The serotonin is then reclaimed back into the neuron so that it can be recycled, or broken down into an inactive substance. Each of the OCD medications delays the "reuptake" of serotonin, allowing it to be available to neighboring cells longer. This biochemical impact results in a progressive adjustment in nervous system functioning, often with accompanying relief in OCD symptoms. It is not clear exactly how or why the medications lessen obsessions and compulsions, as the workings of the brain are highly complicated.

Table 4: Medications for OCD in Children and Adolescents

Generic Name	Trade Name	Dose ranges/day	Number and timing of doses
Clomipramine	Anafranil®	25-250 mg	Between one and three
Citalopram	Celexa®	20- 60 mg	Once per day, a.m. or p.m.
Fluoxetine	Prozac®	5- 60 mg	Once per day, a.m.
Fluvoxamine	Luvox®	25-250 mg	Twice per day
Paroxetine	Paxil®	10- 30 mg	Twice per day
Sertraline	Zoloft®	50-150 mg	Once per day, a.m.

Table 4 shows the six drugs that are currently used to treat OCD. Clomipramine (Anafranil), the first of the OCD medications to be available, is a *tricyclic antidepressant* that acts upon serotonin and also on other brain chemicals such as norepinephrine and dopamine. The remaining medications, *citalopram, fluoxetine, fluvoxamine, paroxetine* and *sertraline,* are known as *selective serotonin reuptake inhibitors* (SSRI's) because they work selectively in only blocking the reuptake of serotonin, and are not believed to have any significant effect on other neurotransmitters. The SSRI's have fewer side effects overall and may be better tolerated than clomipramine.

Among the anti-OCD medications, all but citalopram have received FDA (Food & Drug Administration) approval for treating OCD in adults, and three have FDA approval for treating OCD in children—Clomipramine, for age 10 and up, fluvoxamine for age eight, and sertraline for age six and up. FDA approval allows drug companies to market a drug for a specific indication. Because getting FDA approval is an elaborate and expensive process, drug companies may only seek it if there is a clear financial advantage to them. Having FDA approval does not mean that a drug is more effective than a non-FDA approved drug. Nor does *not* having FDA approval mean that the medications are not safe or effective for OCD in children. Although physicians may prefer to prescribe FDA-approved drugs, many do not limit themselves to these approved drugs. They may prescribe drugs that do not have FDA approval because scientific research and clinical experience support their usefulness and safety.

REASONS FOR CONSIDERING MEDICATION

OCD experts agree that Cognitive-Behavioral Therapy (CBT; see Chapter 5) should always be considered and tried for children, either alone, or in combination with medication. They recommend that medication for children should only be contemplated when OCD is severe and debilitating, and if CBT is not giving sufficient relief (*Expert Consensus Treatment Guidelines for Obsessive-Compulsive Disorder,* 1997).

Medications *are* sometimes necessary for children and adolescents with OCD. If you have diabetes, you may be able to control your diabetes very well with *behavioral* changes such as diet and exercise. However, sometimes diet and exercise alone are not enough and you may need insulin to act directly on your blood sugar to stabilize it. Similarly, medications calibrate the level of serotonin in the brain to help control the symptoms of OCD. Not only may medications reduce OCD symptoms, they may also make it easier for your child to do CBT—like training wheels on a bicycle make it easier to learn how to ride. Medication may be a bonus for children who are too overwhelmed for CBT.

There is a time and a place in which a medication trial may be the best or the only option to give your child a break from OCD. Your decision will be made easier by thoughtful deliberation of whether the potential benefits of medication for your child outweigh the drawbacks. Table 5 presents some reasons to contemplate medication. If you check any of these items, it would be advisable to pursue a discussion of medications with your child's doctor.

Table 5: Reasons to Consider Medication for OCD

☐ Your child is not mature enough to comprehend or participate in CBT.

☐ Your child's symptoms are severe and he is unable to control them sufficiently to engage in CBT.

☐ Your child is unable to function, go to school, or leave the house.

☐ Your child is suffering from depression, hopelessness or helplessness.

☐ Your child is overwhelmed by anxiety.

☐ Your child has additional conditions such as Tourette Syndrome, ADHD or aggressive behavior that complicate his behavior and the treatment.

☐ Your family has such a high level of stress, conflict or distress that you are unable to provide the support that your child needs to go through CBT.

☐ Your child is unable to muster the readiness, motivation, insight, commitment, willingness, time or energy to engage in CBT.

☐ Your child is motivated for CBT but needs the extra nudge to get "unstuck."

☐ Your child has already had a course of proper CBT and still has troublesome symptoms. (The CBT must consist of Exposure and Response Prevention by a trained therapist. Merely being "in therapy" is insufficient).

☐ The aftermath of *not* placing your child on medication may be far more severe than the potential drawbacks of medications.

WHAT TO EXPECT FROM OCD MEDICATIONS

Although medication may be an easier route than CBT for some children, it is by no means a magic potion or universal panacea. In this section, I present important facts of which you should be aware before you go down the path of medication. If you are prepared for all these possibilities, you will be more realistic in your expectations and be able to enjoy the potential benefits that medication may bring for your child. You will also save yourself and your child unnecessary frustration and disappointment.

First and foremost, medications for OCD do not act instantaneously. Although some children benefit from them within two to three weeks, it normally takes between six and 12 weeks to make a noticeable difference. This time period is as long or longer than that required to see gains from CBT. Unlike a painkiller which gives quick relief and can be taken as and when needed, medication for OCD must be taken in steady doses daily to reach an effective level in the bloodstream. In fact, many parents and children are dismayed that it can sometimes be a while before side effects, fine tuning of dosage and orchestration with other medications are ironed out.

Facts about Medication

- ❖ It may be 6-12 weeks before you see any noticeable effect
- ❖ There is no "one size fits all" or best OCD medication
- ❖ Improvements are usually small and gradual, not dramatic
- ❖ OCD symptoms may not be completely eliminated
- ❖ Up to one third of children do not benefit from medication
- ❖ Side effects for each child may vary from non-existent to severe
- ❖ Medications generally cannot be stopped abruptly
- ❖ A medication that is effective may stop working for no reason
- ❖ OCD symptoms usually return when medications are stopped

Second, OCD medications cannot be rated as "good, better and best" because a medicine that worked miracles for one will do absolutely nothing for another. Finding the right medication for your child is a matter of goodness of fit. (See *Finding the Right Medication and Dosage* in the next section). Although all the OCD medications have shown similar overall rates of effectiveness, they vary in the way in which they affect on serotonin.

Besides, each medication interacts with a child's unique symptoms and neurochemistry in its own distinctive way. In short, the effects and side effects of the same medication may be poles apart for different children.

Third, it is rare for medications to stamp out OCD in one dramatic or abrupt move. The changes may be so gradual that you might be tempted to believe that it is not working. It is more likely that your child's symptoms will decrease in frequency, urgency or duration than disappear completely. In other words, although your child is still washing her hands too often, she seems to be satisfied within minutes instead of hours, and your son's book bag may pass inspection after three rounds of checking rather than seventeen. Sometimes the changes are subtle. People have a sense that something is different but can't quite label it. They find that although obsessions are still there, they seem to be easier to resist, and compulsions seem easier to control. Sometimes, they enjoy increasingly long periods of total respite from symptoms.

Fourth, even at their best, medications leave some "residual" symptoms in most cases. Although symptoms may disappear completely for a lucky few, for most they are only reduced to a manageable level. For some, the most that medications do is take the edge off or dull the symptoms. Nonetheless, your child is more likely to be able to return to "business as usual" because residual symptoms are easier to manage and live with.

Fifth, medication does not work for everyone. As many as one third of children may find no improvement or only partial relief on medication alone, even after 10-12 weeks at maximum tolerated doses. There is really no way to predict if medication will work for your child and exactly what changes you may see. *When Medication Doesn't Seem to be Working* later in this chapter offers options if your child encounters this problem.

Next, all OCD medications have the potential for side effects (see *Side Effects of Medications* later in this chapter). Although many children have no side effects, and others experience them mildly, some children find side effects so intolerable that they cannot remain on the medication. The problem is that, in most cases, the medication cannot be discontinued abruptly because withdrawal effects may occur. Typical withdrawal symptoms are dizziness, jitteriness and flu-like symptoms. Withdrawal effects are a function of the drug's *half-life*. Half-life refers to the duration, after the drug is taken, for the blood level of the drug to drop to one half of the highest level reached. Drugs that have a shorter half-life, such as paroxetine (Paxil) leave the blood stream faster and may precipitate more serious withdrawal reactions. Drugs with a longer half-life, such as fluoxetine (Prozac), stay in the body for a longer period and don't trigger withdrawal reactions. However, any negative side effects that occur will also continue even after fluoxetine is stopped, and until it has left the bloodstream, which takes several days.

Even if medications are working "miracles," many parents and children are unprepared for the fact that they may occasionally stop working abruptly for no apparent reason. It is not clear why this happens, because the body does not build up tolerance to SSRI's. The natural waxing and waning of OCD, weight changes, drug interactions, level of stress or depression may be some possible culprits. Although this is not common, it is very disruptive when it happens, because it is usually unexpected. It shatters the sense of security that medication can give.

OCD symptoms usually return when medications are discontinued. About 90% of adults experience a fairly rapid return of symptoms after they stop medication. There are no specific figures for children, but there is reason to believe the numbers are similar. Over the course of a child's lifetime, side effects or life changes such as pregnancy may present reasons to stop OCD medications. At times like this, your child may have no other strategies to manage OCD, if you have been counting on medication alone.

No matter how effective medicine may be, it is not a coping skill. It will not require a child to change habits, make choices, or deal with the repercussions of symptoms. As children grow, they will continue to be confronted by fluctuations and variations in their symptoms. Medicine may not automatically fix the waxing and waning of OCD. Over time, children will need their own competencies and skills to live life with OCD.

Combining CBT (see Chapter 5) with medications may help prevent relapse and provide long-term coping skills when medications are discontinued. Relapse is less likely when CBT is stopped, because the child learns skills that he can apply at any time, even after treatment is stopped.

CBT promotes self-reliance and gives your child skills to fall back on when things get rough. CBT is more durable when the child receives some refresher sessions from time to time. If you are uncomfortable with the prospect of long-term medications, CBT allows you to consider discontinuation of medications once your child has stabilized.

CBT can also address the academic, family and social adjustment difficulties that arise with OCD. When medication is used, it should ideally be a stepping-stone to CBT, not an end in itself. Unfortunately, if medication is the first intervention your child receives, and if it works well, she may lose the sense of distress and urgency that there was in the moment of crisis. She may be lulled into thinking that all is well, and may put off doing CBT or not do it at all. There is a natural tendency towards inactivity when things are going well. Many parents and children have regretted putting CBT on the back burner or ignoring it in favor of the seemingly quicker and easier medication trial.

FINDING THE RIGHT MEDICATION AND DOSAGE

Although there are several OCD medications to choose from, there is no way to predict in advance if there is a right medication for your child. For some, the first one hits the jackpot, but for many it may take several trials and several weeks to find one that works. This is simply because, as already discussed, each medication has its own exclusive qualities that interact with the unique symptoms, brain chemistry and personality of each child. The experience of finding the right medicine and dosage for your child may range from smooth and easy to incredibly frustrating. Being aware of this fact allows you to prepare yourself for all possibilities. Finding the proper medication for your child is a function of your doctor's expertise, experience and comfort with specific medications.

Who should prescribe for your child?

Prescribing medications for children with OCD calls for specific training and expertise. A board-certified child psychiatrist, preferably with expertise in psychopharmacology, is your best bet. However, a nationwide shortage of child psychiatrists can make this a rare find. The American

Academy of Child and Adolescent Psychiatry (AACAP) may be able to help you locate a child psychiatrist in your area. Although it may be more convenient to have your "regular" doctor prescribe OCD medications, many pediatricians, family physicians or general practitioners may not have enough experience with OCD and OCD medications to manage the complexities and subtleties of the arena. Seeing someone without the right expertise may end up costing you more time and money in the long run. If your choices are limited or non-existent, you may have to rely on the physician available to you. It would be helpful if your physician had access to an experienced child psychiatrist with whom he could consult if necessary.

You would be most fortunate to find a physician who provides both CBT and medications for children, but this is a rare luxury. What's more realistic is that a team of two clinicians, one who provides medications and the other CBT, will work together to provide coordinated care of your child. A doctor with a *biopsychosocial* approach to treatment (see Chapter 4) will attend not just to your child's OCD but to his needs as a whole person. Just as it is important for a CBT therapist to be open to the use of medications for treating OCD in children, it is important that your child psychiatrist or prescribing physician be knowledgeable about and supportive of CBT. If not, your doctor is not likely to see when your child could benefit from adding CBT or tapering medications to give your child a chance to try out his newly learned CBT skills.

Which medication should be tried first?

Since medications don't remedy all aspects of OCD, your doctor will select the one he believes will do the best job with your child's most troublesome symptoms, while keeping side effects to a minimum. Starting with a thorough biopsychosocial evaluation will help your doctor narrow down medication choices more effectively. Your doctor will need to understand much more about your child than just her OCD symptoms. Assessing all symptoms, mood or behavioral difficulties, medical history, family history, your child's functioning at school, home and with friends is necessary to this understanding. Your doctor will need to know about your child's responses to other medications, sensitivities, allergies and other medication-related difficulties. Sometimes, a medicine that has worked well for a family member may work well for your child, so your doctor may use that as a starting point, if all other things are equal. If there is concern about potential side effects, she might avoid a medication that might aggravate an existing problem.

The doctor will carefully weigh the pros and cons of each medication to find a good fit for your child. Sertraline (Zoloft) is an option for young children because it has FDA approval for children as young as six, does not interact with caffeine or asthma medications, has a more tolerable side effect profile, comes in pill and liquid form, and is taken only once per day. Many physicians may prescribe fluoxetine (Prozac) because it has relatively few side effects and they have more experience with it. Because it comes both in capsules and in liquid form, it allows the doctor to make dosage changes in very small increments. It is also a good choice for children who cannot swallow pills. Pharmacists can also dilute liquid drugs in sugar syrup; young children may find them more palatable this way. Fluoxetine also stays in the blood stream the longest, which is a plus if you have an adolescent who is forgetful or sporadic about taking the medication regularly. On the down side, if your child needs to stop it due to side effects, it may be a long time for side effects to go away even after it is discontinued. Fluvoxamine (Luvox) was the first SSRI to receive FDA approval for use in children (down to age eight) and therefore has the longest period of established safety for children. However, it usually has to be taken twice a day, which some families may find inconvenient and may increase the risk of missed doses. Paroxetine (Paxil), which also comes in liquid form, has been shown to be effective for OCD in adults but has not been studied systematically in children. It does not stay in the blood stream for very long, which means that withdrawal effects may be experienced if paroxetine is stopped abruptly.

Citalopram (Celexa), paroxetine and fluvoxamine have mild sedating properties whereas fluoxetine and sertraline have mild activating properties. These may be important considerations in your doctor's choice of medication. If your child is drowsy during the day, fatigued, has low energy or is depressed, your doctor might want to avoid giving him a sedating SSRI. On the other hand, if your child were overactive and over-stimulated, he would want to stay away from the energizing SSRI's. Citalopram, which also comes in liquid form, has low potential for drug interactions and may also be effective in treating social phobia and trichotillomania. Although clomipramine is as effective as the other OCD medications, it is generally reserved for those children who do not respond to the other medications. This is due to its higher potential for side effects, as well as the periodic need for blood tests to monitor the level of the medication in the blood. If suicidal tendencies and overdosing are a concern, your doctor will be careful about prescribing clomipramine, which is the most dangerous if overdosed.

What's the right dose?

Once the doctor selects a medication, she must decide on an appropriate starting dosage. Once again, although there are guidelines, finding the dose that works for your child calls for training, experience and clinical acumen on the part of the doctor. When there are no precise instructions as to the right amount for your child, your doctor has to find the balance between too much or too little medication, both of which may be uncomfortable for your child. The dose of SSRI's required to manage OCD is often higher than the dosage recommended for depression.

When deciding on a starting dose, the general dictum is to be conservative—starting with a low dose and making small and slow increases in dosage. Gradual titration over a period of weeks will help keep the side effects low. Starting too high or increasing dosages too rapidly will result in more intolerable side effects. When OCD is very severe or disabling, the doctor may choose to start at a higher dose than customary because side effects are less of an issue than OCD itself.

The best maintenance dose is not known until your child has reached it. (See Table 4 for dosing guidelines). Everyone metabolizes drugs at a different rate. Some children respond to low doses, and some need higher doses, even if they are the same age and body weight. Experts recommend staying at an average dose for at least four to five weeks. If there is no response, the maximum dose should be attempted within four to eight weeks, and if the response is partial, the dose should be increased to maximum in five to nine weeks. A child should ideally remain on the maximum dose for eight to 12 weeks in order to allow enough time for the medicine to reach its full potential. This can seem like a painfully long time, especially if the medicine ends up not working. To know if a medication is truly working, increases, decreases or additions should be made only one at a time, so that it becomes clear what is causing the change.

SIDE EFFECTS OF MEDICATIONS

One of the first concerns for parents and children alike is that of side effects. Like all medications, OCD drugs have the potential for side effects, but, as a rule, side effects are temporary, don't do any lasting damage, and go away completely when the medication is stopped. Most of the side effects are uncomfortable annoyances, but they are not dangerous. OCD medications are not addictive. There are no physical or psychological cravings associated with them. As of now, there is no evidence that they affect growth and development in children. Although there is little scientific research with OCD medications in children, clinical use for several years indicates that they are very safe, even with long-term use. In the forty-odd years that clomipramine has been in use and roughly fifteen years that the SSRI's have been around, they have not given reason for concern about permanent side effects, except for weight gain from clomipramine.

There are two important things to know about the side effects of OCD medications. First, although many children may suffer some side effects, some children may not encounter any at all. It is not possible to predict if your child will experience side effects, and which side effects these will be. Second, most side effects appear when the medicine is first started, and disappear on their own within two to four weeks, as the body accommodates to the medication. Patients tend to adapt more readily to the side effects of SSRI's than they do to side effects of clomipramine. For some, even nuisance side effects are so unpleasant that they are unable to tolerate the medication.

Table 6 offers questions about medication that you may consider asking your doctor.

Table 6: Suggested Questions about Medication

☐ What is the medication and how does it work?

☐ What is your experience in using this medicine with children?

☐ What have scientific studies on this medication for children with OCD shown?

☐ What made you select this medicine for my child?

☐ In what ways will my child improve with this medication?

☐ How soon can we expect to see improvement?

☐ What tests will my child have to undergo before and while taking it?

☐ What are the side effects, and which of them are most likely to occur?

☐ Are there any life-threatening side effects? Any long-term effects?

☐ What should I do if my child has side effects? Which ones should I alert you about immediately?

☐ Is this medication addictive? Will my child come to depend on it?

☐ What are the immediate and long-term effects on my child if he does not take this medicine?

☐ Will it affect my child's growth or ability to do "normal" kid things?

☐ How will it affect my child's other behaviors like tics, attention, hyper-activity or depression?

☐ How will my child function at school on this medication?

☐ Do I need to inform his school? For what should the staff be alert?

☐ How often will my child have to take the medication?

☐ What if she misses a dose? Will that affect her symptoms? What should I do if she misses a dose here and there?

☐ For how long will she need to stay on this dose?

☐ How will you decide when and how much to increase the dose?

☐ How long will it take to get the dosage to the right level?

☐ How often are dosage changes made?

☐ Are there any medicines, vitamins, or foods that my child should not take while on this medicine? Any activities that he should avoid?

☐ How often will you need to see my child?

☐ How can we reach you in between visits or in an emergency?

☐ In an emergency, should we stop the medicine?

☐ Will my child need to take medication for her entire life?

☐ When and how do we decide that its time to stop the medicine?

Serious or life-threatening side effects are rare and not usually associated with SSRI's. The side effects that are listed on package inserts can be alarming, but they list rare probabilities. Drug manufacturers are required to make consumers aware of all the possibilities; it also gives them protection against liability. Ironically, reading about these serious but extremely rare side effects can become a self-fulfilling prophecy of sorts for some people with OCD. Many OCD sufferers tend to overestimate danger and may interpret even rare probabilities as definite possibilities (see Chapter 5 for thinking styles associated with OCD). They may become hypervigilant and over reactive to the slightest physical symptoms, which may then fuel obsessions about harm and catastrophe. The very medicine that is intended to help may actually become the enemy in their minds.

The potential side effects of OCD medications are described below. What should you do if your child has side effects? Start by keeping careful written records of the medications your child is on, when they were started, the doses and increases and any changes observed in your child (see Table 7). Always tell your doctor if you see symptoms or behaviors that are not typical of your child, or if your child complains of them. Some parents may be hesitant to "bother" the doctor until they are certain that the symptoms are severe enough to merit attention. This is not a good strategy—allow your doctor to decide if the symptoms are serious.

Table 7: Medication Diary

Medicine	Dosage/day	Date started	Date ended	Date today	My child's behaviors
Prozac	10 mg	June1	June 30	June 3	Washing a lot. Mild rash?
				June 4	Rash gone. No change washing
Prozac	20 mg	July 1		July 6	Says he feels wound up, can't fall asleep

Generally, side effects resolve by themselves within the first few weeks; so watching and waiting patiently may be your best recourse. If they persist, your doctor may consider a decrease in the dosage or shift in the time of day the medicine is taken. If those don't help, your doctor will probably consider switching to another medication. If the side effects still continue and are not tolerable to your child, it may be time to weigh the benefits of taking medication against the side effects. Which is harder for your child—living with side effects or living with untreated OCD?

The following are potential side effects of anti-OCD medications. Since you will not know how your child may respond to medication until he has tried it, this list should not deter you from considering medication.

❖ *Drowsiness and fatigue*

OCD medications may make your child heavy-eyed and lethargic, but so can depression, overexertion or lack of sleep. It is important to explore all the potential offenders before concluding that the medication is to blame. If it is indeed the medication, waiting for a few days for the body to adapt is the first thing to do. Your doctor may have your child take the medication at bedtime to reduce sleepiness during the day. If your child becomes excessively sluggish, the doctor may lower the dose. If it persists and is bothersome, the doctor may change to another less-sedating SSRI such as fluoxetine (Prozac) or sertraline (Zoloft).

❖ *Insomnia*

Like drowsiness, insomnia may be an artifact of mood disturbance, mania or obsessive rumination at bedtime rather than the medication. If insomnia is due to medication, it can be taken in the morning, so your child is not kept up all night. Sometimes, your doctor may add a low dose of another antidepressant medicine such as trazadone (Desyrel) that has both calming and sedating effects. A glass of warm milk at bedtime, a meal of rice, turkey or other sleep-inducing foods, and some physical exertion may also help your child drift into slumber sooner and deeper. Do not give your child over the counter sleeping pills without consulting your doctor. Their potency wears out in about 10 days, and there might be the risk of adverse reactions with the OCD medication.

❖ Dry mouth

Dry mouth is usually associated with clomipramine because it may decrease saliva production. It can be quite unpleasant and annoying but generally gets better over time. If it is severe, your child may not be able to speak clearly; this reduction in speech flow may have social and academic consequences. Chewing sugarless gum or candy or sipping water frequently may keep the mouth moistened. You may have to ask permission for your child to sip from a water bottle or to chew gum in school. If it is intolerable, the doctor may prescribe artificial saliva agents. Saliva helps irrigate the mouth and protects it from collecting food particles that lead to cavities. Your child may need to brush more often and be more diligent about dental hygiene if he suffers from dry mouth. This is even more important if your child wears orthodontic braces, because the combination of reduced saliva and braces can put your child at risk for tooth decay. Let your child's dentist know that your child is on clomipramine so that he or she can monitor his dental health more closely.

❖ Constipation

Like dry mouth, constipation may be attributed mostly to clomipramine. The most common solutions are a diet high in roughage and fiber, plenty of fluids and regular exercise. Daily consumption of certain fruits, vegetables, yogurt, prune juice, bran cereals and breads can help avert constipation. Unfortunately, parents may often be unaware that constipation is a problem because children may not complain about it for several days. If your child is taking clomipramine, making your child aware of the potential for constipation, asking him or her to inform you if it happens, checking in with your child periodically, and being more alert for signs and symptoms will help. If constipation persists, your child's doctor may be able to prescribe a stool-softening agent. It is best to avoid over the counter preparations until you have checked with your doctor.

❖ Nausea and stomach discomfort

The gastrointestinal effects of anti-OCD medications usually subside on their own in a few weeks. Taking the medication after a meal rather than on an empty stomach may help reduce nausea. Eating small, light and frequent meals may also help. If diarrhea is a problem, foods such as boiled rice, cheese, toast, tea, bananas and apples or apple juice may ease the urgency of trips to the bathroom.

❖ *Changes in appetite and weight*

Weight gain is a big concern for most people, but especially for adolescents for whom the social repercussions can be unpleasant. Clomipramine is associated with increased appetite and weight gain whereas the SSRI's may be associated with weight loss due to appetite suppression, nausea or stomach discomfort. Although a healthy diet and vigorous exercise are the best antidotes to weight gain, adults taking clomipramine have complained that they continue to pile on the pounds despite a rigorous diet and exercise regimen. It is thought that clomipramine may affect centers in the hypothalamus that regulate hunger and metabolism, increasing the former and slowing down the latter. It is not advisable to take over the counter appetite suppression or weight loss products, which may cause anxiety and jitters with continued use. If weight gain is a major problem, your doctor might consider switching to an SSRI.

❖ *Irregular heartbeat*

Clomipramine is the only OCD medication that carries a small risk of causing irregular heartbeats, more so in children who have pre-existing heart abnormalities. It is therefore routine practice for a physician to check a child's heart rhythms before starting him on clomipramine. Your child will have an electrocardiogram (ECG) to measure the heart's electrical activity. Some physicians order an ECG from time to time during clomipramine treatment whereas others do not find it necessary because the risk of heart problems is very small. Ask your child's doctor about your child's risk for heart problems.

❖ *Changes in perspiration*

Sweating is the body's way of keeping itself cool. Clomipramine may cause reduced perspiration, which is usually not a big problem, except that it may result in overheating in children who play active sports. Drinking plenty of fluids at frequent intervals and patting oneself with a cool, wet washcloth when hot are recommended. Citalopram may increase sweating which is uncomfortable for many children.

❖ *Rash*

In rare situations, your child may develop a rash that might be indicative of an allergic reaction to the medication. Report it to your doctor immediately. Your doctor may decrease the dose or change the medication.

❖ *Nervousness or tremor*

If nervousness or tremor occurs, the doctor may drop your child's dosage, wait for about two weeks and then slowly raise it again. If it persists, a change to another medication may be warranted. Alternately, adding an anti-anxiety medication such as clonazepam (Klonopin) or buspirone (BuSpar) may help. Caffeine products such as soft drinks, coffee or tea may increase the chances of jitteriness because caffeine may interact with some SSRI's such as fluvoxamine.

❖ *Headaches*

Headaches are fairly common and are usually remedied with over the counter painkillers such as acetaminophen or ibuprofen. If they continue to be severe, your doctor may consider a prescription analgesic.

❖ *Sexual effects*

All the anti-OCD medications may dampen sexual drive and sensitivity. This side effect is reversed when the medication is stopped but may be a concern for adolescents who are approaching adulthood, and face the prospect of being on long-term medications. They may be embarrassed to discuss this with you, but should be educated about its possibility and encouraged to discuss it with the doctor.

❖ *"Serotonin syndrome"*

This is a very rare condition that occurs if the brain receives too much serotonin. It is a medical emergency and should be reported promptly to your doctor. Symptoms include shivers, headaches, nausea, abdominal cramps, diarrhea, insomnia, profuse sweating, confusion and jitteriness.

❖ *Drug interactions*

It is important to be aware that combining medications of any kind-including seemingly benign over-the-counter or natural or herbal ones-can be potentially hazardous. Parents who are eager to try "natural" remedies in the hope of avoiding the dangerous side effects of medications may inadvertently find themselves in exactly the same situation they feared. Natural and herbal do not mean safe! Conditions such as serotonin syndrome amplify the need for caution regarding natural and herbal remedies. Taking St. John's Wort along with an SSRI may result in toxic levels of serotonin. It is best not to take other remedies of any sort when taking prescription medications, unless it is with the knowledge of your physician.

Many medications such as asthma medications, antibiotics, over-the-counter cough medicines, and anti-acne medications may contain ingredients that interact adversely with OCD drugs. Caffeine can lead to sweating, nervousness, trembling and insomnia. Dextromethorphan, an ingredient in cough medicines, can lead to extreme anxiety, chest, and abdominal discomfort. Phenylpropanolamine can produce extreme nervousness. Keep all your child's doctors informed of every medication your child is taking to reduce the chances of bad interactions.

❖ *Long-term side effects*

OCD medications are relatively new and have not been around long enough for reliable data on long-term side effects. Clomipramine has been around for about four decades, with no major long-term effects, except for weight gain. The SSRI's have been in use for about 15 years in the U.S., and longer in Europe. As of this writing, there is no reason to believe that SSRI's cause long-term damage. While every effort is made to protect consumers from risks of medications, some side effects only emerge after many years, so there are no guarantees. Will these medications affect a child's physical growth and the development of other skills? At this time, they are not believed to affect physical growth and stature. New information may emerge with time, so check with your doctor for the latest facts.

❖   *Medical procedures*

In addition to side effects, medications may involve uncomfortable medical procedures. If your child is taking clomipramine or multiple medications, she may need to have periodic blood tests to check blood levels, because excessive levels can be medically dangerous. If noncompliance with medication is suspected, especially with adolescents, regular blood draws may be required to verify the blood level of the medication. Children are generally not fond of needles being stuck in their arms. Those who have to take clomipramine may also need to have ECGs to monitor heart function. Although ECG's are painless, the sticky adhesive patches that are placed on the chest to hold the wires may trigger obsessions about contamination for some children. Young children may find it hard to lie still for the duration of the test.

BEHAVIORAL SIDE EFFECTS OF OCD MEDICATIONS

You may be surprised to learn that OCD medications can also have side effects on your child's behavior. If your child shows behaviors that are excessive, inappropriate or uncharacteristic within the first few weeks after starting the medication, he may be experiencing Behavioral Side Effects (BSEs). Some parents have described their child as being overly elated or silly. Others have said their child became uncharacteristically rude, impertinent, defiant, uninhibited or provocative. Some have been very irritable or aggressive. It may take some time for parents to recognize BSEs because they may be subtle or difficult to tell apart from normal childhood misbehavior.

BSEs are most likely to occur in young children or when the starting dose is too high. Starting with the lowest possible dose and making slow and gradual increases in dosage is the best preventive approach. Most of the time, these side effects are mild and require no specific treatment, but occasionally they can be severe. Like physical side effects, BSEs also tend to subside over time. If BSEs are severe or persist, they may indicate other conditions such as ADHD or bipolar disorder in a genetically predisposed child. Antidepressants have the potential for inducing manic episodes in children who are susceptible to bipolar disorder or have a family history.

Always let your doctor know if your child's behaviors are noticeably different from baseline after starting medication. Specific examples and instances will help your doctor understand your concerns. The first step to treating BSEs is to lower the dose. If that does not take care of the problem, switching to another OCD medication may be an option. If your child is much improved by the OCD medication, your doctor might consider adding another medication to control the BSEs.

Table 8 offers guidelines for proper usage of medication.

Table 8: Guidelines for Using Medication

☐ OCD medications must only be taken under the close supervision of a licensed physician.

☐ Inform the doctor and pharmacist of drug allergies and all over the counter and prescription medications that your child is taking or has taken recently.

☐ Take the medication exactly as prescribed-the precise dose at the recommended time and in the manner instructed.

☐ Keep careful dated records of any changes in your child's behaviors and side effects. Note all current and previous medications, with dates, dosages, side effects and behavioral changes.

☐ Do not take any herbal remedies, vitamins, supplements or over the counter medications without your doctor's knowledge. Some of the ingredients in cough syrups, decongestants, asthma medications and painkillers can cause dangerous side effects when mixed with OCD medications.

☐ Do not change doses, stop or start taking any medication without first consulting your doctor.

☐ Inform the doctor if you suspect that your child is using alcohol, tobacco or illegal drugs.

☐ Call the doctor immediately if you see any unusual or unexpected reactions or behaviors in your child.

☐ Inform the doctor if you believe that your child is pregnant, nursing, or could become pregnant while taking the medication. The effects of these medications on the fetus are not known.

WHEN MEDICATION
DOESN'T SEEM TO BE WORKING

So your child has started medications and it seems like an infinite wait for it to quell his OCD. Don't despair. Before you throw in the towel, you and your doctor will want to review the following:

Has it been enough time?

Experts recommend staying on an SSRI for up to 12 weeks, of which at least four to six weeks are at the maximum dose, before deciding that the medication is unsuccessful. Often, parents and children who are frustrated and impatient and doctors with less experience in treating OCD in children may be inclined to give up prematurely.

Is the dose adequate?

It is possible that your child may actually not be at a sufficient dose to have an impact on her OCD. The recommended dose of SSRI's for treating OCD is higher than that used to treat depression. Because many physicians may be more familiar with treating depression than with treating OCD, they may not always be aware of the differences in maximum dosing. See Table 4 for dosing ranges for OCD in children.

Did side effects lead to noncompliance or premature termination?

If your child has experienced intolerable side effects, you might have been compelled to terminate the medication before it had a chance to work. Perhaps your child is very drug-sensitive to medication and highly reactive even at conservative starting doses. Perhaps your child's dosage was started too high or built up too fast. Fluoxetine and paroxetine are available in liquid form, which makes it possible to increase doses in minute increments, compared to the fixed doses that pills come in.

Was the medication taken as instructed?

OCD medications need to build up in the system over a few weeks in order to produce the desired effect. Is it possible that your child has missed doses, perhaps more often than you know? This may not be an issue if your child is young and you administer the medication, but could be true for adolescents who take their own medications without supervision, and may be forgetful or uncertain about their commitment to medication. If doses are forgotten or not taken in the full amount and at the given times, the steady build up of the drug in the blood stream is interrupted; that might explain their inefficacy.

Did your child receive CBT?

If your child is not already in CBT (see Chapter 5), it is a good idea to pursue it if available. The combination of medication plus CBT is considered more effective than either option alone. CBT may help your child tackle the symptoms that medication is not impacting. If your child has already been doing CBT, it might be time to change the CBT approach to address the unremitting symptoms. A good CBT therapist will have the flexibility and creativity to fine-tune your child's treatment.

Was another OCD medication tried?

Your child may have to try a second or third medication before finding one that works. About 40% of those who do not respond to one OCD medication have a good chance of responding to a second one. Each medication must be tried for at least 12 weeks with four to six weeks at the maximum dosing. In addition, if none of the SSRI's work, a trial of clomipramine should be attempted. Clomipramine is very effective for OCD but its use is usually deferred due to greater side effect propensity than the SSRI's. However, if two or three SSRI's don't work, clomipramine is worth a try, as it is a different class of antidepressant with a different chemical structure. It acts on other neurotransmitters in addition to serotonin. Some people who do not respond to any SSRI find clomipramine quite effective.

Discontinuing and changing medications can be difficult. A medicine cannot usually be withdrawn abruptly. It must be tapered gradually to minimize the body's reactions to the switch. Often, nausea and fatigue can occur during medication switches. There may need to be enough time for one medication to leave the system and the next to build up. Sometimes, doctors will taper the existing medication and increase the new one simultaneously to curtail these effects. Withdrawal effects may include dizziness and unsteadiness. Children and families can find this a trying time, as symptoms may resurface, increase, new symptoms may emerge, and your child may be more fragile and volatile. It is easy to become disillusioned if you are not prepared for these possibilities.

Has drug augmentation been considered?

If your child's OCD is tenacious, despite trials of two-three drugs and CBT, some doctors may consider drug *augmentation*. This strategy involves combining two or more drugs to produce a more potent overall effect, even at lower doses of both drugs. It is not understood exactly how or why this works and there is virtually no data on this practice for the treatment of children. Augmentation requires a great deal of skill and experience in psychopharmacology. It can be risky, particularly because side effects and drug interactions become more complex to manage.

As you can see, using medication for OCD can be a complex process that requires close monitoring and supervision by an experienced child psychiatrist. Although the benefits can be marvelous, it may take several months before your child's symptoms are well controlled. With the right knowledge and expectations, medications may be a welcome relief to your child and your family.

FREQUENTLY-ASKED QUESTIONS

I just can't get myself to put my child on drugs. I feel like I'm just medicating her symptoms away, and not really helping her find a way to cope.

Most parents with whom I have worked have agonized about medication decisions, so you are not alone. As indicated earlier in this chapter, thoughtfully weighing the pros and cons for your child will help you put your child's needs first. It is not an either-or decision. Trying a medication does not mean that you are committed to using it, especially if the benefits do not outweigh the problems. Making sure that your child also gets CBT in addition to medication will give her the tools to cope with her OCD. Her chances of getting off medication in the future are better if she learns to overcome OCD with CBT.

My son seems too eager to take medication because he thinks his troubles will dissolve into thin air. I am concerned he will use medication as a crutch, and it won't really help him take control.

If your son thinks that his troubles will dissolve into thin air when he pops the pill in his mouth, he is likely in for disappointment. You and your doctor need to educate him about the realities of medication, as discussed in this chapter. Your son also needs to learn about CBT, so that he has a viable option to consider. Perhaps your son does need a crutch for a little while. His eagerness might reflect the fact that he does not have the coping skills to deal with OCD in any other way at the moment. Perhaps he will agree to try CBT along with medication.

My daughter is four years old. Can she take these medications?

Medications are used with great caution with young children. First, it can be quite difficult to make the diagnosis of OCD in very young children. Second, neither doctors nor parents feel quite comfortable with this option because there is little information in the medical literature regarding the use of OCD medications in preschool children. It should only be considered when CBT is not a viable choice, and if the child is greatly affected by the OCD. It may be helpful to get a second opinion.

How often will my child need to see a doctor if she is on medication?

At the beginning of treatment, you and your child may see the doctor as often as once a week, so that symptoms, dosing changes and side effects can be closely monitored. As your child's medication takes effect and he improves, you will see the doctor less frequently. Your visits might become monthly, then every three months, and if all goes well, yearly after your child's OCD is stable. Of course, if anything changes in your child's response to the medication, you should contact your child's doctor regardless of your scheduled appointment.

What if my child refuses medication?

Children usually refuse medication because they have fears or misconceptions about it. Your child might find side effects intolerable, be afraid to swallow pills, have fears that the medications will contaminate or poison her, or change her personality. Some children feel that taking medication is a sign of defectiveness, weakness or failure. On occasion, resistance to medication might be a reflection of defiance to the parent and the display of a power struggle. Giving your child the opportunities to express her reservations in a supportive and non-punitive manner might help you uncover the reasons for the reluctance, and then lay the fears to rest. CBT may help overcome fears of contamination; liquid medications might help the fear of swallowing, and re-aligning the relationship between parent and child may be necessary to eliminate power struggles.

Will my child be able to function at school and do his school work on medication?

If OCD medication works as it's supposed to, it usually helps your child at school because it decreases obsessive rumination, reduces the urge for rituals and thereby allows your child to focus and attend better. However, sometimes, side effects such as sedation may make your child drowsy, tired and unable to concentrate. Sometimes, irritability or restlessness can be disruptive in school. Side effects usually decrease as your child adjusts to the medication. If they do not, your doctor may consider a change in medication.

Will my child have to take medication for the rest of her life?

It is not possible to predict how long your child will need to remain on medication. The chances of stopping medication without a relapse are far better if your child also learns how to overcome OCD using CBT. Typically, a child may need to remain on medication for a lifetime if he experiences two to four severe relapses or three to four mild relapses when medications are discontinued. Experts recommend that a child should be maintained on medication for about 12 to 18 months after reaching a stable phase. This would allow a good period of time during which the child can learn CBT and life can return to normal. After this period, medication may be gradually tapered over several months before it is discontinued altogether. Medication changes should only be made under a physician's supervision. Ideally, tapering should occur during periods of low stress and when a possible relapse would be least disruptive. The school summer break is a typical time for medication tapering, because it is a long enough period, is generally a low stress time, and because any difficulties will not interfere with school functioning. Keep a close record of any changes and side effects during this phase, trying to be as objective as possible. If symptoms begin to return, inform your doctor. Medications can be restarted if necessary and tapering could be deferred until a later time.

My child wants to take medications but is afraid, because one of her obsessions is about drugs poisoning her.

This self-defeating fear is not at all uncommon, especially among adults with OCD. Your child may overcome this fear with some exposure exercises. She may need to try CBT before she is ready for medication.

Are anti-OCD medications dangerous if they are overdosed?

All OCD medications are dangerous if overdosed, although clomipramine is by far the most harmful. Clomipramine overdoses can result in seizures, cardiac arrest, and possibly death. A parent or responsible adult should always supervise a child taking medication, and medication should be kept safely out of reach when not being used. If your child has overdosed on OCD medication, she should be taken to an emergency room immediately. With quick and proper treatment, your child will generally make a complete recovery.

What if my child does not improve after both CBT and medication? What's next?

About 20-25% of children and adults with OCD do not improve after either CBT and/or medication. This does not mean that your child will never be able to benefit from them. Often, the best approach is to try to understand what might have obstructed your child's success, and attempt to remove those obstacles (see *Success in CBT: Who has the Best Chances* in Chapter 5). Sometimes, it is easier to recognize the reasons than it is to remedy them. In such cases, it is best to wait for a better time to attempt

CBT and/or medications again. It is important not to give up hope, because that is the surest way for treatment failure. The advances in the treatment of OCD are so rapid that new options may become available at any time in the future.

Part II:

What to Do

Strategies and Solutions

Chapter 7

The Battle Plan Against OCD

We cannot change anything unless we accept it.

Carl Jung

For about three years, reassurances from his dad and me seemed to satisfy my son's health concerns. But then…more rituals followed. He wouldn't cross the living room without going through a touching pattern. He wouldn't get into the shower for fear of creatures coming out of the shower spigot, faucet or drain. He worried day and night about his health. A headache turned into a brain tumor. A stomachache turned into fear of vomiting. My son wouldn't go into school until my husband promised to give him five million dollars if anything happened to him that day. Nighttime rituals took forever and were driving us crazy! Our son was living in the prison of his mind. My heart broke as I watched my child become more and more limited by OCD."

Sharon, mother of Robert, 12

Watching your child become a hostage to fear can leave you feeling so helpless. You wish you could rescue him from these contortions of his mind. *"What can I do?"* you ask yourself. You are encouraged to know that with the new treatments, there is help and hope for him. How can you harness this help for your child? What can you do to hasten his recovery? Take heart, because there is a lot that you can do, but you and your child must make this journey together.

This chapter offers a master plan to make your child's journey to recovery from OCD more successful. The 10-step battle plan described in this and subsequent chapters will help you *define* your goals, *focus* your efforts, *direct* your energy to where it is most needed and *pace* yourself for the long journey ahead. A battle is not won by chance or luck; it is ultimately won by clever strategy. A good battle strategy against OCD must be *dynamic* and *flexible* to accommodate the need of the hour.

Table 9: The 10-Step Battle Plan against OCD

1. Accept the reality of OCD
2. Lead the charge
3. Be informed
4. Find the right treatment and clinician
5. Simplify your lives
6. Be prepared for the ups and downs
7. Unlock the emotional CAGES of OCD
8. Take good care of yourself
9. Gear up for the RIDE; RALLY for your child
10. Focus on healing and moving beyond.

A good battle plan against OCD encompasses recovery not just from OCD, but also in your child's social, academic, emotional and family life. It includes day-to-day living and coping, not only for your child, but also for yourself and your family. It must be geared towards your family's return to the path of normal life, to getting well and staying well. This chapter covers the first seven steps in the battle plan. Subsequent chapters in Part II describe the remaining steps.

ACCEPT THE REALITY OF OCD

It takes an inordinate amount of courage and hard work to come to terms with any unforeseen adversity in life. Coming to grips with OCD is no different. Acceptance involves facing up to the reality that your child has OCD, and that it is a part of your lives, whether or not you like it. It involves acknowledging that some things can and will change and others will not. You may have to think out-of-the-box and be open to new ways of living than those to which you are accustomed. In addition to OCD, there must be acceptance of your child, yourself and your family as you are, regardless of your faults and failings. Acceptance means knowing that you will continue to make mistakes, that life will continue to be challenging and that you and your child will continue to have good days and bad days. Yet, acceptance is not passive surrender. It is active assertion.

Why is acceptance so important to recovery? Acceptance sets you free to acknowledge and begin to cope with the intense feelings that adversity brings with it—denial, fear, grief, anger and resentment. You can only begin to move forward in your battle strategy when you have started coping with the negative emotions. Intense negative emotions can cloud thinking. You cannot be as logical, rational and realistic as you need to be to overcome OCD. Acceptance allows you to achieve the peace and inner quietude that fosters clear thinking, planning and success in reaching goals. It frees up your energy to problem-solve, take the risks that come with seeking recovery and move forward with hope. Hope is an essential ingredient in the recipe of recovery.

Denial is the opposite of acceptance. Denial allows us to protect ourselves from experiencing the emotional pain and overwhelming burden of difficult situations. But denial is not a good strategy in the battle plan against OCD. *If you don't see the problem, you can't and won't do anything about it!* Denial demands a great deal of emotional energy. Unfortunately, it burns up all the energy you could have spent being proactive and productive in this battle. The clock cannot be turned back on OCD. If you accept that reality, you can move forward. If you choose not to accept it, it can dictate the rest of your life and your child's life.

LEAD THE CHARGE

A battle needs a leader. Someone has to take charge, organize the forces, plan the battle strategy and put it into action. As a parent, *you* are the first person to be in the position of taking charge of the situation. You are not responsible for causing your child's OCD, but you are entrusted with the responsibility of finding him the right treatment and for leading him on the path to recovery.

Your child will eventually have to learn how to overcome OCD for himself and by himself. However, he is not in the best position to orchestrate the process, make good decisions or implement the actions to overcome OCD at the moment. *You must do everything in your power to empower your child to overcome OCD for himself.* Don't lose sight of the fact that you are your child's best advocate. No one is as well acquainted as you are with your child as a person, with all his strengths and challenges.

> You did not choose to have OCD in your lives.
> You *can* choose to get OCD out of your lives.

Many parents and children don't realize that they have the power of choice in this matter. You don't have to passively accept the dictates of OCD. You do have choices and one of the most important choices you are confronted with is that of taking charge. You can make the choice to let OCD rule your child and family or you can make the choice to take your lives back from OCD. As the person in charge, you must coordinate the effort in your child's behalf. You must be ready to put forth the effort and commitment this battle will take, and be willing to take the risk that life ahead is uncertain. In doing so, you will be a role model for your child.

BE INFORMED

One of the first things I say to parents is, "Read, ask, and know all you can," about OCD and its treatment in children. Education gives you the choice of making informed decisions. It allows you to avoid the painful mistakes that lack of information has cost many parents and families. The fact that you are reading this book shows that you are already well ahead in your quest for information. The intent of this book is to make you an informed consumer. Part I is designed to provide comprehensive information about OCD, and Part II to suggest how you can apply that knowledge to expedite your child's recovery.

> Read, ask and know all you can about OCD

Parents of other children with OCD are also a tremendous resource for information about OCD. You can find them through local support groups and affiliates of the OCF or ADAA. If you are unable to locate a support group where you live, don't lose heart. The internet wipes out all geographic barriers with a few keystrokes. You can find a support group of parents that is available for 24 hours a day, seven days a week, from cities and states all over the continent, and even all over the world, in the *ocdandparenting* internet support group for parents of children with OCD (see *Resources*). Here, you will learn from the folks who have been in the trenches. These parents have "been there, done that," and can provide the comfort, empathy and knowledge that comes with being in your shoes.

You can find volumes of information about OCD on the internet. A word of caution: The biggest disadvantage of all this easy access is that there is too much of it, and most of it unregulated and unscreened for accuracy. Along with messages that inspire hope, you will hear and read things about OCD that can be alarming and discouraging. It can be quite overwhelming to sort through and know what's relevant to your situation. To benefit from the information on the internet, you must rate it for *credibility* and *applicability*. Is the source of the information a qualified person or institution? How applicable is the information to your situation? Is it about children? Some of the worst-case scenarios you read about may pertain to adults who are paying the price of not receiving the right diagnosis or treatment for years. Keep in mind that your child and family are unique and that your experience will also be unique.

Finally, your doctor or therapist can address issues specific to *your* child and family. The clinician that diagnoses and treats your child should be an authoritative source of information about OCD. He should be able to help you sort the relevant from the irrelevant and apply some of the broader knowledge to your situation. Ask for clarification or elaboration on topics that raise questions and concerns for you.

FIND THE RIGHT TREATMENT AND CLINICIAN

Your next step is to find the right treatment for your child. (If your child has not been officially diagnosed, your first move should be to get a thorough evaluation by an expert in childhood OCD (see Chapter 3).

After acquiring information about OCD from the internet and discussing Nancy's symptoms with her pediatrician, I was given a referral to a therapist. Nancy was eager to get well and hated the way OCD made her feel. Eight sessions with the therapist proved futile. The therapist had not begun behavior therapy in all that time, explaining that she wanted to gain Nancy's confidence first. During this period, Nancy's depression was so great that I requested we start medication. We went to a psychiatrist who prescribed Luvox and thankfully, referred us to Dr. W, who provided CBT. Within two sessions, Nancy was much improveed and was well on her way to recovery.

Diane, mother of Nancy, age 14

Like Diane and Nancy, countless parents and children have lost precious time, effort and resources going down the wrong path of treatment. Sadly, these lost weeks, months or years of life cannot be recovered. That's why it important to find the right treatment and right therapist as soon as possible. As you know by now, it is *critical* that the therapy your child receives must include Exposure & Ritual Prevention, the cornerstone of treatment for OCD (see Chapter 5). I cannot overemphasize the importance of finding a therapist who provides ERP. In addition, it is important to keep an open mind about medication. Although CBT is the preferred treatment, your child may need medication if he is in great pain and unable to function. It is appropriate to be cautious about medication, but unhelpful to be dogmatic. After all, if your child had a toothache or diabetes, you would not withhold a painkiller or insulin from him.

Unfortunately, it is not easy to find a clinician with the right expertise in treating childhood OCD. There are many different approaches to therapy, and many mental health professionals do not have expertise in CBT or ERP. These are some of the realities that you may face:

❖ It can take far longer than you expect to find an expert in childhood OCD.

❖ There are many more clinicians who can correctly diagnose OCD than there are those who can correctly treat it.

❖ Not all therapists are competent at providing ERP, even if they say they treat OCD.

❖ It may be harder to find a therapist skilled in ERP than it may be to find a skilled child psychiatrist to administer medications.

❖ A clinician's professional degree or license may have no bearing on his expertise in ERP for childhood OCD.

❖ There is no specific license or certification to practice CBT or ERP.

❖ Receiving ineffective treatment can be a painful and costly experience for your child, you and your family.

Although this information is sobering, knowing it will prepare you to have realistic expectations and to look for a therapist with your eyes wide open. Educating yourself about treatment and therapists will help you zone in on the right professionals and save you lots of time, energy and heartache. Your child's therapist must have the *right expertise* and the *right clinical style.*

What you need to know about expertise

You should be looking for a child expert with experience in CBT and very specifically in ERP for OCD. Many different professionals such as psychiatrists, psychologists, social workers and marriage and family counselors provide therapy for mental health conditions. However, these professionals have different training backgrounds and therefore have diverse skills and expertise to offer. Neither the degree they hold nor the years of experience are sufficient to make them the right therapist for you. Knowing these differences will guide your selection of the professional whose expertise is best suited to your child's needs.

Among mental health professionals, *clinical psychologists* are most likely to have training and expertise in CBT and ERP. They either have a Ph.D. (Doctor of Philosophy) degree that involves six to seven years of graduate training in psychology, research, statistics, assessment and therapy or a Psy.D. (Doctor of Psychology) degree that involves four to five years of clinically focused graduate training. Psychologists complete clinical internships that give them intensive experience in assessing and treating mental disorders. Nonetheless, being a psychologist does not guarantee expertise in CBT or ERP.

Psychiatrists are trained as physicians and have an MD degree. After completing medical school, they complete a residency in psychiatry, during which they receive specialized clinical training in diagnosing and treating mental disorders. Some psychiatrists undergo further training to become *child psychiatrists,* and may take examinations to become board-certified. Psychiatrists are trained and licensed to prescribe medications. Some child psychiatrists devote their practices primarily to medication treatment, whereas others also provide therapy, including CBT and ERP.

Social workers have an MSW (Masters in Social Work) degree that involves two to three years of graduate training in psychotherapy and social work. They often have other certification such as ACSW, CSW or LICSW after their names. Their training emphasis is typically in family therapy. They are usually very knowledgeable about accessing social services and navigating the system. Social workers and other professionals with Masters' degrees such as marriage and family therapists, psychiatric nurses and counselors may also have training and experience in CBT.

What you need to know about clinical style

The "bedside manner" of the therapist is important because ERP involves confronting fears, which is exactly what a child with OCD does not want to do! The therapist must be able to elicit your child's trust and confidence and build her readiness for treatment. The therapist must be able to balance compassion and firmness, empathy and direction. It is also important that you feel comfortable with the therapist, because you are a very important player in your child's recovery (as described in Chapters 10 and 11) and will need to have close dialogue with the therapist.

Good therapists convey warmth, genuine compassion and caring. They put you at ease because they understand OCD and your situation and are comfortable in their knowledge and experience. They welcome your thoughts, comments and questions, and take you seriously. They instill confidence and hope. Good clinicians should keep you informed about their assessment of your child's condition and the goals for treatment. They should respect and respond to your inquiries. If they are vague, condescending, annoyed with your questions, or just too busy to give you reasonable attention, it may be time to find another therapist. Therapists should also be balanced and open in their views regarding CBT, medications, and other adjunctive supportive treatments. One who is dogmatic about preferences may not be able to help you work through treatment decisions in the best interest of your child.

Table 10: Suggested Questions to ask a Therapist

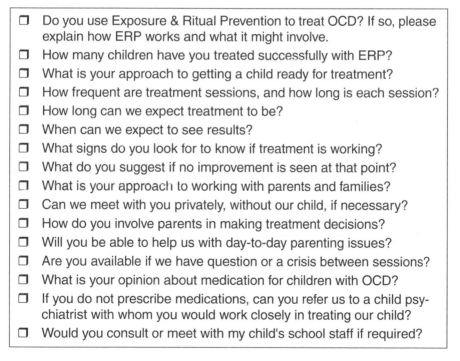

□ Do you use Exposure & Ritual Prevention to treat OCD? If so, please explain how ERP works and what it might involve.

□ How many children have you treated successfully with ERP?

□ What is your approach to getting a child ready for treatment?

□ How frequent are treatment sessions, and how long is each session?

□ How long can we expect treatment to be?

□ When can we expect to see results?

□ What signs do you look for to know if treatment is working?

□ What do you suggest if no improvement is seen at that point?

□ What is your approach to working with parents and families?

□ Can we meet with you privately, without our child, if necessary?

□ How do you involve parents in making treatment decisions?

□ Will you be able to help us with day-to-day parenting issues?

□ Are you available if we have question or a crisis between sessions?

□ What is your opinion about medication for children with OCD?

□ If you do not prescribe medications, can you refer us to a child psychiatrist with whom you would work closely in treating our child?

□ Would you consult or meet with my child's school staff if required?

The *Suggested Questions for Selecting a Therapist* in Table 10 may help your quest for the right therapist to be more focused and fruitful. The questions in Table 10 are guidelines and should be selected according to their relevance to your circumstances. Most therapists will not have the time to answer all these questions over the telephone, so it is best to schedule an appointment if you have a lot of questions.

Your interaction with the therapist when you ask questions will give you a good indication of his or her clinical style. If the therapist does not appear to know about ERP, is not able to describe it to you accurately, is vague, hesitant, or says it's not his preferred mode of treatment for OCD, you should continue your search. If the therapist suggests that your child's OCD was caused by your parenting, childhood conflicts or marital problems, and suggests that treatment should be focused on removing these issues, he or she is not up to date on current knowledge about OCD.

Where to look for therapists

Now that you know what you should be looking for, where do you actually find the most suitable clinician for your child? There are many different starting points including referrals from doctors, family members, friends, the telephone directory, professional or consumer organizations.

Your child's doctor, school psychologist or other healthcare professional may suggest a therapist for your child. However, pediatricians and other professionals may not always know whether a therapist specifically provides ERP, and some doctors may not even know the importance of ERP. The therapist you are referred to, therefore, may provide very effective help for children with a variety of behavioral or emotional problems, but may be of no help at all for your child's OCD.

Parents of other children with OCD are a rich source of personal referrals to therapists. Ask for recommendations from parents you know directly, through friends, family or via a support group or internet group. Other parents will be able to tell you whether their child received ERP and about their personal experience with a therapist. The telephone directory is also a fine place to start, as some professionals advertise their treatment approach, the disorders and the age range they treat. Using the suggested questions in Table 10 may help you dial in the therapists who will be able to provide what your child needs.

Organizations such as the *Association for the Advancement of Behavior Therapy* (AABT), *Obsessive-Compulsive Foundation* (OCF) or *Anxiety Disorders Association of America* (see *Resources*) usually maintain "referral lists" of mental health professionals. Professional members of these organizations may list themselves along with information about what disorders and ages they treat and what approach they use. Two things of which you should be aware: Professionals named on these lists are typically not screened, verified or endorsed by the listing organization. The lists are a good place to start, but it is up to you to do your homework and ask the right questions. Second, the list is not all-inclusive. There are many excellent professionals who specialize in treating OCD with ERP who do not list themselves with these organizations for a variety of reasons. Not being on an organization's list is *not* an indicator of lack of expertise or interest.

You may find this process a long and frustrating one, especially when your child is in urgent need of help. Many parents who have been through it will attest that it is well worth the wait to find the right therapist. They have traveled long distances and many miles, missed days of school and work and spent large sums—all to find the right help. And most say it was worth all that hardship, because it really paid off. Don't give up too easily. You may be surprised at what might surface when you are persistent. If you encounter a dead end, try a different route. Ask for leads and pursue them like a hound. One lead takes you to the next, and the next to several more. Networking pays off. If you give up, you will surely not find a therapist, and you and your child will be the ones to lose.

Your excitement at finding the right therapist might be dampened considerably when you learn that it could be anywhere from a couple of weeks (if you are extremely fortunate) to a few months before you get an appointment. So start now. If you are considering medication for your child, it is just as important to find the right physician to provide medication treatment (see Chapter 6).

Finally, when you have found a therapist and begun the treatment process, remember to make the best use of each appointment or contact with the therapist. Be active, do your "homework," and be prepared with your questions. Every appointment that you walk into "cold" is a wasted opportunity to learn more and help your child.

SIMPLIFY YOUR LIVES

Finally, simplify. It's a time to use survival coping skills. The early stages of OCD are a time of turmoil for the child and family. Established routines are disrupted, and the family is caught up in the upheaval that OCD brings. Until treatment begins and you have the guidance of a therapist, your main goals are to get by and get through the crisis. Have realistic expectations of your child, yourself and your family. You will need to bend and stretch the rules of normal operation in your household. These are not permanent changes to the way your family works; they are only meant as a tide-over to help you get through the crisis. You need a different strategy in a time of crisis than you need in a time of calm. It is enough to keep your child healthy, get enough sleep, and get through the day at school if she can make it. Give your child a "holiday" from all but the essentials for this time in her life. Spare her the chores and activities that add to the stress, but keep those that are relaxing, "normalizing," or distracting.

When you have to make choices, treatment should get first priority. After all, school attendance, grades and soccer will be entirely irrelevant if your child's OCD is out of control. Homework is more important than clearing the dinner table and getting to bed is more important than homework. Set only small, reachable goals each day. Maybe for today, Lucia's goal is merely to get to bed by 10 p.m.—forget about getting into pajamas. And don't add anything new to your child's commitments until OCD and your lives are well under control.

It can be detrimental to make abrupt changes during a crisis, so, for the moment, let things remain *status quo*. It's okay to help your child with his bedtime rituals because, right now, getting some sleep is the most important goal for him. You can help him get through his homework and get to bed at a reasonable hour. You might say, "Wait a minute, I thought I wasn't supposed to do this? Doesn't it make my child's OCD worse?" Be patient and take one day at a time. Don't expect everything to change. Once your child is in treatment, you and your therapist should develop a systematic and gradual plan for withdrawing all *enabling* behaviors, with the full knowledge and preferably the consent of your child. Long-term strategies are discussed in Chapters 10, 11 and 12.

BRACE YOURSELF FOR THE UPS AND DOWNS

OCD has a naturally waxing and waning course. Your child will encounter good days and bad days, good weeks and bad weeks, often for no apparent reason. Stress can also make OCD worse. Knowing what to expect can help you prepare yourself for the unpleasant surprises. If you are prepared, you may be surprised to find that it is smoother than you expected. If not, you may be riding the roller coaster of "Maybe she's getting better… maybe we don't need to see the doctor after all," to "Oh, no! We're back to square one." Brace yourself for a bumpy ride.

What to expect before treatment

For many families, the time before treatment starts is one of mayhem. While some days may be good, many may be very difficult. Your child's OCD may be getting worse everyday and life in the household may be falling apart. Watching your child spin out of control makes you feel like you're in a tempest. It is a time of uncertainty, when you have to rely on faith and hope that there is light at the end of the tunnel. Often, you may be in despair and feel like you are grasping at straws.

Crisis puts us at a disadvantage. It makes most of us look less than our best, and most likely our worst. You may be vulnerable, distraught and anxious-anything but your "normal" self. To make matters worse, you are likely to be easily misunderstood by professionals who do not know the "pre-OCD" you. You may be mistaken for an overanxious, overprotective, over controlling and perhaps even irrational parent. As a therapist, I remind myself when I first meet a parent of a child with OCD that I am meeting "a parent in crisis," a parent with a sense of urgency and often desperation. I try to remember that he or she might not have had a full night's sleep in weeks or months. Compounded stress, relief and eagerness to start treatment may make parents look unusually intense. I usually see the "real" parent emerge after a couple of visits, when the crisis abates.

Getting through this stage calls for persistence, perseverance and hope. You must *stick it out* until it gets better. That's exactly what your child will be called on to do during treatment. Each day can be different and doesn't predict the next. You will encounter many lessons in patience and fortitude. If you spend a lot of energy focusing on how bad things are, you won't have enough left to focus on moving forward. Pace yourself, because this journey is not a sprint—it's a marathon. If you expend your energy in one burst, you won't have the stamina for the long haul.

What to expect during treatment

You may be immensely relieved to have found a CBT therapist and finally started treatment. Now that you've finally started therapy, why isn't your child getting better already? Progress appears to be achingly slow, like you're swimming in molasses. It may seem impossible to believe that things can get better someday, when they only seem to get worse. Is it working? Did you make the right decisions? Pick the right therapist? The doubts and questions begin to creep in.

A good rule of thumb is to expect to see the beginnings of change within five weeks of treatment and to wait for at least 10 weeks to see a substantial change. Many parents and children are not aware of this time frame, and become disappointed and disillusioned within the first week or two. They may easily abandon treatment prematurely because they think "it's not working." If you are prepared for the following possibilities, you will understand that they are part of the process of treatment.

❖   *Turtle steps*

Progress in treatment can often be likened to Aesop's tortoise that was slow and steady, but surprised everyone by winning the race. When you are eagerly awaiting recovery, you may watch and wait, but the "tortoise" does not seem to be moving at all. Yet, it is taking small, almost imperceptible steps. The initial phase of treatment can seem achingly slow, because the time spent in preparation for ERP does not yield immediately visible results. Yet, progress may be happening under the shell. Turtle steps will eventually lead your child to the finish line. If you believe that progress is slower than you expect, discuss it with your therapist, so that you can understand the possible reasons for the delay.

You may be tempted to rush into the new things you have learned about treatment and to try them at home as soon as possible. Don't be too hasty. Use the guidance of your therapist to decide how and when you should intervene with your child's OCD (see Chapter 10 for more details). Don't push beyond the goals your child has agreed to in treatment. He needs to set the pace for exposure exercises. Abrupt or rapid changes may be too taxing for your child if he is not yet adequately prepared to confront his OCD. If you are too hasty, the whole endeavor may backfire. The "tortoise" may recoil into his shell and it may take a lot to draw him out again.

What to expect during treatment
☐   Turtle steps
☐   Fits and starts
☐   The extinction burst
☐   The cognitive lag

❖   *Fits and starts*

Your child's rate or pattern of improvement cannot be predicted in advance. It may occur unevenly and can take place in fits and starts. For some children, there is an almost immediate burst of improvement. Just the relief of a name, a diagnosis, being absolved of blame and guilt is enough to jumpstart improvement. For others, it is like a stalled car that won't move for a while, then suddenly decides to come to life. Yet others just make fairly steady progress throughout the process.

❖   *The extinction burst*

This term, derived from behavioral learning research, describes the intense initial *increase* in a behavior that you are trying to *reduce*—the *opposite* of what you want. When you say, "No more chocolate. You can have an apple instead," to your child, he doesn't dutifully say, "I understand, Dad. Thank you for making healthy food choices in my behalf." He is more likely to say, "Please, c'mon Dad, just one more," in the hopes that you will cave in. Worse yet, he may throw an embarrassing tantrum in the grocery store aisle, and you have to scurry away from the disapproving eyes of customers who obviously haven't experienced the joys of being a parent. That's what the extinction burst is about. When you try to extinguish a behavior, the child puts more energy and effort into resisting the change, because he'd much rather have the chocolate than the apple.

Likewise, when the comfort and familiarity of the OCD routine is disturbed, your child may resist the changes that treatment brings. Treatment can rock the OCD boat. Even though your child may be intellectually ready and willing, she may not be quite ready when it actually happens. Your therapist tells you to scale back on answering the reassurance questions. When you try it, your child goes ballistic. "Please, just answer this one, then I'll stop," she pleads. She puts the old "You don't love me" guilt trip on you. She yells and screams and tells you she hates you. She falls apart completely. You have never seen your child like this.

You are in for a big shock if you have not been prepared for the extinction burst. "She's gotten much *worse* since we started, not better." Has the exposure backfired? Were you misdirected? Did you do something terrible to your child? Assuming that you have a good CBT therapist and that the exposure was conducted as prescribed, this behavior is most likely the extinction burst. *This is when it's most important to stick it out. It will work if you don't give in.* When parents don't know about the extinction burst, they may be more prone to give in and give up. When your child realizes that you will not revert to OCD's rule, she will come to terms with it and realize that it will ultimately benefit her. If you cave in, you will teach your child that she can get her way by protesting-the louder the more effective.

❖ *The cognitive lag*

It might surprise you to know that your child may be doing better in treatment than either of you realizes. It is an intriguing but true fact that although there is tangible progress in treatment, there is a *lag* time in sufferer's and families' recognition and acceptance of that progress. This "cognitive lag" is another reason that people give up treatment prematurely, because they do not perceive improvement that may actually be occurring. Rituals respond fastest to treatment, followed by anxiety, and finally by a change in the belief system. The cognitive lag may reflect a sense of cautiousness about celebrating success, perhaps for fear of failing again. There is also a natural tendency to expect dramatic improvements and get distracted from the small goals that are the focus of each week's treatment.

"How have things been this week?" I asked cheerily when Lucia and her mother Elena walked into my office. I recalled that it had been a very productive session last week. Lucia and Elena had been reenergized when they left my office.

"Oh, pretty much the same. Another terrible week."

I sighed inwardly. "How so?" I asked.

"She's still not sleeping in her bed and I'm not getting any sleep either," lamented Elena.

"That sounds rough," I replied. "You must be exhausted."

"I can't take it much longer." Elena looked weary and worn. Lucia looked dismal.

"Okay," I said, "let's take a look at what we were working on last week and go from there." I pulled out my notes. "Lucia had two goals this week. The first was to go to bed without asking you to straighten the wrinkles on her comforter and the second was to wash her hands without using soap. How did she do with the wrinkles?" I asked.

"Okay, I guess."

I persisted, "Well, how many times this week did she ask you to fix her comforter?"

"Hmmm, let me see. Probably twice this week."

"Twice all week? She used to do it about 10 times a night—that adds up to 70 times a week. How much improvement is that on a scale of 1 to 10?"

"I guess it's down from a nine to a two," replied Elena, taken aback at the sudden realization that her "turtle" was way ahead of her. A look of relief crossed Lucia's face.

"What about the hand washing?" I asked.

Elena thought about it for a moment. "80% better, down from 20 minutes a day to five."

"That's absolutely terrific," I exclaimed, "What a victory for Lucia! She deserves to be so proud of herself. Now, let's see about sleeping in her bed all night—that's not been on her goal list yet. Let's talk about whether it should be for this week."

Lucia's rituals had definitely improved, yet neither she nor her mother had realized it—an example of cognitive lag. Thanks to quantifiable data, they were able to accept tangible evidence of improvement. There's nothing like the power of real numbers to settle differences of opinion.

What to expect after treatment

Life is usually much calmer and more manageable after therapy, depending on the level of success in treatment. Nonetheless, you may still see ups and downs. These ups and downs may be due to the natural "waxing and waning" course of OCD (see Chapter 1) or due to stress and transitions. The periodic escalations in OCD symptoms are known as "slips" when they are relatively minor and time limited, and "relapses" when they are major and chronic. By this point in the treatment, your child and you should have learned a set of tools to handle slips and relapses, so they should be far less disruptive and easier to recover from than the initial untreated OCD. Once your child has undergone CBT, she has a far more effective repertoire to overcome OCD than she did before. Chapter 14 presents strategies for handling slips and relapses.

UNLOCK THE EMOTIONAL CAGES OF OCD

As discussed in Chapter 1, your child may be trapped in the emotional CAGES of OCD. She may be *Confused, Angry, Guilty, Embarrassed* and *Sad*. Although you did not cause your child's OCD, your reactions and responses can either help free her or keep her trapped for longer. As parent and child, your lives are inextricably intertwined.

How can you unlock the emotional CAGES of OCD for your child? At this time, what your child needs most consistently from you is unconditional love and acceptance. Your child needs understanding and empathy. No matter how upsetting your child's OCD or the oh-too-frequent meltdowns are to you, remember that OCD feels much worse for your child. He is the primary victim of OCD; you are the secondary victim. The more unlovable your child acts, the more he needs your love and understanding. Remind yourself, especially when upset, that what you are seeing is not your child, it's OCD playing havoc with your child. If you can separate the two, you'll be able to keep the perspective you need to help your child. You must stay calm, focused and in charge.

Give your child hope. Hope is essential for motivation, and motivation is essential to recovery. Why would you want to work hard and take great risks if there's no hope of getting well? Your child must know that there is light at the end of the tunnel, even though it might seem like a remote possibility at the moment. You must convey to your child your belief and confidence in her ability to regain control of her life from OCD and to be "normal" again. Even if you doubt this at the moment, keep it to yourself. Air your fears in private. Your child needs to believe in himself to be able to take on the challenges of treatment. When in doubt, your child will be looking to you for affirmation. You are her barometer and she will pick up your cues. If you look hesitant, doubtful, tentative or discouraged, your child may pick up your nonverbal signals and begin to lose hope. Never give up on your child and never give up hope.

Keep a balance between optimism and reality, and encourage your child to be positive and realistic. Sometimes, even when you don't really feel it, "acting" the part can help. Have you noticed that when you do fun things, you feel better? Remember the time you had to drag yourself off the couch to do something, and were surprised at how much you ended up enjoying it? Back to the old Behavior Therapy principle—when you change your behaviors, you can change your feelings. Act "happy" and feel happy.

Sometimes, it's necessary to step back and look beyond the OCD. There's a lot more to your child than this illness. Your child is not just a problem to be solved. The danger of becoming too caught up in OCD is that you forget that your child is so much more. OCD and your child become almost synonymous. Don't lose sight of the fact that every day is precious. Valuable time is lost when you forget your child is a beautiful person, regardless of his strengths or afflictions. You have not lost your child; he is only shrouded in a nasty disorder. You must help him emerge from behind the cloak of OCD.

Release your child from guilt and shame. Blame and criticism will keep your child trapped in the emotional CAGES of OCD. He will hardly want to confide in you, ask for your help or trust that you are acting in his best interest. Don't compare your child with Noel, Michelle or Nigel when he is not doing well. Comparison results in alienation, not motivation. You need to battle the OCD, not each other. Your child needs to know that you will do all you can to help her get through this.

You may wonder if your child has control over his OCD because he does well at school, at his friends' houses or when he's on the computer. Sometimes, he can go up the stairs without twisting and turning and at other times it takes him an hour of writhing and gyrating. You may accost him about the discrepancies. Your child will sense your anger and rejection and will withdraw from you. The chasm between you will be difficult to cross. It is essential that you and your child be on the same side of the fence if you want your child to succeed in CBT. In fact, a poor alliance between parent and child is one of the reasons for treatment failure. You jeopardize your child's chances of success in treatment.

Finally, remember that children are far more resilient and brave than we expect them to be. Trust your child to come through. With the right help and support, your child may surprise you with his courage and endurance. When the time comes, you must hand over the charge of overcoming OCD to your child. If you don't, your child will never learn to fight for himself. Chapter 8 discusses how you can take care of yourself so that you can give the most to your child. Chapters 9, 10, 11 and 12 discuss specific ways in which you can help your child on the journey to recovery.

FREQUENTLY-ASKED QUESTIONS

What are the most important things I can do to help my child?

After unconditional love and acceptance of your child the way he is, perhaps the most important thing you can do is to give your child hope. Hope is the basis for effort and for motivation. Without hope, there is no point in trying. You must infuse hope not just by your words but also by your actions. Your demeanor and your behavior must convey the purpose, will and determination that are born out of hope. You must show your child that you are a survivor, not a quitter. Survivors make the choice to conquer and move beyond.

We were told that there's a long waiting list for CBT. What can I do while we're waiting for treatment?

First, ask your therapists' office to place you on a "cancellation list." Be ready to accept an appointment at short notice. Call periodically to affirm your interest in an earlier appointment. Your calls will be a sign of your interest. In the meanwhile, you can help your child get ready for treatment. Using the suggestions in this chapter, you can build a strong alliance with your child, so that you are prepared to fight OCD together. Teach your child about OCD and treatment, using the suggestions in Chapter 9.

We just found a CBT therapist who came highly recommended. But I didn't like his style. He made me really uncomfortable and I'm not sure what to do now.

If your antenna is up, ask yourself what might be driving your uneasiness. Was it a comment, demeanor or something in the way the therapist interacted with you or your child? If you can pin it down, you can decide whether it is trivial or significant. Don't dismiss your instincts, but don't give up too quickly either. Go to your next appointment and ask questions to clarify any potential misunderstanding. If you'd rather not do it in person, call and discuss your concerns by phone. You have to weigh the pros and cons—if the therapist has a high rate of success in treating children with OCD and your child and the therapist appear to have good rapport, you may need to think about setting aside your discomfort in the interest of your child. It's important to have good "vibes," but they don't always happen instantly. Some parents are fortunate to click with a therapist in the first encounter, but for others, it takes some time and work. If you believe that your discomfort will linger and will be detrimental to your child's treatment, you may need to find another therapist.

Our therapist says she does CBT and ERP, but she's spent the first three sessions talking about our family's and our daughter's feelings. I'm not sure if she does ERP, because I thought we should not focus on feelings.

CBT and ERP do not preclude the discussion of feelings. It is important to talk about feelings, especially in the early stages of treatment, because it may be necessary for the child and family to overcome negative or hostile feelings, to be primed to begin ERP. However, talking about feelings is not the ultimate goal of CBT. It is merely a stepping stone to the action element of CBT. I suggest that you ask the therapist about the purpose of your discussions about feelings. A good CBT therapist will always be open to questions. Ask about the treatment plan, when ERP will be started and how the focus on feelings fits in with the overall goals. If the therapist is evasive or annoyed, then you have something to be concerned about. CBT is time limited and goal focused, so if you hear "We'll just have to see how things go," your concerns would be justified.

The therapist says we need family therapy and parenting training. I thought these were not helpful for OCD.

Again, these are not the primary approaches to treatment of OCD, but may be necessary in some measure to prepare a child to get the most out of CBT. Remember that parenting, marital relationships and family communication also become victims of OCD. If a therapist suggests that working on resolving these issues is in order, it is likely that these problems are impeding your child's ability to engage in CBT. Attending to these troubles may make CBT a lot more successful, because a tumultuous family environment can dampen motivation and participation in treatment. What's important to clarify is that the therapist does not view family therapy or parenting as the only or final goal of treatment.

I found a highly recommended doctor, but he's always busy. Is he the right one for us?

No matter how compassionate and dedicated the professionals you find, resources are limited, and your child is one of many patients in great need. Doctors are often forced to attend to the most urgent crisis. If you believe your child's doctor is not attending to your needs as closely as you would like, be assertive and speak up when you need his involvement. Don't assume that he knows you are patiently waiting for your turn. If your doctor does not return calls, answer your questions or address your concerns despite your best efforts, you might want to consider finding another doctor.

I can't find a CBT therapist. We already have a great therapist, but he doesn't do CBT. What should we do?

Since there is a severe shortage of CBT therapists for children, your situation is quite common. However, don't give up because you never know when an unexpected lead might materialize. In the meanwhile, perhaps your current therapist can help you and your child cope and get by. If your therapist is willing to learn CBT, there are training manuals for therapists and training institutes by the OCF that can get her started. It would also be advisable for your therapist to obtain consultation from an OCD expert by phone, email or in person while working with your child.

We can't afford either CBT or medications. What recourse do we have?

Once again, ask yourself if you have assigned your child's treatment the priority it deserves with regard to expenses. Assuming you have, and you are still not able to afford it, don't lose hope. There are many avenues you can pursue although they will mean more work for you. Find out if your child is eligible for federal or state funded health care options such as the Children's Health Insurance Program. Parental income and the child's diagnosis (an official one) are usually the defining criteria. Large universities or medical centers often offer sliding fees based on income level (you may need to furnish proof). They may also have research studies that offer medications or CBT free in exchange for participation. Many therapists and hospitals will make allowances for hardship via an installment pay-

ment plan or reduced fees. Universities and graduate psychology depart-
ments often offer lower fees because they have "doctors in training."
Although trainees are less experienced, they are often enthusiastic, committed and eager to learn, and often make excellent therapists. Make sure
you ask who is supervising the trainee, how often, how closely and what
his/her credentials and expertise are.

Pharmaceutical companies may offer financial assistance to those in
need. Ask your prescribing doctor about this possibility. The doctor will
need to speak to the drug company and find out the process for accessing
such services when available. You may also be able to get "starter" samples
until you find the medication that works for your child, so you are not
spending on medications that aren't effective for your child.

Chapter 8

Taking Care of Yourself

I know God will not give me anything I can't handle. I just wish that He didn't trust me so much.

Mother Theresa

We either make ourselves miserable or we make ourselves strong. The amount of work is the same.

Carlos Castaneda

When your kid is behaving in bizarre ways, parents are filled with many emotions. Confusion and fear are right up there because you don't have a clue what's going on. When you get a diagnosis and, if you're lucky, get your child to the right person for help, other emotions surface. Gratitude, hope. These are emotions that relate to your child and what the future looks like for them. Parents rarely have the luxury of looking at themselves in all of this - their own feelings. Mostly because they don't have time; they're consumed with their emotions for their child's well being. I think it's important for parents to understand their own emotions because they, in fact, do have an impact on their children and how their children will cope. I think all parents go through a grieving process for their child; loss of their own dreams for their child; acknowledging that their child is not the "perfect" being they expected; grieving for an uncertain future.

What's interesting about the process for parents is that, like the waxing and waning of OCD symptoms, every bout of OCD can re-trigger those feelings of loss. Acknowledging this has been helpful for me and maybe has even helped ease some of the difficulties we encounter with Robert. I think I'm also coming to accept Robert more as I allow myself to feel bad without feeling guilty. Writing this made me feel better!

Sharon, mother of Robert

If you are the parent of a child with OCD, this chapter is about you and for you. You are also a victim of OCD. Although you may not *have* the disorder, you are forced to *live* with the disorder. The web of OCD extends far beyond the child who is afflicted with it. For every child with OCD, there are at least two family members, and usually more, who have to live with the fallout of OCD. Although some parents and families absorb the impact of OCD with relative composure, for many, living with a child's OCD is an ongoing chronicle of tumult and trauma. Yet, you may be neglected victims of OCD.

In this chapter, I present Step 8 in the Battle Plan against OCD: Taking care of yourself. I will discuss the many ways in which OCD affects parents and suggest ways to tend to yourself so that you can take better care of your child. Many parents find it helpful to write down some of the strategies suggested here on an index card and carry it with them. The card comes in handy as a reminder when discouraged and in doubt.

WHY YOU NEED TO FOCUS ON YOU

As Sharon's poignant account suggests, parents can get lost in the storm of OCD. They are lost to themselves. Many parents feel that they are being selfish if they focus on their own needs when their child is suffering. In reality, taking care of your needs is *altruistic* because the better you care for yourself, the more energy you have to give for your child. By taking care of yourself, you are taking care of your child.

When you are drained and depleted, you compromise your ability to lead the charge against OCD. As you will learn in Chapters 10 and 11, you have a lot to do with your child's recovery from OCD. Your child's needs continue to evolve during the process of treatment. You must be prepared to shift gears quickly and frequently to accommodate to his changing needs. You must have enough reserves to take you and your child through this journey. There will be many times when your child may want to quit, and you may want to follow suit. You will need to have the strength and the courage to carry both of you forward through the times of doubt and despair. Tending to yourself is part of your commitment to help your child overcome OCD. It is not an easy role.

How do you know when it's time to take care of yourself? You will know when you feel spent, burned out, worn and weary. You have nothing left to give anyone else. You want to throw up your hands and throw in the towel. You pinch yourself repeatedly, hoping to wake up from this awful nightmare. That's when it's time to give something to yourself. But taking care of yourself is a choice that you must make; no one else can make it for you. You must be motivated and committed to do it, just like your child must be motivated for treatment. You can continue to run yourself ragged and take everyone down with you or you can choose to replenish your reserves. You have the power of choice.

Why wait for burnout to take place? Why not attend to it before it strikes? It will take you more than twice the effort to recover from burnout than it will to prevent it from happening. Prevention is better than cure, or as grandma said, "A stitch in time saves nine." When you start nurturing yourself, you'll start feeling more energetic, invigorated and renewed. You'll have more hope and optimism in the face of adversity. You'll find yourself more compassionate towards your child, your family and yourself. You'll bounce back much faster from the aftershocks of OCD.

THE WEB OF OCD

Some of the numerous ways in which OCD can envelop your life along with ways to counter the negative influences of OCD are suggested below.

The tumult of emotions

Although many parents do not and cannot afford the time to introspect on their own emotions, they experience a tumult of feelings. Like your OCD-stricken child, you may also be in emotional CAGES of *Confusion,*

Anger, Guilt, Embarrassment and *Sadness* (see Chapter 1). You feel your child's pain so much that you cannot distinguish it from your own. You may only allow yourself fleeting glimpses of your emotions before it's time to put them away and move on. If you indulged in your feelings, you'd likely be overwhelmed with their intensity.

Confusion: Confusion, worry and uncertainty about the future may cast dark shadows on your life. Worry is a fact of parenthood. We always worry about our children's welfare. It helps us look out for them, keep them safe and teach them how to protect themselves. When your child has OCD, you are in new and uncharted waters. You don't know how to look out for him anymore. How do you teach him to protect himself when there is no safe haven from OCD? You know he has OCD, but deep down inside, there may be a small voice that whispers, "What if he really is crazy? Psychotic?" There's overwhelming worry about the future. "What if he never gets better? How will he do on his own? After I'm gone?"

I worry about the future. When the teen years begin and the search for identity heightens, will he decide to stop using the medications? Will he turn to street drugs or alcohol to deaden his anxiety and to feel more like a group? Will he be able to tolerate living in a dorm when he goes to college? Will he have to stay home and commute? All of this has me very concerned.

Nina, mother of Bob

Anger: If you give yourself a moment, the anger and resentment may seep through. OCD gives plenty of opportunities for anger. You may be angry and bitter at the unfairness of the situation. Why me? Why my child? You are resentful for the imposition on your life and for the disruption and destruction of your hopes and dreams for your child and family. You feel trapped when you are unable to disentangle from the OCD and frustrated at your child for making things difficult. You may be angry at your spouse who didn't listen or didn't understand when you knew something wasn't right, at the doctor who brushed you off because he didn't have the expertise to discern OCD, or the therapist who didn't know how to treat OCD but kept going anyway. You feel angry at the betrayal you feel by family members who suggest that all your child needs is some firm discipline, or those that think it's all in your child's mind. The friends and family you counted on haven't been there when you needed support, understanding, encouragement and hope. You envy the families all around you who seem to have it so easy. They complain about how hard it is to find the right size shirts for their child or how the moles have dug up the lawn! If only they knew what you'd give to have things like that to complain about!

Guilt: *Maybe I could have prevented this, if only...if only, I had seen it earlier, if only I had trusted my instincts. I wish I hadn't yelled like that last night. I wonder if I pushed her over the edge.* Anger is followed by guilt and self-blame. You may look back and regret having missed the early signs. You may feel guilty at having put your child through so much unnecessary turmoil and regretful for the seemingly wasted time, effort and finances. You only wish you had known earlier, so that you could spare your child every day of agony that she didn't need. You try to help your child, but often, it seems like you make him feel worse. You can't seem to do or say the right thing. More guilt. Fortunately, children are usually willing to forgive parents faster than parents forgive themselves.

Most parents do the best they can in their circumstances. There are no perfect parents and there are none who are exempt from mistakes. To stumble along the way is part of our journey as parents. It gives us the opportunity to learn from our lapses.

Embarrassment: It's embarrassing to even admit it, but sometimes you feel mortified and maybe even ashamed about your child and your situation. Going to a family gathering, to the mall, church or the soccer field is like traveling with a ticking time bomb. When is it going to blow up? How long before you have to hang your head in shame and make a hasty retreat because of some ridiculous OCD-fueled scene? You've endured too many fiascos already and enough humiliation to last a lifetime. You wish you could explain what's really going on, but you are stopped cold in your tracks when you hear, "What that child really needs is a firm parent with a strong hand." Relatives and friends oblige you with unsolicited advice. Your child is merely a spoiled brat in their eyes. On the heels of shame comes the guilt about being ashamed of your child.

Sadness: Then there's the deep, painful sense of grief and loss that you feel for the child you have lost. You are in mourning for the child that was and would have been. Your child who was full of promise and hope has been cheated of his childhood. Your heart is heavy for him. You feel disappointed, demoralized, depressed, helpless and hopeless.

I do not have the words to describe the great sadness and anguish we felt as we watched Nancy go through this period before finding the right help.

Diane, mother of Nancy, age 12

What do you do with the pain? Where do you put it? How do you get past it? The key is to find ways to release the hurt constructively rather than destructively. It's not the feelings that are the problem; it's what we do with them that is critical. It's easy enough to blow up and take out your anger on anyone who's unfortunate enough to be in your path, but that doesn't take you forward; it sets you back. You must be able to get past the pain so that you can divert your energy to where it is really needed-to getting well, staying well and living well. If you can't move past the feelings, you can't harness your energy to move onward. Your energy will be spent running in circles. There must be a place for grief, but there must also be a place for moving on.

The following are several constructive approaches to coping with emotions. You will have to find the ones that suit your style and work for you.

❖   *Acceptance*

First of all, accept the feelings as natural and normal. You are human and being human entails having feelings. Feelings cannot always be controlled; they are natural reactions to the situations we encounter. They are not reflective of weakness or lack of resolve. You're okay and your feelings are okay. Even bad feelings have a place in our lives because they can motivate us to change the situation. Feeling bad about your child can drive you to make things better for him.

Allow yourself to acknowledge, "I'm really furious right now. I could just explode." You may need to shed tears or have some quiet time to contemplate and come to terms with your feelings. Permit yourself to experience all the pent-up emotions—grief, anger, resentment and worry. Don't "stuff" the feelings-they will simmer and resurface periodically until you find a productive way to get them out of your system.

❖ *Find someone with whom you can share your feelings.*

Recognizing and talking about feelings can often be more upsetting than trying to keep them at bay. That's why some people avoid discussing feelings. However, the more you talk about the anguish, the easier it is to get through it. The pain may never fully go away, but it will subside to the point where you are not engulfed by it. In talking with another, you may find validation, acceptance, comfort, empathy as well as a balanced perspective. A spouse, trusted friend or family member, counselor or other parents of children with OCD may be confidants to help you work through the feelings.

❖ *Work off the angst*

A constructive physical activity is a good release for feelings. When you feel the tension building, take a brisk walk or a jog. Do the gardening or the spring-cleaning. You may like to bake or cook. Rake the leaves, prune the bushes, swab the floors or scrub the tub. It is well known by now that physical exertion stimulates feelings of well-being. And throw in an added bonus-get the piled-up chores done at the same time.

❖ *Keep a diary*

Like Sharon, whose account you read above, you may find that writing allows you to sort through and express the thoughts and feelings you didn't know you had. Write out your deepest thoughts, fears and feelings. The mere process of writing is a cleansing and healing experience for many. As you write, the jumble of emotions within you is released into thoughts and words that take on meaning. Many parents find it reaffirming to read their diaries later and look back on the path they have traveled.

❖   *Stop the guilt, blame and shame*

It's important not to feel guilty because your child has OCD. As soon as the burden of guilty feelings was lifted from me, I had so much more energy and drive to help my son overcome his OCD.

Nina, mother of Bob

Regret is only worthwhile if you use it as a stepping stone to learning. It is no good if you use it to blame and berate yourself. Forgive yourself for doing things that may not have been helpful for your child. Be compassionate—treat yourself as you would have others treat you. Although a measured amount of guilt is a good motivator to act differently, excessive guilt is destructive. It destroys self-esteem and tears down relationships. What's been done cannot be undone, except by doing it differently the next time.

Accept that you have made mistakes and that you will continue, like every one else, to make mistakes despite your best intentions because you're not perfect. Perfect parenting is not a reality. You will make mistakes as you figure out what works and what doesn't. Sometimes, this is the only way to learn. The intent of your behavior is more important than the actual behavior. If you acted with good intentions, then mistakes are a "no-fault" occurrence. If you did not intend well, you must examine the motives for your behavior and make amends accordingly.

Don't be ashamed of your child. He did not concoct this bizarre and complicated illness just to make your life miserable. Nor is he being deliberately ungrateful when he happens to embarrass you in public. In fact, your shame may add to the unfortunate belief in our society that mental illness is a weakness or a flaw and something to be hidden. Your child will also come to believe this and feel unworthy. He cannot succeed in treatment if he feels inferior and unworthy.

❖   *Don't sweat the small stuff*

When you are tired and emotional, even the molehills become mountains. Recognize that like you, others are not perfect and make mistakes without malicious intent. Don't hold them to unreachable standards. You must learn how to let some things slide. Try to be picky about what you are going to get upset about. It's a big drain on your energy to react with intensity to everything that comes your way.

❖ *You can't change what others think, but you can change what they know*

What will other people say or think? The fact is, other people say and think whatever they please, and there's not a thing we can do to control it. Spending your energy trying to engineer public opinion may be a waste of time. Instead, your time may be better spent in education about OCD and mental illness. When you are ready, you can help people learn more by being more open about your child's OCD and de-stigmatizing OCD. Be prepared for the fact that some of the people will listen some of the time.

❖ *Avoid the thinking traps*

Be careful about going to extremes such as blaming all of life's troubles on OCD. Remember that life probably wasn't perfect before OCD. Some problems may have preceded OCD and may be independent of OCD. OCD is not the reason for every problem. "All or none" thinking fosters helplessness and hopelessness, neither of which are helpful to recovery.

❖ *Act happy, feel happy*

It may surprise you to know that you can be happy if you begin to *act* happy! Behave as if you're happy, even if you have to "fake it," and pretty soon, you'll begin to believe yourself. Remember the times you have to drag yourself to get dressed and go out when you'd much rather stay at home? When you did, you enjoyed yourself more than you expected. Likewise, notice how you feel like a couch potato after you sink into the couch? Get up and move around and you feel much better. When you feel like sinking into bad feelings, get up, start acting happy and active and make yourself feel good again. Don't just wait for it to happen to you, *make* it happen for yourself. Feeling good is not a matter of passive expectation; it's a matter of active assertion.

❖ *Draw on your spiritual reserves*

If you have a spiritual or religious source of strength, reach for it. For many, reliance on religious or spiritual beliefs provides the fortitude and endurance to cope when there are no easy explanations or solutions. Faith in a higher power gives people the courage to carry on in the face of great odds. Western medicine is only recently beginning to acknowledge the importance of faith, spirituality and prayer in the way people cope with life's illnesses and adversities.

❖ *Get therapy or medications for yourself*

If you are unable to cope with your emotions and feel unduly dejected, demoralized, hopeless, helpless or suicidal, you may be suffering from depression or anxiety. It is best to seek an evaluation and appropriate treatment. Getting help is not a sign of failure or weakness. Seek CBT to learn how to cope with the feelings and think your way out of depression. Some parents find that they benefit from medications.

Obsessed with OCD

Your child is the one with OCD, but sometimes you feel like you have become obsessed with his OCD! It is your personal crusade. OCD is all consuming, not just for your child but also for you. You feel like you must be immersed in OCD, or else you're not doing enough. You read everything you can lay your hands on. You can think of little else. Your whole world revolves around the OCD. While education and involvement are healthy and necessary to give you control and move you forward, they can be carried to a level that defeats their purpose. When your involvement with OCD makes you feel out of control, you have probably crossed the line from the realm of helpful to unhelpful. You may be exhausted and overwhelmed because you can't possibly sustain that level of intensity for too long. What you are doing is not helping anymore, but is hurting you or your child. How do you step out of the quicksand?

❖ *You don't always have to have the answer!*

Life is full of questions that don't have answers. Accepting and living with uncertainty and ambiguity is a fact of life. Often, you won't have the right answer or solution to a problem despite your best efforts. Accept that it's okay and that it does not reflect on you as a failure. Sometimes, you may learn better from hindsight. Don't be so hard on yourself.

❖ *Take a break from OCD*

Plan to take some time away from OCD. When you have the urge to read more, pick up a novel or the newspaper instead. Call a friend, get out of the house or do catch up on something you've put on hold for a long time. Seek a relaxing hobby to take your mind away from OCD periodically. Take some time to do something enjoyable for yourself.

Unwitting accomplice to OCD

You've been trying to make it easier on your child as he struggles through his laborious compulsions and cruel obsessions. You stay one step ahead of him, clearing his path of trouble. You help him check the closets, to wash one last time and fold his shirts the right way. You answer his questions over again—anything to help his fear go away. You think ahead of what's coming his way and you try to eliminate any triggers from his path. You tiptoe around so that you don't set off any alarms for your child. Your child relies on you to help him steer clear of trouble. This daily rigmarole is exhausting and draining for you, both physically and emotionally, but you would do it again for your child. Ironically, it doesn't seem to help the situation much and perpetuates your sense of failure.

Then comes the shock and dismay of realizing that you've been aiding and abetting the OCD all along! You may have inadvertently been fostering avoidance, which makes OCD stronger (see Chapter 4). This is the last thing you want to hear when you're beleaguered, defensive and tired. You've defeated your own goals—how could you have been taken in? You feel dim-witted because you didn't see it for yourself. You feel guilty and angry that your best efforts only hurt your child.

❖ *Step back and get perspective*

You must be able to step out of the web of OCD and become an observer of the process rather than a participant. When you have the urge to help your child with his rituals, resist the temptation to rush to the rescue. See how far he can go on his own.

❖ *Catch yourself in the act*

Start playing "psychological detective" and paying attention to the ways in which OCD has taken control of your behaviors and beliefs. You will be surprised at what you find out when you increase your awareness to behaviors that were previously automatic. Write these down in a diary or keep a list. Learn to detect the early warning signs and catch yourself before you head down the wrong path.

❖ *Recognize unsustainable commitments*

Recognize and accept that you can't do all of it all of the time. You won't be there to rescue your child when he's at school, on the playground or when he leaves the home. He needs to learn the coping skills to get through these challenges on his own.

❖ *Use your therapists' guidance to ease your way out*

If you have gotten to the point where you feel consumed by your child's OCD, you probably need a CBT therapists' help to ease your way out of it. It won't happen overnight and it will be more successful if it is planned and systematic, rather than "cold turkey." Chapters 10 and 11 offer more specific ways for extricating yourself from OCD.

The brunt of the burden

It is not at all uncommon for one parent to shoulder most of the day-to-day burden of a child's OCD. It is most typically the mother, although it may sometimes be the father. The mother is often, by societal role evolution, the one to take care of the household, attend to illness, doctor's visits, school issues and homework. Chances are if you are reading this book, you are the parent who is taking charge of the situation. You may be overwhelmed and fatigued with the running around you have to do to get your child through the day. Then there are the rituals that keep you up until the wee hours of the morning. After you micromanage your child's needs, you are the lucky recipient of his anger when he unleashes his frustration on you. When everyone's mad at everyone else, you are the peace-keeping force in the family. You may feel the responsibility of holding it together for everyone, with the fear that the family will fall apart if you don't. You are exhausted and unable to sustain your involvement alone. You may be resentful of your partner's seeming lack of participation.

❖ *Evaluate your role in the family*

Before you confront your spouse of shirking responsibility, stop a moment to think about whether you have assumed the role of "caretaker" in the family. Perhaps you have been doing it so well and for so long that your spouse assumes you will do it with grace like you always do. Your spouse may not stop to consider that OCD is not an everyday challenge.

❖ *Ask for help*

Talk to your spouse and let him or her know that you need help. Some partners may be in denial, but there are surely many who are dedicated, but aren't aware that they need to help. Don't assume your spouse knows what you need. Be direct in your request. Don't keep him or her guessing. Of course, your request for help will be best received if you "ask nicely" rather than resort to character assassination. Your spouse may be surprised to learn that you are frustrated. Some could use specific direction about where and how you need help. Ask your spouse to participate in your child's treatment, or keep him or her informed of the process, so that you are not entirely spent.

❖ *Recognize the difference between "I want to" and "I need to"*

As discussed in Chapter 7, accept the fact that it's not possible to accomplish all that you would like to do. Prioritize your responsibilities into categories A, B or C with A being essential and C being discretionary. Do only those things that you *need* to do to survive the tough times, and put aside the things that you *want* to do until later.

❖ *Divide and conquer*

Remember that while you may be the primary caretaker, your spouse may be the primary breadwinner. Think of and list all the things your "uninvolved" spouse may be doing to help the family that you aren't. Parents often need to have different roles in the family in order to make efficient use of resources. There is no purpose in duplication, when there is so much to do and so little of you. This division of labor allows you to be more productive. Sometimes, it may even be helpful to have one parent less involved, to maintain a different perspective. However, given the circumstances, this may be a good time to reconfigure the division of roles and responsibilities between you and your spouse. It is a time of crisis, and the status quo may not work.

❖ *Know your limits*

Learn to recognize your limits of tolerance. Accept that you can't contribute much to the family when you are pushed beyond your limits. Learn to detect and respect those limits. Learning to detect early warning signs of burnout is a valuable skill—it can save you unnecessary grief. As discussed in Chapter 7, it's necessary to scale back and go into survival mode when you are in crisis. Trying to get everything done may well end up in getting nothing done.

❖ *Buy your way out*

When possible and affordable, buy your way out of chores that are impossible to complete but necessary. It's automatic to balk at having to spend money when you already have more expenses to take on. But if you think about it, time is money too. There are some things others can do for you for a fee and some things no one but you can do. It may be worth your while to pay the relatively inexpensive price of these services while you devote your valuable time to the really important things that can't be done by someone else. You may find it worth your time and money to buy easy to cook or ready-made meals, find someone to clean your house once a month or pay the teenage next door to mow the lawn or be a "mother's helper." Your time will be freed up to take your child to doctor's appointments, pay bills or help your child with homework.

Sonya had to come home to all the chores after a busy and stressful day at her job. She didn't ask her husband for help with the kids, dinner or dishes and she resented him because he didn't volunteer to help. She figured he should know she could use the help. After we discussed things, Sonya realized that she didn't have to do it all. She needed to be realistic, not a super parent. Sonya asked the teenager next door to be a "mother's helper" while she got dinners ready and laundry done before her husband got home from work. For a few dollars, Sonya was able to get all her chores done and still have some time to herself. It was money well spent. At her request, Sonya's husband helped with homework and baths for the children. The daily grind didn't seem so daunting after that.

❖ You don't always have to answer!

Even simple things like answering the phone can be too much on the days when you are straining at the limit. Let your answering machine or voice mail do the job for you. If it's important enough, the caller will leave a message, and you can return the call when you are truly able to attend to it. With today's technology, you can distinguish the important calls from the less important with a gadget or a "distinctive ring." Likewise, you don't have to be at the beck and call of every member of the household. It's neither realistic nor sustainable. When you pander to every whim and fancy, your family becomes less self-reliant. Dependence is not a good long-term strategy for your family. Teach and expect everyone to pitch in by doing things for themselves and sharing the chores.

❖ Believe in yourself

We are able to deal with much more in life than that for which we give ourselves credit. If you stop to think about it, you have most likely been through at least one thing as bad as or worse in your life than OCD.

Marilyn was struggling with her daughter Rebecca's OCD. Rebecca wasn't getting to bed until 2 a.m. and she insisted on being awakened at 5 a.m. so she could be ready for school on time. Of course, if Marilyn didn't help her through her rituals, Rebecca would be up the entire night. Marilyn was exhausted from sheer lack of sleep, not to mention the worry and the anger. "I can't bear it anymore," she sighed. "I've really been trying, but I simply don't have it in me. I'm just not that strong."

I reflected with her on how cruel and unrelenting OCD was. I asked if she could think back on her life and remember even one thing that had been worse than Rebecca's OCD. Marilyn thought momentarily. "Well," she recalled, "I guess there was. It was when Rebecca was born a two-pound "premie." It was the worst time of my life. It was my first pregnancy, my first baby. I was so excited but everything went so wrong. We thought we'd lose our baby."

"How did you get through that time?" I asked, as Marilyn recounted the agonizing days of not knowing if Rebecca would stay alive from hour to hour. "I've never really thought about it that much," she replied. "I guess I just knew I had to, and I did it. I found the strength that I didn't know I had. I guess the OCD pales in comparison, doesn't it? Rebecca and I got through that and we can get through this now. I'll find the strength I need. I know I have it in me, but sometimes I don't even want to reach for it."

❖ Get some R & R (rest and relaxation)

Relaxing is incompatible with being stressed, so when you choose to relax, you choose not to be stressed. But relaxing doesn't come naturally when you are stressed. It requires a planned, concerted effort. It involves making choices and decisions to rest and relax. Make at least 15 minutes a day of "prescribed R & R" for yourself. Try to catch up on your sleep. Easier said than done when your child is up till the wee hours washing and checking. But you can't survive on cumulative sleep deprivation, so you must replenish your fuel. Catch forty winks if and when possible; make the time to sleep in lieu of chores or activities. Spend a fraction of the time you consume in negative emotions doing something good for yourself instead. Take a craft class, sign up for painting, learn a new piece on the piano, play a game of tennis or meet a friend for coffee.

Steal your moments of peace. Sometimes, it's the little things in life that bring the greatest joys. A cup of tea with your feet up, sitting on the porch and breathing the fresh night air, a hobby, exercise, walking, listening to music or talking to a friend. Take care of your physical and mental health. When you eat healthy foods, get enough sleep and exercise, you feel better equipped to deal with the rest.

❖ *Expect and plan for rough times*

Know that rough times will happen again and again and again. You will be caught in turmoil and be taxed beyond your limits. If you can plan for these times and think through your reactions and responses ahead of time, you won't just succumb to your impulses and react in the heat of the moment. There will be fewer opportunities for words or actions that cannot be taken back. On occasion, a child's difficulties are so severe or complex that a parent may need help in the home to get respite. Severe aggressive or destructive behaviors are some examples. Check with your local social service agency for resources for respite care.

At odds with your spouse

OCD, like any other adversity, can bring couples closer together or tear them apart. Some are fortunate to bond together strongly in the best interest of their child. But serious stressors like OCD can de-stabilize even the most secure relationships. They can accentuate differences in coping, communication and nurturing styles that might have been dormant in the absence of stress. Dealing with OCD is hard enough when parents see eye to eye on OCD-related matters. It adds a new dimension of complexity to the marital relationship when parents disagree about their child's OCD. Those who have had marital problems prior to OCD may find that the polarization increases.

Spouses may have differences of opinion on everything from whether the child has OCD to how much soap he should be allowed to use. One parent may not accept the child's OCD for what it is and adopt a "no nonsense" approach to the child's rituals and fears. One parent may be the enabler and the other the enforcer. One parent labels the other as "in denial;" the second belittles the first as an "armchair psychologist." As already discussed, the other parent may be far more intimately involved with the child's day-to-day OCD.

OCD devours so much energy in the here and now that spouses don't have the time or the focus to nurture their relationship. Instead of the alliance that is necessary for recovery, there is alienation. Parents become mad at each other instead of at OCD. Over time, they begin to drift apart, each consumed in putting out the fires that confront them.

❖ *Accept different styles of coping*

It is well known that men and women may have different approaches to handling the vicissitudes of life. In general, women prefer to talk about and discuss the things that trouble them. Sometimes, they look for solutions but often they are just looking for someone to listen to them. Women seek solace from others when they are in distress. In contrast, men may be more prone to rely on themselves to work through a difficulty. They may retreat and actually shun help or interaction with others. These styles are often at odds with each other, resulting in marital conflict when spouses can't seem to find their niche. Coming to terms with these disparities while keeping the relationship vibrant and strong may be a lifelong challenge for couples even in the best of times. Men and women have to learn to reach compromises, accepting that each way of coping is meaningful and valid, and respecting the other's need to do it his or her own way.

❖ *Put yourself in your spouse's shoes*

Remember that just because your spouse doesn't handle feelings the way you do, it doesn't mean that he or she doesn't feel the pain. When you are tempted to conclude that he or she is not empathic or responsive, put yourself in your spouse's shoes. If you are unhappy about what's going on with your child and your family, it's unlikely that your spouse is enjoying any of it. Start listening to the other's point of view. Perhaps your spouse feels unheard. If your spouse feels accused or blamed, he or she may become more defensive.

❖ *Nurture your relationship*

Make time for yourself and your spouse to enjoy something relaxing, even if it's a weekly video movie after the kids are in bed. Focus on the good things in your relationship and make it a point to remind yourselves of these during the difficult times. It's easy to get so caught up in the children's needs that you neglect your own relationship. Yet, your relationship is what you will rely on to sustain you through the rough times with OCD.

❖ *Save your arguments for your ears only*

Avoid nasty arguments in front of the children. Disagreements are a natural and normal part of family life. When you deal with them by yelling, screaming and insults, the children are affected. They may become scared, feel insecure and learn that it is the only way to resolve differences. It is necessary for children to learn how to negotiate differences of opinion, so show them that it can be done by discussion, listening, respecting and compromise. Agree to disagree and respect each other's decisions or interventions until you have a chance to discuss them in private. Pre-plan an "it's urgent, we need to talk" sign and a place, so you can work out urgent issues quickly without arguing. When there is a crisis, the children need to see a unified front. It is confusing and makes them feel less confident and secure if you are in sharp disagreement.

❖ *Avoid saying the things you can't take back*

Avoid saying things you know you will regret later—they can't be taken back. Ultimatums breed mistrust, resentment and insecurity in a relationship. Even if ultimatums result in some changes, the hurt remains in the background. When you think you may spew angry and hurtful words, leave the room, say them to your computer, your diary or out loud on a walk.

❖ *Find marital counseling or therapy*

Some parents need an objective moderator to work out their differences. If you are not able to go it alone, seek help from a family therapist or spiritual counselor. You may not be able to attend to this in the midst of the chaos of OCD, but sometimes, your child will not be able to participate in treatment if you and your spouse are up in arms all the time.

Alone in a crowd

Sadly, the stigma of mental illness still pervades our society. It's a dark and lonely place that no one walks in, except those who have been in your shoes. Having a family member with a mental illness is a different experience than having one with a debilitating physical illness. If your child has diabetes or cancer, you may be able to discuss it openly with family and friends without repercussion; you will generally meet with sympathy, not suspicion or blame. Tell someone your child has OCD, and you will get a hundred and one opinions, and very little understanding. Even close family and friends may assume that OCD is a character flaw or weakness that can be corrected with good discipline.

It's almost impossible to explain OCD to others because it's so bizarre and unreal. It's so far from most people's normal experience that they simply cannot relate to it in the abstract. So you are left alone and lonely, longing for someone to talk to and understand, but with little support or empathy. Suddenly, even family and friends seem so remote and distant, because there is little overlap between your world and theirs.

❖   *Find strength in numbers*

Even though it may be difficult to find someone who understands, make an active effort to connect with other parents, family or friends. One way of sharing the burden, as well as getting more useful tips about everyday life with OCD is to join a support group. The OC Foundation may be able to direct you to a support group in your area. If you can't find one geographically, support groups are also available on the Internet. The *Ocdandparenting* group (see *Resources*) is one where you will feel validated and supported. What you will derive from this group is the real-life experience of parents and families who walk in your shoes. They can relate to you as the parent of a child with OCD like no one else can. They can give you many different perspectives on the myriad of emotions, challenges and decisions that you encounter on this journey. There are parents who are beginning the journey, those who are in the throes of it, and those who have found the light at the end of the tunnel.

❖ *Start a support group*

If you can't find a support group—start one! Ask your child's therapist to inform his or her other patients and their families about your group, and you'll be surprised at how many parents will be eager to sign up.

Parental anxiety or OCD

Gail writes:

I look back and realize that I probably have OCD and a lot of anxiety, and have had it since my childhood. I just never knew my quirks and fears had a name. Now, my son is struggling with severe OCD. You would think I could be more understanding and I try to be, but sometimes I don't have the patience. I can't help feeling guilty that I passed it on to him. Poor kid—he didn't have a chance.

Like Gail, your child's OCD may lead you to recognize that the fruit has not fallen far from the tree. Or perhaps you were officially diagnosed with OCD long before your child developed it. Many parents struggle with the guilt for having passed on OCD, even though they had neither the choice in the matter or the intent to pass it on. In other words, there is no reason for guilt; yet, it is an intuitive emotion. If you have OCD or an anxiety disorder, you might also wonder if your parenting has led to your child's OCD. Your own illness and struggle to cope may have compromised your parenting skills or your availability to your child. You fear for your child's future and you want to protect him from the suffering that you have experienced. You may be a far more understanding parent because you know what it's like firsthand. On the other hand, perhaps it's harder for you to handle because you can't take any more of it. It may make you more impatient with your child, particularly if you have overcome it and your child does not seem to be able to do it. Sometimes, you may exacerbate each other's symptoms.

If your OCD is active, you may not be able to give your child clear reference points for "normal" washing, checking or worry. You may be hypervigilant, overly cautious and risk avoidant. To be clear, children who learn such cautions do not necessarily learn OCD from their parents. Rather, it becomes part of the way they view the world. It is their experience of "normal" because they may not have any other reference point.

Sheila, an adult woman with OCD, grew up with two parents who had OCD. She described her mother as particularly preoccupied with cleanliness and there were rules, rules and rules about how things were done around the house. Sheila only realized when she left the nest as an adult, that most people didn't use separate hampers for unwashed and washed laundry. By her mother's rules, if washed laundry ever touched the hamper in which dirty laundry had been, it was as good as dirty again.

Sheila's OCD exploded after the birth of her first child. She washed and sanitized for hours on end until her knuckles were raw and bleeding. She held her three-month-old baby over the sink and scrubbed her hands with antibacterial soap for three minutes each time, up to six times a day. Changing diapers was a nightmare of contamination fears and rituals. It got worse after her second child came along, but between bottles, diapers and sleep-deprived nights, Sheila had neither the time nor the money to get help. But one day, Sheila knew she had to get help. It was the day her four-year-old returned from preschool and announced, "Joey and Jenna don't know how to wash their hands properly. I showed them how to scrub until all the germs are gone." Sheila knew she couldn't let her children suffer the same fate as she did. She came to treatment, for the sake of her children.

As we went through treatment, Sheila struggled to understand the threshold between normal cleanliness and OCD. She confessed that having had a mother with OCD cleaning rituals had deprived her of the reference point that most children have. Sheila had to now learn what "normal" cleanliness was. How many times and when did people wash their hands, for how long, how often did they sweep and mop the floors, vacuum the carpets or clean their babies' hands?

❖ *Get therapy or medications for yourself*

The most important thing you can do for yourself and your child if you have OCD or anxiety is to get treatment for yourself. Research has shown that parents who obtain treatment for their own anxiety help their children make greater improvements in treatment. CBT can teach you the skills you need to overcome your own anxiety or OCD; moreover, what better way to role model for your child what you are asking of him. Dr. Herb Gravitz' book, *Obsessive Compulsive Disorder: New Help for the Family* is a good resource for families struggling to live with OCD in a loved one.

Chapter 9

Readiness for Treatment

Confidence is contagious. So is lack of confidence.

Vince Lombardi

Throughout this difficult ordeal, Nancy was determined to help herself. I think her attitude helped in many ways to help speed her recovery."

Diane, mother of Nancy

As described in Chapter 5, overcoming OCD with CBT is like riding a bicycle Up and Down a Worry Hill. Riding up a hill requires effort, participation and practice. Above all, it takes the will to do it. If you wanted to succeed, you would try to prepare for the ride in advance by knowing what to expect, building up your stamina, keeping your bicycle in good condition and wearing the right riding gear. If you rushed into it without proper preparation, your chances of making it to the top of the hill would be slim. Likewise, the chances of success in CBT are greatly increased when there is proper preparation; rushing into it may jeopardize the odds of success. Your child must "gear up for the RIDE" if he is to have the best chance at recovery. It is a critical step in the battle plan against OCD.

In this chapter, I will discuss preparation for treatment. I will present tried and tested methods that I have used successfully for my patients and their families for many years. I will also present an approach to help children overcome reluctance or refusal to engage in CBT. The strategies in this chapter must be applied in collaboration with a CBT therapist.

WHY IS READINESS IMPORTANT?

How many children actually enjoy living with OCD? I have yet to meet one. Although most children have a wish to be rid of OCD, they also need to be *ready* to participate in treatment. To be ready, they need to be able to channel the *desire* to get well into the *action* to get well.

Readiness is crucial because CBT involves actively learning and using a set of skills to overcome the urges and injunctions of OCD. Readiness drives active participation and compliance, which are the keystones of success in CBT. Learning the skills of CBT is quite similar to learning how to ride a bicycle. You can help your child learn how to ride a bicycle, but eventually, your child must learn to ride for himself. Likewise, your child must learn how to overcome OCD for himself—you cannot do it for him. He will only learn when he's ready. Ironically, when your child feels pressured, he is less likely to want to do it for himself.

Carefully getting your child ready for treatment is an important investment with huge dividends. I devote a lot of time and effort to this preparatory stage of therapy and it really pays off. Although the time spent in laying the groundwork may seem to slow down treatment initially, treatment subsequently proceeds a lot faster and easier than anticipated by the child and the parents. Most of all, it is more likely to be successful. In fact, I have found that when a child is well prepared for the RIDE, the total number of CBT sessions for a child with moderate to severe OCD may be as few as six to 10, compared to the average of 10 to 15.

THE KEYS TO READINESS

In my work with children and adolescents over the years, I have found that the keys to readiness are effective *stabilization, communication, persuasion and collaboration*. Your CBT therapist must work closely with you and your child to build readiness for treatment.

```
┌─────────────────────────────────┐
│      The Keys to Readiness       │
│   ❑   Stabilization              │
│   ❑   Communication              │
│   ❑   Persuasion                 │
│   ❑   Collaboration              │
└─────────────────────────────────┘
```

Stabilization

Stabilization comes first. A child who is overwhelmed and struggling to get through the basics each day simply does not have the wherewithal or mind share to consider CBT. Just getting through each day with OCD consumes all his energy. Your child needs some respite from the dual challenges of OCD and everyday living. Flexibility in expectations, accommodations at home and at school can ease the initial pressures on your child. In severe situations, some children may need medication to reach a reasonable level of functioning before they can even entertain the thought of CBT. Families need stabilization too. Blame, shame and conflict don't help a child feel safe enough to risk the challenges of CBT. Calm, supportive and understanding families set the stage for treatment readiness.

Communication

Effective communication about the primary CBT concepts of *exposure*, *habituation* and *anticipatory anxiety* is essential to preparing a child for treatment. OCD is overcome by confronting fears (exposure), experiencing habituation (getting used to the anxiety, much like you get used to the cold water in the swimming pool) and understanding that confronting fears seems harder *before* you do it than when you actually do it (anticipatory anxiety). Exposure may appear both counterintuitive and daunting at first glance; a child who is afraid does not exactly want to hear that he must *face* his fear to overcome it. When children don't understand CBT, they are unnecessarily intimidated by it. In fact, if the child is not well prepared, CBT may backfire, and the child may be unwilling to attempt it again. Effective communication dispels misconceptions about OCD or CBT.

As you might guess, communicating the concepts of exposure and habituation to children can be challenging. As if it isn't hard enough explaining OCD to a child, it's even harder explaining the paradoxical nature of exposure therapy. The metaphor of the *Worry Hill* grew out of my efforts to convey these concepts to children in child-friendly language. Almost any child or adolescent can relate to the image of riding a bicycle up a big hill. Exposure feels like the ride up the hill. It can be hard to huff and puff up a hill, but if you don't quit, you can get to the top of the hill. Once you get to the top, it's smooth sailing down the other side of the hill. You can only coast down the hill if you first get to the top. Likewise, you can only get past your fears if you face them. When you do, you find out that they are not even half as scary as you imagined.

When a child understands the Worry Hill, it's an *"aha!"* experience. It has been heartwarming for me to see the anguished look in the eyes of a child change to a glimmer of hope as she says, *"I get it! It makes perfect sense."* Specific examples of child-friendly language from *Up and Down the Worry Hill* are presented in the next section in this chapter.

Persuasion

Third, effective persuasion helps children see the *necessity* for change, the *possibility* for change, and the *power* to change. Once children understand what OCD and CBT are really about, they are more readily persuaded. Your child must be helped to see the benefits of overcoming OCD; this convinces him of the necessity for change. When he learns that OCD can be successfully overcome, and that many others have done it, he sees the possibility for change. Finally, the child must know that he has the power to change. He must understand that he can take charge and take control of OCD instead of letting it control him. OCD is such a coercive force that it leads your child to believe that he has no choices; he is a prisoner of his mind. The recognition that he has the power to change is a liberating experience for the child. Remember Bob, the youngster you met in Chapter 5, who conquered OCD after a five-week crash course in CBT? I remember his words when I asked him what led to his success: *"I didn't know it was even possible to get over OCD. I thought I just had to do what it told me. When you told me it was my choice, I knew I could do it."*

Collaboration

Finally, *collaboration* makes your child a vital partner in treatment. After all, he is the star performer. With your therapist's guidance, your child must become a key player in his own treatment. He must be involved in setting goals and deciding the pace of treatment, as is suitable to his age and maturity. When your child is a collaborator in his treatment, he takes ownership of it. He becomes more invested, committed and enthusiastic. The journey to recovery becomes his.

In my practice, I do not proceed with treatment until the child is ready. I test the child's readiness by giving him the freedom to decide if he wants to go ahead—with no pressure from his parents or me. I may say, "If you decide you want to do this, don't do it for me. Don't do it for your parents. Do it only for yourself." I tell the child that I do not want an answer immediately. I do not put him on the spot because he may not be able to back out gracefully. Instead, I ask him to go home, think about what he has learned about OCD and the RIDE, sleep over it and call me with an answer, or tell me at the next appointment.

I've rarely had a child refuse to participate in treatment when he is given the freedom of choice. When children make their own decision to participate, they are far more invested and committed than if they have been "dragged" into it. On the other hand, when a child says "No," it probably means that he really is not ready for CBT. If he isn't ready, he won't be able to do what it takes to succeed in CBT. More work needs to be done to get him ready or other options such as medication may need to be considered. For some children, CBT may have to be deferred temporarily and attempted later when the child is older, more mature or more willing.

EFFECTIVE COMMUNICATION WITH YOUR CHILD

I use excerpts from *Up and Down the Worry Hill: A Children's book about OCD and its Treatment* (see *Resources*) to illustrate how to explain OCD and CBT in child-friendly language. The metaphors and analogies presented here may be used for children as young as four or as old as 16. Older adolescents and adults also find them meaningful. It is important to seek your therapists' guidance in this process.

Casey looked at his plate. He had seven bites left and he had to finish them in the right order. "I can't eat any faster, I have to do it exactly this way," he whispered to himself. Jenny laughed at him. "C'mon Casey-man, what's the matter? Can't you hurry, slowpoke? I saw you this morning, touching and counting things…you're weird!"

At school, Casey began to draw all the planets. He wanted his drawing to be perfect. The circles didn't come out right, so he erased them and drew them again. His drawing still wasn't perfect. Casey erased it again. The paper tore. Pete said, "Hey, how come you're always the last one to finish anything, Casey? Laura ran over and said, "Let me see your drawing! The paper's torn. How come you have to erase everything?" Casey looked away. He didn't know what to say. He wished he could hide somewhere or disappear. He couldn't wait to get home. Casey was confused, overwhelmed and scared by his feelings and urges. He was sad when his sister teased him and embarrassed when his classmates noticed his rituals.

Casey is your average child with OCD. Most children experience some or all of the fears, uncertainties and emotions that Casey encounters. He has a hard time understanding what is happening to him, let alone trying to explain it to someone else. Casey knows that he's different from the other children, but he's not quite sure how. Worse yet, he thinks he's the only one who's weird and crazy. Who else could have these absurd and ridiculous fears and rules to follow? He suffers in silence because he does not know that anyone else could possibly understand his experience. It would be a huge relief to him if he knew that he wasn't the only one, and that he wasn't crazy.

Effective communication allows you to convey several important messages to your child. He needs to know that you understand and accept his feelings about OCD. He needs to know that he is not losing his mind, it's not his fault, and he can talk to you without shame or fear. He will be reassured to know that he has a real problem, with a real name and a real fix. He needs to know that there is hope for recovery.

Goals for Effective Communication

✓ Talk about OCD without shame or fear
✓ Explain OCD and CBT in child-friendly language
✓ Correct misconceptions about OCD and CBT
✓ Dispel feelings of shame, guilt and fear
✓ Instill hope and optimism
✓ Build confidence and readiness for treatment
✓ Build an alliance to optimize recovery

It is easy to overlook the importance of these messages and to forget to say them altogether. Although these ideas may seem obvious to us, they are not intuitive to children. Some children need them said clearly and repeatedly. Talking to your child also allows you to provide support and build an alliance with your child in preparation for treatment. As you will see in the next chapter, having a strong alliance with your child can make a world of difference to treatment.

TIPS FOR SUCCESSFUL COMMUNICATION

Effective communication doesn't just happen on its own—you have to make it happen. A planned, thoughtful approach is more likely to be successful. When OCD takes over your household, it is easy for your interactions with your child to be focused on the unpleasant aspects of OCD. This is especially true in a time of crisis, which is what most families encounter at some time or another. It is very hard to find positive things to focus on when your world has been turned upside down.

I suggest You and Me Alone or "YAMA time" with your child as a way to preempt the natural default to unhelpful exchanges. YAMA time is a special piece of quality time with your child with no agenda at all-other than spending positive time together. It's a time to relax and "yammer" about nothing in particular. The goal of *YAMA* time is to build rapport, comfort and trust by being together to listen and share. Talking about OCD or other "bad" things is off limits. Once you lay the groundwork for a comfortable positive relationship, talking about the tough stuff of OCD will come more naturally.

YAMA
You and Me Alone
Positive time with your child

Parents must make a commitment to spend at least 15 minutes (and preferably more) of YAMA time with their child daily. For many families, those 15 minutes represent a minute fraction of the time that is spent in distasteful interactions with their child. When parents say, "But I have other children and so much to do. Where am I going to find the time?" I reply, "You're already spending that time (and much more) on your child anyway, except that it's mostly *negative*. Just take 15 minutes of that time and change it to positive. You spend it with her in one way or the other-wouldn't you rather it's positive?"

YAMA time should be planned so that it is consistently and regularly available and is private and uninterrupted. Young children are generally very pleased to have "special" one-on-one time with a parent or parents. Although adolescents may not be as enthusiastic, parents can find ways to engage them by spending time learning about their adolescent interests, such as the computer or music.

Tips for Successful Communication

✓   Think ahead, be proactive
✓   Make YAMA (You and Me Alone) time
✓   Listen, accept, support and encourage
✓   Put yourself in your child's shoes
✓   Acknowledge your own anxiety and uncertainty
✓   Use metaphors and analogies
✓   Pace information to your child's readiness

Acknowledge your own uncertainties and fears to your child-within reasonable limits. There is a tricky balance between showing that you are also vulnerable and giving your child the security of knowing that you can take care of her. The message that is important to convey to your child is that you are also human and therefore also feel afraid, uncertain, sad or angry. However, you will find ways to cope with and conquer your feelings. You will not give up, but have hope and optimism and keep going. You model for your child the appropriate ways in which to handle adversity and negative emotions. If you break down and lose control, your child's faith in your ability to be her anchor may be shaken. (See Chapter 8 for suggestions on *Taking Care of Yourself*).

As discussed earlier, metaphors and analogies are a very effective way to communicate OCD and CBT concepts to children. Younger children can relate better to concrete and tangible events that are part of their everyday lives. Older adolescents usually comprehend direct explanations of OCD and CBT. Information about OCD and CBT should be delivered at a measured pace. It can be overwhelming to be inundated with information that is complex and somewhat scary to begin with. As adults, we seek as much knowledge as possible because we have the skills to comprehend, filter, assimilate and cope with it. Children are not equipped with those skills, so they should only be given what's helpful for them to know. Your child does not need to know all the facts at once, so give him only as much information as necessary at any given time. That will give him time to digest and absorb it. Let your child give you the ready signal when he wants to know more.

CHILD-FRIENDLY EXPLANATIONS FOR OCD AND CBT

The following are some "universal" metaphors and analogies I have developed and used successfully with children as young as four, adolescents and even parents and teachers. The exact wording may need to be modified slightly to suit your child's maturity and understanding, but the core concepts remain the same. Read *Up and Down the Worry Hill* with your child. Discuss these ideas, elaborate on them and tie them into real-life experiences that are meaningful to your child. (The concepts of CBT are described in Chapter 5).

What is OCD?

In describing OCD, it is important to try to define it succinctly and to explain it as an illness like any other, not a character flaw. The following excerpt from *Up and Down the Worry Hill* describes OCD, obsessions, compulsions, why and how OCD happens and who's responsible for it. It also addresses issues of feelings and negative self-perceptions.

*"Casey, you're just like any other kid except that you have an illness called **Obsessive-Compulsive Disorder**. It's called **OCD** for short. Let me tell you a little bit about OCD. You see, Casey, OCD is something that happens in your brain. Your brain is like a computer. It does many things and is very busy. When you have OCD, your brain's computer tells you to worry about things that are not true and tells you to do things over again even when you don't need to. It happens because some chemicals in your brain don't work right, and your brain gets "stuck." It's like it would be if you rang the doorbell and the button got stuck. The doorbell would keep ringing and ringing loudly and wouldn't know when to stop. OCD is like a "worry button" in your brain that gets stuck. The worry thoughts that OCD puts in your brain are called **obsessions**. The things you do over and over again to make the worry thoughts go away are called **compulsions** or **rituals**. They are the things you do to try to "fix" the doorbell button that's stuck."*

Young children may be encouraged to give OCD a nickname to differentiate it from themselves. Older children and adolescents may prefer to call it OCD.

Whose fault is it anyway?

"So it's not just my fault that I do weird things, is it Dr. Greene?" Casey asked. "Not at all! Having OCD is not your fault. It's not your parents' fault either. It's like having allergies or asthma—it happens to you because you're more sensitive to it. Sometimes there are other people in your family who are

also sensitive and have OCD. OCD doesn't happen because you've been bad or because you do it on purpose. Sometimes, your parents or your teachers and friends may think that you are just being stubborn or annoying. It's hard for them to understand that you don't want to do it, but you can't stop."

"Why me? It's not fair!"

It is natural for children to want to know why OCD assails them and not their siblings or friends. There is a sense of injustice and unfair punishment. In response to *"Why me?"* children need the assurance that they were not singled out for OCD as punishment, that they did not do anything to deserve it and did not bring it on themselves. Each person, young or old, has different blessings and challenges and OCD happens to be the challenge that your child received. It may be helpful to detail her blessings, so that she recognizes both sides of the picture. "You are good at math and piano, and Jimmy is good at soccer." Name other children your child may know who also have OCD, so that your child does not feel alone. Knowing that other children like her have OCD can be of tremendous help.

Older children and adolescents can appreciate the bigger picture and have more perspective. They understand that life doles out both the good and the bad. They can accept the fact that even though OCD is difficult, there could be many worse things in life. Ask your child to name one classmate or friend who seems to have it "easy." Ask him if he really believes it is that way, or whether that child may have some adversity to bear of which your child may simply not be aware. Ask him to name one child who seems to be less fortunate than himself. Ask if it's because that child is a "bad kid." Help your child identify the blessings and challenges of siblings, peers or other family members, to the extent that is appropriate. Some children have diabetes, others cancer, and some have disabilities that are more severe. Although OCD is a difficult illness, there are many illnesses that are just as difficult or more so.

CBT and ERP

The metaphor of the Worry Hill describes CBT and ERP in child-friendly language.

Dr. Greene smiled at Casey and his parents and said, "I have some good news for you. There are some ways to fix your "worry button" when it gets stuck. One way is to learn how to tell OCD to stop bothering you by learning some special exercises. This way is called Behavior Therapy. In Behavior Therapy you learn some exercises that teach you how to face your OCD worries and find out that they are not true. Then you learn to stop doing the things OCD tells you to do. It's a lot like learning how to ride a bicycle. Do you ride a bicycle, Casey?"

"Yes, yes, I just rode up a big hill yesterday and then I came coasting down. It was hard work to get up the hill, but lots of fun coming down," said Casey with sparkling eyes.

"Well, Casey, learning how to stop OCD is a lot like that. In the beginning, facing your fears and stopping your rituals is like riding up a big Worry Hill because it gets harder. If you keep going and don't give up, you get to the top of the Worry Hill. Once you get to the top, it's easy to come down the hill. You can only coast down the hill if you first get to the top. Getting to the top of the Worry Hill takes patience and hard work. Saying, "I want to" makes it a lot easier. The more you practice, the easier it gets.

The exercises that help you go up and down the Worry Hill are called exposure and ritual prevention. I will help you learn how to do these exercises. They teach you how to face your fears without doing the rituals. You will learn that nothing bad happens if you stop doing the things OCD wants you to do."

Habituation

I describe habituation as follows: "When you face your fears and don't do the rituals, you find out that nothing bad is going to happen. Pretty soon, you start getting used to the things you fear and they don't bother you anymore. Remember, you can't coast down the hill if you don't get to the top, right? Another way to understand how we can get used to our fears is to think about taking a swim. How does your skin feel when you first jump in the pool?"

"Shivery and cold."

"Well, does it stay that way? What happens after you've stayed in the pool for a few minutes?"

"It feels warmer."

"Why does it feel warmer—is it the water that got warm all of a sudden?"

"I get it! My skin gets used to the cold water!"

"You will get used to your fears in the same way. You just have to stay in the pool to feel warmer and you just have to stay with the things you fear to get used to them. That's what happens during behavior therapy. Gradually, you realize that you are not as worried about germs when you do not wash your hands. The next time around, you find it a lot easier to eat without washing your hands, and you get used to the worry feelings faster. The hill becomes smaller and smaller. As you continue practicing your ERP exercises, your fear of germs will bother you less and less."

Gradual Exposure

I describe gradual exposure as riding up little hills in preparation for tackling the big hill. "You don't have to ride up the biggest hill first. In fact, that's probably not a good idea because you may not be able to get all the way up right away. You may need to practice a lot and build up the energy to get up that hill in one try. What would be the best way to prepare for going up that big hill?"

"Try some smaller hills first?"

"Yes, exactly. You start with the little hills and you work your way up to the big ones. That way, you get stronger with each hill, and you can be sure that the biggest hill will not be quite as hard. Likewise, you face your fears gradually, not all at once. We will make a list of all your fears and start with the ones that are the least scary—the littlest hills."

Getting ready for treatment

"Before you go up any hill, big or small, you would probably want to make sure you are ready for a good ride. It's probably not a good idea to ride up a big hill without the right accessories—a helmet, good sneakers and comfortable clothes. You would want to make sure you've eaten enough to have the energy to ride. You would have a good drink of water and carry some with you to sip as you huff and puff up that hill."

The therapist's role in treatment

"I'm your therapist and that means I'm like your coach or instructor. I am here to teach you the best ways to get up that hill. My job is to give you a map, guide you and give you suggestions about the best way to get to the top of the hill. But I can't ride up that hill for you. How well you ride will depend on how well you use the tips and ideas I give you. My guidance to you will only be as useful as you want to make it."

The child's role in treatment

"Only you can ride the bicycle; only you can be in the bicycle's seat. You are in charge and you have to decide if you want to ride up that hill. In the same way, only you can face your fears and make them go away. No one else can do it for you. You have to want to do it, actually do it and practice often. You may not learn it instantly but you have to keep trying because if you give up, you'll never learn. Once you learn it, you'll always know how to do it. Once you've got your balance on the bicycle, you don't even have to think about it and you can enjoy the ride. ERP may be hard work at first, but it gets easier when you do it again and again. Once you learn how to do it, it will become automatic, just like it is when you learn how to keep your balance on a bicycle."

The parents' role in treatment

"Your parents can help you a lot as you get ready to ride your bicycle up the Worry Hill. First, they can get you the right kind of bicycle—one that is sturdy and in good condition. They can make sure that the tires are inflated properly, the brakes are working and the bicycle is tuned up. If you are just learning how to ride, your parents can hold the seat of the bicycle to keep you steady. When you are ready, they give you a gentle push and let go so that you can ride on your own. Your parents can never ride the bicycle for you."

What to expect during treatment

"Learning how to face your fears doesn't happen overnight. On some days, the ride is easier and on other days, it is harder. Some hills are harder to tackle than others. Sometimes, you may be more tired, hungry or sleepy; it may have been a tough day at school or at home. That will make the ride more challenging because the hill can seem much steeper when you're not in the best shape. Days like that will come and go. They're not important, because you will conquer your hill in small steps, not in giant leaps. If you stick it out, you will eventually learn how to face your fears."

Casey began to see Dr. Greene every week after school. He learned the exposure and ritual prevention exercises. Little by little, Casey learned how to walk down the stairs without stopping and counting, wash his hands only once before eating, take big bites of his muffin and go to the bus stop without checking his book bag. Dr. Greene was right! At first, he felt worried and scared when he didn't do the rituals, but pretty soon, he found that the scared feeling just went away!

Casey practiced the new things he learned everyday. The more he practiced, the less worried he felt, and the easier it became. His "worry button" didn't seem to get stuck so much anymore. Dr. Greene also talked to Casey's parents to teach them ways to help Casey face his OCD, and to be patient and understanding.

What to expect after CBT

"To be a good bicycle rider, you must take good care of yourself and your bicycle. You must practice often so that you stay in good shape. Just like that, sometimes, you will need to face your fears as often as possible, or you will find it harder to deal with them when they arise."

Slips and relapse

"No matter how well you ride and how much you practice, there will be some times when you wobble or fall off the bicycle. That happens to everyone at some time or the other—there are no guarantees that you will never fall. Falling off the bicycle isn't your fault. It doesn't mean that you are a terrible rider or that you were careless. Sometimes, it may be because you ride over a pebble that you didn't see in time. Sometimes, the road could be bumpier than usual. Perhaps the big truck barreling down the road in your direction unnerved you a bit and you lost your balance."

"So what do you do when you fall off the bicycle? Would you just sit there and decide that you'll never ride a bicycle again? No, you probably wouldn't. Instead, you would try to pick yourself up, brush yourself off and get going again. If you have a bruise or a cut, you attend to it. Occasionally, the fall may be a pretty bad one and you may sprain your ankle or fracture your arm. You may have to go to the hospital. The doctor will put your broken bone in a cast and give you medicines to ease the pain. It will be difficult for a few weeks as you wait for your body to heal. You may be impatient, but the healing will take its time. Then, the cast will come off and you will eventually ride that bicycle again.

Having an OCD "slip" or "fall" is no different than falling off a bicycle. You wouldn't do yourself any good if you stayed down and gave up. If you get discouraged and think it's all over and you can't deal with your OCD anymore, you will probably be right. You must pick yourself up, assess the damage, fix the problem and get going again. You must start riding up that Worry Hill again."

Chapter 14 provides a strategy for Slip Recovery.

Medication

"Some children need medication to help make the ride up the Worry Hill easier. Medication is like the training wheels on a bicycle—they help you learn until you can do it on your own. Not everyone needs training wheels, because many children learn to ride a bicycle without them. If you want to learn how to ride on your own, though, you will have to let go of the training wheels when you are ready."

Recovery

Casey started feeling a lot better. After a few weeks, he noticed that he didn't worry as much or feel sad anymore. He didn't have to touch things four times any more. He could eat his muffins just as fast as Jenny did! His clothes didn't feel so funny and slippery now. His hands didn't feel so "germy" anymore. He even forgot to check his book bag before he ran off to school! Most of all, he found out that that he didn't have to be perfect! He was having fun like the other kids.

Then one day, Casey rode his bicycle up the Big Hill all by himself! He wasn't huffing and puffing as much anymore. He got to the top quickly and looked around. He was so proud of himself. Then it was time for his favorite part—coasting down the Big Hill. As he breezed past the bushes and trees, he whistled a tune and thought to himself, "I learned how to ride up the hill and I learned how to face my OCD. I wish I could tell other kids with OCD who feel alone, ashamed and sad, "Don't give up! You too can learn how to ride up and down the Worry Hill and beat OCD. Casey began singing to himself, "Up the hill, down the hill, on my new bicycle…"

PERSUADING THE RELUCTANT CHILD

Therapy was a three-hour drive for us each week, but we would have traveled even further at that point in our lives for help. The first month, things were shaky. We weren't seeing any improvement. My son said he wanted to go, but he wouldn't do his exercises.

Sharon, mother of Robert

If your child is like Robert, you are in good company. It's easy to become frustrated if you assume that your child's reluctance is intentional. But, when Robert says he won't do his treatment exercises, it's hardly like saying he won't pick up his room or take out the garbage. In reality, it may not be a matter of intent or will; like Robert, your child may not yet be *ready* for treatment. The problem of reluctance is generally averted by proper preparation for treatment, as described earlier in this chapter. However, your child may already have begun therapy and may be past the point of preparation. Watching your child while away his chances at regaining his life can be heartbreaking, when you know that a chance at recovery is within arm's reach. You may feel helpless and thwarted as you struggle to move ahead and he stalls.

Sharon and Michael knew CBT would help Robert. They took a day off work each week to make the three-hour drive. They pulled Robert, age 10, out of school for a day each week because his health came before school. It was a big investment. Imagine how frustrating it was for them to see him while away the time and the opportunity. Yet, ironically, the more fervently they tried to motivate Robert, the more impervious he seemed to their pleas. In our sessions, Robert would participate, express readiness, choose exposure targets and commit to the exercises, but when he went home it was a different story. Robert and his parents didn't see eye to eye on the matter. Sharon and Michael didn't see Robert do his homework exercises. When they asked or reminded him about them, Robert would insist that he had done them and that they were bothering him unnecessarily. They offered to help but he said he didn't need it. A family of frustrated people would return for the next appointment.

As Robert's therapist and guide, I made the decision that it was not wise to proceed until we had cleared this roadblock. We stopped the RIDE and began to work on uncovering the reasons for Robert's reluctance. Robert revealed that he harbored a secret fear that therapy would change his personality. There were some "habits" that he liked and chose to do and he was afraid that therapy would make him relinquish them. We learned that Robert needed to have more control over his treatment and that his parents needed to give him the space to set his own pace. Their well-intentioned efforts to help Robert were not what he needed at this time. Once we cleared these hurdles, Robert made rapid headway in treatment. We had to work together to make it happen. Each of us had a part to play.

Later, we came to understand that Robert was afraid the therapy was going to change his life;the fear kept him from doing the exercises. He worked through that with our therapist. Another breakthrough happened when my husband and I stopped taking part in my son's rituals. Gradually, he started the exercises. When he saw progress, he gained confidence in treatment.

Sharon, mother of Robert

Robert is now a successful 14 year-old who is doing well in all areas of his life. But his path to success was not easy. I tell you Robert's story because I think it is heartwarming, and gives hope that even a bad start does not mean a bad end. Robert and his parents went through the pain, anguish and despair that you may know, but through it all, they held on to their hope and commitment. Along the way, they learned what helped Robert engage in treatment and what didn't. As is true for most OCD sufferers, Robert's OCD waxes and wanes. Some times are worse than others. About once or twice a year, he needs a "CBT tune up" for new symptoms or challenges. Yet, in the four years since his treatment was completed, Robert has blossomed into a fine young man. He has accomplished many milestones that were hard to imagine under the shadow of OCD. He is active in many extra curricular activities, takes on leadership in the classroom, has acted in school plays and celebrated his Bar Mitzvah with pride and grace. He even landed a small part in a movie filmed in his town!

Robert's family's experience illustrates the point that you cannot do CBT for your child. But knowing when and how much to push and when and how and when to let go can be a thorny issue for many families. Don't be dissuaded by refusal. You have to see past it. It may be the voice of OCD that is driving your child. Remember that your child just doesn't quite have the skills to get it all together to reach the goal.

Like Robert, many children who are initially cautious about treatment have come around and done it for themselves. It has been so much more effective and powerful for these children, because they have been more invested and committed when they have made the decision for themselves. As described in the following sections, you have a very important and indispensable part to play in undoing your child's reluctance.

Collaborate with your child's therapist

It is not a good idea to hammer away at your child's reluctance on your own. There are many reasons why you, as the parent should not take on this role single-handedly. Trying to make your child agree to therapy is an undue and unnecessary burden on you, when you have to deal with all the other aspects of OCD's impact on your lives. You are your child's parent, not his therapist. You and your child have a long, intertwined history together. If your child is reluctant, you have undoubtedly locked heads already on the issue. Continuing that role will invariably evolve into a power struggle. It will undermine the alliance that you and your child need to so carefully nurture for treatment.

I recommend that you work with a CBT therapist to guide and moderate the process. If you don't already have one, it is time to find one. A therapist's relationship with a child involves a different set of parameters than that of a parent. A child may open up and divulge to a therapist what he is hesitant to disclose to you, because he knows the therapist is unlikely to have a personal reaction to the information. There are also issues of confidentiality that make it easier for a therapist to engage a child than it may be for you as a parent. A good CBT therapist has the training and skill to elicit trust and participation from your child and may be able to uncover and address the reasons for his reluctance. A skilled therapist may even be able to make your reluctant child very eager and enthusiastic to begin therapy by making it appealing to her age and interest. If your child is unwilling to even meet the therapist, go ahead and meet the therapist without her. You can help the therapist know as much as you can about your child, so that the therapist can help you with a strategy.

Go through the PACES

Treatment reluctance is often experienced as the dragon that cannot be tamed. Going through the *PACES* allows parents and children to systematically dismantle the dragon. It is a matter of collaboration, not coercion.

> ## *Persuading the Reluctant Child*
> **Plan** a strategy
> **Ascertain** reasons for reluctance
> **Correct** and remove obstacles
> **Empower** to take charge
> **Stop** enabling

❖ *Plan a strategy*

You may have run out of patience. Ironically, you must now do something that's counterintuitive—take it slowly. You have learned that you cannot plow through your child's reluctance. So you must now find a way around it. A thoughtful, planned approach may take a little longer to execute, but will be far more effective than one that emerges in the heat of the moment. Impulsive reactions of anger and frustration, threats, ultimatums or coercion are unlikely to charm your child into participation. Your CBT therapist and you must work together to figure out a strategy that is best suited to your child's age, symptoms and particular context. You must together define each of your roles in trying to optimize your child's willingness to engage in therapy. You will together decide how and when it is "safe to proceed."

When a child's reluctance is interpreted as purposeful resistance, callous disregard or defiance, it can make parents angry and frustrated. As you will see below, reluctance is most often due to other reasons. When your child perceives your anger and frustration, he becomes more alienated from you and from treatment. He may suspect that you have your own agenda and don't have his best interests at heart.

❖ *Ascertain reasons for reluctance*

In my experience, reluctance to participate in treatment is generally due to misinformation, misunderstanding and misconceptions about OCD and treatment. Don't be surprised if your child who is reluctant to engage in therapy is also reluctant to disclose why. You are more likely to hear, "I don't know, I don't care, I just don't want to," than some clearly conceptualized and articulated answer. Others may protest, "I don't need therapy. I can do it myself. There's nothing wrong with me." The bravado often reflects fear, misunderstanding or plain old embarrassment. The reasons for your child's reluctance may be just too overwhelming or embarrassing for her to divulge. It may take lots of patience and some creative sleuthing to unearth the barriers to treatment.

There are countless different reasons for treatment reluctance. If children haven't been prepared properly (as discussed earlier in this chapter) they may have incorrect information about OCD, its origins and their role in it. Children may not know that OCD fears are invalid and untrue and may not quite grasp the idea that they can indeed overcome it. They do not want to take the chance that their worst fears will come true. Maria does not want to take the risk that she will spread hepatitis if she doesn't wash her hands thoroughly. Young children often personify and attribute great power to OCD and are afraid of retribution if they do not comply with its dictates. They may believe that OCD may actually become worse if they "mess with it."

Another common misconception that children may have is that having OCD makes them "defective." This may happen especially if a child hears that OCD is a "brain disease." It is a big blow to self-esteem and the sense of identity. He may actually misconstrue it to mean that his defectiveness cannot be treated or corrected. He may see it as his destiny and believe that he has no choice in the matter.

When children misunderstand what OCD and CBT are all about, they may fear that going to therapy confirms that they are "psycho" and need to go to a "mental" doctor. They may feel that it forces them to admit their worst fears and to acknowledge that they are indeed mentally ill. They resist the social stigma of going to therapy. It further alienates them from the "normal" lives around them. For some children, it is far more palatable to suffer the disorder in secrecy than to allow the world of peers to have any inkling that they are "crazy." Older children and adolescents don't want to have to deal with explaining to peers their frequent absences from school and social events for therapy appointments.

For some like Robert, there is the fear that therapy will alter their basic personality. Despite the problems OCD brings, there is comfort in familiarity, and rituals may have become so habitual that they are not so bothersome. They may not always recognize the boundary between OCD and their own "habits and preferences." In such cases, children do not want to rock the boat with therapy. Robert was afraid that therapy would turn him into another person against his will. He was unwilling to risk the change that therapy might impose on him. He had clearly misunderstood what therapy would do. It would give him control, not take it away, and it would restore his personality, not destroy it.

If children have not been given the message about the power of choice, they may be afraid that they will be forced into exposure exercises against their will. When they don't know about habituation, they may be afraid that they will not be able to survive the anxiety of confronting their fears. This can be a frightening prospect for a child who goes to great lengths to avoid those fears. A good CBT therapist will reassure the child that exposure exercises will only be conducted at the pace for which the child is ready and willing with full knowledge and consent.

Strange as it may sound, some older children and adolescents with debilitating OCD may even be afraid to get well and face the challenges of the world from which they have retreated. After all, there are many challenges on the social and academic scene, particularly when there is a lot of catch up to do. Children who have bowed out of it due to OCD may find it formidable to think about reentry. It may just be a little easier to stay sheltered and relieved of the challenges that abound in the world.

For some children, the therapist or therapists' office itself may trigger OCD. Emily wouldn't come into my office because she couldn't possibly sit in a chair that had been "contaminated" by all the unknown people and their germs that had previously been acquainted with that chair. Paul couldn't imagine how he would tackle the extra doorways he would encounter at my office, given that he could barely get through the ones in his daily path. Of course, neither Emily nor Paul recognized or labeled these fears as their reasons for reluctance.

There is a saying that goes, "In order to change, we must be sick and tired of being sick and tired." Sometimes, OCD may just not be bothersome or cumbersome enough to the child to warrant all the effort required in therapy. Perhaps life is reasonably comfortable because the OCD is mild. More likely, perhaps the child does not feel the full brunt of OCD because his parents are protecting and rescuing him from it. The parents are worn and weary from trying to ease the child's burden, so the child can afford to be complacent. For instance, if your child insists on changing into fresh clothes seven times a day because they have "germs" on them, and you do as many loads of laundry to keep up with her demands, you are "rescuing" your child and bearing the burden of her OCD. As long as she has her fresh clothes, she is quite happy and unperturbed. It's only when she has no freshly laundered clothes available that she experiences the distress that often drives motivation for treatment. (See Chapter 10 for more about rescuing your child).

Some children may be more focused on immediate relief from compulsions and less willing to change an established routine. They are less able to anticipate or appreciate the long-term consequences of OCD and their actions. For other children, there might be a sense of futility, hopelessness and helplessness about recovery. They may believe that it is not worth the effort. Often, children who are depressed or have other comorbid conditions may be overwhelmed by their symptoms, and lack the energy, organization or focus to comprehend or accept CBT.

Refusal from young children is often due to fear and misunderstanding. Younger children generally don't question or challenge their parents' decisions to take them for treatment and are more accepting of parental authority. However, some may be prone to be defiant and blame everyone else for their problems. They are not receptive to the idea that they may actually have to make an effort to take control and change their behaviors.

For some children, treatment refusal may be a reflection of conflict and tension in the household. It may indicate a lack of alliance and trust among family members, both of which are deterrents to success in treatment. It may evolve into a power struggle for dominance. Your child may view your wishes and desires as suspect. Reluctance in teens and adolescents may also be expression of the need to assert independence. The mere fact that *you* want them to go to treatment is sufficient to make them dig in their heels. They are simply not as accepting or trusting of your views, wishes and desires as they used to be a few years ago. The more you try to talk them into it, the less likely they are to listen. Teens are easily prone to becoming defensive, and if it makes them feel defensive, they won't do it. Your teen may say—"You go to therapy first, you're more messed up than I am." Or you may hear, "You don't really care about me, you just want me to go so I don't embarrass you. You want to send me to that shrink so you don't have to deal with me. How come I'm always the bad guy in this family? How come you don't make Jamie go to therapy when she mouths off so bad and flunks all her classes?" They must save face in front of siblings who are only too eager to pick on them.

Finally, there are a few questions you must ask yourself: What messages are you conveying to your child about the importance of therapy? Are you clear and consistent in your conviction about the need for and the importance of CBT? Are you optimistic and hopeful that it will work? Or are you ambivalent and unsure of CBT or the therapist? Have you inadvertently been giving mixed messages? Whether you have verbalized this in front of your child or not, children can often read their parents' emotions and subtle cues. If you are half-hearted about your convictions, your child will not feel safe enough to go ahead. She needs to know that you have "approved" the treatment and the therapist.

Don't be discouraged if your attempts at uncloaking your child's reluctance meet with failure. It does call for patience and fortitude. Sometimes, they don't intend to withhold their reasons from you-they may not even know for themselves what is holding them back. They may not have the introspective skills or may not have taken the time to figure it out. Even if you never figure out why exactly your child is stonewalling, you can still use the following strategies to address the potential holdup.

❖ *Correct and remove the obstacles*

Once the reasons behind the reluctance are uncovered, each must be thoughtfully and systematically tackled. Misunderstandings about anxiety and CBT should be corrected with carefully constructed explanations at the child's level of comprehension. Metaphors and analogies such as the *Worry Hill* are understandable to most children. Most importantly, children and adolescents may need to hear clearly that they have the power of choice to overcome OCD by changing their behavior. Unlike epilepsy or other illnesses that cannot be changed by choosing a different behavior, they are not destined to live with OCD. Sometimes, children just need a little nudge or a boost of confidence to get through the *anticipatory* anxiety.

Your child might benefit from talking to other children with OCD who have gone through treatment and overcome OCD successfully. There's nothing as powerful as a personal testimony. Your child will recognize that he is not alone and that other children just like him also struggle with the same issues. Hearing the experiences of peers also dispels the doubts of some children who don't really trust adults to tell them the whole truth.

You might have to backtrack and rebuild a positive relationship with your child that fosters trust and mutual respect. Perhaps your child needs to be unlocked from the emotional CAGES of OCD (see Chapter 7) or needs more YAMA time with you. You may also need to take a long and honest look at parental responses and reactions that convey unhelpful messages. You may need to seriously consider if there's any truth to your teen's claims that you may be unsupportive. If there's a power struggle between you, it's time to end it. Does conflict and tension in the family interfere with treatment? You and your child may need a few sessions of family therapy if discord is stalling therapy.

❖ *Empower*

When your child is learning how to ride a bicycle, your role is to find her a good and safe bicycle, the best riding gear and spend hours preparing and coaching her. Finally, you have to let go of that bicycle seat and empower her to ride for herself. Likewise, you have to empower your child to get well. CBT is a process of changing the way of thinking and behaving and works best when it is an internal process. A child has to participate actively in CBT for the best results. You are in charge of deciding what is best for your child and conveying that clearly and firmly, with encouragement, hope and enthusiasm. Your child must be given the power to change.

Provoking the child's desire to get better fosters the need for change. The child loses perspective of reality when caught up in OCD. Instilling and cultivating the desire to be well again and to have a chance to enjoy life will reduce reluctance. The child must consciously recognize and acknowledge the ways in which OCD steals the pleasures of his life away. "Yes, I'd rather spend three hours playing soccer than three hours washing my hands." The child must see how life can be different without OCD. Show him pictures and videos of himself *before* and *after* OCD and let him see the contrast. List all the pros and cons of going through CBT versus remaining anxious. "Even if you could get 1% better, isn't that better than nothing? Why would you not want to get better?"

Giving the child as much tangible evidence as possible regarding the effectiveness of treatment allows him to see the possibility for change. A powerful way to do this is for the child to interact with other children who have been through treatment successfully (with informed consent from both sets of children and parents). Finally, the child must know that he is trusted and given the space and the time to think, and the power to make the choice. Rewards can be helpful motivators for most children.

❖ Stop enabling

So you've done all of the above and your child is not particularly impressed. She still refuses to even accept she has a problem. Now it may be time for you to stop "enabling" your child's OCD. Enabling or assisting includes helping the child with rituals, providing continuous reassurance, complying with demanding rules and going out of the way to shield the child from anxiety triggers. Don't lose heart—if your child will not change his behavior, you can still help him by changing your behavior.

You may need to allow him to experience the full impact of his OCD without shielding, protecting and rescuing him. It is important that your intent must not be to punish your child, but to help him realize exactly how much OCD disrupts his life. Enabling behaviors should be withdrawn gradually, with calm, purposeful resolve. Make your child responsible for himself, consistent with his abilities. Stop participating in your child's rituals. When you start weaning your child from the safety net, he will begin to feel the discomfort and distress that OCD brings. He will begin to encounter "natural" exposures when you stop removing them from his path. He will see how unpleasant OCD makes his life when you stop rescuing him. This will spur him on to want to get rid of the OCD.

Let me not forget to add that this step can be very hard on you as a parent. Your child will not be expressing gratitude and thanks to you when you make this move. Be prepared for serious retribution when you stop helping your child. You will be confronted with the *extinction burst* (see Chapter 7). You may be beleaguered by your child's pleas and meltdowns and feel guilty about being "the meanest parent in the world." It is *only* when you are firm in your commitment to help your child learn the right behaviors that he will begin to make the effort. Buckling under pressure merely reinforces and rewards him for his resistance. (See Chapter 12 for other effective parenting strategies).

That's why it is really important to have the guidance of a therapist. Don't implement any of these steps too abruptly. Plan ahead and inform your child of what and why you are doing it, and hopefully you will get his agreement. If you don't, you must go ahead anyway. (Chapter 10 offers specific strategies to stop enabling). Dennis' story illustrates how stopping participation in your child's OCD can make a difference.

Dennis was the "wash police" for his family. He lay in wait for family members emerging from the bathroom, looking for signs that they had washed their hands. Wet sink, damp towel, the smell of soap, cold fingers—if Dennis didn't have these confirmations, he started with the questions. Had they remembered to wash their hands after using the bathroom? Did they really? Well, could he smell their hands to be sure? They would oblige him to quiet him. It wasn't enough because there would always be one more time. His sister would scream to get him off her trail. It was driving his family crazy.

Dennis didn't think his concern about germs was excessive at all. As far as he was concerned, it was just good hygiene and he wasn't about to do anything to change that. "Okay," I said to Dennis, "so it's not OCD. It's just normal cleanliness and your family is just sloppy and unclean." "Yes," he replied. "Okay, then it shouldn't bother you if they don't answer your ques-

tions, should it?" Dennis was taken aback, but replied, "Yeah, that's fine."

I sent Dennis' family home with the instruction that they were to walk away without a word when Dennis asked his questions, because it wouldn't bother him. I asked Dennis if he agreed to this. He faltered but agreed. Needless to say, it bothered him tremendously when they didn't oblige him with the customary inspection routine. He picked up the pace; they wavered and gave in sometimes, but generally held their ground. In a couple of weeks, Dennis stopped the questions. He had undergone "natural exposure." He saw that nothing happened even when his family didn't wash up. Ironically, a few weeks later, the family brought home a much-awaited puppy, and Dennis was it's most loyal playmate. I gently asked if he washed his hands each time he touched the puppy. "No," he replied, somewhat shaken by the thought.

Finally, all said and done, some children and adolescents (and many adults too) are just not ready to make the leap. All is not yet lost. As Winston Churchill said, "Never, never, never, never give up." If you do, you have everything to lose and nothing to gain.

Your child may benefit from medication, if he isn't already taking it. You may need to take a hiatus from CBT for now. The cessation of pressure on your child may allow things to sink in, diffuse the power struggle and let maturity work its magic. Your teen may need to figure it out for herself; sadly, she may have to suffer needlessly until she comes to the conclusion you've known all along. She may need to experience more unnecessary pain before she realizes that she is ready for help. You can always revisit CBT at any time when your child is older, more mature or more ready. Or, less fortunately, when your child is more debilitated by OCD. Even if your child won't go to therapy now, you and your family should, by all means, go without him or her. You can benefit tremendously from learning how to cope with your child's OCD and supporting her without enabling. You can work on adjusting and fine-tuning your communication, problem solving and other life skills to accommodate the situation.

It is a very painful process to stand back and watch helplessly as your child endures pointless pain. But in reality, you have not been standing back helplessly. You have done everything in your power to help your child, but he has not been ready to accept the help. When he is ready, you need to support and facilitate his entry into therapy. Don't let your grief, anger or frustration send him into retreat again. Saying, "Well, it's about time," or "I told you so," would be a step in the wrong direction.

STRATEGIES THAT IMPEDE READINESS

Don't you have the right to decide what your child needs to do for his own good? Should you not just insist that your child go to therapy and enforce it? Your child is neither old enough nor wise enough to make such decisions, so should you not be the one to decide for her? After all, her brain is giving her false messages, so she is not thinking clearly or acting rationally and is not able to act in her own best interest. Doesn't it undermine your parental power to have to ask her permission to engage in therapy? Yes, you have the right—in fact, the responsibility—to decide what's best for your child. Yes, you must let him know this in a matter of fact manner without fear of repercussion. However, some ways of exercising this parental authority can backfire.

Coercion

CBT teaches people to help themselves. It is a process of changing the way of thinking and behaving and works best when it is an internal process. You can't force a person to change the way they think or behave, the way you may be able to enforce surgery or taking a pill.

OCD takes over a child's control. Your child is losing control of his life and is clinging on to the little piece of float to keep himself from drowning. If you try to coerce him at this time, you are taking away that little piece of control that he hangs on to for dear life. If you want your child to learn how to take control of his life and OCD, you are giving the wrong message when you attempt to control his decision. Coercing is like saying, "Why don't you just stop it?" Remember the power of choice. In a funny way, you may have to let go of the control in order to get it back. To paraphrase the far-eastern proverb, if you try to catch the butterfly it will fly away, but if you stay still and wait, it will light on you.

Coercion may work in the short-term, but it does not help your child learn to make the right choices in the long term. Your child may "go along" to every therapy session, but she will neither be invested nor committed to learning how to overcome OCD. And she will never really adopt the strategy for herself. Eventually, you may be successful at getting your child into the therapists' office to do CBT, but it will be at the cost of your relationship. This damage can be lasting and difficult to undo.

Ultimatums

Ultimatums involve threat. Threats involve anger and retribution. Ultimatums and threats undermine trust and hurt your long-term relationship with your child. You have to be a coach, not a bully. We are not given control over people's will. When you feel the urge to give an ultimatum, see it as a cue to step back, recognize your frustration and see if you can figure out what's driving it. OCD gives ultimatums. You don't want to add yours to the ones your child already experiences.

Tricks

Don't trick your child into the doctors' office and don't sugarcoat treatment unrealistically. Your child will sooner or later become wise to the truth, and you will surely lose his trust. Just be straightforward, positive and confident, not hesitant or ambivalent. CBT is collaborative, not confrontational. Your child will eventually respect you for your honesty.

Power struggles

You don't want to battle your child to do CBT; neither do you want to beg for your child's permission. You have to find the middle ground that establishes your authority but also gives your child control. You need to tell your child what you believe is best for him in a matter of fact manner. But you know that it's futile to get into the "No, I won't," "Oh, yes you will," repartee. That merely disintegrates into a war of words and test of the pecking order. As a parent, you need to be at the top of the pecking order, so stop the power struggle while you are still ahead.

You cannot force your child to internalize changes, but you can send a clear message about how far you are willing to let him stray down the path of no return before you will intervene. It's a tough decision, and an individual one for each family. If things get really bad, you may have to make a plan without your child's agreement, for her own good. There are other options. If your child is functioning reasonably well, you may have to wait for a better time and place. If your child's functioning is severely limited, he may require hospitalization or a day treatment program, to which she may be admitted against her will.

FREQUENTLY-ASKED QUESTIONS

We told David that he has OCD. He listened to what we had to say and that was that. He doesn't want to talk about it anymore. I said that was okay and when he was ready to talk or ask questions to let me know.

You are doing the right thing. Give him the time and the space to digest it all. Let him know you are there and ready to help when he needs you. If your child doesn't want to talk to you about OCD, remember that this is not a rejection of you. Each child handles the information differently. Young children may just not have a whole lot to say about it, and adolescents may prefer to work things out for themselves. Asking specific questions rather than general ones, and avoiding Yes/No questions will get you further in your attempts at conversation.

My son is six and insists that it's not OCD or "somebody else" putting fears and rituals in his head. He says it's just him. It's clear to his doctor and to me that he has OCD, but he just doesn't get it.

Your child may be having trouble with the concept of "externalizing" OCD. At the age of six, it is quite common for children to be literal about things, and he might be a bit confused about "something else" in his head, because he might envision this entity literally. Don't push the issue. Accept his understanding of it and focus on whether the fears, even if they are his, bother him and whether he would like to learn how to send them packing.

Chapter 10

GUIDE, RIDE and RALLY:
Critical Roles in CBT

What lies behind us and what lies before us are tiny matters, compared to what lies within us.

Ralph Waldo Emerson

Every day my son would barrage us with concerns about his health. He was constantly worrying about something. At that time, I wrote in my diary, "Worrying about shots—says he can't get them off his mind even though he knows he doesn't get them until age 15. This is after a week of worrying about health. He's constantly seeking reassurance. "Now, I'm absolutely healthy, right?" He has episodes with breathing, "Is this a deep breath?" He says to himself he knows he can trust me when I tell him he doesn't need them, but he can't help it. He told me that reassurances don't really help him.

Sharon, mother of Robert, 12

Your child often relies on you to get him through his daily fears and dilemmas. Like Sharon, you may be eager to learn how you can help your child through these daily struggles with OCD. Now, finally, your child is on the verge of beginning CBT. It's been a long road to this point, and you are poised and ready. You are full of expectation, enthusiasm and relief that the time is finally here.

In this chapter, I present the roles that you, your child and your child's therapist will play to help your child get the most out of CBT. I also suggest what *not* to do—the strategies that are unhelpful to your child during his treatment. Examples describing each of these roles for children of different ages and with various forms of OCD are in Chapter 11.

GUIDE, RIDE AND RALLY

If your child is in CBT, your child's therapist must GUIDE, your child must RIDE and you must RALLY. These three roles are essential to treatment success. Your therapist's role is to teach and guide your child along the RIDE. The therapist must also be your guide in developing your role in your child's treatment, dealing with day-to-day parenting challenges and handling the larger issues of coping and healing. Your therapist must provide the map, plot the route, point out the roadblocks and prepare you for the hairpin bends on this journey. Your child must RIDE *Up and Down the Worry Hill* for himself. Your contribution as a parent is to RALLY for your child. You can help make the RIDE easier by supporting, cheering and standing behind your child as he embarks on this journey.

The average CBT session takes about one or two hours per week. The rest of the time—*a whopping 166 hours a week*—your child is on your watch. You are the one who must help your child cope with OCD between CBT sessions. Your role in helping your child through OCD cannot be overstated. As discussed in Chapter 4, your responses to your child's OCD can affect the way in which your child manages and copes with it. In fact, recent studies have found that children may do much better in therapy when their parents are actively involved compared with being bystanders.

The RIDE (Rename, Insist, Defy, Enjoy) is described in Chapter 5. Your role in rallying for your child is described in detail later in this chapter. But before you take on the rally, you must hand over the charge.

HANDING OVER THE CHARGE

When you developed the battle plan for tackling your child's OCD (see Chapter 7), you undertook to lead the charge. You made all the important decisions for your child, sought the right treatment(s) and therapists, and orchestrated the whole show. Your child's role will now change and so will yours. Your child must now learn how to overcome OCD for himself. Your involvement as a parent is very challenging, because it must be dynamic and evolving to meet the need of the hour. You must continually adjust the part you play to accommodate to your child's changing needs in the process of recovery. Providing the right kind of help requires great flexibility, patience and commitment on your part. It is sure to keep you on your toes!

It is now time to hand over the charge to two key players. The first is your child's CBT therapist, and the second is your child. You, your child and your child's therapist must work together synchronously, yet in clearly different roles. When you have consistent expectations and common goals, the road to the finish line will be much smoother. You will pre-empt the frustration and conflict that comes from stepping on each other's toes. You cannot face your child's fears for him. He must do it for himself. You cannot be the therapist either. Your expertise is that of a parent, not a therapist. However, your parental expertise is essential to the therapists' ability to be a good guide for you and your child. A good CBT therapist will rely on your input to develop a good map for treatment. GUIDE, RIDE and RALLY are complementary roles.

Knowing when to hand over the charge is not always intuitive. Some of it will depend on your child's age, maturity, independence and the severity of OCD. Your child's therapist will help you gauge his readiness. As discussed in Chapter 9, to be ready, your child must have a clear understanding of exposure and habituation and know that he has the choice and the power to overcome OCD. Your therapist will also help you develop a plan for shifting the charge from you to your child gradually with his knowledge and preferably, also with his consent.

When the therapist has prepared your child and she is ready, you must hand over the task of overcoming OCD to her. She has to complete the last and most important lap of this marathon—she must do CBT for herself. You have laid the foundation and prepared the ground. You have selected the bicycle, gotten the right gear and held on to the bicycle seat while she learned how to keep her balance. The finale is hers. You cannot ride the bicycle for your child, although you can ride alongside. Eventually, you must let go, and she must ride away on her own. If you don't, she will never ride a bicycle on her own.

As parents, it is intuitive and normal for us to have "fix it attacks." We want to take care of our children's problems for them. It would be so much simpler and less grief for all if we could take it right out of their hands and attend to it swiftly and surely. Fix it attacks are as prevalent as the common cold. It's not hard to see how parents who are in the midst of one can make the RIDE their own. The next time you have a "fix it attack," remember that the more you do for your child, the less she will be able to do for herself. In other words, "helping" turns into "hindering" when you do "too much" for your child. You cannot overcome OCD for her, no matter how much you'd like to and be ready to. Letting go can be difficult, especially after you have just mastered the role of leading the charge.

> The more you do for your child,
> the less opportunity she has to do it for herself.

HOW TO RALLY FOR YOUR CHILD

The specifics of your child's RIDE and your RALLY will be unique to you. Each child's needs are different due to age, maturity, readiness for CBT, specific OCD symptoms, and the nature and extent of parental entanglement in the symptoms. The following are general guidelines. Your CBT therapist must help you negotiate the nuances, subtleties and actual application of these guidelines in your situation. Examples of the RIDE and RALLY in action are in Chapter 11.

> *RALLY for your child*
>
> **Recognize** OCD episodes
> **Ally** with your child
> **Lead** your child to the RIDE
> **Let go** so your child can learn for himself
> **Yes**, you did it! Reward and praise

Recognize OCD episodes

Recognizing involves opening yourself up to observe, reframe and come to terms with an OCD episode. It involves putting things in perspective and being able to separate yourself and your child from OCD. When your child says, "Ugh, don't touch me! Your hands are dirty," you can't help but bristle at the insult he's just heaped on you. That's if you believe it's a deliberate insult. If you can separate the OCD from your child, you will be able to accept that it was OCD getting the better of his judgment. Separating your child from his OCD can be much harder than you might expect in times of crisis. When you don't take the defiance, insults and rejections that stem from OCD personally, you can help him and yourself move to the next step.

Stop, think and then proceed—don't act too hastily on your gut reaction. Just as your child is learning to rename OCD, so must you, in order to be impartial and objective in helping your child. When your child is being stubborn, unreasonable and irrational, remind yourself that you might be dealing with OCD, not your child. This will allow you to target your actions and emotions at OCD, not your child.

Recognizing does not mean that you have to condone or approve of the behavior. You merely have to accept that the intent of the behavior was not malicious. You may be angry with your child and tempted to assume that he is being insolent. When you put things in perspective you realize that your child is not being himself. He's not at his best, and may be his worst when in the throes of OCD. He doesn't listen to you anymore; he listens to the voice of OCD. The more astute an observer you are of OCD's influence on your child, the more adept you will become at detecting "OCD moments." When you are not sure, give your child the benefit of the doubt.

Ally with your child, not the OCD

Being an ally calls for empathy, reflection of feelings, availability, respect and effective communication. Although it might seem obvious that you would ally with your child instead of OCD, it is not always that straightforward. OCD has a natural aptitude for pitting family members against each other, because it clouds reason. In order to ally with your child, you must put yourself in his shoes, feel what it is to be him in that moment, to have fear welling up inside you and to believe that you must do senseless and ridiculous things to quiet it.

When you and your child have a good alliance, treatment can proceed faster and more smoothly. Consider Carlos, age 15 and Shana, age 14, who had similar symptoms and level of severity. Both were equally motivated and understood the treatment well. But the alliance with the parents was very different—Carlos and his mother had a close, supportive relationship and worked as a team. Shana and her mother were easily frustrated with each other and engaged in many push-pull interactions. Guess who did well? Carlos was able to use his mother's support and encouragement and completed his homework exercises easily. In contrast, when Shana ran into a problem at home, she rejected her parents' help, which made them very frustrated. Her progress in treatment was slow and erratic.

Reflect your child's feelings and struggles with empathy. When you do, you are more likely to focus on your child's needs at the moment than your own, or to get distracted by the OCD.

"It must be so hard, I'm trying to understand what it must feel like for you so I can be there for you."

"I'm guessing it must make you feel pretty out of control."

"I wish you didn't have to suffer so much. Let's see what we can do together."

When reflecting, it is best to wonder out loud rather than put words in your child's mouth. If you say, "You're mad and scared," you're likely to hear, "What do you know about what I'm feeling? Leave me alone. Don't tell me what I think!"

Engage your child positively with gentle encouragement and steadfast support. Let your child know that you are there for him, as and when he needs you. Be supportive but firm, kind but steadfast. Let your child know that you are helping him, not the OCD. Let him know that getting better happens in small steps. Let him know you understand how hard it is and how much patience it requires. His effort is what counts, not his achievements. Role model patience and "turtle steps" for him by showing the same behaviors yourself.

Paradoxically, being available might mean that you must recede to the background at times. Your child may be more overwhelmed if you hover, direct and prod. How do you know if you need to stay and participate actively or leave and give him space? When you are allied, you are in tune to your child's cues and communications and respond accordingly. It's essential to develop and practice a signal system to communicate at difficult times. You are unlikely to have rational conversations in the heat of the moment. A proactive, prearranged system for brief but clear communication saves a lot of hassle. It must be done during a time of calm. You might have to ask,

"Is OCD bothering you?" "Do you want to do this on your own, or would you like my help? It's your choice."

One way to use signals is to use the "Feeling Thermometer" (see Chapter 5) as a "Help Thermometer." Zero might mean that your child is fine and dandy, and 10 might mean, "Help, I'm in deep trouble." A five might mean "I'm not doing too well, but I'd rather work it out myself." When such a system has been worked out ahead of time, you and your child merely need to resort to numbers,

"What's your help temperature?"

"Six."

"Okay then, I'll be back in 15 minutes to see how you're doing then."

You and your child, with the guidance of your therapist, can come up with other creative ideas or possibilities for a signal system.

Humor can sometimes break the tension that pervades OCD moments. When you and your child are comfortably aligned on the same side, you may find opportunities to laugh at the absurdity of OCD. Although humor is a wonderful antidote to many of life's troubles, it must be used judiciously because it can ally or alienate. Humor must be directed at OCD, not at your child. You must laugh *with* your child, not *at* your child. Remember that it is only funny if your *child* finds it funny.

Lead your child to the RIDE

Leading your child to the RIDE involves reinforcing the guidance provided by your child's therapist and helping your child stick with the exercises prescribed by the therapist. There are many ways in which you can encourage, cheer and help your child negotiate the twists and turns of the RIDE. Your child's therapist will guide you through the details of your involvement in the RIDE. The RIDE steps are summarized below (see Chapter 5 for more details).

RALLY for your child

Rename the thought. "It's simply OCD, not me."
Insist that YOU are in charge! "I'm in charge, not OCD."
Defy OCD, do the OPPOSITE of what it wants.
 "I will ride up the Worry Hill and stick it out."
Enjoy your success, reward yourself.
 "I did it. I can do it again."

You can help your child recognize and relabel OCD episodes:

"Who's talking, you or OCD?"

"Is it you that's afraid, or is OCD telling you to be afraid?"

"What percentage of you really believes what OCD is telling you?"

"Are you praying because you like to pray or because OCD tells you that you must pray?"

"Do you want to say sorry or is it OCD that's telling you to say sorry?"

Your child may sometimes get annoyed, because OCD can sometimes become strangely "comfortable" for him. When you attempt to get him to recognize and relabel OCD, you may be disrupting the sense of comfort that comes with familiarity and stability.

Reaffirm the power of choice for your child. Let him know that he has the power to take charge and to defy OCD.

"Who's going to be in charge? OCD or you?"

"Remember what we talked about before? OCD can't make you do anything if you decide you won't let it."

"You can choose to do what you want to do or what OCD wants you to do. It's your choice."

Give him the space to decide for himself and to feel in control. Give your child the power to get well. Let him know you trust him to make the choice that's good for him.

Take treatment seriously and make it a "project." You can try to make it more fun and interesting by helping your child pick out "RIDE gear." After all, when your child joins the hockey team, you go to the store together to pick out his helmet and other equipment. Take your child to the store and let him pick out a binder or folder and personalize it with his own decorations—stickers, drawings, pictures or the like. Make sure there are enough copies of the fear thermometer for convenient access-one in his binder, on the refrigerator, another in his backpack and one in the car. Give him a set of colored index cards to write down his successes, tips or reminders. Use the feeling thermometer whenever possible to communicate about fears, successes and the need for help.

When it's time to defy OCD and start exposure, you must reinforce the guidance provided by your child's therapist. Help your child review the RIDE steps with his *Worry Hill Memory Card* (see Chapter 5). Support your child all the way with encouragement. Stay close enough but not too close. Be available to clarify any misunderstanding he has regarding homework exercises. Provide positive statements and encourage constructive self-talk. "You can do it. You just have to do your best." Encourage your child to stick it out when the RIDE gets tough.

In some situations, your therapist may define your role as that of a "co-therapist," helping your child with exposure exercises under the guidance of the therapist. This role is suitable when you have a good alliance with your child and when your child is young and needs help getting through the steps of the RIDE. It is typically not suitable if your child is older, is an adolescent or if the alliance with your child is shaky.

A very important part of your role is to give the therapist feedback on how the treatment is working. Your child's therapist relies on you and your child for information to design, implement and fine-tune the treatment. If you don't let your therapist know how things are going, she will not be able to design ongoing treatment effectively. Continue the log that you began at the time of your child's evaluation (see Figure 3 in Chapter 3). It will give your therapist a more objective description of your child's progress in CBT, from your perspective. Note down your child's symptoms, their frequency, triggers, contexts, time involved and other notes before treatment starts and as it progresses.

Part of leading your child to the RIDE is to *role model* the behaviors you would like to see him display. Are you excessively worried, overcautious or highly reactive? How do you take on responsibility and face adversity? You must become aware of your emotional states and the manner in which you handle them. If you are tense or stressed, you may need to contain and change your own thoughts, self-talk and behavior patterns before attempting to help your child with his. When you take control of your feelings and actions, you model the same for your child. If you want your child to take risks and be fearless, show him that you are willing to do everything you ask of him.

Teach and model "normal" anxiety and help your child recognize the difference between normal and excessive worry. Your child needs to know that anxiety levels of three to five on the *Fearmometer* may be quite normal and appropriate, depending on the circumstances. As a parent, you can also model for your child what constitutes normal washing, wiping or checking—when your child is ready to accept this, of course. Teach your child that uncertainty is a fact of life. Give him examples of all the uncertainties with which he lives everyday and that he might take for granted. Use the same strategies to cope with your fears as your child is learning.

Let go; let your child RIDE for himself

Finally, you must let go and let your child learn for himself. By doing so, you convey your trust and reaffirm faith in your child's ability to overcome OCD. You give him hope and optimism. You let him know that *he* has the power to change.

There are no guarantees about safety in life; there is no certainty about outcomes. To overcome OCD, your child must learn to live with uncertainty, trust his own instincts, to take reasonable risks and exercise reasonable caution. He must accept mistakes, imperfections and their consequences. To learn these lessons, he must learn to violate the rules of OCD. He (and you) will live to tell the tale.

Let your child, in collaboration with the therapist, decide the hierarchy and targets for treatment. Let him set the pace for treatment. The goals that are set in treatment should be his goals, not yours. They should focus on what your child can be most successful at, not what's most distressing to you. Imposing your goals can result in failure, if your child does not have the same goal or does not subscribe to it. Your child will be more motivated if given some control. Give your child the room to grow, just like you did when he was a newborn and toddler.

Letting go also involves letting go of OCD as the organizing force in your lives. Now that you've reached a point where he is taking charge of it himself, it's time to pull back and step out of the web of OCD. Recognize your child's strengths and personality aside from OCD; begin to normalize him and your lives again.

Yes! You did it.

Reward and celebrate your child's successes. This is an important but easily forgotten part of the treatment process. We learn so much from the feedback we receive about our performance. Don't forget to reward and praise for *effort*, not necessarily the end result. Celebrate the smallest successes, no matter how small they are. Every success should be a victory. It is so easy to focus on what's not going well. You may make weekly ratings of progress on a chart or a graph. Perhaps your child can collect tokens in a jar and redeem them for things he wants. Teach your child how to reward herself for effort. Find relaxing things to do, get ice cream or watch a movie together. Recall and review past successes to shore up your child's confidence in himself. Retrace your child's steps and reaffirm small improvements, no matter how small. For more about how to reward your child's behaviors, see Chapter 12.

The biggest challenge of the RALLY is that it is not so much a task as it is a dynamic relationship between you and your child. It evolves and shifts continuously. You and your child influence each other's movements. As the older of the two, the onus of adapting to the shifting role really falls on your shoulders. Even if you do your best to follow the guidance of your therapist, there will be times when things don't go well. What works one day may not work the next; what works in the morning may not work in the evening. You will make mistakes along the way and you will learn by trial and error. Just as it takes time for your child to prepare for and learn the RIDE, it will take you time to learn how to RALLY.

WHAT TO AVOID: STRATEGIES THAT DON'T HELP

As discussed in Chapter 8, you can sometimes become an unwitting accomplice to OCD. You reassure, accommodate, make excuses, assist, participate, protect and shield, all in the name of kindness and compassion. Often described as "enabling," it is "when you seem to be doing all the wrong things for the right reasons," in the words of psychologist Dr. Herb Gravitz. You find that it is intuitive to default to these strategies more than you intend to. Some of it comes naturally to you. The rest is because you don't know what else to do! The intent of this section is to make you aware of the many ways in which you may be innocently aiding and abetting OCD, and to suggest ways to break out of the vicious cycle.

You may resort to enabling during times of crisis when you have no choice but to survive. Perhaps you are deeply mired and cannot find a way out, even though the crisis is long gone. Recognize and accept your enabling behaviors as well-intentioned parental mistakes; the kind that none of us are exempt from. It is a fact of parenthood that we learn by trial and error. Although we act with the right intentions, our actions sometimes help and sometimes hinder.

Advice and good logic

If you haven't found out already, OCD and logic are mutually exclusive. Although children with OCD are perfectly rational and logical at most times, they subscribe to the warped logic of OCD with tenacity when caught in an OCD episode. Remember that it is the nature of OCD *not* to make sense. You may be very tempted to lecture your child and to become annoyed when it doesn't seem to sink in. Saying things like, "Don't you get it?" or "Just stop it" is of no avail. In fact, it may aggravate your child's behavior because she is already struggling to follow OCD's "orders;" your directives add further stress and confusion. Your child would have stopped the silliness already if it was possible. When she starts CBT, she will learn logical reasoning skills at a pace that is suited to her needs.

Reassurance

Did you ever think that comforting and reassuring your child when she is afraid would actually make her OCD worse? This news comes as a shock to many parents because it defies a very basic and intuitive task of parenting. It is the most natural thing for a parent to console and reassure a frightened child. Ironically, whereas reassurance is both appropriate and effective for a normally anxious child, it functions as a ritual for the child with OCD. Reassurance is a form of escape from the fear because it helps the child avoid facing the fear and finding out for himself. This avoidance provides only very temporary relief and perpetuates the vicious cycle of OCD. You have found this out already because your child asks again, almost before you have gotten the last words out of your mouth. Of course, if you have reassured your child excessively, you have only done so with the best intentions and for lack of a more effective strategy. See Chapter 11 for the steps to break free of reassurance seeking.

Distraction

Like reassurance, distraction provides only temporary relief from OCD because it prevents the child from confronting the fear. There are times when distraction can be helpful to get through a crisis. Getting your child to play a computer game or watch a funny movie may be the only way to get him out of the bathroom. Nonetheless, it is not an effective long-term strategy for OCD, because the fears return when the distraction is over.

Avoidance

By now, you may have gotten to a point where you allow your child to avoid the things he fears. You have learned that it is the only way to get your child through the basics of his day, and to get to school. When you have attempted to encourage your child to confront his fears, you have dealt with his fury. You may therefore default to avoidance as the only way to get by. "Okay," you say to your son, "don't take that backpack if it bothers you," or "You don't have to walk through the kitchen if it makes you afraid." Life is just a lot easier when you don't rock the boat. But as you learned in Chapter 4, avoidance feeds the fires of OCD. Compassion may lead you to protect your child from encountering OCD triggers, but shielding your child actually prolongs OCD.

Assistance and participation

You and other family members may also become unwitting accomplices to OCD when you assist and participate in your child's rituals. You follow your child's "orders" by doing the laundry six times a day to keep a fresh supply of towels ready. You check the closets with him at night. The entire family uses only plastic forks because metal forks "leak poison." These are some of the ways in which you may assist and participate. You do it to keep the peace because it's been too traumatic for the rest of the family when you don't submit. You intend to ease the burden for your child, but then you realize that you have been taken for an "OCD ride."

Ironically, the assistance that is intended to help your child prevents him from encountering "natural" exposures and learning how to help himself. It merely strengthens his OCD. Children who take reasonable risks, persist in the face of mild to moderate anxiety and are resourceful in coping tend to be less anxious. Your child must eventually learn to develop self-reliance in negotiating day-to-day challenges. You walk a fine line between helping your child and "enabling" OCD.

Criticism, scolding and punishment

You couldn't get your child to stop her asthma, diabetes or short sightedness by punishing her, so don't expect OCD to vanish into thin air when you strip your child of his TV or computer time. True OCD is not a willful misbehavior and therefore cannot be easily turned off by the child with a scolding or two. Not only that, harshness will turn your child against you. He will believe that you don't have a clue about what's going on with him. Since he cannot "just stop it," he will become secretive and withdraw. He will engage in clandestine rituals. To the burden of OCD will be added the burden of being surreptitious.

However, it is often very tricky for parents to sort out true OCD from typical childhood misbehavior, because children with OCD are not immune to the latter. When you know it is misbehavior, handle it the way you would at any other time. When you're not sure, you may sometimes have to give your child the benefit of the doubt. Chapter 12 discusses matters of parenting at greater depth.

Taking control of the therapy

As you know already from reading this chapter, you must hand over the charge of implementing therapy to your child's therapist. Your role is to support your child under the guidance of your child's therapist. Resist the temptation to speed your child along of your own initiative or to try some exposure exercises at home without your therapist's input. Your child will become confused about what he is supposed to do if you and your therapist are not working in harmony. Your zeal may hurt your child's chances at success. If you are concerned that therapy is progressing too slowly, that your child is not working on issues of greatest importance, or that therapy is not what you expected it to be, don't wait patiently to see what happens. Discuss it with your therapist sooner rather than later, so that a small problem does not become a big problem that is difficult to repair. Ask for clarification of the goals and process of treatment.

As a parent, you have a special and unique relationship with your child. Taking on the role of a therapist can be unduly complex and burdensome to you and confusing to your child. The therapist enjoys the objectivity of a neutral third party. You are also not trained as a therapist, unless that is your profession. Reading all about OCD does not give you the background or skills to become a therapist, in the same way that it does not give you the expertise to treat your child's asthma or diabetes. Nonetheless, you play a pivotal role in helping keep your child's asthma or diabetes under control by overseeing your child's diet, exercise and medication.

Abrupt changes and new rules

Finally, even if you are horrified at how you have been aiding and abetting OCD all along, don't change anything abruptly. How you go about withdrawing your enabling behaviors is just as important as the fact that you are changing them. Even if you now know what you should be doing instead, don't surprise your child with any new interventions. Unpleasant surprises won't make you popular. Don't break loose abruptly because that can cause upheaval for your child. With your therapists' guidance, you will learn to wean yourself systematically and gradually. It will not be easy and it will not happen overnight.

When you want to change your response to your child's OCD, it should be a planned change rather than a reactive one (unless it is a safety situation or other emergency). When you plan, your intervention must be part of a bigger scheme of intervention (e.g., a hierarchy of behaviors) rather than a response to an isolated behavior. Give your child fair warning of a change in your response. When your child is prepared, she is not thrown off, and it will save both of you a lot of unnecessary grief. Your child must first have the tools to cope with the change. If you act without giving her some coping strategies to get through the change, you will leave her high and dry and she may fall apart. Your child must first understand what exposure is, what habituation is, how to survive exposure and stick it out until the anxiety passes. If you take away something that has been soothing to your child, be sure to give her something to replace that need. She will not know what to do with the internal angst if you don't.

When possible, seek your child's agreement and willing participation in the change. If not, you are forcing your child to comply and that prevents her from being in control of the behavior herself. You take away her choice to overcome the behavior. The manner in which you make the change is of utmost importance. Are you calm and encouraging or are you annoyed, impatient and holding your ground for the principle of the thing? If it is the latter, you compromise your alliance with your child.

FREQUENTLY-ASKED QUESTIONS

How do I know if my son is having obsessive thoughts if he won't tell me? He looks preoccupied, but he won't tell me much. How can I help him?

As long as you have given your child the message that he can talk to you as and when he is ready, you will have to give him the space to think about it. Often, rituals are a good indicator that a child is having obsessions, because rituals are the counteraction to the obsession. So if your child starts tapping, touching, washing or counting, you can be sure it's in response to a fear or urge. That's when you can offer to help. Another way to communicate is to use a signal system that allows your child to say if he needs help or would rather figure it out for himself.

Should I let my son do an activity that will make him anxious?

In general, it is important to let children take risks and learn how to cope with the anxiety. When you let him take risks, you give him the important message that you believe in him and his ability to cope with a challenge. Avoiding situations that will make him anxious will reinforce fear. The risk depends on the nature of the activity. Of course, you would not let him take real risks like walking on the train tracks! Are you anxious about him being anxious? When you are too anxious, you may be overprotective, and give your child the message that there is more danger in the situation than he has gauged. You may unwittingly reinforce his anxiety. If you are anxious about it, perhaps you should consider taking the risk too and learning how to manage your anxiety.

Will it be too traumatic for my child to interrupt rituals once begun? Shouldn't the anxiety have a way to get worked out of his system?

It may be traumatic if the child is not prepared for it, does not understand why you are doing it or if it is done brashly. If the child is prepared and ready, it is rarely traumatic. The rituals can be gradually tapered or shortened, instead of stopping them altogether. The anxiety will work its way out of his system automatically when habituation occurs.

My child is seven years old. Is she too young to use a hierarchy? She picks an item low on the hierarchy but when it's time to do it, says she can't.

Some children of this age grasp the concept of a hierarchy perfectly and others don't. Even older teens may have trouble with the notion of ranking, so it's not just age that is of relevance. Remember that the hierarchy is just an aid to gradual exposure. It is not an end in itself. There are many alternative ways to select the tasks for gradual exposure. Instead of using numbers to rate items, colors could be used instead. A thermometer with colors such as red for "too hot," orange and yellow for "pretty warm" and blue for "ice cool" fulfills the same purpose. Sometimes, using only three categories or "piles" such as "pretty easy," "kind of hard" and "really tough" make the sorting task easier for children.

If your child is too afraid to attempt an exposure exercise that's low on the list, she may not have understood the concept. She also needs to understand that she will feel at least some discomfort during exposure to easy tasks. It's important to go with what she's telling you and adjust the tasks accordingly. Over time, she and you will become more astute at gauging the difficulty level of various tasks.

We started CBT after a great deal of difficulty. Now my son wants to quit and I'm ready to quit myself.

It is normal to have occasional doubts and second thoughts during treatment. Take a few moments to figure out what is driving your desire to "quit." Remember that treatment is a commitment in terms of time, effort and perseverance. Even if your child makes a 5% improvement, it is better than 0%. Think about what you have to gain versus what you have to lose if you stop treatment. Be sure to have a frank discussion of your concerns with your therapist and other family members. Remember that it is fine to get a second opinion or work with a second therapist, if you believe that the first is not the right one for your child's needs.

Chapter 11

CBT With Your Child:
The RIDE And RALLY In Action

They conquer who believe they can.

John Dryden

This chapter presents examples of the RIDE and RALLY for commonly seen variations of OCD. The way in which the RALLY steps apply in your specific situation will depend on your child's age, maturity, readiness for treatment, the closeness and trust you enjoy with your child, the type of symptoms he has, and the nature of your involvement in his symptoms. A younger child will need you to *Lead* more than to *Let go*, and to lead for longer than with an older child. If your child is a teenager, you may have to let go more than you lead. Allying with your teenager may involve backing off and trusting him; he, in exchange might indicate a positive alliance with a "grunt" of approval. Your therapist and guide will help you arrive at the right balance of leading and letting go, when and how much to praise, and in what fashion to ally with your child.

CONTAMINATION AND CLEANSING

Maria, the 12-year-old you read about in Chapter 1, was hounded by thoughts that she would contaminate others. At first, she had feared that she might have contracted hepatitis. The news report the night it all started had been quite alarming. An employee at a local food store had been found to have hepatitis. So had the donuts he had apparently handled. Several customers had become seriously ill. *"If you don't wash your hands, you'll get hepatitis,"* whispered OCD. Maria did due diligence to washing her hands before she ate and after she used the bathroom. But it wasn't enough. *"More, more, more, not enough, not enough, not quite enough,"* urged OCD.

By the time Maria and her parents Carl and Elaine came to see me, they were desperate. Their happy little girl's life was now a miserable drama that revolved around the bathroom—from toilet to sink to shower, Maria was caught in an interminable cycle of cleansing rituals. Maria's initial fears that she would get ill were soon replaced by fears that she would spread the illness and be responsible for the deaths of others. She refused to touch anyone—no hugs, no kisses, no shaking hands. Next came the creeping doubts that "vaginal wetness" would contaminate the seats on which she sat at home, at school and on the bus. Maria began wiping herself dry to the point where she was chafed and bleeding. She barely made it to school most days. Most of Elaine's waking hours were spent in the bathroom with Maria—assisting, checking, reassuring, prodding, pleading to get her to move on. If she didn't, Maria would not emerge from the bathroom for hours. Carl didn't know how to help anymore. Maria seemed to understand her father's logical explanations, the education about hepatitis and the reasoning. Yet, when it came time to clean, the look of panic crossed her eyes. OCD prevailed. Her parents were heartbroken.

Maria was nervous but ready to undertake the RIDE. I coached and guided, explained and reinforced. It would be well worth the risk, I assured Maria and her family. Her parents were committed and dedicated. They knew it would be a tough few weeks, but they each had a role to play and they were ready to do it. They needed a surge of confidence and optimism, because theirs had long since run out.

CBT for contamination fears involves learning how to appreciate the difference between *unpleasant* and *dangerous*. Maria learned that although she didn't *like* the "dirty" feeling, not washing her hands was hardly calamitous. In fact, there are germs everywhere, and our immune systems overcome them all the time without our knowing it!

Maria and I made a hierarchy of her fears and began the RIDE. She had tremendous courage, determination and trust. We read medical books about hepatitis. Maria repeated the word "hepatitis" several times in a conversation. She touched her parents with unwashed hands. She used the toilet and used only four squares of toilet paper instead of an entire roll. Immediately after, she sat on all the chairs in my office. Her parents and I then sat on the chairs that she had just "contaminated." She struggled to get to the top of the Worry Hill; she wavered at times, but she always made it.

How could Carl and Elaine RALLY for Maria? Their roles differed. Maria's mother was deeply entwined in Maria's rituals. Maria would get stuck and be unable to move forward if her mother didn't participate in and assist her with her rituals. She would never have made it out of the bathroom, out the door, on the bus or to school if her mother didn't hurry her along, if that was even possible. Whereas her mother had to gradually extricate herself from Maria's rituals, Maria's father's role was that of support and encouragement. He kept Maria and her mother steady in their progress by encouraging, praising and being steadfast in his commitment to be there all the way.

We made a hierarchy for weaning Maria off Elaine's help with rituals. With Maria's knowledge and consent, Elaine gradually decreased the number of reminders, the physical assistance and the extra checking she did for Maria. Step-by-step, they went through each exercise. It was difficult in the beginning, but when they stuck it out, it got easier. Carl and Elaine were there by her side, steady and stable in their conviction. They rallied for her as follows:

Recognize OCD episodes: Elaine reminded herself that Maria was not doing this to drive her crazy, and that it was driving Maria more crazy.

"Maria, is it you or your OCD that's saying you're not clean enough?"

Ally with your child: They devised a communication system that involved hand signals.

"We are here with you. It must be really hard to stop washing right now. What can I do to help you stop OCD right now?"

Lead your child to the RIDE: They gave her the power of choice.

"Remember that you can choose to be in charge, and to tell OCD to go

take a hike! Let's together try to stop OCD from making you wash one more time. Go on, now, you can do it, defy OCD. Climb that Worry Hill. Come on, huff and puff, huff and puff. Remember what happens if you stick it out? Pretty soon, you'll be coasting."

Let Go so your child can do it:

"Remember, if I help you wash, I'm helping OCD, not you. See, you can do it yourself! I'm here if you need me, but I'm going to let you see for your-self how strong you are. You can face it!"

Yes! You did it! Reward and praise:

"You are awesome. What a fighter you are! You don't give up too easy, do you? Wow, after that round, we could all chill with some ice cream and a movie. What do you think?"

At the end of eight weeks of CBT, Maria and her parents reported 80% improvement. The OCD was not all gone, but things were just so much easier. Fears were now a passing thought rather than paralyzing fear. As we were nearing the end of treatment, I asked Maria if she would write an article for the school newspaper. I suggested a story about contaminating the chairs on which she sat in school. I asked Maria to be creative and truly imagine the disastrous consequences she feared. Maria wasn't quite sure if I was serious and I assured her that I was. At our next appointment, she showed me her piece entitled, *Students Die of Wetness.* It was a dra-matic description of a horrible tragedy, all because of the selfish unconcern of one girl who spread the wetness. She dissolved into laughter as she read it out loud; Carl and Elaine wiped the tears from their eyes. Maria had made a mockery of OCD.

"BAD THOUGHTS" AND MENTAL RITUALS

Fifteen-year-old Jessy had ugly thoughts. A soft-spoken, gentle teen-ager, she sat in front of me one day with tears streaming down her face. When she could finally summon up the words, she told me with anguish that she had seen a pregnant woman walk by at the mall, and suddenly wished that the woman's baby would die. Or be deformed. Jessy was sure she was a horrible person for wishing something so repugnant, especially on someone as helpless and innocent as an unborn baby. She had to make it right by "canceling" the abhorrent thought. She stopped, mustered all her concentration, and conjured up the image of the pregnant woman walking by. Then she closed her eyes and muttered to herself, "You'll have a beautiful, healthy, bouncy baby," again and again, until it felt right. It was only the "mental rituals" that kept Jessy from falling apart altogether.

But that was not all, Jessy poured out, weeping by now. The "evil" she had within her was going to destroy her and everyone else, she was sure. When she was babysitting, she had the thought that she wanted to put the baby in the microwave along with his bottle. She opened the microwave door to make sure she hadn't actually done that. Then she ran to the crib; she heaved a sigh of relief to find the baby gurgling contentedly. But the thought kept nagging her. Before long, she was racing back and forth from the microwave to the crib, because she could not afford to take the chance that she just might have acted on her impulse. Jessy was a mess of sweat and tears and struggled to regain her composure when the baby's mother returned. She stopped babysitting altogether after that episode; she couldn't trust herself enough.

And there was more. Sometimes, she had the urge to poke her eyes out with a fork or stick her finger in a plug, to stab her mother with a knife or to kill her dog. Worse yet, she was sure that she had touched the "privates" of the boys in her class. She had been sure she was possessed. What else could this be? Such deeply wicked thoughts could only come from an evil power. She was ashamed and chastised herself constantly. Yet, deep down inside, Jessy knew it wasn't her and that something was terribly wrong. Sometimes, it felt like she was just crouching in a corner, shielding her mind with her hands from the next ugly thought that would assail her. Jessy's break came when she learned about OCD on a news show. She confessed her shameful secret to her parents and was immensely relieved to learn that she was not the only one.

Jessy's parents shook their heads in disbelief. They knew she was incapable of the horrendous acts and thoughts that plagued her. A gentle, loving and sensitive child, she had always been kind and thoughtful. She had always been fond of babies and animals and compassionate towards the less fortunate. How could these violent thoughts and impulses be hers? Surveys show that 90% of us experience unwanted, violent or upsetting thoughts. For the majority of people, these are passing thoughts. We may be briefly alarmed at their occurrence, but, for the most part, we are able to forget or dismiss them with relative ease. We don't dwell on them. In contrast, OCD sufferers experience them as a constant assault of horrific and loathsome thoughts; they can neither be dismissed nor controlled.

Sufferers need to learn that thought is not equivalent to action. We have thoughts of all kinds all the time. Merely thinking them does not make them come true. We would need to have magical powers to make our evil thoughts materialize merely by thinking them. People with true OCD don't actually carry out their malicious thoughts, even though that is their worst fear. OCD expert Dr. Lee Baer has written a wonderful expose of "bad thoughts OCD" and its treatment in his book *The Imp of the Mind.*

CBT for this form of OCD is focused on helping the child distinguish *voluntary* thoughts from *unwanted* OCD thoughts. Children are often alarmed at their ugly thoughts and assume that they must be evil and will suffer punishment for their wicked ways. Children need to be taught that they are not evil because they neither desire nor enjoy these ugly thoughts and have no control over their emergence. Would Jessy hurt babies or poke her eyes out? The answer was a plain and simple "No," because Jessy abhorred her thoughts and was doing everything in her power to prevent herself from acting on them.

The RIDE for Jessy involved *facing* her bad thoughts instead of trying to suppress them. She needed to recognize and rename them as OCD, not herself. She would have to actively take charge of her own thoughts instead of passively succumbing to OCD's dictates. Jessy realized, when she understood how habituation worked, that when she kept trying to fend off OCD thoughts, they took on greater importance and meaning. Exposure for Jessy involved thinking about those nasty thoughts *deliberately* and graphically until they become boring and ridiculous. In fact, saying those thoughts out loud instead of suppressing them would take away the emotional charge, the taboo and the power of the thoughts. Because the thoughts were too hard for Jessy to say out loud initially, we started by writing them out and listening to me recite them.

Jessy wanted an assurance from me before she was ready to begin. "Are you sure I won't actually do these bad things?" she asked. I asked Jessy what she thought the chances were that she would actually put the baby in the microwave. Very, very slim, she conceded. "That's the best guess you or I have about it and that's what you have to learn to live with. I can't promise you that you won't do it, because I don't know for sure, so I'd be lying if I gave you a guarantee. But I have no guarantees that I won't commit a horrible crime tomorrow either. The fact is, there is no certainty in the world and we have to live with our best guesses. If we spent our time chasing certainty, we'd be miserable. You can never enjoy today if you're always worried about tomorrow."

We stood looking out of my office window one nice summer's day, watching passersby on the sidewalk and cars idling down the street. I took the lead: "I hope that old gentleman gets hit by a car as he crosses the street," I said out loud, as he began to cross. Jessy winced and covered her eyes. She peeked out of the corner of her eye as the gentleman started walking across the street. A car came speeding by, seemingly at breakneck speed. Jessy let out a gasp. It slowed and stopped, and the gentleman made it to the other side comfortably. And safely. Like he had done so many times before. Just the way millions of people cross millions of streets every minute of the day. My thought and wish did not come true.

"Well," I commented, "I couldn't seem to make my wish true, no matter how hard I thought about it." "I understand," Jessy conceded. "Thoughts don't just happen like magic. But it's still so *awful* to think those things and say them. How could you say that and not feel bad?" "If I really wished those things, I would feel bad," I replied. "You see, I was just saying a bunch of meaningless words. Those were not my thoughts or wishes. I said it to prove a point. When you believe they are *your* thoughts, you feel bad. When you believe they are meaningless words, you can recite them with no feeling."

As we gazed out the window, we saw the same gentleman get ready to cross the street again. Jessy looked at me expectantly. "Here's your chance, Jessy," I said softly. "Ready for it?" Jessy steeled herself, clenched her jaw and muttered, "Get hit by a car, hit by a car..." She didn't "undo" the thought, pray or slap her cheek to make the thought go away. She allowed it to pervade and infuse her thoughts. Her face was ashen; she held her breath. "Keep going," I encouraged her. "You'll be coasting down that Worry Hill pretty soon...just stick it out..." As Jessy watched nothing happen, she seemed to relax a bit. In another minute, she was laughing with relief. Our gentleman was strolling along in the sunshine, blissfully unaware of our "death wishes" for him. His life had not been altered by the power of our ugly thoughts.

How did Jessy's parents rally for her? In Jessy's case, because she was 15, and because her OCD thoughts were quite personal, her parents rallied for her on the sidelines rather than in the foreground.

Recognize OCD episodes: When Jessy seemed preoccupied and far away, they helped her "catch" herself by asking if she was okay. Their gentle reminders helped Jessy realize she was getting carried away and helped her stop the runaway train of obsessive thoughts.

Ally with your child: Jessy's parents were steadfast in their support. They let her decide when and how they could be of help. They gave Jessy the space and time she needed to get through the RIDE.

Lead your child to the RIDE: Jessy's parents learned about the RIDE, about exposure and habituation. But because they were not actively involved in Jessy's rituals, they did not play an active part in helping her through the RIDE. When Jessy told them she was thinking ugly or hurtful thoughts, they helped her reframe them, "Do you mean OCD is telling you to think about hurting yourself?" They encouraged her to ride up the Worry Hill and reminded her of the coast that would soon follow.

Let Go so your child can do it: This is where Jessy's parents played the most important role. They trusted her to do it for herself. They let her use her new wings. "You can do it, Jessy, we know you can."

Yes! You did it! Reward and praise: Jessy's parents let her know how proud they were of her courage, faith and commitment. They celebrated her successes with her.

MORAL DILEMMAS AND CHECKING

Bob, whom you have met several times already in this book, was 10 when I met him. He had a host of different obsessions and compulsions. His mother Nina's notes read:

"Even as a toddler, he was concerned with cleanliness and orderliness. He started making lists when he was seven years old. He made elaborate Lego creations that had to be "just right." He was so concerned they would never be the same again that he refused to dismantle them. When I suggested taking photographs to have a record of them, Bob insisted on taking them from every angle possible, sometimes taking 10 shots for each set up. A couple of months later, Bob started cleaning his drinking glass with his fingers, determined not to waste a drop. This led to licking plates clean at every meal and snack, so he wouldn't waste a morsel of food. Bob became obsessed with avoiding wastage. He stopped eating so that he didn't have to go through the elaborate cycle of checking for wastage. He started losing weight...Then came the dilemmas: What goes in the garbage and what goes in the recycle? There were lots of questions and lots of checking to ensure nothing was in the wrong receptacle.

This has now progressed to checking faucets and shutting them off forcefully, turning them again and again to make sure they are not dripping and wasting water. He checks under the sinks repeatedly and has to say the alphabet to ensure that there are no drips. Bob checks to see that each light in the house is turned off and that the radio, stereo and TV are off—there must be no wastage of electricity. All this checking takes an hour or more, delaying bedtime. He sits on the toilet for an hour before bed, pushing and straining to the extreme, just in case he didn't "get it all out." He uses an entire roll of toilet paper and wiping until he bleeds to be sure that there "isn't any left behind." When Bob finally ends up in bed, it is often past midnight."

When I asked Bob why wastage bothered him, he had to think about it for a minute. It wasn't that something calamitous might happen, such as a flood from a leaking faucet or decay and illness from leftover food. It was simple: Wasting wasn't morally right. Bob was so motivated and ready to take control of his life again that I wasn't fast enough for him! He seemed impatient with my explanations and ready to move on. "Okay," I said, after we made a hierarchy, "Let's go!"

We selected exposure targets and I suggested to Bob and his parents that he could proceed up the hierarchy during the week, at a comfortable pace, as and when he was ready. When Bob and his parents came in to see me in a week, there was jubilation written all over their faces. Bob's success at the exercises had taken all of them by surprise. All those months of struggle, all those hours of torture every night and in one week, Bob was able to go to bed leaving the lights and the radio on all night! He had habituated to the bad feeling. It no longer bothered him. You see, Bob understood that he wasn't going to have to leave lights on all night for the rest of his life. He just had to do it until he could get used to the feeling. Once he did, he could go back to the "normal" way of checking the lights.

Bob volunteered for his next big challenge: Not only was he not going to check the faucet more than once, he was going to deliberately leave it dripping all night! Just one week ago, it would have been unthinkable. Armed with the confidence of success and the sweet taste of victory in his mouth, Bob went on to RIDE not just hills but mountains. He conquered his fears of dripping faucets. The following week, he tackled and overcame doubts such as, "I'm not sure if I have to poop." When Bob returned to see me the following week, he was spending five minutes on the toilet instead of an hour, and wiping seven times instead of 50 or more. Bob and his parents were ecstatic. So was I, because I was going on maternity leave the following week, and we had undertaken a "crash course" of CBT. Bob's success surpassed all our expectations.

What role did Bob's parents play in his recovery? A critical one. Bob's parents were divorced and he lived with his mother, with whom he was very close. Both parents came to each session with Bob. Bob did not feel comfortable divulging many of his symptoms, especially those involving the bathroom, to his father. Bob's mother was typically encouraging, supporting, prodding and helping him get through rituals into the late hours of the night. Whereas Bob's father would have liked to be more helpful, Bob wasn't ready to share much with him. Bob's parents therefore rallied for him in different ways. Bob's father gave him verbal support, encouragement and praise and came to all sessions. He was willing to take on whatever role was most helpful to Bob in the moment. Bob's mother played a wider and more involved role.

Recognize OCD episodes: Both parents acknowledged OCD episodes for what they were. When Bob lounged on the couch and needed many prompts to get up and get ready for bed, Nina knew it wasn't just laziness or uncooperativeness. She recognized that Bob was reluctant to start the whole bedtime rigmarole of exhausting rituals. It was easier to just avoid them, delay and hope they would just go away. Nina helped Bob recognize and relabel his procrastination and avoidance.

Ally with your child: Nina and Bob had a tremendous alliance that made the world of difference to his ability to RIDE. She understood, she didn't blame or shame. Because she had so much empathy, she didn't get frustrated or angry with *him*—how can you get angry with someone when you really know what they are going through? She saw him as a victim of OCD, not a perpetrator of defiance. She was ready to help when he was ready to go. Bob trusted her implicitly. He confided in her. He knew he could count on her as his greatest advocate and ally.

Lead your child to the RIDE: Nina led Bob to the RIDE by leaving the faucets on, turning up the radio and otherwise setting up the exposure scenarios. When he wanted to check the medicine cabinet one more time, she closed it. When he asked one more question, she didn't answer it. Between visits, she helped him make choices about exposure exercises. Because of the strong alliance between them, the role of "co-therapist" was a suitable and fitting role for Nina. I coached Nina to become Bob's "co-therapist" in my absence due to my impending maternity leave.

Let Go so your child can do it: Nina let go, and let Bob take the risks he needed to take. She took the risk that he might fail and it paid off.

Yes! You did it! Reward and praise: Bob's parents were both there to acknowledge and celebrate his successes. They reinforced his effort, his courage and his victory.

CONFESSING AND APOLOGIZING

Anna burst in the door from school. "Mom, I'm sorry I was rude to you this morning. I'm really sorry, I'll try not to do it again. Did I just interrupt you? Were you trying to say something? Sorry, sorry." She turned to her father and said, "Dad, I didn't mean to ignore you. I'm sorry. Is that okay? Are things okay between us now?"

Anna's parents grimaced. Why, you might wonder, when most parents of a 13-year-old would give their right arm to hear the word "sorry" emerge from their teen's lips. What a sensitive, empathic and caring child! But that was exactly the problem. Anna was too caring and conscientious for her own good, or that of her family. It would have been fine if she really had something to be sorry about, but this was only the twentieth time today they had been through the apologies—for things she hadn't even done! No, she had not been rude to her mother, nor had she ignored her father that morning. The transgressions were all in her mind. A mind that had been consumed by OCD in the past few months. OCD that sat on her shoulder and whispered her "sins" into her ears. "You didn't treat Mom and Dad equally. Kiss them an equal number of times or you'll hurt their feelings. Better tell them how you were disrespectful to the late Mr. Harris today when you referred to him as "that dead guy." And how mean you were to the dog because you called him "lazy" in your head."

Anna knew she was overdoing it when she confessed her every thought and apologized ad nauseam. She knew she hadn't really, really been mean or nasty. Yet, the nagging doubts remained. She'd best just clear her conscience by confessing or apologizing. Her parents had gotten tired of it. First, they accepted the apologies, then they reassured her that she had not sinned or erred, and finally, they had thrown up their hands in despair. They didn't know what to do and it was driving them batty. No peace at the dinner table ("Please excuse me, I think I might have burped"), watching a little TV ("I think I was staring too long at that man's chest"), or just relaxing together ("I should be doing something useful instead of just sitting here"). The declarations of guilt echoed through the evening.

"I also have these other weird thoughts," Anna confessed sheepishly when she came to see me. "I think…I feel like…inanimate objects also have feelings, and I'm hurting them. Like, I can't decide on an apple after dinner, because if I pick one, the others will feel hurt. Or, when my Dad brought home a coconut from the store, I couldn't bear to see him crack it open, because it was like he was cracking it's head open. And that must have been painful to the coconut." Anna peered into my face, looking for that confirmation that she was indeed "crazy." She was immensely relieved when I matter-of-factly said, "Oh, yes, I've heard that one too. You haven't shocked me yet." "And then," she went on, "I have to pray. I have to pray for two hours to make sure I've prayed for everyone that I know, and throw in some extra prayers as insurance in case I missed someone. It's pretty tiring."

We made a RIDE hierarchy to enable Anna to get used to the bad feelings. Anna's exposure exercises included "provoking" OCD by deliberately doing the things it didn't want her to do. Anna said rude things to her parents on purpose, interrupted their conversations and burped loudly at the table (oh, joy)! She hugged one more than the other, just to be unfair. While she engaged in these exposures, she had to stick it out without doing any rituals until the guilty feeling passed. No more apologies, recantations or praying marathons.

While it might jar you to know that treatment would involve "prescribed rudeness," remember that it is the *feeling* of discomfort that is being targeted. To overcome OCD, Anna needed to do things that triggered her OCD and made her uncomfortable. What about her parents? Weren't they horrified and offended? On the contrary, they applauded Anna's brazen disrespect. That's because they understood perfectly what the Worry Hill was all about. They knew that Anna did not mean to offend them and had to merely "get the words out of her mouth" to realize that they were meaningless. They rallied enthusiastically for Anna as she exercised insolence. They knew that there was not a chance in the world that this child of theirs would be permanently impertinent.

What about praying? Was it appropriate to stop someone from praying if they wanted to? The fact is that Anna's "prayers" were not true spiritual experiences. Anna was not praying by choice; she felt compelled to pray to appease unfounded bad thoughts. True prayer is experienced as a satisfying and uplifting experience. Prayer as an OCD ritual is tormenting and threatening. CBT does not disturb the purpose or fulfillment of true prayer. It only restores what OCD has hijacked.

How did Anna's parents rally for her?

Recognize OCD episodes: When Anna began to confess or apologize, they put aside their impatience and acknowledged that it was OCD that she could not control.

Ally with your child: They tried to remain calm and composed and to separate their frustration with OCD from their support of Anna.

Lead your child to the RIDE: Anna's parents willingly accepted "insults" from Anna. Their willingness to become the targets of exposures made the RIDE even possible for Anna. Is it right to condone a teenager's insults to her parents? No, it isn't, but Anna wasn't insulting her parents. She was merely voicing her nonsensical thoughts so that she could see exactly how meaningless they were. Exposure would not have been as powerful if Anna could not have overcome feeling bad about saying "rude" things to her parents.

Let Go so your child can do it: Anna's parents did not reassure Anna when she began to waver. They did not accept her apologies. They turned a deaf ear to her confessions. They had to let her find out for herself that she could overcome her bad feelings without their assurances. She had to ride the bicycle on her own.

Yes! You did it! Reward and praise: They were at the finish line, cheering her and celebrating her success. A special family dinner at which everyone burped out loud to express their satisfaction!

"JUST RIGHT" AND REPEATING

Alyssa was only five when it began. She remembered that she had to count everything she saw. Things on the wall, on the floor, on the TV, cars going by, people on the road. She couldn't stop even if she tried. She had to count even while she talked or sang. She had to touch things a certain way to "feel good." There were many scary things, like witches and ghosts and spiders, behind her, in front of her and at the foot of her bed. She had to sleep in a fetal position to keep the "scary things" away from her feet. The hardest thing by far for Alyssa was "the underwear thing." Alyssa felt that if her underwear didn't come up far enough, it would fall down. She had to pull it up often, "like 80 times a day" to keep it from falling. Then it was socks that had to stay up at her knees. It became harder and harder to find the right underwear and socks. Mornings became a dreaded time of indecision, arguments, tears and refusals. A drawer full of socks and another of underwear, but none could be worn. Special shopping trips to find underwear and socks with tighter bands—not good enough either. Alyssa would be late for school if it weren't for her mother hurrying her along, helping her pick underwear and socks that would be "just right." Alyssa finally quit wearing underwear altogether. She wore her swimsuit under her clothing when she went to kindergarten.

Alyssa was a bright five-year-old, already reading at a second grade level, playing the piano and dancing tap, ballet and jazz. She knew something wasn't right. "Why does my brain make me think these things?" the insightful youngster asked her mother. She had begged her mother to find a doctor to help her. She couldn't wait to get to our first appointment. We talked about OCD and the weird and scary things it made her think. She decided to call her OCD "Mr. Problem." Although she was eager to overcome OCD, she was initially skeptical and reluctant to do the exercises.

We started with the lowest items on the hierarchy. Stopping the counting and touching was easy. Alyssa's mother brought in a bagful of assorted socks and underwear to our session one day. She brought in a hand puppet that Alyssa had chosen to be "Mr. Problem." Alyssa picked out the "least of the evils." She slipped on a pair of socks and pulled them taut, all the way up to her knees. She walked around the room, allowing them to gradually slide down her legs, resisting the temptation to reach down and grab them. I put on my best skills as a puppeteer and played the role of Mr. Problem. At first, Alyssa's fear temperature was a nine, but she talked back to "Mr. Problem" and told him to stop bothering her. Alyssa was artistic, so we drew pictures and played board games until the urge to pull them up passed. It wasn't longer than 10 minutes. First, she inched down to a seven, then a six, and soon enough, a two on the *Fearmometer*. Then, she chose a looser pair of socks and repeated the steps. Each time, she was nervous but got through it. Soon, Alyssa was jumping up and down so that her socks would slip down easily. She watched the socks slide down slowly but surely. And finally, she wore her socks bunched up at her ankles. At the end of our session, Alyssa went home in the loose socks and "not right" underwear that had entered my office in a bag.

Because of Alyssa's young age and the fact that her symptoms interfered with her ability to get dressed and get to school, her mother Claire was more actively involved in the RIDE.

Recognize OCD episodes: Claire had to get Alyssa through the morning routine. She was able to recognize the pickiness and tantrums as OCD, not willful fussiness. Despite the frustration she felt, she was able to step outside the emotional circle and keep perspective.

Ally with your child: During calm times, Claire sat down with Alyssa and they talked about Mr. Problem. They talked about how annoying he was and how they would work together and do their best to get rid of him. Claire reiterated her commitment to help Alyssa overcome OCD.

Lead your child to the RIDE: Claire reviewed the steps of the RIDE with Alyssa to keep her focused and on track. She took her to the store to allow her to pick out a special "CBT folder" and a "Mr. Problem" puppet. She helped Alyssa save her drawings, Fearmometer and other CBT work in her CBT folder. I coached Claire to be a co-therapist so that she could guide and coach Alyssa through the same exposures at home. She gave Alyssa the power of choice in selecting the exposure exercises and deciding if she wanted to go ahead. Claire helped Alyssa stick with the exposures that she had chosen, and encouraged and cheered her along the way.

Let Go so your child can do it: Claire knew that eventually, Alyssa would have to get to the top of the Worry Hill on her own. She gradually gave her more leeway to make decisions on her own.

Yes! You did it! Reward and praise: Praise and encouragement abounded. But these successes were rewarded with a stop at the bagel store-a very special treat for Alyssa.

JUST SO OR NOT AT ALL: PERFECTIONISM

Eight-year-old Leo's mother Rita's note to me read: "Leo is nine and has increasing difficulty getting work done in school. According to his teacher, he rarely participates in class and practically refuses to do work. The frustrating part is that he is an intelligent child. We have had frustrations with Leo at home, but assumed it would pass with age. But it's getting worse, and only now we are realizing that there may be more to it than maturity. Here are some examples of what Leo's been doing:

❖ *As a toddler, Leo would do a puzzle over and over and over…15, 20 or 30 times. If he ran into trouble, he would get very angry, but would not accept help.*

❖ *He has tried piano lessons, video games, bike riding and the skateboard and never learned any of them. He gives up right at the beginning because he can't do them right away the way he thinks he should. If he can't do them perfectly, he would rather not do them at all.*

❖ *He won't eat lunch unless he has had breakfast, and no supper unless he has had lunch. The rules can't be broken. For example, if he gets up late and doesn't get around to breakfast and then lunchtime rolls around and I offer to make him a sandwich or soup, he gets very angry with me because he didn't eat breakfast. So he'll eat cereal or a bagel first, <u>then</u> eat a sandwich!*

❖ *He has an art kit that has markers, colored pencils and markers. He won't use the colored pencils because they will change length…they must all be the same length...and he doesn't want to get them out of order.*

❖ *I ripped a page out of a magazine the other day to use the coupon on it. He was very upset. He said that I had to put the page back. I asked him why and he didn't know...but I just had to tape the page back in.*

❖ *He hates to do school work, in school and at home. Each and every movement of the pencil requires prodding. If it's not perfect instantly, it's not any good at all.*

❖ *He can't decide what to eat at a restaurant. In fact, he sometimes won't order at all and shuts down completely. It's quite a scene.*

❖ *If he forgets something at school, folds a paper airplane wrong or his pencil needs sharpening, he just melts into a pile of tears—even in school, in front of all the other kids.*

❖ *He just can't take it if he makes a mistake. One word wrong on a spelling test, and he can't get over it. He has to blame the teacher because he can't accept that he made a mistake: Mom, he asked me words I didn't know how to spell.*

I feel compelled to tell you the good things about Leo. He is so bright, exceptionally witty and can be so much fun to be around. He loves to draw, he's so loving and caring and sometimes excessively worried about little things. For example, he is incredibly worried that the dog will get out and get away...I used to think, 'Oh, well, he'll get over it.' But he hasn't. He cries for the longest time over the littlest things. We need help."

Leo's obsession was about making mistakes. Mistakes that would cause fatal errors and drastic consequences. Ironically, it was not the really big mistakes in life that troubled him—it was the small matters that made his world fall apart. He couldn't risk those mistakes because they might be impossible to undo. It was just easier not to do things at all than to deal with that fear all the time. Leo's parents, particularly his mother, had become quite adept at protecting Leo from the potential for mistakes. She was nimble and quick-footed in staying one step ahead of him, smoothing the path, tearing down obstacles and fixing potential pitfalls before Leo reached them.

Why did Rita run around in a frenzy to make life easier for Leo? Because, although it wore her out, it was far less exhausting than enduring one of Leo's all-out "meltdowns" when he was thwarted. Leo crumbled into a sobbing, screaming mess quite readily when things didn't go just the way he had envisioned them. Homework was a scene. It didn't matter that they were in public; the scenes were there for all to see. Family outings were ruined; dinner at a restaurant felt like paying a big bill for an embarrassing drama. Clearing the path would have worked well enough, except that, pretty soon, she simply couldn't keep up with anticipating and fixing everything. New and unexpected things seemed to crop up all the time. Leo was so used to being "rescued" by his mother that he made no effort to get through a difficult situation. He simply expected his mother to work it out for him. He had not a clue as to what to do when things weren't perfect or didn't go his way. He had been deprived of that learning opportunity.

In order to overcome OCD's unrelenting demands for "perfection or else…" Leo had to learn to make mistakes and to live with being "good enough." He would have to come to terms with imperfection and uncertainty. The goal of CBT was to increase Leo's awareness of his OCD need for perfection, then teach him to deliberately break the rules and do things "just wrong" instead of "just right."

Leo wasn't too enthused at first about having to make mistakes on purpose. After all, hadn't he been trying so hard all these years to avoid blunders? But he begrudgingly conceded that life was no fun the way he lived it, and there were many things he'd rather do than be preoccupied with perfection. After the first week, Leo really got into it. It wasn't quite as bad as he'd expected, he confessed. In fact, the exercises went pretty well. Leo even proudly brought in his own version of the "Fear Thermometer" that he had made for himself on the computer. The pencils were sharpened into uneven lengths and paper planes were folded incorrectly on purpose. Leo even agreed to spell a few words incorrectly on purpose to find out the worst thing that would happen as a result. At the end of it all, Leo realized that blunders, bloopers and slip-ups were not the end of the world.

Leo's parents were critically involved in the RALLY. They worked together, using the same approach to handle Leo's OCD. Leo's father, Martin was able to keep perspective and not get drawn into Leo's demands. Rita, on the other hand, had to work hard to extricate herself from the role of "rescuer." She had meant well, trying to save her son from the grief he encountered; she was aghast when she realized that she had inadvertently fed his OCD. Learning how to handle his tantrums and tirades was a big part of their role.

Recognize OCD episodes: Leo's parents had to identify and label the episodes where he got "stuck" or dissolved into tears as OCD stumbling blocks, not deliberate difficultness on Leo's part. Making this distinction allowed them to help Leo label and rename OCD episodes too. It helped them extricate themselves from the storm of frustration that followed.

Ally with your child: In order to ally with Leo, his parents had to step back and take perspective. During moments of calm, they let Leo know that would need to step out of the tornado's funnel so that they could stand on their feet and be available to help Leo make it through the episode. They had to let Leo know that their disengagement was not lack of interest; rather, it was necessary to help him.

Lead your child to the RIDE: Leo's parents were there to support and cheer Leo on as he went on the RIDE. They let him make mistakes so that he could learn to live with them. Leo's parents talked about the mistakes they made and lived with everyday, both now and in the past. They talked about and condoned imperfection. They talked about learning how to live with uncertainty. They gave him examples of uncertainties they and he lived with everyday, of which they weren't always aware.

Let Go so your child can do it: Perhaps the most critical step in the rally was letting go. Rita had to recognize that she couldn't fix everything for Leo. She had to let him meltdown and figure it out for himself. She had to let him habituate to the uncomfortable feelings. She had to let him learn how to problem solve. She stopped the rescue mission. Martin and Rita learned how to channel Leo's negative energy into a productive learning experience using *Corrective Learning Experiences* (see Chapter 12). To their surprise, Leo's meltdowns were far less intense or prolonged when they let him learn how to cope with his anger.

Yes! You did it! Leo's parents were there when he made it through the RIDE. They gave him a lot of credit for what he had undertaken and for the courage and perseverance he showed. Leo felt a surge of self-confidence that he had never quite experienced before. He knew he had it in him. He could let things slide without becoming so upset.

FEARS OF HARM AND REASSURANCE SEEKING

"Is that blood in my spaghetti?" Four-year-old Danny examined his dinner as he sat down. "No, Danny, it's spaghetti sauce." "But it looks like blood—are you sure it isn't blood?" "Danny, I just told you, it's spaghetti sauce, see? Right out of this jar," replied his grandmother. Danny turned to his grandfather. "Grandpa, is this blood in my spaghetti?" Grandpa repeated what grandma had just said. "But it's gross, it looks like blood, it smells like blood. I can't eat it," said Danny as he ran from the table. Danny's grandparents sighed collectively. They'd been through this routine a few dozen times already.

If it wasn't the questions about blood, it was, "Is there poop in my pants?" Danny would ask repeatedly and check his underwear, sure that he had soiled it without his knowledge. At night, it was, "Is there a monster under my bed?" which would only be quieted after they bent down on fours and checked under his bed, in the closet, and behind the door. Every night, at least five times. Even as an infant, Danny had very rigid bedtime rituals and would "flip out" if the covers were not tucked in just right or if his mother or grandparents didn't say goodnight in the right sequence. They said to me with puzzlement written all over their faces, "He's such a smart boy too. He already knows the answers."

Danny was only four when we met, and a busy, active four-year-old at that. As an only child of a single working mother, Danny's grandparents David and Helen were "second parents" to him. A very bright and articulate youngster, he needed constant engagement with his mother or grand-parents. It was challenging to have a conversation without many interruptions, even after we arranged to take turns speaking. Danny seemed not to listen or attend, but it was clear he was taking it all in.

We talked about "silly worries" that kept coming back even after he knew that they weren't true. The silly worries chased him around the house. Why did he let the silly worries chase him, I asked. Had he thought about chasing them instead? Danny stopped for a moment; it was clear that that option had not occurred to him. He liked the idea. We agreed that there was no reason he should put up with being bullied around by the silly worries. Instead, when they came to scare him, he would turn around and scare them instead. It worked. We made it visual—silly worries with faces, arms and legs. Danny realized that he didn't have to passively accept the worries and look to his caregivers to take care of them—he could now do it himself.

Among other OCD fears, we tackled the "blood" fear. Danny didn't want to hear the word blood, see it written or see anything that resembled blood. "What would happen if I said the word "blood" out loud?" I asked. Danny wasn't sure what exactly would happen; only that he wouldn't like it. It would make him feel "yucky." "Okay," I replied, "do you want to keep feeling yucky about it, or do you want to chase it away?"

I remember the day Danny, his mother Sarah and I sat in my office, reciting the word "blood" over and over again, louder and faster, until it became a tongue twister. We sang the "Blood song" that we had invented on the spot. I lead the chorus, then Danny's mother and finally Danny joined in. We raised our voices to a crescendo and sang it in many octaves. At first, Danny was afraid of how he would feel, but we did the RIDE very gradually. His fear temperature at first was a 10, and within three minutes, he had habituated to a two. By that time, it felt very *silly*, but it wasn't scary anymore. We laughed about it. Danny's mother said, "I had no idea that this was what therapy was about." After weeks of avoiding blood, Danny was done with it in less than five minutes. The piece de resistance was when spaghetti was served for dinner. Danny ate it without batting an eyelid—no questions asked.

Being the "reassurance-giver" is a very taxing role for parents of children with OCD. It can drive many to distraction because it's a bottomless pit. Giving reassurance doesn't appease the questions because they are not *rational* questions; they come from the relentless doubts of OCD. It is normal and intuitive for parents to nurture their children and to assure them of their safety. Providing reassurance is therefore a tricky proposition-it is necessary in appropriate amounts, but you learn that you must draw the line when it begins to defeat its purpose.

Danny's mother and grandparents were intensely involved in his treatment. Given his young age, the family dynamics, as well as Danny's need for reassurance, of which they were the targets, they had to change a lot about their way of interacting with Danny. They had done their best, with the best of intentions, and Danny's best interest at heart. They had not realized how giving constant reassurance and participating in Danny's rituals was only sending him further into the depths of OCD. They cared so much, yet they had not found a way to help appease the relentless doubts.

Danny's family rallied for him in the following ways. They had to stop giving reassurance to OCD, and they had to learn new strategies for giving Danny comfort, assurance and control over OCD. We developed and discussed the following plan with Danny in advance, when he was calm and rational, and so that he would not be surprised or upset with any abrupt withholding of reassurance. With this plan, Danny's family learned how to put his questions in perspective and help him conquer his fears.

Recognize OCD episodes: Danny's family kept his questions in perspective. It was OCD asking the questions, not the rational Danny. They helped Danny keep the same perspective by asking him, "Is that you asking, or is that a silly worry?"

Ally with your child: During moments of calm, they helped Danny understand why answering the same question a million times only helped the OCD silly worries, not him. They prepared him for the change in their response that was soon to begin. They explained that they would stop answering his questions, not because they were mean and nasty, but because they were going to help him chase away the silly questions. Danny understood and accepted the change in plan.

Lead your child to the RIDE: They worked out a "weaning plan" with Danny's input. They would initially answer the same reassurance question no more than five times (instead of the usual 20), then twice, and finally, no more than once. They rehearsed and role-played with Danny exactly how they would respond to his questions henceforth. By doing so, Danny was prepared for the real thing when it happened. He was not rudely surprised and couldn't protest that he did not know.

Then, when the questions came, they asked Danny, "Do you want us to help you or help the silly worries? They asked if he already knew the answer to his question and encouraged him to answer it for himself. They encouraged him to chase the silly worries away instead of letting them chase him. They had a list of pleasant activities for Danny to engage in while waiting for the question urges to pass. They had to help him remember that the uncomfortable feeling would pass if he just waited it out. It wouldn't last forever and it would become easier each time he tried. He needed to hear that if he could stick it out, he would find out that nothing bad would happen. He would get used to the feeling. Their role was to remind him supportively of how the feeling would pass, and to help him stick it out until it was gone. When Danny was well on his way, they gave him more opportunities for exposure by talking about blood often and using the word in conversations as much as possible.

Let Go so your child can do it: Then it was time to let go. They had to give Danny a calm, supportive but firm response if he persisted with questions. When he got distressed, they had to stick it out, until their anxiety passed! They had to climb their own Worry Hill. It was a good experience for them to be in his shoes briefly and see how hard it could be to stick it out. When they felt frustrated, they "took space" and exited the situation.

Yes! You did it! Reward and praise: They were there to reward Danny with praise, and small goodies for any *effort* made in the right direction. They let him know that they noticed; they acknowledged how hard he was working. When he experienced *any* success, they reminded him of that in future situations, so that he built more confidence about being able to face OCD.

Danny's family also learned the strategies they had to AVOID. The following responses are just as important to other forms of enabling or participation in your child's rituals as they are to reassurance seeking.:

> *Parenting Responses to Avoid*
> ☐   Abrupt withdrawal of help with rituals
> ☐   Anger and frustration
> ☐   Going solo
> ☐   Surprises

1. Stopping reassurance abruptly: The "cold turkey" approach can be a shocking jolt into reality for most children, who are not equipped with either the cognitive or emotional resources to tide them through it. The "weaning" approach was the right one.

2. Anger and frustration: Yelling at Danny to "stop the silly questions" would only hurt his feelings and further alienate him. He would think they were mad at *him*, not OCD.

3. Going solo: Danny's family learned that it was best to enlist Danny's participation and consent to the weaning plan. Giving Danny some input made him feel more in control. He was more invested in it because it was a cooperative venture. Changing their response without his cooperation would have been less effective and more painful.

4. Surprises: Danny's family learned that Danny, like most children with OCD, didn't exactly care for surprise changes in parenting strategies. They found out the hard way when it threw off his routine. Preparing him ahead of time took the shock out of it. That meant that they couldn't be impulsive, spontaneous or reactive. They had to plan ahead for any changes they wanted to make.

MAGICAL THOUGHTS

Every morning, every night, it was a struggle. What to wear, what way to go down the stairs, everything was a game. Nobody knew. How could I tell

anyone that I couldn't wear my blue sweater because I might become fat?
Nobody at school could tell, and I wanted to keep it that way. Eventually, it
got unbearable. Everyday was another set of head games—if I didn't touch
the doorframe, I would gain 10 pounds. If I didn't wear the "right" socks,
people wouldn't like me anymore.

By the time Nancy, age 12, came to treatment, she was quite jaded about receiving any help for her OCD. She had initially been eager to get well and motivated for treatment, but the experience with her previous therapist had left her disillusioned. Eight weeks had gone by and Nancy didn't have any strategies for dealing with her OCD. She didn't quite trust what I was saying; she remained reserved and skeptical. It was clear that it was going to take her a while to trust me enough to open up and tell me her thoughts and fears. And yet, in order to devise exposures, I would need to know the details of her obsessions and compulsions. An intelligent, independent and determined young girl, I knew that Nancy would have to make her own decisions and be in charge of her own recovery.

I was forthright with Nancy in describing the Worry Hill and the RIDE. I told her that she would be the one to decide whether or not she wanted to undertake the RIDE, when, how far and for how long. I would be able to guide and coach her, if she was ready and willing. I assured her that there would be no pressure or coercion from her parents or me. Nancy's jaw seemed to relax a little. I sent her home to think about it. I asked her to call me with her decision. Nancy was back in my office the next week, after having called to say she was ready. She had had it with OCD. She was going to send it packing.

We started listing her obsessions and compulsions and making a hierarchy. "I have to touch the walls as I walk by and I have to walk through the doorway six times, or else…" "Or else?" I asked. "I'll become someone I don't like, I'll become a bad person," she replied, trying to hide her embarrassment. "OCD is pretty ridiculous, isn't it?" I asked. Nancy seemed relieved at my comment. "And if I wear my blue sweater, I'll become fat. I'll gain 10 lbs if I wear certain clothes. Or, sometimes, if I don't touch something, arrange the bathmat a certain way or run my foot over the carpet in the same spot, the kids at school won't like me or I'll fail my test."

Nancy's OCD was of the superstitious or "magical" variety. Her fears didn't have any logical connection whatsoever to her rituals. How does one become fat by wearing a blue sweater, or by forgetting to touch a wall? Nancy was well aware of the absurdity of her thoughts; yet, she was inexplicably trapped into following their injunctions.

Nancy started the RIDE. She was grateful to be given permission to consider OCD as an entity separate and distinct from herself. She wanted no part of it. She despised it. She had little trouble taking charge and making the choice to overcome OCD. We constructed an imaginal exposure exercise. Nancy imagined herself walking around in school, "fat, ugly and unpopular." She tried to talk to the other kids, but some ignored her and others smirked at how distasteful she looked. She tried desperately to pursue her peers and they began running from her. "Fat, ugly, horrible," they sneered. As Nancy allowed herself to say the words out loud and think about them, they didn't seem so potent anymore. Her anxiety began to fade. The "feeling" of being uncomfortable just seemed to pass, as she habituated to the thoughts. Nancy walked through doorways without going back and retracing her steps. She decided she would risk not touching the walls—she didn't turn fat or ugly, and her friends didn't seem to treat her differently. Then, one day, Nancy came in wearing her blue sweater! She had conquered OCD.

How did Nancy's mother Diane help her daughter through treatment? Although Nancy was only 12, she was mature, independent and self-motivated. She was also embarrassed to disclose her "senseless" thoughts or discuss them at length.

Recognize OCD episodes: Diane only helped Nancy recognize OCD episodes when she seemed to be stuck or perplexed. When Nancy's grades were dropping, Diane tried to take perspective and discern if it was OCD-related or typical adolescent stuff such as excessive socializing instead of studying. She asked Nancy directly and trusted her answer.

Ally with your child: Diane helped her daughter by giving her the freedom and the choice to take charge of her treatment. Allying meant understanding and trusting her to do it on her own, and giving her the space to do it without pressure or inquiry. It meant allowing Nancy to take responsibility for setting goals, expectations and consequences for herself.

Lead your child to the RIDE: Diane brought Nancy to all her appointments, was active in scheduling, and made efforts to reduce Nancy's workload and chores.

Let Go so your child can do it: The most important thing Diane did for Nancy was to let go, so she could do it on her own. She did not directly participate in exposures or homework exercises, given Nancy's age, maturity, and need for privacy.

Yes! You did it! Reward and praise: Diane was there to reward and praise, to let Nancy know she was proud of her courage and effort. Nancy was an avid and top-notch horseback rider and musician. Diane made an effort to give Nancy more opportunities to attend riding lessons and viola concerts, both very rewarding for Nancy.

HOARDING

"Michael can't let go of anything. He hoards everything, even his germs!" Michael was 14 at the time his exasperated parents brought him into my office. He had always been very possessive of his toys and belongings, even as a toddler. They had just thought it was rather charming, and didn't make much of it. As he grew, it wasn't so cute anymore. It became a nightmare of battles and tears to get Michael to let go of outgrown clothing, torn sneakers or broken toys. He stored them in bags in his room, even though there was almost no room in his closet. Then he began checking the garbage, lest something he wished to save had been thrown out.

When Michael's father remodeled his room, Michael was a mess, because his dad was hauling away the old drywall. He didn't want to let it go. He began bringing home the plates and utensils he had used in restaurants, as well as left over food that was fit only for disposal. He even carefully brushed the crumbs he had dropped from the table and brought them home in a napkin. "Why?" they asked, but Michael couldn't quite say. It was embarrassing to his family when others saw what he was doing, but it would have been more mortifying to have them witness the ruckus that would have ensued had they prevented Michael from his elaborate ritual. Michael starting staying home more and more and refusing to go out. He did not want to leave the house, he said, because he did not want his germs to leave the property. He wouldn't use the bathrooms at school, because he didn't want to leave his waste behind. He brought home bits of paper and other trash from school.

A few months prior to our meeting, Michael's mother had finally sold the swing set that the children had long outgrown. Michael had been furious at the time, because he didn't want it to go. Now, five months later, he had not gotten over it. He had been crying hysterically about it, saying he had been tricked and no one asked his permission. He wanted his mother to retrieve the swing set from the family that purchased it at the garage sale. Michael wished he could be dead so he could be with his belongings and not worry about losing them.

The last straw came on a trip to the grocery store. Michael reached into the pockets of his jacket and found sand in them—remnants of a trip to the beach in the summer. As he drew his hand out, a fistful of sand spilled to the floor. Michael bent down to pick it up. An unsuspecting store employee, trying to be helpful, came over right away with a broom and swept it away with a gesture of courtesy. Michael was beside himself with panic. His parents decided to leave right away, fearing a scene. All the way home, Michael cried, kicked and screamed in the car as if his world was coming to an end. He wanted the sand back. He couldn't leave it at the store. "Call the manager," he demanded, "Tell them to send my sand back to me. Call them right now. It's mine, I don't want to leave it there."

Was Michael afraid to let go of his "germs" because he might contaminate others? When I asked him what would happen if his germs were scattered about, Michael had to think hard about it. What would his germs do if they were left about? "Nothing," he replied. "I'm not worried about others getting sick. I just want my germs. They belong to me, no one else." It was about *possession*, not contamination.

Michael was initially defensive. None of it was a problem. It didn't bother him and he didn't see why it should bother "them." I spoke to

Michael privately, without his parents present. "Do you really like spending all your time worrying about what you left behind where?" I asked. Michael agreed begrudgingly. He had gotten tired of being the "troublesome one" at home. "No blame, no shame," I said to Michael and his family. We have to work together here if Michael is to get rid of OCD. They were ready and willing.

I described the Worry Hill and the RIDE. It seemed to make perfect sense to Michael. It was as if a light bulb went on. "I just never thought of it that way before," he confessed. As always, the next step was to make a hierarchy of Michael's fears. "Have you ever tried leaving your things behind on purpose and seeing how that feels?" "No," he replied. "I've always been too scared." Michael agreed to start with the easiest things possible. He left a pencil shaving on his desk at school and survived it. He dropped a juice carton into the garbage can at the mall and lived to tell the tale. His confidence grew and he was enthused about moving up the hierarchy. He took used napkins from home and dropped them in trash receptacles at stores, school and restaurants. He even flicked a crusted piece of dirt off his shoe at the grocery store and left without a backward glance.

One morning, Michael's mother was bursting with excitement. "You are not going to believe this," she exclaimed. "Michael and I packed five big bags of clothes and toys from his room to take to the Salvation Army! He just decided to do it, on his own. I didn't even bring it up. We dropped it off on the way here too, and he didn't even make a fuss. Oh my goodness, I've been waiting to clean up his room for two years—I can hardly believe what I'm telling you." Michael beamed with quiet pride. "That was something very high on my list," he confessed. "But I thought about some kids who really need clothes and toys, instead of them doing nothing in my room." By the end of treatment, Michael was helping his father haul the drywall from his room. He was enthusiastically picking out wallpaper and furniture. The "never-to-be" remodeling project was finally underway.

Recognize OCD episodes: Michael's parents had to work hard to hold their instinctive angry reaction to his absurd rules and demands. They had to stop, think and proceed, realizing that Michael was reacting to OCD.

Ally with your child: Michael's parents let him know that they would support him in his battle against OCD, and would be available in whatever way he needed them. They abandoned the power struggles and arguments that were typical of OCD episodes at their home.

Lead your child to the RIDE: Michael's parents helped him externalize and reframe OCD episodes and reminded of the power of choice. He could do it if he wanted to!

Let Go so your child can do it: For the most part, Michael handled exposures on his own.

Yes! You did it! Reward and praise: Michael was praised and given positive attention for his efforts. He even chose the décor and wall hangings for his newly remodeled room!

FREQUENTLY-ASKED QUESTIONS

We started therapy a few weeks ago. My daughter did well for the first few sessions. She stopped washing her hands and counting. But now, things seem to be creeping back in. Is this normal? What should I do?

Discuss the matter with your child's therapist. Your daughter's OCD may be "waxing" and she needs to do the exposure exercises with greater vigor. It is also possible that your daughter may not have habituated during exposure. Perhaps she just "went along" with the exercises, but did not truly allow herself to face the fear, or engaged in mental rituals instead.

My daughter just started CBT. We came home and started doing the exercises the therapist suggested. My daughter is kicking and screaming like she's "possessed." Her OCD has taken a turn for the worse! It's scary and we don't know what to do.

It must be really frightening to see your child become a different person. It is not necessary for a child to become so upset although it can sometimes happen. You may be witnessing the extinction burst, as discussed in Chapter 7. There is a certain level to which a child and parents have to struggle through the challenges of CBT, but there is a threshold—if your child becomes too frightened, it can backfire, and the child may refuse to do CBT altogether. A CBT therapist will try to optimize this balance between challenging and pushing too far and will make continuous adjustments to the CBT program to keep this balance. Call your therapist immediately and explain what is happening. Perhaps your daughter did not understand the changes that were going to occur or perhaps the exercises are too high on the hierarchy for her. CBT should be paced gradually, so that children can be introduced to it gently. Your therapist may suggest ways to modify the exercises, explain things to your child, give her breaks periodically, and most of all, help you find ways to persist through the rough times. There might be nuances of the exercises that have to be adjusted. Don't give up—CBT is very effective for up to 80% of children, but there are many glitches to be worked out initially. It is a dynamic and evolving process, not just a prescribed formula.

How long should an exposure exercise last?

There is no time limit for exposures. An exposure should last long enough for the anxiety to subside. When that happens, it is a sign that habituation is setting in. Exposure is only effective when it results in habituation. If it is ended before anxiety subsides, it is no different than a ritual or escape. On average, children habituate to their OCD fears within 10 minutes, although it could be as little as two minutes for a minor fear and longer than 10 minutes for a fear that is high on the hierarchy.

Chapter 12

Parenting Challenges

Some days you tame the tiger. And some days, the tiger has you for lunch.
Tug McGraw

Having a child with OCD can be frustrating, trying, aggravating and rewarding. Things that any "normal" child should be able to do quickly can be a struggle. For instance, it can take many redirections and positive talk to get my 11-year-old son to brush his teeth in the morning. He may look lazy or unmotivated. Part of it is that he doesn't want to fall into the "trap" of a compulsion and it's also fatiguing and scary to fight off the unwanted feelings, so it's much safer to lay on the couch than to start up something.

Nina, mother of Bob

Parenting is such a joyous but humbling experience. It is one of those things in life for which we can never be completely prepared. Even the best primed among us will encounter many trials along the way. For many, parenting may feel like a precarious tightrope act. Just when we think we have it down pat, the rope shifts from under our feet as our children grow and change. Our parenting skills need to be dynamic and flexible to fit their evolving needs. Even at the best of times, it takes hard work, patience and fortitude. It is never easy.

No parent is prepared for the upheaval that OCD can bring. Like most parents, you are caught off guard when it comes to OCD. The good common sense that got you through rough spots in the past doesn't work with OCD. In fact, it may even seem to work against you now. You don't have a good benchmark against which to compare your situation or other parents from whom you can learn. Family and friends tell you that all your child needs is good old-fashioned discipline. You may feel a sense of despair.

The intent of this chapter is to help you map your own parenting expertise to a new and uncharted territory. It is geared towards helping you build your confidence to sustain your parenting efforts through the difficult times. The more confident you are, the more effectively you will be able to put your skills to good use. I will discuss the nuts and bolts of everyday parenting—the foundation on which you build the skills to parent effectively in the world of OCD. I will discuss strategies for specific problems that you might encounter on this parenting journey. You will learn how to get yourself and your child through the tough times, take back control from OCD and restore your household to its normal functioning. Parenting strategies for children with other forms of anxiety are described in *Worried No More: Help and Hope for Anxious Children*, listed in the *Resources* at the end of this book.

THE PERFECT PARENT

Before we proceed, I would like to discuss what we all aspire to be: The Perfect Parent. The perfect parent knows what's best for his or her child at all times, never acts in haste, never makes a mistake and never needs a break from the children. Erma Bombeck puts it in perspective so aptly:

"The art of never making a mistake is crucial to motherhood. To be effective and gain the respect she needs to function, a mother must have her children believe that she has never engaged in sex, never made a bad decision, never caused her own mother a moment's anxiety and was never a child."

As you read this, you know I am talking about the myth of the perfect parent. Perfect parents are what we are *before* we have children. It's the only time we can be perfect parents because myth meets reality when we have children of our own. The truly perfect parent is one who accepts his shortcomings and humanity with realism and does the best he can in the circumstances.

DAILY DILEMMAS: DID I DO THE RIGHT THING?

"I hate you! You're the worst mom in the world!" Your child clearly needs some convincing that you are the perfect parent. You cringe as you hear the painful words from the child for whom you would give your life. You have worried yourself sick, compromised your performance at your job, given up things you enjoy and humiliated yourself for this child. And you get these words in appreciation, just because you didn't hold the door open long enough for her to pass through without touching it.

You might be relieved to know that this scenario and many similar ones are common in many households with OCD. The child you knew as gentle, loving and sensible has suddenly turned into someone you don't recognize. It seems like she doesn't recognize you either, because she has stopped heeding your words. Instead, she follows the ridiculous rules of OCD: *Wash your hands 23 times. Change your clothes every hour. You can't go to sleep until you have checked your room and arranged all your belongings. No rest until your homework is perfect and you've said your prayers for an hour*...and so on and so forth. How do you get your child to bed before midnight, get her up on time in the morning or get her through homework without becoming public enemy No. 1?

Like so many other parents, you may wonder, *"Am I doing the right thing or am I making things worse for my child? Is she doing her best? Is she taking advantage of the situation? How do I know when to set limits and when to look the other way? How do I know when to shield her from paralyzing fear and when to urge her to confront reality? When do I push harder and when do I back off? How do I know how much to protect and how much to let go? How do I extricate myself from the dependency of OCD?"* You struggle to find that balance of kindness and firmness, empathy and reality, protection and the freedom to learn, support and indulgence, helping and enabling. You make many mistakes along the way as you try to find that middle ground.

Whereas the right balance is every parent's goal, it can be an elusive one because it is not static. It shifts continuously in response to the circumstances. The tightrope walker has achieved just the right balance, until the rope moves. Then, he must carefully regain his balance to adjust to the shift in the rope. If he doesn't react quickly, he will lose his footing and fall.

When OCD disrupts the equilibrium of your home, everything changes. Your parenting skills have to adapt to the changes that OCD brings in order to regain that balance. It might mean that the expectations you have for yourself and your child must shift. The laws of your home might have to be rewritten.

Before we talk about how to parent your child through the crises of OCD, let me cover the essentials of everyday parenting. Many or all of them may be familiar to you, although you may have conceptualized them differently. You may find these a helpful refresher or you may recognize that you need to substantially realign your style of parenting to tried and true principles.

THE NUTS AND BOLTS OF PARENTING

Raising your child to understand the dos and don'ts of life in a constructive and nurturing way can be a challenge. The strategies that help children learn these lessons of living can fall under two broad umbrella categories: The Three S's—*Security, structure and stability*—and the Three P's—*Proactive, positive and preventive*.

The Three S's and the Three P's provide the foundation for constructive parenting. It is on this foundation that your approach to handling the tough times will be built. It provides the stable base from which you operate. Parenting is not a task; it is a relationship between you and your child. It is dynamic and evolving. Because you and your child continue to learn, grow, change and influence each other reciprocally, your parenting style and skills will mirror this process. Like any other parent, you will not be able to follow all of these guidelines all of the time. It is only important that you attempt to keep to them as much of the time as is humanly possible. The rest of the time…you will do very well if you are willing to learn from your mistakes.

The Three S's: Security, structure and stability

Security, structure and stability are the essential backdrop against which children grow and flourish. When children feel loved and nurtured unconditionally, they trust their parents and feel secure. When your child recognizes that you have his greater good at heart, he is more likely to want to please you and abide by your expectations. He is also more ready to learn from his mistakes when he feels safe enough to make them. Structure refers to having fair, reasonable and consistent expectations and routines for all members of the family. Structure makes the child's life more predictable and gives him a sense of stability. Expectations must be suitable to your child's age, developmental capabilities and temperament, because he can only meet them if he can understand them and has the ability to meet them. The following strategies help build security, structure and stability:

❖ *Do as you would have your child do*

Children learn in many ways, but a great deal of how they learn to negotiate the emotional challenges of life comes from seeing us do it. Children witness the manner in which we cope with the ups and downs of life. They see our reactions when we are happy, sad, angry, disappointed, frustrated, overwhelmed or afraid. They are perceptive to our subtle, non-verbal anxiety cues even when we think we are hiding our feelings from them. You may not realize how much your child emulates your actions and your beliefs. If you want to be a positive example, you may first need to become more self-aware of your behaviors. It is easy to become accustomed to reacting in automatic ways without thinking. If you want your child to learn healthy ways to handle disappointment, resolve conflict and problem-solve difficulties, teach him not just by your words, but also by your deeds.

❖ *Set kind but firm limits*

The more enjoyable moments of parenthood are those when you can say "Yes" to your children and experience the satisfaction of witnessing their pleasure. But along with that pleasure comes the responsibility of saying "No," which is not something parents generally enjoy doing. Yet, it is often necessary to say "No" to our children. Although children protest restrictions and rules, *kind but firm limits* teach children that not everything they desire is necessarily available or good for them. We set limits because we care. We do it to protect them from the dangers of which they are not yet mindful. You say "No" when your child wants to ride his bicycle without a helmet, stay up past his bedtime on a school night or eat one too many cookies. You set limits because your child does not always know what's in his best interest either at the moment or in the long-term. You risk your child's displeasure because his safety and well-being are more important.

Kind but firm limits help children feel safe and secure

Just as it is a parent's responsibility to set limits, it is a child's responsibility to test those limits! All children test the boundaries to see if they hold true. Knowing that there are safe and sturdy boundaries within which they can operate helps children feel more secure that someone is watching out for them. Limits must be sensible and practical. You must let your child know how far he can go for his own good. When your child feels secure and loved, he understands that the limits are for his own good. He may not like them, but he is willing to accept them because he trusts your intentions.

❖ *Say it, mean it and do it*

Say it, mean it and do it highlights the need for consistency in parenting. Choose your words carefully, because you must honor them. When you do, your child knows you are reliable and predictable. The rules of his world are steady and constant, not erratic. He will push the limits to suit his own preferences. If you fail to follow through on your word, your child will know that he does not need to take you seriously. You confuse your child with mixed messages. You lose your credibility with him and thereby your parental authority. Don't promise anything that you can't deliver. Don't make empty threats in a moment of anger. If you recant your position because your child's protests wear you down, you give him the message that the louder he protests the more likely he is to win.

You must be consistent from one time to the next and one situation to the next. There must also be consistency between parents. Both parents must apply the same rules and consequences. If not, the child will find the loopholes and the parent whose rules (or lack thereof) suit him the best.

❖ *Allow your child natural opportunities to handle disappointment*

When you set limits, you deny your child something he wants. He may therefore be unhappy and disenchanted with you. Although you might feel bad about letting him down, it is important to remember that learning how to deal with disappointment is a very crucial coping skill in life. You are doing your child a favor if allow him to learn these lessons gradually in the safety and security of your home. When your child encounters obstacles, he learns how to problem solve, seek alternatives, develop patience, delay gratification and work hard for the things he wants—skills that are necessary to live in our world. Share your experiences (within reasonable limits) with your child, so he sees that you are no stranger to stumbling blocks, and that these are a part of life.

If you allow your child to have his way with everything and go out of your way to shield your child from disappointment, you are doing your child a disservice. He won't be prepared for setbacks when he is older. Rearranging the world to appease your child is neither realistic nor sustainable. Sooner or later, you won't be able to fend off every obstacle for your child.

❖ *Believe in your child*

Lady Bird Johnson once said, *"Children are likely to live up to what you believe of them."* Have faith in your child. Believe that he can soar high and allow him to spread his wings and fly. Although we must help our children make the right start, we have to eventually let them put their own skills and resources to the test. We teach them how to take appropriate and measured risks and survive dangers. We encourage them to face healthy and necessary challenges. We teach them that they can cope on their own and problem solve. We encourage independence and adventure in good measure. We push slightly above their comfort limits. We foster self-reliance because we won't always be at hand to take care of them.

The Three P's: Proactive, positive and preventive

You will be on the right track in teaching your child the dos and don'ts of life if you think the Three P's: proactive, positive and preventive. All children sometimes behave in desirable ways at times and misbehave at other times. Since it is hard to behave and misbehave at the same time, the more you can get your child to behave, the less time and inclination he has to misbehave. When you are proactive, positive and preventive, you can focus on developing and increasing your child's good behaviors so that there is simply less room for misbehavior.

❖   *Be proactive*

Being proactive is the opposite of being reactive. It involves using foresight rather than hindsight. Don't wait for a bad situation to arise to teach your child how to handle it. Think ahead about what you would like your child to learn. When possible, give your child the guidance and the tools to handle the situation *ahead* of time. Teach your child what she *should* be doing instead of what she *shouldn't* be doing. Sometimes, we forget that children don't automatically know how to behave in new situations. We get upset when they misbehave and tell them what is *not* acceptable, but neglect to tell them what *is* acceptable instead. We assume that because, as adults, the appropriate action is obvious to us, it is similarly evident to a child. It's intuitive to say, *"Don't do that, that's not okay,"* but we neglect to tell children what is okay to do instead.

We are setting children up to misbehave when we don't let them know in advance what to expect and how to respond. Then we penalize them for walking into the trap we set. You are engaging in proactive parenting when you prepare your child for new situations, provide clear expectations, give appropriate information, invite and respond to your child's ideas. Engage your child in setting goals and consequences for himself. He will be more invested and responsible when he has input into the matter.

Megan's parents want to make sure that their experience at the family get together is a pleasant one for them and for Megan. They want to reduce the element of surprise and give Megan the advantage of preparedness. They give her some general guidelines about what to expect at the family gathering and provide guidance on how she could handle herself in a variety of situations. They coach her in social graces and table manners. They prepare her for the fact that there might be uncomfortable moments. They invite Megan to brainstorm with them the ways in which she could respond if Aunt Rita gushes excessively or cousin Patrick teases her. Megan now knows what to expect and feels more confident in handling herself independently. The pressure of navigating her way through the event entirely on her own has been eased. Megan can direct her energy to having a good time.

❖ *Be positive*

Being positive involves teaching your child to believe that he is fundamentally a good person. When you focus on your child's strengths, talents and abilities, you nurture his sense of worth and self-esteem. You divert your energy and his to the good things rather than the undesirable. Attention gives children feedback about their performance. Greater attention results in a behavior being strengthened; less attention weakens it. Becoming aware of the ways in which you pay attention to your child is necessary to ensure that you channel it only towards desirable behaviors.

Spend some *YAMA* time (see Chapter 9) every day with your child. It involves committing at least 15 minutes a day (and preferably more) to relax and "yammer" about nothing in particular. (If you cannot find 15 minutes in a day to do this, you should take a serious look at your priorities). During this time, do nothing but be with your child physically and emotionally, allowing him to enjoy just being with you. Try not to let your chores and tasks occupy your mind because your child will be aware that you are distracted. Appeal to the good person in your child (every child has one) by talking to him about caring, love and give-and-take among family members.

Create family rituals that build positive memories for your child. Your child will be able to draw on these memories when he is older and find solace and comfort in them. Family rituals include things like the weekly trip to the library, baking cookies on rainy days, putting up holiday decorations together and other such events.

It is human nature to want quick results, but good behavior doesn't develop overnight. If you want your child's behaviors to improve, you must *shape* or mold the behavior in the right direction by working at it in small, manageable steps. Small steps lead to big changes. Select one or two behaviors to focus on at one time. When your child is successful, move to the next step or next behavior. Give your child choices. Let him know what consequences will follow each choice. Teach him to weigh the consequences that follow his choices and help him make the choice that is best for him. The way in which you attend to your child is a major influence in shaping her behavior. Types of attention, rewards and punishments are discussed in the next section.

❖ *Be preventive*

Linda knows that her son Alex is quite tired and irritable when he returns from school. It takes him a lot of energy to get through the day. She has learned that if Alex does not get some quiet time to "unwind," the evening deteriorates into a crescendo of squabbling, bickering and punishment. Nothing is accomplished. Linda and Alex now have a routine that prevents things going from bad to worse. Alex has a healthy snack immediately upon his return and then watches his favorite show on TV for half an hour. There are no interruptions, no questions asked and no provocations from his sister, who is in another room doing her homework. The healthy food and half hour of rest works wonders for Alex's demeanor. He is relaxed, refreshed and far more pleasant to be around.

Linda has averted an evening of censure and failure for Alex by using a preventive strategy. She has made it possible for him to self-calm by *taking space*. Taking space is a way to terminate over stimulation by moving to a quiet place where interaction is suspended. It allows the intensity of the child's emotions to abate without any further irritation from the environment. It allows the child a safe way to release the pent-up emotions of the day. Although it may appear similar to a time-out, it is really quite different because it is a *voluntary* behavior that is preventive in nature. It is not a punishment for misbehavior.

Teach your child to voluntarily take space to calm down. Ask him, "Would you like to take space now?" and provide a pre-designated safe place for him. Offer him deep breathing or other calming and soothing activities such as music to hasten the process of calming down. Teach calming self-statements. Encourage him to initiate taking space on his own. When your child seeks taking space on his own, he begins to take control of terminating his own escalation. Gradually, he learns to recognize early warning cues and to avert them before they accelerate into a crisis. Reward him when he makes the effort to self-calm.

Alex now knows that he can take space whenever he gets irritable. He can ask for a break from the situation by exiting to a quiet place where he can calm down. It allows him the time to "chill out" and feel refreshed. Linda stays one step ahead of the situation, catching distress early and nipping it in the bud to prevent unnecessary misbehavior.

Being preventive involves being alert to the context, time of day and triggers that trip the switch for misbehavior in your child. Being alert at times of undue stress and pressure can help avert many undue crises. There are often simple reasons for misbehavior. In fact, they are so simple that they are easily overlooked or discounted. When your infant cried, you knew that he was probably hungry, sleepy, soiled, bored or lonely. You went through and eliminated each of these basic needs systematically. If you were fortunate, he stopped crying. As children get older, it's easy to forget that these same needs continue to operate to drive distress and irritability. Because crying was the only way your infant knew how to communicate, you actively tried to ascertain and fix the reason for his discomfort. Just because your child now has language skills does not mean that he knows how to recognize or express these needs directly. Teach your child to become aware of his bodily needs and cues, and to use words rather than indirect actions to communicate them. Instead of whimpering constantly, he learns to say, "Mom, I'm hungry." Instead of taunting his sister, he learns to say, "I'm frustrated. This homework is too hard."

YAMA time can also be used preventively. Some children need to be "reoriented" when they wake up in the morning, to start their day out right. Others need it to decompress when they return home from school. Some need it at bedtime, so they can get all the stresses of the day off their chests and sleep easy. Yet others may need all three. It is helpful to review what the day holds or what has transpired with your child. "What went well for you today? What did not go so well?"

Table 11: The Three P's: Proactive, Positive and Preventive

Be Proactive

❖ Negotiate or set expectations child ahead of time, not after the fact
❖ Tell your child what you expect her to do instead of what not to do
❖ Invite your child to set expectations and consequences for himself
❖ If your child does not participate, set expectations without his input
❖ Rehearse and role-play potentially challenging situations

Be Positive

❖ Let your child know often that you notice his good behavior
❖ Build your child's self-esteem by focusing on his capabilities
❖ Focus on one or two desirable behaviors to develop in your child
❖ Commit to daily You and Me Alone (YAMA) time with your child
❖ Appeal to the good person in your child
❖ Teach your child the Power of Choice
❖ Give rewards for making good choices or taking the initiative
❖ Be credible—say what you mean and do what you say

Be Preventive

❖ Stay one step ahead of your child in anticipating problem situations
❖ Praise your child when he does not misbehave, instead of noticing him only when he does
❖ Give your child fair warning of changes; prepare him to cope.
❖ Be consistent and predictable
❖ Learn to detect early warning signs of misbehavior
❖ Identify patterns in misbehavior and find remedies accordingly
❖ Use daily YAMA time with your child to steer him back on track
❖ Teach your child to detect his own early warning cues
❖ Give face-saving reminders
❖ Teach your child to use words to communicate rather than actions
❖ Teach your child to "take space," self-calm and release negative feelings appropriately
❖ Avoid arguments, lengthy explanations and power struggles
❖ When you child misbehaves, take action quickly, quietly and firmly

Being preventive also calls for anticipating and averting situations that are ambiguous and confusing to the child. When you are consistent, predictable and steady, you provide clear cues for your child. When you are inconsistent, you create situations that are a "set up" for the child because he is not sure what behaviors are appropriate. Being preventive also involves paying attention to your own reactions and responses that add fuel to the fire. Many futile power battles and arguments can be easily avoided with some conscious forethought (see *Corrective Learning Experiences* later in this chapter). Arguments make you more frustrated and reinforce your child's misbehavior. Give your child reminders when bad behavior begins, so that he has the chance to correct it without losing face.

ALL ABOUT REWARD AND PUNISHMENT

Some parents are concerned about using rewards and punishment as incentives for their children to behave in the right ways. They believe that children should learn to do things because they are internally motivated to do them, not because they are externally "bribed."

The fact is that it is really not an either-or proposition. We are motivated both internally and externally. In the early years, children rely more on external rewards to motivate them. Internal motivation develops with age and maturity. External rewards help children get *started* on the right path. Over time, the intrinsic satisfaction of doing "good," pleasing parents and oneself takes the place of pleasure derived from external rewards.

Some consider rewards and punishments a thing of the past, associated with corporal punishment and raps on the knuckles. For others, it conjures up images of rats in cages pressing levers for pellets in an animal laboratory. These associations are unfortunate because positive or negative consequences are so much more than that. The fact is that reward and punishment are an integral part of our daily lives, whether we recognize it or not. We are influenced by them everyday in more ways than we realize. Don't we all like to receive approval and positive feedback? Don't we work hard to avoid censure? We work harder for recognition and praise from bosses, spouses and friends. Our behaviors have natural consequences that are either pleasing or unpleasant to us. These consequences influence our decisions to continue or stop the behaviors. Much as we may love our jobs, we work for a paycheck. A bigger paycheck is usually more attractive than a small one. We encourage our children to get good grades because the world generally offers more rewards for academic success.

Rewards and punishments are not inherently wrong. They only become wrong when they are given for the wrong reasons or in disproportion to the action. If you are rewarding your child for doing something that is in his best interest, you are okay. If you are rewarding your child because it suits your convenience, because you want him to do something for you that you would rather not do, or to buy his affection, you should rethink your motives. Parents who reward excessively and disproportionately to the context must be watchful that they are not compensating for their own anxiety or guilt. If you buy your child an expensive gadget to make up for having yelled at him or if you promise your teenager a car for taking out the garbage you should probably stop and reconsider your intentions. Likewise, punishment is misused when it is used as a vehicle of your anger and is meted out as vengeance.

Rewards and punishment can actually do more harm than good if they are used haphazardly and inconsistently. However, this is a "user problem," not a problem with the rewards or punishment themselves. Say what you mean and do what you say. Always give your child a reward to which you have committed—if not, your child will not take anything you say seriously. You let down your child and do damage to your parental authority when you cannot follow through. Why would he listen to you when you renege on your promises?

Types of rewards

There are different types of rewards and punishments for behavior, as described in this section and the next. Praise, planned rewards and unplanned rewards are "behavior starters." They help children initiate and continue to engage in certain behaviors. In contrast, planned inattention, natural consequences, logical consequences, time out and planned penalties are "behavior stoppers" because they act as deterrents to the behaviors in question. In most cases, you can rely on "behavior starters" to increase your child's desirable behaviors. However, if undesirable behavior recurs and continues, you may need to use a combination of "starters" and "stoppers" to prevent it.

A few things to keep in mind before I describe various forms of reward and punishment: Rewards should be given for a child's *effort* rather than actual success or final performance. This ensures that it is the child's *behavior* in the right direction rather than the eventual outcome that is of importance. Outcomes are not always successful, for a variety of reasons, but a child's effort to succeed is what counts most. Rewarding for effort also recognizes the fact that the child might not have *wanted* to do the right thing or did not enjoy it, but made the effort anyway. It would probably have been easier for your child to continue to misbehave than to exercise self-control, share, be polite or wait until later to do something. Rewards and punishments should be practical, feasible and proportionate to the achievement. They are not universal but specific to each child, and may change over time. In other words, what one child likes may not appeal to his sibling, and your child may like one reward for a week and then lose interest in it.

> Reward for effort more than for success

❖ *Praise and attention*

We often complain that our children take us for granted, but we are just as often guilty of doing the same. We take our children for granted when we don't acknowledge the times they behave well and don't appreciate the effort they put into it. In fact, we conveniently forget all about them when they are quietly going about their business, not making any trouble for us. This is when it's most important to praise and attend to your child—when he is doing what he needs to be doing and not clamoring for your attention negatively. Make an active, deliberate effort to recognize, acknowledge, praise and encourage any behavior that is in the right direction, regardless of how minor it is. Be spontaneous and surprise your child with praise when he least expects it. "I noticed how well you did your homework with only one reminder today." "Thanks for having dinner with us and having a pleasant conversation." "It was really nice of you to help your sister with her project." "I really appreciate your help in the kitchen." "It was very thoughtful of you to pick up the books that fell off the shelf."

Noted psychologist and child expert Haim Ginott reminds parents, "If you want your children to improve, let them overhear the nice things you say about them." Praise nurtures children and builds their self-concept. Eventually, children learn to recognize their own desirable behaviors and praise themselves. We need the ability to believe in ourselves even when things don't go well. Don't be concerned about being too generous with praise and attention—there is much less potential for harm from too much praise than there is from frugal praise.

❖ *Planned rewards*

Planned rewards are those that are negotiated in advance to follow a desirable behavior. "You can have a cookie after you eat your dinner." "You can have an hour of computer time if you do your homework without reminders." Planned rewards may be *material, social* or *activity* focused. Material rewards include toys, food, clothing and other possessions. Social rewards involve time with other family members or friends. Activity rewards may include a trip to the pool or dinner at a favorite restaurant. Social rewards are preferable to material rewards because they also pro-vide increased positive interaction time within the family. Children may enjoy rewards such as a bicycle ride with dad, a board game with mom or ice cream for the family.

Younger children need immediate and more tangible rewards, as their ability to wait for even short times is limited. They also respond well to sticker or star charts. Older children prefer privileges such as later bed-times or curfews, additional computer or phone time, or an outing to the mall with friends. They also like to earn tokens or points that can be traded for different types of rewards, much like paying money to buy goodies. Adolescents can be involved in negotiating privileges and in "contracting" for rewards in exchange for meeting responsibilities.

Some parents say, "I can't do this. It's too much work." Yes, it is defi-nitely work, but it is probably a lot less work than trying to undo "bad" behavior later. As with most things in life, it comes with hard work and commitment. Will you be tied down to rewarding your child forever? Not by any means. Once your child's behavior is well established, you can start scaling back on the rewards. Your child's intrinsic motivation should kick in by then. You may need to periodically reinstate a reward system to get your child back on track if her motivation seems to be waning.

❖ Unplanned rewards

Many parents are surprised to hear that they may be giving their children *unplanned rewards*. Unplanned rewards occur when you inadvertently reward your child for behaviors you should be deterring. You shower your child with attention when he whines or teases his sister or give in to his demands when he has a tantrum. When your child refuses to go to school, you let him stay at home and watch TV. You also give your child unplanned rewards when you rescue him from his responsibilities. When he refuses to do his homework, you do most of it for him. When he sulks, you do his chores for him.

Parents often say, "Oh, nothing motivates my child. He doesn't care enough to work for anything." Although this might be entirely true, it is often a simple case of getting too much too easily. You also give your child unplanned rewards when you give her toys, gifts, clothes, gadgets, outings with friends or other "goodies" regardless of how she behaves. Your child gets everything she wants too easily, so there is no incentive for her to work for anything. To eliminate unplanned rewards, scale back and portion out the goodies to your child so that there is something that he desires. When your child misses school and stays home, he must remain in an environment that resembles school as closely as possible. He must do his schoolwork at home, and there should be no computer, TV, sleeping or talking on the telephone. If he refuses to do his homework, let him face the music at school the next day.

Types of consequences

There are different types of behavior deterrents that are suitable for different situations. Usually, you may need to use all in combination as appropriate to the behavior and the context. Corporal punishment is not recommended for children, as there are many other less harmful or severe ways to achieve the same effect. Consequences must be immediate when-ever possible and proportionate to the infraction. They must be consis-tently applied.

❖ *Planned inattention*

Minor infractions that are unlikely to cause any harm are best ignored. We have a "knee jerk" tendency to respond to every negative behavior. Not every behavior is worthy of the effort it takes to respond; further, respond-ing and attending may actually strengthen the behavior. The intent of ignoring is to reduce attention and thereby extinguish unwanted behavior; it is not to be unpleasant to the child. When your child makes provocative statements, ignoring him will deprive him of the attention he is seeking. On the other hand, scolding reinforces him if he is trying to attract atten-tion. It is important that a strategy for ignoring should be planned ahead of time, so that it is not an act of haste or anger. When you ignore an unde-sirable behavior, try to shift the focus immediately to a positive behavior in which your child may have just engaged or could engage. Naturally, behaviors that present real risk of harm to your child or someone else can-not be ignored. More strategies are presented later in this chapter.

❖ *Natural consequences*

Minor misbehaviors can also be deterred if you allow your child to face natural, real-world consequences. If your child doesn't get dressed on time in the morning and misses the bus, let him walk to school. If it's too far or unsafe to walk, drive him at your leisure. Let him explain to his teacher why he is late. Don't do it for him. If he fails to do his homework, let him deal with the consequences of a poor grade or failure. If he breaks a toy, he experiences the loss of the toy. If you protect your child from natural con-sequences, he will not learn how the real world works. Again, if harm and danger are involved, you cannot let natural consequences operate. You wouldn't let your child run out in the street and let him experience the nat-ural consequences of being hit by a car.

❖ *Logical consequences*

Logical consequences are sensible sequences to bad behavior. "Abuse it, lose it," sums up what logical consequences are. If your child rides his bicycle into oncoming traffic, you cannot allow him to suffer the natural consequences of being struck by a car. But you can impose the logical consequence of putting away the bicycle so that he cannot ride into the street. When your child throws the toys, you put them away. When she breaks the computer, you don't repair it. When she destroys something, you don't replace it. If she spills a drink, she cleans it up. If she is a sore loser during a board game, you stop the game and resume it only when she can agree to abide by the rules.

❖ *Time out*

Time out is a very effective way to end misbehavior for children as young as two or as old as 12. It literally means taking time out from the pleasurable or reinforcing situation in which misbehavior occurs and placing the child in a dull, boring and quiet place for a brief period. When correctly used, time out is both harmless and highly effective. Unfortunately, it is often both misunderstood and incorrectly applied. To be effective, time out must be applied quickly and calmly. The child should get no attention or reinforcement of any kind during time out. You should be able to carry your child to time out if he refuses to go. A good rule of thumb for the length of a time out is one minute for each year of your child's age.

❖ *Planned penalties*

Planned penalties include taking away points, tokens or privileges such as the computer, phone, TV, time with friends or a late bedtime. When your child fails because he didn't do his homework, he may not care about it too much. The fact that he will pay for it later in life does not impress him in the here and now, because children are not able to appreciate the future in the way we do. Giving him a planned penalty will make him "feel the pinch" in the moment.

One major reason for the failure of planned penalties is the fact that parents can't enforce the ones they give. Parents unwittingly select penalties over which they have no physical control. When they aren't able to enforce the penalties, the child realizes that they are meaningless. There-fore choose only those penalties that you know you can control and enforce. Refusing to drive your youngster to places she wants to go, for-feiting the ball game or placing selected toys under lock and key are some consequences over which you have control.

One cardinal rule about using consequences is that they should always be planned and measured, not impulsive, hasty or disproportionate. If you punish in a moment of anger, you will undoubtedly over-punish. Let the punishment fit the crime—try to make your consequences proportionate to the misbehavior. Don't make empty threats that you don't or can't carry out—they undermine your credibility.

Table 12 summarizes the foundation on which good parenting is built. Now, to return to the issue of the daily parenting challenges that OCD may bring on parents.

Table 12: The Nuts and Bolts of Good Parenting

❖ Children thrive when they have security, structure and stability

❖ Trust between parent and child lays the foundation for parental authority

❖ Be proactive, positive and preventive

❖ Age-appropriate, clear, dependable and predictable expectations make it easier for children to learn

❖ Do as you would have your child do

❖ Kind but firm limits help children feel safe and secure

❖ Say it, mean it and do it—be consistent

❖ It may take many attempts for children to learn new behaviors

❖ Small steps lead to big changes

❖ Rewards are a more powerful incentive for learning than punish-ment

❖ Reward for effort rather than success

❖ Expect ups and downs during any disruption to the normal routine

❖ Teach your child self-reliance

❖ Learning to cope with disappointment is a normal and necessary part of growing up

❖ The earlier you lay the foundation, the easier it is for your child to learn it

PARENTING THROUGH THE TOUGH TIMES

OCD makes children behave in ways that are not typical. Their misbehavior is far more complex than voluntary, planned or malicious. Parents of children with OCD often talk about how baffled, frustrated and in despair they feel around parenting issues because nothing they do or say seems to help. They are completely at a loss about which way to turn. Many parents swing the pendulum from understanding and empathy to anger and rejection. If you were used to "coasting" through parenting issues, you may be in for a rude shock. Parenting a child with OCD takes energy, incredible patience and quick thinking. Your old comfortable ways are out the window! Yet, most parents are generally on the right track. They just need to learn how to adapt and fine-tune their own expertise to accommodate the vagaries of this sinister illness.

When OCD disrupts your household in unexpected and unpredictable ways, you feel out of control. Yet, you can impose some semblance of control in this chaos, if you remind yourself that *you*, not OCD, are still in charge. You have to handle each issue moment-by-moment and day-by-day. Although this section provides the strategies that are effective in such situations, you will still need to use your judgment in applying them to your situation.

Each parent's needs are different. Perhaps all that you need is a refresher and a validation of your approach. Or perhaps you realize that you have been sidetracked into unwittingly supporting and "enabling" your child's OCD. Although you know what you need to do, your attempts to extricate yourself may have been draining and futile. Perhaps you need the help of a therapist to get you back on track. What will help you most is your readiness to be flexible, your insight into your "parenting style" and your willingness to try other approaches. It takes courage, commitment and risk-taking to change familiar and comfortable ways. It is the same courage, commitment and risk-taking that is asked of your child when he has to confront his OCD.

Guidelines for the challenging times

The following guidelines apply not just for parents of children with OCD but also for those who struggle with other challenges such as severe defiance, aggression, separation anxiety, panic or Tourette Syndrome.

❖ Take care of yourself first

If you are stressed, you are more likely to lose patience and become frustrated easily. Your anger and annoyance can get in the way of being logical and giving your child appropriate and reasonable consequences quickly and firmly. If you want to be in charge of your household, you must *act* as if you are in charge. You must get your feelings under control. You must be calm, collected and sure of yourself. Chapter 8 describes how you can take care of yourself so that you can take better care of your child.

❖ Rely on the essentials of good parenting

The nuts and bolts of good parenting that were discussed earlier in this chapter will continue to be the basis for your parenting during tough times. Those principles still apply, even though they may not appear to at first glance. You just have to learn how to adapt them and to change your beat with the music.

❖ Seek the positive

It can be really hard to be objective when you are caught up in your child's OCD. It's so much easier to focus on the bad stuff because it's in your face all the time. Yet, even your child with OCD does something nice and positive everyday. These little things might pale in comparison with the grief he puts you through. These little things will add up to much, if you *allow* them to. Seek out the good in your child and the positive steps he is taking, no matter how small they are. It will help you keep the balance that is so essential to getting through the tough times.

❖ Act quickly; don't wait for things to get out of hand

Be proactive, positive and preventive. Don't wait for things to get out of control before you decide it's time to do something about them. The sooner you take action, the easier it will be for your child to accept it and the easier it will be on you to implement the change.

❖ *Priority A, B, C behaviors*

Sometimes, everything seems to be going wrong and your head is spinning. You may not know where to start because all of it is urgent. You may feel completely weighted down by the magnitude of the situation. A very effective way to get through this mess is to sit down calmly and make a list of all the behaviors that need attending. Then, put each one into one of three categories—A, B or C—as follows:

Priority A behaviors are those that are essential to your child and family's safety and health. These include behaviors such as aggression, destruction of property or self-injury. They represent the line that cannot be crossed. They must be attended to immediately and firmly because failure to handle them can have grave consequences.

Priority B represents behaviors that are of moderate impact and importance. You can attend to them when you've got the Priority A behaviors under control. These are the behaviors where you will pick your battles. They vary from family to family but may include things like getting homework done on time, getting to bed at a reasonable hour or arguing.

Priority C behaviors are those that you will consciously and deliberately let slide at this time. They are not worth your limited time and energy during the tough times. It is far less important to have good table manners than it is to get homework done or go to school.

When you are done separating each problem behavior into a category, you will systematically start with Priority A and work your way down to C. Priority A behaviors need immediate and firm action; they are the subject of the next section in this chapter. Priority B may need a combination of rewards, punishments and negotiation to iron out and Priority C can be attended to when your lives are back to "normal."

❖ *Tackle one problem at a time*

When you are in crisis, you only attend to the most urgent situation at hand. That's your Priority A behavior at the moment. Don't worry about how you're going to fix the rest. The time for those will come before you know it. Focus on only one or two "target" behaviors at a time. Trying to address more than two can be overwhelming and distracting for both of you. When your child is successful, move to the next target behavior. Small steps lead to big changes.

❖ *Be prepared for the backlash*

Remember the *extinction burst* discussed in Chapters 7 and 9? It's what happens when you try to change your child's behavior and your child would rather not change it. I usually tell parents, "Oh, let me not forget to mention that your child's behavior may get *worse* before it gets better. Oh, and another minor detail, when that happens, it may be very hard for you to deal with." You will meet with bargaining, negotiating, cajoling, threatening. Disengage from all of these completely, assuming that you have set clear expectations ahead of time and have not sprung a nasty surprise on your child. Getting caught up in arguments is both distracting and exhausting; it will derail your resolve.

This is when you have to stick it out. It is a very difficult time for parents, but you must have faith and conviction that what you are doing is the right thing and it will get better. If you waver and give in, it will undermine your credibility with your child. Many parents are not prepared to expect the extinction burst, which is why many behavioral management programs fail. If you give in and give up now, you will merely have succeeded in reinforcing your child's sense of control over the situation. If you can get through the anguish, the behavior will extinguish. Always prepare your child ahead of time for a change in your response. Surprises don't go over well. Preparation gives your child the chance to make the right behavioral choice, since he knows what to expect if he doesn't.

❖ *Be flexible*

As you know, OCD waxes and wanes. It gets better and it gets worse. Your child's behaviors will move in parallel. The unpredictability of OCD and its accompanying roller coaster behaviors is difficult for parents to adapt to. The good days give hope and the bad days are discouraging at best. If you keep in mind that this is the *normal* course of OCD, you will be able to take these ups and downs in stride. Be flexible and be prepared to switch gears quickly and often as the need arises.

❖ *Take one day at a time*

Thinking about the future can be overwhelming when it looms large and uncertain. But as Abraham Lincoln wisely put it, "The best thing about the future is that it comes only one day at a time." And one day at a time is how you deal with it.

❖ *Trust your instincts when in doubt*

There will be many times when you are in a situation and aren't sure of the best way to handle it. When in doubt, trust your instincts. Neither this book nor any other can prepare you for every possibility that might arise with your child. That's because your child, you and your circumstances are unique and there is no way to predict what you might encounter. Use the principles described here as the foundation on which you base your decisions; the rest is your best judgment. Don't second-guess your decisions. Give yourself credit for doing your best in the circumstances.

❖ *Expect to make mistakes*

As discussed before, mistakes are a fact of life. Far more important than the mistakes you make is your willingness to learn from them. As Will Durant said, "Forget mistakes. Forget failures. Forget everything except what you're going to do now and do it."

❖ *Do as you would like your child to do*

Remember, more than ever, that your child witnesses the manner in which you handle the crises you encounter. This is a real challenge for parents because you may be taxed to the limit and aren't likely to respond calmly either. Yet, if you yell and scream when your child is being obnoxious, he will only do as well as you do in handling his own distress.

❖ *Take space when you need it*

Your child is not the only one who needs to take space when he needs to chill or vent (discussed earlier under Be Preventive). You also can benefit from taking space when you are pushed to your limits. By taking space in an appropriate way, you can model the right response to being overwhelmed. Instead of saying, *"I'm getting out of here. I've had it with you,"* which may confirm your child's view of herself as "bad," you can say, *"I'm feeling too stressed now. I need to take a break so I can calm down and think clearly and be more helpful to both of us."* You can use the *Feeling Thermometer* as a barometer of your own anger or frustration. It allows you to be aware of your feelings and to make a graceful exit before you succumb to regrettable words or actions.

❖ *Don't expect gratitude*

It can be most demoralizing when your child neither sees nor appreciates what you are doing for her. The sacrifices you make, the price you pay and the grief you endure all go unnoticed. This is a fact of parenthood, so don't expect gratitude from your child—at least, not at the moment. It may come many months or years down the road. It may only happen when she becomes a parent and encounters similar challenges.

DEALING WITH FRUSTRATION, ANGER AND PANIC

Perhaps one of the hardest things for parents to deal with is the unexpected and intense explosive behavior that some children with OCD experience. Parents often refer to these episodes of rage, panic and confusion as "meltdowns." They appear to come out of nowhere with little provocation and no warning. There may be intense frustration, anger or aggression. Some children may scream, cry uncontrollably, hit their parents or siblings, throw things, kick down doors and destroy property. Others take it out on themselves by banging their heads against the wall or hitting themselves. When the storm is over, there is equally dramatic remorse and regret. Your child may be mortified and promise that it will not happen again—a promise that is short-lived because he loses control repeatedly.

It is as if your child is suddenly transformed into a toddler throwing a tantrum. The problem is that your child is not two or three years old but seven, 12 or 16. It can be quite jarring and frightening to witness this dramatic regression to a previous age. Not to mention fear for the safety of the child or others. Your child is not recognizable or reachable. It is shocking and disturbing because it is feels like someone or something else has taken over your child's body and mind. You wish you could tear off the mask and reveal the gentle, loving and rational child who used to be happy.

Why do children with OCD lose control in this manner? Is it one of the symptoms of OCD? These episodes of loss of control are not of themselves symptoms of OCD. Rage attacks are not a diagnostic symptom of OCD. It is not necessary to have rage attacks to be diagnosed with OCD, nor are rage attacks experienced by all children with OCD.

It is not clear why exactly these meltdowns occur, but there are many possible reasons. Meltdowns are most likely to be the result of the coping challenges that OCD places on children. Sometimes, an accidental encounter may trigger fears of the worst catastrophe, leading to state of panic. Jason, a 15-year-old with OCD "lost it" and hit a peer in the cafeteria line at school because the other child touched him on the shoulder. That sounded like unprovoked aggression to Jason's school principal, so he was suspended. It was only when someone took the time to talk to Jason that the real reason emerged. The touch had triggered Jason's obsessions of contamination and death from hepatitis. Jason's belligerence was a gut reaction of self-defense from a threat that was very real to him.

Children with OCD commonly erupt in rage or panic when others knowingly or unwittingly thwart their rituals. The child is unable to complete rituals to appease anxiety, and either does not have or does not use the tools to overcome the anxiety of the unexpected exposure. The child screams in a panic, "You don't understand. I have *got* to finish this the right way or my whole day will be ruined!" or "If I can't finish counting, my mom will die and it will be my fault." To the child with OCD, these dangers are very real.

Paul, the 15-year-old you met in Chapter 1, helped me understand what drove his frequent rage attacks. This is how he described it to me:

I feel like I'm in a room with no windows and no fans and the air conditioning doesn't work. It's a blazing hot day and the sun is beating down on the roof. I'm trying to do my school work or homework or just even trying to get some sleep. It gets hotter and hotter and I take off my shirt to cool down. I sip at my water bottle. The heat keeps increasing. Pretty soon I can't breathe. I'm sweating bullets and I've just finished the last drop of water I have. I can't leave because the door is locked. There is no escape. I'm alone in the room and the people in the next room can't seem to hear me. I keep yelling, "Help, let me out of here," but it's useless. Finally, I can't take it anymore. I'm going to combust if I don't get out of here. I pound down the door, kicking, screaming, using every ounce of energy I have. The door bursts open and I fall out, gasping for breath. Everybody stands far away from me, looking at me like I'm crazy. They look cool and comfortable, not hot and bothered like me. It's because they have windows, fans and air-conditioning in their room.

Paul's poignant rendition of being trapped with no escape is an experience shared by many children with OCD. The unrelenting din of alarm bells and evacuation orders from OCD results in information overload. It is altogether too much to handle. The rage attack represents a way of escaping and letting out all the frustration. Gabriela, who was plagued by "just wrong" thoughts that she had undo all day long with mental rituals, said she couldn't shut off her brain. She often wanted to scream—"*Stop, I can't take it anymore!*" For some children, guilt and shame about "bad" thoughts or acts makes them irritable and sick to their stomachs.

Children who have ADHD, Tourette Syndrome or impulse control problems in addition to OCD may be more prone to flying off the handle. They have the mix of frustration coupled with impulsivity. Often, these children struggle during the day to keep it together in school. They may suppress their tics or rituals and be polite, courteous model students. Their teachers and peers would never know. All this hyper-control takes an inordinate amount of effort and then takes its toll. When the child gets home, he walks in the door and falls apart—and parents get the brunt of it.

The sheer emotional and physical strain of keeping rituals and tics hidden all day can be exhausting. They release all that pent-up emotion with a great sense of relief. Home is a safe place to do that—where else would they do it? Alex, who had OCD and TS came home from school and tyrannized his mother and younger sister with his verbal abuse and tirades. They dreaded his return each day.

So the next time your child melts down "for no reason at all," "out of the blue" or "completely unprovoked," stop for a moment and remember Paul, Gabriela or Alex. It is hard to understand what's going on in your child's mind unless you have OCD yourself. Ironically, you are the one to take the bullets. It might surprise you to know that if you want your child to stop having meltdowns, *you* have to begin to change how *you* behave. You have to take the first steps and do most of the work—at least initially. The fact that your child has reached the point where he explodes may mean that he does not have the skills at the moment to be more functional than that.

Think of the kettle of water on the stove. The water starts out cold, but with the heat of the stove, it warms up steadily and then comes to a boil. As the heat continues, it boils frantically, until it releases a blast of steam. The kettle "screams" at you until you take it off the stove or turn off the heat. Then the whistling stops and the kettle gradually returns to a simmer. The water remains hot for a while and eventually cools down. If you don't do anything about it, the kettle will keep screaming for respite.

The one thing I would change about my parenting style and approach since my son's diagnosis is that I would not have let him get away with outbursts of anger and meanness to others because they weren't following his (OCD) rules. In the past, I shrugged it off as part of his illness, but I should have taken action at once by taking him aside, explaining that however you feel is okay, but not to yell at friends because of MINOR transgressions. This is such a difficult thing to teach a child with OCD. To learn this control at a younger age probably would have helped him have more and better friendships. Now, he has a few close friends, but he's so tough on them to follow his rules and so argumentative that he isn't as well liked as he could be.

Nina, mother of Bob

Dealing with meltdowns involves four major steps that are proactive, positive and preventive: Set the ground rules, find an effective way to communicate in crisis, be prepared to switch gears often and offer your child *Corrective Learning Experiences.* The most important thing to avoid is reacting to your child's meltdown with one of your own.

Set the Ground Rules: Safety & Respect

Even though your child's unbridled rage and destructive behavior is *understandable,* it's not *acceptable.* No matter what he is experiencing, it does not give him permission to endanger himself or other family members. Children must learn how to live in and participate in the rules and norms of family, school, community and society. There are consequences in the real world for aggression, and they're not what you want for your child. You are being a better parent when you intervene now to set limits on your child's aggressive or violent behavior. Not doing so would prevent him from learning the essential survival skills of self-control and respect for the rights and feelings of others. The longer he waits to learn these skills, the harder it becomes. Little do you realize it, but you may be unwittingly doing your child a disservice when you don't set limits—you are depriving him of preparation for living in the real world, the one that is not under your roof.

It's time to set the Ground Rules. Every member of the family has a right to *Safety and Respect.* That is a value that cannot be compromised. Every member of the family must live by these rules. Your child needs to know this in unequivocal terms. Any threats or actions that compromise safety for your child, you or other family members are unacceptable. Respect refers to treating everyone in the family with basic human dignity. It means not having to live with verbal or emotional abuse and threats that are emotionally damaging. You must have a zero-tolerance for violation of Safety and Respect. The sooner you set the Ground Rules—no threats, no violence, no verbal or emotional abuse—the easier it will be to implement them. Yet, many parents are so afraid of triggering their child's rage that they avoid dealing with the issue proactively and firmly.

You may need to spell out the Ground Rules. Spelling them out makes them more official. Be concrete and specific and include the exact behaviors or categories of behaviors that are not excusable in your home. Describe the words, actions and innuendoes that are not okay to use. Write them down on an index card and post them in the kitchen, your child's room, in his backpack and in the car. When you have the rules in writing, all over the place, there is no room for excuses like "I forgot" or "I didn't know that." Draw attention to them often, especially when your child appears to be heading down that path. Reserve the right to add to or subtract from the list. Will your child find loopholes? Of course he will. Should that stop you from doing it? Of course not. Most children actually appreciate their parents taking a firm stance on these issues much as they may protest. At least someone is setting boundaries and stopping them from feeling out of control.

> Ground Rules: Safety and Respect

So what is your child supposed to do with his frustration and anger if he can't express it by exploding? There are several options which are described in the following sections. Most importantly, your child needs to learn that although he may not be able to control his feelings, he can learn how to control his behavior. You will teach him how he can channel his rage or panic in a more productive way using *Corrective Learning Experiences*, as described later in this chapter.

Find an effective way to communicate

One of the biggest challenges during crises is communication. A lot of disasters could be averted if parents and children could communicate effectively in the midst of a crisis. The problem is that when a child is caught in an OCD moment, he is easily over aroused and over reactive. Emotion overpowers logic and reason. Your child's upset, you're upset and you try to reason with your child. He doesn't respond, so you cajole, beg, threaten and yell. It still doesn't help and it's downhill from there. There may be too much talking and yelling and too little listening. Logical messages are therefore wasted on an upset child. The fact that your child seems impervious to reason is intensely baffling and frustrating; you may see it as stubbornness or deliberate dismissal of you. You may intensify your attempts to convince your child. Ironically, the more you intercede, the less opportunity the child has to think and problem-solve for himself. The situation spirals out of control.

When your child is in meltdown mode, he is already on information overload. If you continue to talk, reason, chastise or plead, you add another barrage of sensory input that he cannot tolerate. You are turning up the heat in the windowless room from which he cannot escape. Can you recall a time when you have clearly, rationally and effectively resolved a conflict or a problem in the midst of chaos? It was only after you calmed yourself down that you could begin to think productively. We don't think well when we are extremely aroused—how can we expect a child with OCD to do it?

How do you communicate with a child who won't listen to you? You don't. You communicate after the storm is over. You talk when he and you are calm. That's the cardinal rule. Wait until he and you are calm enough to understand each other. What you have to say should be concise and clear. One brief and simple explanation or request should suffice. It should be free of equivocal messages, in order to reduce room for confusion, mis-interpretation or misperception. Your child needs "quiet" time to ponder and digest the information that you have given to him.

Find a system of communication that does the "most for the least" in a crisis. The *Feeling Thermometer* (Chapter 5) is one good way to quickly and briefly communicate using numbers rather than words. Teach your child to rate his level of distress on the thermometer. Select a number such as seven or eight that represents the point at which communication is going nowhere. That's the cue to disengage. Agree on a number that represents "calm enough to talk." That's the cue to work out the problem.

Be prepared to switch gears often

Remember when your child was a newborn? Amidst the joy of the arrival of your precious bundle was the disruption of having everything change. You had to rearrange schedules, routines and relationships to make room for another person in your life. You had advance warning of your baby's arrival, so you could get yourself as ready as possible. You read parenting books and talked to other parents. But when your baby arrived, you still had to figure out a lot as it happened by trial and error. It was a big and challenging change, yet it was a largely positive one.

OCD, on the other hand, is an unexpected and unwelcome visitor and you are not prepared for its arrival. OCD does not bring the joy and the warmth that a newborn brings. You have to muddle your way through it because you can't turn to your usual supports. Your mother, best friends and neighbors don't know about caring for a child with OCD the way they may know about newborns. The old system you lived by has to be re-established but you are often the pioneer beating the trail. There are often no easy right or wrong answers, only guidelines that you can be applied to your own situation.

Prepare yourself to switch gears often and without warning. You will be better equipped to traverse this path when you can be more open instead of rigid, willing to learn instead of set in your ways, and focus on today instead of yesterday or tomorrow. It is not an easy road to travel.

Offer Corrective Learning Experiences

Corrective Learning Experiences (CLE's) are a systematic approach to shaping a child's unacceptable behaviors into desirable behaviors. Undesirable behaviors present *teachable moments* to help children learn self-control and responsible behavior. CLE's focus on *when* and *how* to intervene to break the cycle of distress in a productive rather than destructive way.

As you might surmise, simply meting out punishment to children for OCD-fueled meltdowns does not teach a child how to handle the OCD-fueled trigger for the meltdown. On the other hand, punishment might alienate him further. Your child will be convinced that you don't understand him and can't help him. A CLE approach does not imply that a child should be allowed to get away with misbehavior with no consequences.

The goal of a CLE is not merely to punish, but to help the child learn something positive and valuable from the experience.

Corrective Learning Experiences teach your child
❖ How to self-calm
❖ Why the behavior is not acceptable
❖ Feelings cannot always be controlled
❖ Behaviors can be controlled
❖ Acceptable ways to express feelings
❖ Acceptable behaviors
❖ Accountability for actions
❖ To make amends
❖ Ways to prevent recurrence

Your child already knows from you how she should *not* be expressing anger. Using CLE's allows you to offer her alternatives for how she *could* appropriately express anger. Children do not automatically figure this out, and we instinctively tell them what they can't do, while forgetting to teach them what they can do instead! The next time he does the same thing, the parent says, *"How many times have I told you not to do this?"* which implies that he is doing it willfully, knowingly and in defiance. When kids are young or immature, it takes "readiness," maturity and repeated training to learn seemingly simple things.

Corrective Learning Experiences, which can be used at home or at school, follow the sequence described in Table 13. (An example of the use of CLE's in school is in Chapter 13). Just as your child will learn to overcome OCD in small steps, he must learn to conquer angry behaviors in small steps. These steps are guidelines that must be adapted to fit your circumstances. Before you hasten to put them into action, read this section carefully and think about how these steps might apply in your situation. Discuss them with your child during a moment of calm and invite his input into designing a plan for your home. Write down the specific steps and examples that you will apply and rehearse them with your child.

Alex's mother used the CLE approach to teach Alex to control his verbally abusive behavior towards her and his sister.

Table 13: Steps in Corrective Learning Experiences

- ❏ Anticipate and dissipate
- ❏ Understand underlying triggers
- ❏ Deflect and defuse
- ❏ Foster self-calming
- ❏ Timely disengagement
- ❏ Timely reengagement
- ❏ Ways to reduce recurrences
- ❏ Accountability
- ❏ Ways to make amends

❖ *Anticipate and dissipate*

You may be able to ward off unnecessary crises by being consistent and predictable in your parenting. Being proactive in preparing your child for what to expect in a situation ahead of time also helps avert pointless disasters. Watch and learn the early signs of an imminent meltdown and nip them in the bud. Does your child become quiet, sullen, irritable or flustered? Ask your child if he is okay, if something is bothering him, if he needs help or would like to talk about it. Ask your child to rate his anger, frustration or sadness on the *Feeling Thermometer* (Figure 7 in Chapter 5). Spending YAMA time (see Chapter 9) each day with your child will cue you in to the subtleties of his emotions and give you guidelines on how to channel them. Alex's mother "saw it coming" when Alex appeared flushed, perspired and had a little more "stomp to his step."

❖ *Understand underlying triggers*

Try to gauge what's driving the behavior. "Bad" behavior is not necessarily deliberate, voluntary, or malicious in intent, even though it might appear that way. Ask your child what is bothering him. Be prepared for the fact that he might not be able to tell you. If the behavior occurs repeatedly and the triggers are not obvious to him or to you, keep a log or journal for about a week (see Figure 3 in Chapter 3) to identify patterns and themes in your child's behavior. You might be surprised to learn that there are certain times of day, triggers, contexts or people associated with the anger. Over time, Alex and his mother realized that the energy of keeping it together at all costs at school was too much for Alex. He erupted when he got home.

❖ *Deflect and defuse*

When you find patterns and triggers, you know that you need to problem solve to circumvent them. If it's "after-school" anger, you have to find ways to refuel that pent-up emotion. Have a designated stress release time and place every day after school for at least 30 minutes. Find activities that are "releasing" such as punching a pillow or those that are soothing such as music, reading, a favorite board game, physical chores, raking, shoveling, mowing, vacuuming, going for a walk, bike ride or run. Alex and his mother agreed that he would spend half an hour in the basement upon his return from school. He would have his snack by himself and have to time to "chill" with the pool table, punching bag or Nintendo. He would have no interaction with his mother or sister until he was ready to be civil.

When a situation is escalating, consider whether the behavior is Priority A, B or C, and act accordingly. Have a list of these behaviors ready ahead of time. Give your child simple face-saving choices. He may just need time to leave the situation and vent or to "chill out" in a safe place. Don't add fuel to the fire by becoming rigid and inflexible around relatively trivial issues such as Priority C behaviors. Avoid power struggles, arguments and negotiation when the child is upset. When the kettle starts to boil, turn off the heat.

Introduce cue words or signals to communicate easily when you see early warning signs of a meltdown. Let your child know that responding to a signal can give him a "face-saving exit." Encourage your child to verbalize your feelings rather than act them out. "I'm going to explode." Reward your child for making the right choices.

❖ *Foster self-calming*

A very critical part of a CLE is teaching your child how to self-calm. It's an important skill for your child to learn because there will be many situations where you will not be available to help him get through a tough spot. First, *you* must self-calm. If you don't, you cannot expect your child to do it. How do you teach your child to be rational and calm if you role model the opposite? Besides, you may say and do things you will regret later. Walk away when you are too angry to be nice.

The first step in self-calming is to remove oneself from the situation in order to reduce over-stimulation and regain self-control. Teach your child how to "take space" in a designated quiet place away from the distressing context. If your child does not take space, give your child two choices— one that allows him to make a positive choice and take control, and the other that is your choice, and not so favorable to him. For instance, when Alex refused to take space, he was offered the option of going into the backyard and kicking around a ball or waiting in his room with the door closed. Once you state you your choices, say them, mean them and do them. No further negotiation, bargaining, engaging and caving in—this is the trap in which most parents get caught. If he refuses both choices, he suffers a penalty such as the loss of computer time.

❖ Timely disengagement

If the child does not move into a self-calming mode, you must recognize the "point of no return" at which to disengage from interaction. As discussed earlier under *Find an Effective Way to Communicate*, trying to placate or persuade an over aroused child only adds fuel to the fire. You will become increasingly frustrated when your child is unresponsive and unreceptive to reason. A *Feeling Temperature* of 7 or 8 is usually a good indicator for timely disengagement. If you are frustrated and angry, you can leave the room and take space in the same way as the child. By doing so, you can show your child that you too are human, vulnerable and get frustrated and you too need space.

❖ Timely reengagement

It's not over when you or your child take space and disengage. When the storm has passed, it is critical to reengage with your child. This is the time to review what just transpired and discuss how things can be different or better next time. This "coaching" process will, over time, teach him to think ahead and incorporate these ideas into his repertoire of action. You and your child need to try to understand what was upsetting to your child and to identify feelings and triggers in the situation. The *Feeling Thermometer* is again a very handy tool to help your child quantify the severity of his emotions and of the triggers.

Engage your child in talking about his feelings. If articulating feelings is difficult, use "feeling faces" to draw emotions such as a "smiley," sad, mad or scared face. Help him understand that all emotions are normal and healthy; however, whereas feelings cannot always be held back, actions can and must be controlled. Regardless of the reasons behind the behavior, your child must learn to channel emotions in an acceptable way. Discuss the notion of coping with disappointment because, "life just doesn't always let you have what you want when you want." Review what could have been done differently and evaluate the potential effectiveness of alternative solutions. In Alex's case, his mother helps him problem-solve alternatives to hitting when upset. They include verbalizing his frustration, mulling over it in the safety of his room or working it out through physical exercise.

❖   *Ways to reduce recurrence*

Triggers and disappointments will always abound and cannot and should not be eliminated altogether. Children must learn ways to cope with this reality. Brainstorm ways to prevent future recurrences with your child. Make a list of potential triggers and identify ways to handle them. Try to identify a proactive "stress-release plan" to handle the negative energy. Just like your child will learn to conquer OCD in small steps, he must learn to conquer angry behaviors in small steps. Teach your child what kinds of things it is okay to say when angry and frustrated and write them down so that he can rehearse them and recall them in need. You and your child can generate a hierarchy of steps that lead to eventual self-calming and self-control. For ideas on the hierarchy, ask your child—letting her come up with hierarchy items will make her feel more invested.

An "EWS" or *early warning system* is one example of a preventive measure. The child and parent (or teacher) agree on cue words or phrases to signal the need for an exit from the situation. The *Feeling Thermometer* may be used to identify a number that warns of an impending meltdown. Colors may also be used as signals. Red represents *"Stop, leave me alone,"* yellow means *"Slow down,"* and green reflects, *"I could use your help."* Alex can pull a red card out of his pocket instead of having to verbally communicate with the mother. His mother knows that the red card means he is upset and needs to leave. Other potential options are to leave the scene, take deep breaths or count to 10 before reacting.

❖ Accountability

Children, like the rest of us, need to be held *accountable* and *responsible* for their actions. They need to accept and acknowledge the impact of their behaviors. All actions have consequences and we have to live with them. Your child must learn that he cannot impose his frustration on others via verbal or physical abuse or by destructiveness.

Some situations result in natural consequences, which are the obvious outcome of their actions. For instance, if Alex was having a meltdown at the same time that he should have been on his way to the soccer game, he endures the natural consequence of missing the game. Parents can also impose logical consequences. If Alex destroys his toys in anger, the *"Abuse it, lose it"* principle applies. The toys are not replaced. When he kicks a hole in the door, he pays for the repairs. With older children or teenagers, planned penalties such as curfews or the removal of privileges such as the computer or car are usually effective. The penalty should be proportionate to the magnitude of the behavior. Consequences are more effective if parents *say it, mean it and do it.* Empty threats undermine parental credibility.

❖ Ways to make amends

The child must recognize how his behavior might have offended or hurt someone, apologize and make restitution for damage done. Alex must seek out and apologize to his mother and sister for pushing them. When a child destroys something, he needs to clean up the mess or repair the damage in some appropriate fashion or make up in some other way for inconvenience done. Sometimes, physically active chores such as mowing the lawn, raking the leaves or vacuuming the house helps children put the pent-up physical energy to good use. The child is rewarded for going through the CLE process with praise.

Your CBT therapist can help you modify and fine-tune your CLE plan as you go along. If, after using the *Corrective Learning Experiences* approach described here, your child still endangers the safety of the household, you may have to take the unpleasant but necessary step of getting help from outside the family. Remember that it is not fair or right to subject other family members to your child's violence. Your child must know ahead of time what will happen if he crosses the line of Safety and Respect. Let him know that you will call on the local hospital or the police to handle it when he is unable to control his behavior. If you decide to do this, *you must follow through*! Don't cave in at the last minute because your child pleads or you suddenly have a change of heart. If you change your mind, you will lose all your credibility with your child.

Parents and teachers who handle frequent or intense meltdowns and explosiveness in children are referred to an excellent book entitled *The Explosive Child* by psychologist Ross Greene. Dr. Greene presents a sensitive, insightful and practical method for working effectively with children who are frequently explosive.

STRATEGIES FOR EVERYDAY CHALLENGES

The following scenarios are common in many households. Suggestions for handling each are presented below:

Is this OCD or just misbehavior?

All too frequently, you may struggle to understand whether your child's behaviors are driven by OCD, manipulation, need for control, or plain old defiance. Is your child making excuses, purposely being difficult or trying to avoid expectations? You want to give her the benefit of the doubt, but you have the nagging suspicion that you are being taken for a ride. You could spend hours trying to sort this out and never arrive at a satisfactory conclusion. When in doubt, you have to trust your parental intuition and experience. If you end up being wrong, you can learn from hindsight. If it's dangerous behavior, you must take action regardless of the cause, as described earlier in this chapter.

Trying to understand the underlying reason for each behavior will divert too much of your energy to the wrong place. Don't try to understand your child's OCD intellectually—OCD is not a logical or consistent illness. Ask your child directly whether the behavior is driven by OCD or another reason. Tell your child you trust him and expect him to be honest about telling you what's OCD and what's not. When your child responds, you must accept and trust his response. You may have to consciously pick your battles and let the rest slide. Avoid abrupt and drastic actions at this time. You can't make everything right at once, but it will happen in due time. If it's obviously manipulation, you should handle it the way you would in any other circumstance.

"I can't help it, it's my OCD."

This issue is a tricky one for parents because it's never quite clear how much one can and should expect of a child with OCD. Part of the problem is that the standard keeps shifting as your child progresses through different periods from diagnosis through treatment and after. In general, a good rule of thumb is that you can't expect too much of a child with OCD, but you can't expect too little either. It's that fine balance between supporting and enabling. It's important not to have an "all or none" approach—your child must either do everything or nothing. A good way to gauge what may be the right amount is to push your child one notch above what you perceive to be his limit. Remember too, that your child's limit will vary from day to day or week-to-week, so you have to adjust your expectations to these changes.

Your child rejects your help

Your child may unload all her frustration and distress on you, but when you try to suggest some remedies, she says you don't understand and rejects your help. Discuss this "help seeking-help rejecting" behavior with your child during a moment of calm. Tell her that it is confusing and frustrating to you because you don't know how to help her. Ask her what she is expecting of you when she seeks you out. Ask what kind of response from you would be helpful for her. Your child may just be looking for a place to vent or a shoulder on which to cry. Perhaps she needs to figure it out for herself and will do it in due time.

Walking on eggshells

You may be walking on eggshells to prevent outbursts, bending over backwards to please and appease, but it's still not enough. You may be stressing yourself with caution, nervous anticipation and expectation. Don't keep rescuing your child from opportunities to learn how to handle disappointment and frustration. You are unwittingly doing your child a disservice because you are preventing her from learning critical coping and adaptive skills. How is she going to do it when she's older and you can't be there all the time to rescue and protect her from the real world?

It is impossible to anticipate and prevent everything that will trigger either your child's OCD or a meltdown. You have to draw the line somewhere—talk to your therapist about where that line is for your child and in your situation. It will be a difficult transition to change your behaviors, but the sooner you do it, the easier it will be for all of you.

Mood swings

Children with OCD commonly become demoralized, irritable and frustrated due to the challenges of managing OCD. However, moodiness is not uncommon, particularly among adolescents, even when they don't have OCD. Is your child's irritability and edginess typical adolescent behavior or should you be concerned about something else? Look for the most parsimonious or simple explanation first. Is your child irritable because he skipped his lunch and is starving? Did he have a bad day at school? A breakup or fight with a friend? Has he been sleep-deprived lately? Neither children nor adolescents can be counted on to recognize the relationship of their mood with their physiological needs, so you must actively rule them out first. Getting your child's blood sugar to a stable level and sleep deprivation remedied via a catnap may do the trick. If it doesn't, you may want to consider the possibility that your child is depressed. Discuss your child's moods and behaviors with your child's therapist or doctor.

Sleep difficulties

When your child doesn't sleep you don't sleep either. Sleep problems are very disruptive, because they make everyone more irritable and less functional during the day. Your child may be getting to bed in the wee hours of the morning because he cannot break away from rituals. Perhaps he lies awake in bed for hours absorbed in obsessions. Sleep is one of those Priority A items that should be at the top of the list because of the cascading effect that sleep deprivation has on everyone. It is best to discuss sleep difficulties with your child's therapist or doctor so that a systematic plan can be put in place to get your child and family back on track. If rituals are the issue, they should become part of the child's RIDE hierarchy. The use of a timer to limit rituals may help get the child through them and to bed faster. Relaxation strategies may help calm a child who is too anxious or uptight at bedtime. Soothing music is often an effective sleep aid. Some parents also find that the aroma of lavender leaves in a pillow are calming and sleep-inducing. A brisk walk or bicycle ride up the hill one hour before bedtime may be the right amount of fatigue to do the trick. Cut back on non-essential commitments to reduce the workload on your child. If sleep continues to be a problem, discuss the possibility of medication with your child's doctor.

Outings and social occasions

OCD can quickly send children into the closet to hide away from friends and family. Help your child socialize as and when sensible by lowering the bar on social activities. Encourage your child to visit friends or attend a social gathering. Start with short visits and work your way up to longer periods. Be proactive and discuss with your child what he might expect during these visits. Anticipate potential OCD-related problems and rehearse with your child alternative problem-solving strategies to tackle them. Provide opportunities for your child's friends to visit if your child is unwilling to venture too far from home.

Late for everything

"I'm late, I'm late, I'm late..." The harried words of Lewis Carroll's White Rabbit echo in households with OCD like a familiar refrain. Like sleep disruption, being late has a cascading effect on the entire family. Parents are late getting to work after they've spent the best two hours of the morning hustling their child through rituals. Families are late going to events or outings because the child with OCD isn't done washing up or getting dressed. With your therapist's guidance and your child's knowledge, it may be necessary to set time limits on rituals, after which the rest of the family may need to proceed with their schedule. Practical strategies like having clothes picked out ahead of time, instead of just before the event may take the pressure off the right choice when the clock is ticking.

Siblings "neglected by default"

This book is dedicated to helping you help your child with OCD. But you may have other children, siblings to your child with OCD. OCD can be very hard on siblings. They may end up being neglected by virtue of the fact that all your energy, time and effort is consumed by your child with OCD, leaving little to spare for the "low-maintenance" siblings. This situation is true of any family with a special needs child—the other siblings automatically get less of your time. The squeaky wheel gets the grease. You are grateful that your other children are going about their business, but they may be suffering the effects of OCD as much as you are. In some families, the patient, quiet sibling who has dropped into the background suddenly explodes from the cumulative stress of OCD. This unexpected reaction may send the family into a tailspin.

Make it a point to spend some quality time with your other children, apart from the child with OCD. Engage your child with daily YAMA time, go on outings or invite his friends over to play. Some families find that everyone gets a fair share of quality time when each parent rotates taking one child on an outing once a week. Don't put your other children's life on hold for OCD. Their lives need to go on too. Keep family routines normal when possible. Getting your routines back to normal will help the rest of the family feel attended to. You may have to set limits or negotiate with your OCD child to make time for siblings.

Educate your other children about OCD when possible. Create a family culture of empathy, support and teamwork to get through a challenge. It may help them to understand why their "attention-seeking, demanding, immature" sibling is making such a fuss about every little thing. I offer families the opportunity to bring siblings in for selected therapy sessions to allow them an opportunity to share how OCD affects them. Siblings who feel heard and understood may be more likely to listen and understand as well. If you give rewards to your OCD child for good behavior, be sure to do the same for siblings, especially for working or playing cooperatively and maintaining positive sibling relations. Allow the siblings the time and space to vent. Teach siblings to target their anger and resentment at OCD, not at their OCD sibling. Turn that energy into something good. When siblings say hurtful and destructive things to each other, have them apologize and exchange compliments to make amends.

FREQUENTLY-ASKED QUESTIONS

I told my son that if he didn't go to school, he couldn't go swimming. He really enjoys swimming, and he doesn't seem to have any OCD when he's in the pool. He would rather be in the pool than in school. Am I doing the right thing?

Much of how you handle this situation will depend on why your child is not going to school and what efforts he is making to get himself back there. If your child appears to be making no effort to get well, it would be more understandable to withhold going to the pool. On the other hand, if your child's OCD is crippling and the pool is his only source of pleasure right now, it would not be advisable to deprive him of it. It might be his only respite from the storms of OCD. What you could do is to offer him additional time at the pool as an incentive for trying to get to school or engage in treatment.

We've tried all this "behavior modification" stuff like rewards, tokens and time out before and it's never worked for us.

You are certainly not alone. Many parents throw up their hands in despair because "it just doesn't work." These techniques are not guaranteed to work for everyone, but they are highly likely to be effective if they are *applied properly.* Remember, the behavioral management techniques are only guidelines, not a recipe. To be effective, they must be tailored to your situation. This is where an experienced CBT therapist will do you far more good than one who doesn't have CBT skills. Once the strategies are tailored to your needs, they must be carried out consistently over a period of time. The relationship between you and your child is dynamic and evolving and the approaches you use must move in accordance. There are many "glitches" to be problem-solved as you go along; many parents give up too soon when things don't go right. The "extinction burst" (discussed in this chapter) is one big reason that behavioral management plans go awry— parents who are not prepared for it give up in haste because their child is getting "worse, not better."

How will OCD affect my child's ability to handle stress and transitions?

We are all more likely to reveal our vulnerabilities during times of stress and transition. Your child may have more frequent or severe OCD episodes during an unsettling period in her life, when routines are disrupted. However, the good news is that when the stress and change stabilize, OCD usually stabilizes with it. In other words, things usually return to the way they were prior to the stress or transition.

How do we get through the holidays with our daughter? She falls apart at these big events and ruins it for all of us.

While the holidays are supposed to be a time of good cheer and excitement, they fall short of the "Hallmark Holiday" experience for many families. I like to think about the "50/50 Rule" for situations that involve a lot of expectations: 50% of it will turn out the way you expected, and 50% won't, but you don't know which 50% it will be. Holidays are wrapped in expectations. Breaking free of ideas of how the holidays "should be" may ease some of the disappointment and disenchantment that follows.

Most of us want to relive, with our children, our fond recollections of holidays of *our* childhoods. It's a time to create new memories and let our children play a role in forming them. It may be helpful to be proactive, preventive and positive. Try to spend more YAMA (You and Me Alone) time with your child. Make a list of the situations that typically trigger stress—big family gatherings, lots of noise, change in routine). Anticipate these situations and tone them down if possible. Sit down with your child and ask her what's special about the holidays for her, what she would like to do to make it special and come up with a way to incorporate your child's ideas to make the holiday memorable (if it's within reason).

During your YAMA time, let your child know the plans, what to expect for each day, give her a chance to express apprehensions, and try to rehearse potentially sticky situations. Set consequences ahead of time for behaviors over which your child has control. Decide if your child is prepared to get through some of them or whether it's better to do something different. Give your child incentives and rewards for effort in the right direction. Acknowledge every positive step your child takes. Build in some time for yourself to get a break from all the hustle and bustle and to gear up to handle the unexpected.

Chapter 13

OCD Goes to School

Children learn and remember at least as much from the context of the classroom as from the content of the coursework.

Lawrence Kutner

Patrick woke up each morning with dread. He would have rather stayed under the covers than face another day of torture. How could he ever explain to anyone that he had to get all his things ready in the right way so that the words "See you later," sounded just right? The wrong intonation, the wrong emphasis, any interruption, including that of the bus, and he would have to start all over again. It was really tricky, because he had to say it before the bus turned the corner and drowned out his words, but his parents usually wanted to say their goodbyes after the bus arrived.

Like Patrick, about half the children with OCD are saddled with the daily challenge of figuring out how to get through another school day. Some children have to devote every ounce of effort to keeping it together at school. They do such a remarkable job that teachers are often surprised when they are informed that they have OCD. For many children, OCD may be minimal at home and severe at school. The other half are fortunate not to have to contend with OCD in school. Some may even experience relief because school keeps them busy enough to keep OCD out of their minds. Tara loved school—it was the one place she could count on to find respite from OCD. *Count on?* Funny, because she had to count, count, count everything at home, but for some inexplicable reason, the urge to count ceased at school. Children usually aren't able to explain why they seem to be able to control their symptoms in some settings and not in others. Generally, this discrepancy in control is not planned or intentional, so give due pause before you grab your child by the collar and give him a piece of your mind.

This chapter is written both for parents and for school personnel. In this chapter, I describe how OCD may affect your child's life at school, your child's rights to a free and appropriate public education, and the complex and sensitive issues that OCD raises in the context of school. As a parent, you have to decide whether or not you should tell the school about your child's OCD. Can the school help your child? How can schools and parents work collaboratively in the best interest of the child with OCD? In this chapter, I propose a *home-school partnership* and specific strategies to address your child's OCD-related school problems. If you decide to inform the school about your child's OCD, please consider sharing and discussing this chapter with your child's school.

THE FALL OUT OF OCD AT SCHOOL

Schools strive to provide children with the opportunity to learn, make friends and have fun—the most important "developmental tasks" of childhood. School is the "real world" for the child. Yet, when OCD enters this world, the tasks of learning, making friends and having fun can be disrupted to the point where the child is unable to grow and mature. It is most heartbreaking for parents to witness the wasted time and wasted potential that envelops their OCD-ridden child.

When OCD begins to encroach on your child's day at school, he usually cannot *start, proceed with* or *complete* what he needs to be doing. Obsessions may result in children getting "stuck" or fixated, unable to refocus or move on. They may be excruciatingly slow in completing assignments. The interference of OCD may show up in drastic changes in performance, erasing, re-reading, trips to bathroom, difficulty taking notes, completing tests, unlocking lockers or arranging books repeatedly. Children may seek reassurance with repeated questions that perplex and annoy teachers: *"Is my math correct? Is it okay if I sit here? Are you sure I'm not going to vomit? Is it time for recess yet?"* Not only does OCD disrupt the child's own work, it creates demands on teachers and peers. Teachers who do not know about the child's OCD may question the child's motives. Does the child have control over the behaviors? Is he using them when convenient? Is he trying to shirk work?

Unfortunately, these OCD-related behaviors can be quickly and incorrectly pegged as laziness, disorganization, poor motivation, noncompliance, defiance or attention problems. In fact, *ADHD is the most common misdiagnosis for children who manifest OCD symptoms in school.* Children with OCD appear distracted and inattentive because they are preoccupied with their obsessions. They are not daydreaming willfully. They are merely unable to control the meanderings of their minds. Their machinations to surreptitiously complete rituals may be seen as fidgetiness or hyperactivity. When Patrick moved around in his seat and opened and shut his book bag to count his pencils and check his books, his teacher thought he was restless, disorganized and inattentive.

Many children with OCD are hardworking, diligent and persistent and therefore manage to get by in school due to a huge personal effort. Nonetheless, it is at great cost to them and is both exhausting and discouraging. Their creative potential is diverted to the drudgery of getting through a routine day. When OCD is severe, children may not be able to keep up this heroic level of effort. As a result, it may result in incomplete work, failure on tests, and even the need to repeat grades or be schooled at home. Drop out rates may be high, but may incorrectly be attributed to substance abuse and truancy, which may mask untreated OCD or anxiety.

TO TELL OR NOT TO TELL SCHOOL PERSONNEL?

Should you tell your child's teacher or counselor that she has OCD? There is no simple right or wrong answer to this question. It is a personal decision for each family because there are plusses and minuses to each choice. Some parents and children are ready and willing to disclose OCD to the child's school, whereas others are cautious and hesitant. Some parents are pleased with their decision and its outcome; others regret it, regardless of what they decided. Knowing some of the benefits and risks of disclosure will help you be prepared with reasonable expectations. Here are some guidelines to help steer you to your decision.

In essence, you must consider your goals and your expectations, how realistic they are in the constraints of your child's school environment and whether you are prepared to proceed without guarantees about the outcome. Will telling the school result in greater good for your child, will it make no difference, or can it have the potential to hurt him? Writing down the benefits and disadvantages may help you see them more clearly. After you weigh the pros and cons, consider which way the scale tips. Your decision will be guided by what's best for your child in the big picture. With either decision, you will take the risk of not knowing if you made the best choice until after you have made it.

Perhaps the two biggest considerations are: To what extent is OCD getting in the way of your child's ability to function at school and how do you expect the school to respond to the disclosure? If OCD is not affecting your child in school, you may decide that there is no point in mentioning it at all. However, some parents feel that they would rather be proactive and preventive and disclose early, before their child needs help urgently and it isn't available.

If OCD is getting in your child's way at school, you may want to give some serious thought to telling the school. Most teachers are enlightened and would like to know, understand and help when possible. Parents have sometimes been pleasantly surprised to find out that teachers may know more about OCD than they expect. They may have worked with other children with OCD and may be both understanding and helpful. Disclosure may make your child's life easier because he will not be misunderstood and mislabeled as lazy, oppositional or unmotivated. Teachers may be able to teach better, attend to your child's specific needs, implement strategies to assist with your child's challenges and make adjustments to expectations. If an emergency arises, the teacher is more likely to know what is going on, what to expect, how to handle it and when to seek help. If your child is on medication, it might be good for teachers and nurses to know so that they may be alert to side effects. One thing is clear: School personnel cannot help your child if they don't know what's happening!

How do you expect the school to respond to your disclosure? Has your experience with your child's teachers, school counselors, principal and other staff in the past been positive? Have they been responsive to your child's needs and to your concerns? Have they taken appropriate steps to help your child get the most out of school? What is the school's track record for helping children with other disabilities? Although schools are mandated to identify and provide services for children who aren't able to learn in school, this is easier said than done. Some schools are excellent in responding to a child's needs quickly, whereas others may be wrapped in red tape for months while your child is barely getting by each day.

What are some reasons for caution in telling the school? Fear of being misunderstood, mislabeled or stigmatized are the biggest holdups. You take a risk. There is no guarantee that people will understand. Unfortunately, stigma, even in subtle forms, still exists when it comes to mental illness. Some parents may have many misgivings about letting the school know about the child's difficulties, due to concerns about the implications. They may be afraid to have their child labeled because they do not know the immediate and long-term repercussions of the label. They do not want their child to be treated as different or "inferior," or to incur peer ridicule. Will the label and record follow their child to college and to the workplace? It is against the law for school labels to be disclosed to colleges without written permission from the child and parent.

Many parents are concerned that if they inform the school of their child's difficulties, there will be an immediate push to place the child on medication. Parents may view this as schools opting for the "easy way out." Many parents are very reluctant to place their children on medication, and don't want the school to influence their decision. Parents may be struggling to decide what course of action is best for their child at the moment and in the future. Parents may also be hesitant to disclose if rapport with the teacher or other school personnel is weak. They may believe that the child's teacher may misunderstand or downplay their concerns.

Like many parents, you may be understandably concerned about confidentiality. You may be reluctant to divulge sensitive information about your child to the school. "School" is a lot of people, most of whom the parents may not ever encounter directly. What are the limits of confidentiality within the school system? What are the safeguards against information being accessible to personnel who have no need to be informed? Will your child's needs be discussed among school staff with respect and dignity? What is the guarantee that peers will not find out? Although school personnel are bound to laws of confidentiality, there are no guarantees because even the best systems and the best intentions fail at times.

When, how and whom to tell?

If you are leaning towards disclosing your child's OCD, your child's therapist or doctor may be useful guides in deciding when, how and who to tell at the school. Most children whose OCD affects their school functioning need a therapist anyway. One big advantage to having a therapist work with you is that you can have the input of an objective professional. Second, an official diagnosis of OCD made by the therapist or doctor will definitely carry weight when you present your child's case to the school. On the other hand, if you choose to inform your child's school before you find a therapist, school personnel may be able to recommend a therapist.

Whenever possible, let your child know why it might be important to inform the teacher or school about his OCD. For very young children, informing them that the teacher knows may be sufficient. For older children, it is important to involve the child in the decision. Children may be reluctant because they feel embarrassed, worry about peers knowing or fear being singled out by the teacher for special attention. Your child's fears and misconceptions should be allayed before he will be fully willing to participate. Teach your child all about OCD first; let him read *Up and Down the Worry Hill* (see *Resources*) which will help him dispel shame and guilt, feel more confident, advocate for himself when necessary and help others understand what his illness is all about.

You may want to tell only as many school personnel as need to know to help your child. "School personnel" is a broad and encompassing term that includes a wide variety of professionals such as teachers, administrators, counselors, social workers, special education teachers, school psychologists, nurses, occupational and speech and language therapists. In some situations, it may be enough to tell the homeroom teacher. In others, it may be best to inform the school counselor or psychologist.

Write a brief summary of your child's symptoms, her diagnosis, her strengths and talents, how her illness might affect her schooling, what kinds of support she might need, and the actions and words that might help or hurt your child. Request a meeting with your child's teacher, counselor or other staff with whom you would like to share this information. If your child has new teachers, request to meet with him or her before the school year begins and make sure all important school personnel attend. Give your child's teacher, counselor and each staff member present a copy of your written summary for their files. Briefly describe what you have written in your summary. Present your child as a person with strengths, interests, skills and pleasures. Give them credible sources of information about OCD to read, a list of resources or other helpful contacts.

Figure 9: My Child's Needs in School

Name: *Maria G.*	Grade: *6*	Teacher: *Mrs. Kelly*
Diagnosis: *Obsessive-Compulsive Disorder*	Date: Sept 15	Made by: Dr. W.

What OCD is: An illness consisting of repeated fears (obsessions) and rituals (compulsions) that are severe and uncontrollable.

My child's fears and rituals: Worries about germs and disease; hand washing rituals.

How OCD affects my child at school: Maria may appear preoccupied and distracted with obsessions. She won't use the toilet at school and will avoid touching other kids, door knobs and other objects that she fears have germs on them.

Responses that help my child:Giving her extra time and space, gentle redirection

Responses that may hurt my child: Penalizing her for being tardy or avoiding things or people

My child's strengths and talents: Conscientious, wants to do well likes school

School support requested: Accommodations and 504 Plan: Extra time to complete assignments, last in line for gym and cafeteria

Resources about OCD: Obsessive-Compulsive Foundation, Obsessive-Compulsive Information Center. See attached list of books on OCD.

Should classmates know about a child's OCD?

Classmates should never be informed without explicit permission from the child who has OCD and his parent. Ideally, classmates should only be informed if there is a specific advantage to letting them know. Most children are embarrassed to have personal information divulged to peers because it sets them apart. If your child's OCD is not apparent to classmates and does not disrupt classroom activities, there is probably no real advantage to disclosing. However, classmates may notice your child's symptoms or be curious when your child is habitually late for school or missing classes for doctor's appointments. If your child's symptoms are obvious to classmates and are raising curiosity or concern, it might be wise to preempt the chances of being misunderstood or of teasing by giving some planned, systematic information at their level of comprehension.

Classmates may be introduced to a health curriculum that includes OCD, anxiety, depression or stress, during which each disorder or condition is described, along with its impact on children and families. Books like *Up and Down the Worry Hill* can be read to the class. Such a teaching module allows facts to be shared in a general way, without particular focus on a given child. It also allows children to develop empathy and understanding for children afflicted with such conditions. A role-play module could include a "walk in my shoes" exercise, during which a child pretends to have a given condition to experience what it might feel like.

WHAT SCHOOLS CAN DO TO HELP

There are many ways in which schools can help children with OCD optimize their learning potential, academic achievement, social interaction and overall adjustment. The following contributions include both short-term and long-term ways to help children with OCD. It is the responsibility of school personnel and pupil services teams to delegate each of these functions to appropriate members of the staff.

> ### *What School Personnel Can Do to Help*
> ❖ Education and training
> ❖ Early detection
> ❖ Forging home-school partnerships
> ❖ Assessment
> ❖ Consultation and appropriate referral
> ❖ Provision of a safe environment
> ❖ Management of OCD in school
> ❖   Phase I-Stabilization
> ❖   Phase II-School-based intervention

Education and training

Parents are often dismayed to learn that their child's teachers and even counselors know and understand very little about OCD. Because childhood OCD has only recently emerged from the closet, there is vast variability in the knowledge and awareness of OCD among school personnel. Some are well informed and others may know next to nothing. There is also wide variation from school to school and district to district. Schools can take a proactive approach to education about OCD, anxiety and other mental health issues in children via continuing education curricula for staff. Experts in OCD may be invited to present training sessions to educate staff in the recognition and management of OCD in schools. Such training would allow school personnel to:

❑ Increase awareness of OCD, its symptoms, course and treatment.

❑ Recognize OCD as a legitimate disorder rather than misbehavior.

❑ Increase awareness of the immediate and long-term negative effects of OCD on children, families, teachers and peers.

❑ Increase acceptance and tolerance and reduce misunderstanding and mishandling of children with OCD.

❑ Use appropriate skills and strategies to manage OCD in school.

❑ Educate parents of children with OCD.

❑ Educate students in order to increase acceptance and reduce teasing.

Table 14: Red flags for OCD in School

❑ Excessive focus on having things neat and tidy. Lining up, ordering or arranging items on desks, in backpacks or lockers repeatedly

❑ Undue distress and frustration when things are disorganized, when interrupted or when routines change unexpectedly

❑ Uncharacteristic sloppiness or carelessness in assignments

❑ Rigidity about "perfect" performance and inability to reach excessively high self-imposed standards

❑ Erasing repeatedly until the paper has holes in it, the ink is smudged and the writing or drawing is illegible

❑ Very slow and deliberate work, resulting in incomplete assignments

❑ Tardiness or school refusal. Arriving late to school habitually or missing school altogether. The child is at home, not truant

❑ Inability to proceed with or complete tasks. Assignments or tasks that are clearly within the child's capability are not completed due to repetitive rituals such as checking, re-reading or counting

❑ Drowsiness from lack of sleep or staying up late performing rituals

❑ Frequent trips to the bathroom. Frequent urinary urges for which no medical problem can be found may be obsessive urges to "clean out" the bladder. (Medical cause for the urges must be ruled out)

❑ Counting or focus on lucky and unlucky numbers

❑ Sudden avoidance of familiar things or reluctance to try new things

❑ Fears of contamination, death or harm may coerce children into avoiding potential triggers that are not always intuitive or logically connected to the fear

❑ Odd behaviors: Walking in specific patterns through doorways, counting tiles or syllables, touching or tapping in symmetry or sitting and standing repeatedly

❑ Frequent checking of the book bag, lockers or under the desk

❑ Opening doors, lockers, desks, or books with elbows or with tissues, holding hands in the air to avoid physical contact, refusal to shake hands or share pencils and supplies

Early detection

School personnel may have the opportunity to be the first to recognize when a child may need help, even before parents or pediatricians pick up cues that all is not well. Teachers, counselors, school psychologists and other school personnel spend thousands of hours with thousands of children. Parents rarely have as many comparison points as school personnel do. Teachers and other classroom staff are privy to a view of the child in a variety of activities, settings and interactions. Over time, they develop a keen sense of what's normal and what's not for a given age or circumstance. When they are informed and aware of OCD, they are in the prime position for early detection, which can make a world of difference to a child with OCD. Yet, in many instances, school personnel who are not educated about OCD may not be aware of it, even if it significantly impacts the child's functioning in the classroom.

When OCD presents in classic ways such as excessive hand washing, it is relatively easy to detect. More often than not, OCD is difficult to spot in school, because many rituals may be hidden. Surreptitious and unusual behaviors may be an attempt to hide or camouflage embarrassing rituals. For instance, if your child is clowning around and being "fidgety" in class, it may be because he is trying to disguise checking and touching rituals. Many children with OCD are overly responsible and conscientious. They work very hard to function properly in school. Teachers may have trouble believing it when they are informed that the child has OCD.

Table 14 lists some of the ways in which OCD may manifest in school (see Chapter 2 for other signs and symptoms of OCD).

Forging home-school partnerships

Children spend roughly half their waking hours in school and the other half with family. It only makes good sense that the adults with whom they spend the most time-parents and teachers-should work in concert to help them grow and mature to their potential. Parents and school personnel are experts in their own arenas. Schools can help forge partnerships with parents to combine this wealth of resources in the best interest of the child. The *home-school partnership* approach recognizes the fact that parents and school personnel each have important and complementary roles to play. It is a farsighted, practical and sensible approach because schools and parents will be hard pressed to be effective if they work in isolation. Further, neither schools nor parents appreciate carrying the brunt of the burden alone.

Partnerships are more realistic and effective when schools and parents have similar goals, perceptions and approaches to working with the child. When a good partnership exists, schools and parents work cohesively to develop and use a consistent approach to managing the child's OCD at home and at school. Rather than being passive participants, parents today are eager to work actively with school personnel to advocate for their child's needs.

Home-school partnerships work when parents and schools have a common purpose, respect each other's expertise, communicate regularly, and interact with *"no blame and no shame."* School personnel should attempt to anticipate and eliminate potential difficulties in the partnership in advance. Parents should be approached thoughtfully, objectively, and without judgment. Some parents may be anxious and stressed; others may be defensive.

An effective partnership must include the child, parent(s), school personnel and the child's therapist or doctor (as applicable). Partnership with the child in question is implicit. Parents and school staff are merely *instrumental* in helping the child master OCD and cannot actually do it for the child. No one but the child can eventually learn how to overcome his OCD. The child is therefore a necessary and vital partner. The exact nature of involvement of the child will depend on the child's age and maturity.

It is helpful to have a "Case Manager" or equivalent person within the school assigned to the child. The Case Manager may be the teacher, counselor, nurse, school psychologist or social worker and is responsible for ensuring that the child receives appropriate care at school. The Case Manager acts as the "point person" through whom all communication is channeled. The *internal* collaboration among relevant school personnel-teachers, school psychologists, counselors, social workers, special education teachers, speech and language therapists or the pupil services team-is also very important. Good communication is at the core of healthy partnerships. A systematic plan for communication is necessary to keep all relevant personnel "in the loop," so that they can be consistent in their perceptions of and responses to the child. Having a Case Manager can reduce communication "gaps and mishaps" among school personnel.

Partnerships develop when school personnel meet with parents in a timely manner, are supportive and receptive and invite and welcome their input and suggestions. They discuss and share information and resources about OCD that would be beneficial to the child. In an effective partnership, parents and school personnel listen to each other and respect each other's contributions. Teachers must appreciate the scope of the problems that parents may face with a child's OCD and give them due credit for their efforts at management. Parents must understand that teachers and school personnel have many other children under their care, and reinforce and credit them for effort, time and devotion to their own child.

Partnerships also extend beyond the home and school to healthcare professionals in the community who are involved in the child's care. These *external* partnerships may include pediatricians and child psychologists, child psychiatrists or social workers. Most children whose OCD affects them in school need a therapist. Community partners provide treatment and support to the child and parents that may be beyond the scope of the school's capability. They complement and supplement the efforts of parents and school personnel. School-based interventions for a child with OCD must be implemented in conjunction with the therapist. The therapist can help orchestrate perceptions of the child across settings, establish realistic and meaningful treatment goals, reduce overlap and promote efficient sharing of information.

In addition to direct treatment, community partners can provide consultation to school personnel in developing and implementing school-based interventions. They can provide continuing education workshops and training experiences to school personnel in general mental health issues, as well as specific training in OCD and its treatment. Experts in childhood OCD can provide training using a *"Train the Trainer"* model, whereby selected school staff are trained to treat children with OCD within specified parameters.

Assessment

A child with OCD may need to have a school-based assessment to determine the ways in which OCD affects his functioning at school. An assessment can provide a "baseline" of the child's behaviors with which to compare progress over time. An accurate understanding of the child involves understanding him as a person, not as a problem. It is necessary to recognize the child's strengths, talents, interests and personality as well as his difficulties. A child's strengths, social and psychological competence can be tremendous resources that can be tapped on the road to recovery. It is just as important to appreciate the needs and strengths of the family and classroom environment because these are significant influences in the child's life.

School psychologists have specialized training in evaluating children. Assessment tools include interviews, psychological tests, self-report questionnaires and parent and teacher rating instruments. The assessment must also examine the need for school-based or community services. The results of the assessment and appropriate recommendations are then shared with the parents and other members of the partnership.

Some of the questions that a proper assessment must address include:

❑ What is the specific behavior that is problematic?
❑ When did it begin?
❑ When does the behavior occur and in what circumstances?
❑ What is the frequency and duration of the behavior?
❑ How distressed is the child?
❑ What is the child's developmental level?
❑ Is the behavior normal and expected for the child's age?
❑ What factors in the classroom, school or home appear to affect the child's behavior?
❑ How is the child's academic, social and personal functioning affected?
❑ How do peers, teachers and parents respond to the child's behavior?

❑ What responses calm the child and what seem to escalate anxiety?

❑ What are the child's coping skills?

❑ What are his resources and personal strengths?

❑ Does the child seem to be improving without intervention?

❑ What are the risks and side effects of different types of treatment?

❑ How do the parents and child feel about therapy and medications?

❑ Are the child's treatment needs within the purview of the school?

❑ Is there access to a community professional who treats OCD?

Appropriate referral

A child with any kind of physical or behavioral symptoms should always be referred to his or her pediatrician for an evaluation to rule out medical reasons for symptoms, and to obtain the pediatrician's impressions and recommendations. School personnel can provide appropriate and timely referrals as necessary to community healthcare providers.

Table 15: Guidelines for Referral to Mental Health Clinicians

❑ There are no qualified school personnel to conduct an assessment or school based intervention
❑ OCD or anxiety is impacting the child's school functioning
❑ The child's symptoms are complex and involve multiple diagnoses
❑ The child has suicidal thoughts or intentions
❑ The child's OCD extends outside the school, such as the home
❑ School-based interventions are not helping the child
❑ The child's needs exceed the scope of the school's resources
❑ The focus of intervention may need to extend to family members
❑ Interventions at school may compromise the privacy of the family

Since OCD is fairly complex to treat and because schools are primarily educational rather than treatment settings, children with OCD should receive treatment from a qualified therapist who can provide CBT, and/or a child psychiatrist to provide medications. Parents may initiate these contacts, either at the recommendation of the school, or of their own choosing. Parents, school personnel and community providers should be able to have regular dialogue during the child's treatment. Chapter 7 provides guidance on finding a CBT therapist. Schools and parents must understand and accept that receiving therapy from a mental health provider is not a sign of weakness of character. Parents and schools need to work together to eliminate the stigma associated with mental health care. Table 15 presents rules of thumb to guide referrals to mental health clinicians.

Provision of a physically and emotionally safe environment

School personnel have a responsibility to develop and maintain an atmosphere of *Safety and Respect* for all children within their walls. Every child should be ensured of a healthy and safe school environment and should not have to endure ridicule or humiliation for any problem or disability. Teachers should model respectful behaviors and convey the sense that each child is fundamentally a good person. Interactions with the children should be supportive and encouraging. Children with OCD (and other problems) should feel emotionally safe to make mistakes that are driven by their difficulties. If they do not, the effort they put into suppressing their disability is emotionally draining and detracts from their ability to attend to schoolwork. A child's worries or fears should never be dismissed or belittled. They may appear senseless or unwarranted, but they are still real to the child. Children with OCD often recognize the incongruity between their fears and reality but simply do not have the skills to refocus and manage their anxiety.

Safety and respect grow from an appreciation of diversity and individual differences. Schools can foster understanding, tolerance and appreciation of OCD and its impact on children. They can work to increase awareness about OCD by making it a part of the regular curriculum. Age-appropriate descriptions, books, videos and talks by parents or local experts are helpful. Introducing children's books such as *Up and Down the Worry Hill* (see *Resources*) and other books about OCD may help peers understand what it might be like to have OCD. Peers can be educated without compromising a child's confidentiality by providing information in general terms. If the child's OCD symptoms are conspicuous and raise questions from classmates, school personnel may seek permission from the child and parent to educate peers. Some brave parents and children with OCD opt to speak to the class to let them know and understand OCD. Children often respond with surprising compassion and sensitivity.

Children with OCD often have low self-esteem and poor peer relations. They may even be isolated. School personnel can help boost the child's self esteem by recognizing and acknowledging the child's strengths and talents. Classroom practices or school policies that exacerbate anxiety should be closely examined and remedied. Punitive discipline, uncontrolled peer teasing or aggression and a high rate of negative interchanges must be eliminated. Children with OCD should be assigned to teachers who understand the disorder and have a "kind but firm" approach.

Children with OCD might incur ridicule, teasing and bullying if their symptoms are conspicuous. They may be among the 15 to 20% of students who are bullied in schools each year. Bullying may be the most prevalent form of violence in schools and can have very damaging consequences. Adult attitudes about bullying and teasing have often been that it is "just the way kids will always be" and victims need to learn how to "deal with it." In recent years, our attention has been drawn to tragic school shootings that were perpetrated by teenagers who were bullied and ostracized, and who described their actions as retaliation against the humiliations to which they were subjected. Although these are extreme instances, they should help us realize that victims of teasing suffer tremendously and are not always be able to "deal with it" and "move on."

A "zero tolerance" rule for bullying and aggression is well advised. School personnel should be vigilant for teasing and set limits quickly and consistently. However, peer group norms may be a far more powerful tool in the war against bullying than are school policing policies. That's because bullying carries on in locker rooms occurs regardless of the school's policies. Building awareness of the harmful effects of bullying, changing peer group norms, attitudes and acceptance of bullying and increasing peer empathy for victims are helpful strategies. Role-playing the victim of bullying for a day can greatly increase children's sensitivity and empathy. They become more receptive when they can simulate and "walk in the shoes" of victims. Reframing bullying as a sign of immaturity, weakness or cowardice rather than heroism can go a long way towards protecting innocent children. Bullying thrives because it can remain hidden and unreported. Changing the culture of disdain for those who tell on bullies is just as important.

Peers and teachers should also not be subject to the aggression or anger of a child with OCD. These children also need to learn how to express anger, anxiety, and other negative feelings safely and acceptably. Angry episodes and lashing out should be targeted for a *Corrective Learning Experience* (see Chapter 12). Figure 10 describes the use of a Corrective Learning Experience in the school setting.

Management of OCD in school

There are two types of school-based interventions that may be suitable for children with OCD. The first is *Stabilization*, which is an immediate and short-term response. Its goal is to recognize the limits of the child's abilities during a crisis and to ease pressures sufficiently to allow him to continue to learn until treatment can take effect. The second type involves *CBT interventions* that will give the child the skills to overcome the OCD fears and rituals that impede school functioning.

❖   Phase I: Stabilization

A child in the throes of OCD does not have the skills to cope and function adequately in school. Until he does, the responsibility of easing the pressures on him rests with the adults in his life. Stabilization involves setting realistic expectations about what a child can accomplish in a time of crisis. It involves letting the child deal with one challenge at a time. It may be necessary to adapt classroom expectations to allow the child to achieve success on the most essential tasks—getting an education and getting well.

Figure 10: Corrective Learning Experiences

Child's Name: Alex   **Teacher:**Mrs. Logan   **Date**: September 22.

SITUATION: Commotion in cafeteria line; Ryan jostled Alex.
CHILD'S BEHAVIOR: Alex punched Ryan in shoulder, swore at staff.

1. **ANTICIPATE/DISSIPATE**
    Early cues: Alex was mildly irritable in the line. No other signs.
    Strategies: Ask Alex if he's okay. Be vigilant for other signs of distress.
2. **POSSIBLE TRIGGERS** Crowded hallway, touch provoked fear of contracting hepatitis.
3. **DEFLECT/DEFUSE:** Increase space in line, ask students to spread out.
4. **SELF-CALMING**   **Feeling temperature**: Six
    Cues for need to self-calm: Irritable, raised voice, fidgety
    Where/how child will take space: Leave the room and take space in
    hallway or library.
5. **TIMELY DISENGAGEMENT:**   **Feeling temperature**: 8
    Cues for disengagement: Agitated, not listening, argumentative.
    What/how: Stop talking or reasoning. Leave scene, ask Alex to take
    space.
6. **TIMELY REENGAGEMENT:**   **What happened?** Alex hit a peer.
    What feelings? Fear and anger.   **Feeling temperature?** 10
    Were feelings okay? Yes.   **Were actions okay?** No.
    If not, why not? Peer was unaware that he was provoking; aggression is
    not acceptable
    How could feelings be expressed appropriately? Verbalize, tell peer.
    How could actions be different? Walk away, find another spot, ask staff
    permission to come back later.
7. **WAYS TO REDUCE RECURRENCE**
    Early warning signals: Restless, Fear temperature of 6.
    Trigger: Touch   **Solution**: Keep distance. Alex last in line
8. **ACCOUNTABILITY: Impact of actions:** Unsuspecting peer injured,
    chaos in cafeteria, rudeness to staff.
9. **WAYS TO MAKE AMENDS:** Apologize to peer and staff.

Accommodations are generally temporary and should be flexible enough to be modified or discontinued when child is doing better or treatment is taking effect. However, they may need to be continued when a child's symptoms are not responsive to treatment or when he is chronically ill. Accommodations and adaptations to the curriculum, instructional methods and the pace of delivery can provide relief from routine expectations and reduce the child's responsibilities to the essential. They make it easier for the child to do what's most important. For example, when Emily struggles to write perfectly, it may be helpful to excuse her from writing in cursive or writing at all. She may be permitted use of the computer or audiotapes to get the work done. In the big scheme of things, what is important is that Emily learns the material, regardless of how she learns it.

Accommodations allow the setting of goals that the child can achieve and not fail. Anxious children need the experience of mastery, not further failure. Children should not be punished for behaviors that are clearly driven by OCD. For instance, if your child is late for class because he has a two-hour long grooming ritual each morning, he will not benefit from being punished for being late. Rather, being excused temporarily while he is learning how to overcome OCD is a more helpful response. Likewise, being punished for being inattentive or preoccupied with rituals will not help the child overcome the preoccupation. Strategies that are effective for a child should be recorded in a *"Skill Diary"* or notebook in which successful techniques are documented. The Skill Diary should be easily accessible to the child and parents, to allow quick referencing when needed.

Parents and teachers alike may be concerned that accommodations are not fair. They may be bothered by the fact that it makes things too easy, promotes excuses or sets a bad precedent that cannot be followed. OCD, like asthma or diabetes, is a legitimate illness that impairs coping and functioning. Children with OCD don't derive any pleasure from their condition and are not doing it just to be difficult. They are genuinely anxious and do not have effective coping skills.

There is a difference between *fair* and *equal*. The belief that all children are homogeneous in their needs is a myth. Each child is unique and different and not equal to any other. Fairness refers to meeting each child's unique needs, whereas equality refers to treating every child in the same way, regardless of needs. A child with a reading disability is given remedial assistance. The additional help is fair, but certainly not equal. Likewise, the accommodations made for an anxious child are *fair but not equal.* When parents and schools are rigid and inflexible about school expectations, the child may give up on school altogether. It is wise for school personnel to recognize the point of no return and the futility of damaging "power struggles." Schools are encouraged to make necessary accommodations before the child finds it so aversive that he quits school altogether.

❖ *Phase II-School-based intervention*

School personnel may implement school-based CBT interventions *in conjunction with the child's CBT therapist.* It is critical that school interventions occur in partnership with the therapist, so that they are consistent and directed at the same goals. If not, the outcome could be disastrous. The child's OCD may actually become much worse if the child gets confused with counteracting interventions. Pressure to "fix" all the child's difficulties as "soon as possible" can come from many directions. Parents, teachers, other school personnel, and perhaps even the child herself may be impatient for results. The sense of urgency can blur clarity and actually set back treatment. The child's CBT therapist, in partnership with the child, must determine the treatment goals and the pace of treatment. All interventions must be planned and systematic, and must be implemented with the child's prior knowledge. For example, the child's CBT therapist may suggest that the teacher help the child overcome reassurance questions in the classroom. With the therapist's guidance, the child's teacher may inform the child that she will only answer the same question twice a day instead of 20 times.

It is necessary to have the following issues clarified, agreed upon, and communicated among parents, school personnel and therapists before school-based interventions are implemented.

❑ Who is responsible for implementing and monitoring each intervention?

❑ What are the precise parameters of each intervention?

❏   What specific roles are to be played by the child, parent, teacher, other school staff and community provider?

❏   What resources and services will be needed to put the plans into action?

❏   Do staff or parents need to be trained before proceeding?

❏   Has the child been prepared adequately for each intervention?

❏   Where and when will each intervention occur?

❏   What exactly will happen when the intervention is carried out?

❏   How will the child's response to each treatment be recorded?

❏   How will the plan be scrutinized?

❏   How will the need for modifications be determined?

❏   How will changes be incorporated and executed?

BARRIERS IN THE HOME-SCHOOL PARTNERSHIP

Partnerships don't always come easily. Although they may be ideal for optimizing resources, they can be challenging to develop and maintain. Parents, schools and clinicians often have different goals, expectations and means. There are many instances in which partnerships between schools and parents are weak or nonexistent. There are two sides to this picture: Schools who perceive parents of a child as unwilling to cooperate, and parents who perceive school personnel as uninformed or disinterested.

Home-school partnerships can be challenging to maintain when parents and school personnel don't see eye to eye about the child's needs. Gaps and mishaps in communication may lead to serious miscommunication. Failure to follow-through with mutually accepted accommodations or interventions is a major reason for problems in the partnership. For example, Casey's parents and school counselor agreed that Casey should be given additional time to complete all assignments. Yet, the next day, the math teacher penalized Casey for not handing in his work on time. He had not received communication about the accommodation that was being made for Casey.

Power struggles may emerge when parents and schools lock heads about the child's need for services in school. Parents are more educated than ever about their children's conditions and needs, and more actively involved in advocating for their children in school. They are more likely to propose their own views and to challenge the recommendations of the school if they do not see them fitting. They are less likely to simply accept what they hear from school personnel.

There are many reasons why schools may sometimes be less than ideally helpful to children with OCD. Their inability to mobilize or organize may not be willful. Instead, it may merely reflect lack of knowledge and understanding about OCD. In addition, many schools may not have adequate resources to help children with special needs, even though the law requires that they do. Teachers may be overwhelmed trying to attend appropriately to all the children in the class. They may be frustrated and isolated in dealing with the child with OCD. In many cases, the disruptive or defiant child commands far more of the teacher's attention than the child with OCD. Mental health professionals in schools may be overburdened. Some schools have school psychologist to student ratios of 1:2500, counselor to student ratios of 1:550 (the recommended ratio is 1:250) and social worker to student ratios much higher than the recommended 1:800.

Further, there are differences in philosophy. Some school personnel subscribe to the viewpoint that schools should attend to children's academic needs only. Others may see the child's emotional well being as inextricable from the child's academic functioning. Some staff may be empathic and understanding of the child's distress whereas others believe that the child is being manipulative and needs only firm discipline. Sometimes, there may be a mismatch in styles between a teacher and child or parent. Some educators may be strict, rule-bound and inflexible whereas others are willing to go the extra mile to help the child.

Working through the obstacles

A preventive approach can preempt many obstacles from arising. Schools that proactively foster a culture of partnership with parents in every area of a child's functioning will encounter fewer problems in working with parents when a child has difficulty. Many crises can be averted when good partnerships are in place ahead of time. Schools can anticipate and prevent problematic partnerships by initiating meetings with parents before the school year begins, providing a welcoming environment and sending the message that parental involvement is valued. Parent participation increases when it is invited and promoted, rather than passively accepted. Schools may foster open dialogue and provide opportunities for parents to have decision-making roles in school issues. Schools can educate parents in order to allay concerns pertaining to confidentiality and labeling. Schools must adhere strictly to laws and guidelines regarding confidentiality. In an environment of collaboration, a child's problems become a shared responsibility that is addressed jointly by parents and school personnel.

Teachers, who are on the front-line of teamwork with parents, may need a range of resources to facilitate optimal alliances. Schools may need to release time for teachers to meet with parents in order to build better collaborations. It's a process that takes time and needs to be started well before a crisis arises. Teachers may also need support and consultation on how to handle a child with OCD. Although many teachers now have training and experience in working with special-needs children due to mainstreaming, they are primarily educators, not mental health personnel. They may need specific resources such as "how-to" strategies and an aide to provide an extra pair of hands, eyes and ears. Teachers may also benefit from peer social support to relieve the sense of frustration and isolation they might experience.

Schools and parents must be willing to take an honest look at problems on *both* sides of the fence. They must be open and willing to engage. Parents may need to acknowledge and change parenting practices that are detrimental to the child's development. School personnel may need to examine disciplinary practices, classroom atmospheres and school policies that adversely affect the child. Parents must have an accurate understanding of the school's capabilities and constraints. A militant attitude on either side of the partnership is detrimental. Parents who are waiting for the school to make a mistake to prove their incompetence are unlikely to be able to work with the school. It is important that parents not get overly focused on procedural errors that were accidental. Parents should pick their battles, focus on the most important issues and let go of the trivial.

SPECIAL SERVICES OR NOT?

Children with OCD have a right to appropriate school-based services. For some children, OCD may be so debilitating in school that they need formal services. The Individuals with Disabilities Education Act (IDEA) and *Section 504 of the Rehabilitation Act of 1973* mandate a *Free and Appropriate Education (FAPE)* in the *Least Restrictive Environment* (LRE) for all children from preschool through high school. Public schools in the US are mandated to abide by these regulations whereas private schools are not required to comply. State and education agencies must actively seek out and identify children who have special education needs. In theory, the laws bring significant benefits. In reality, it is far more complicated than that. There are specific guidelines and procedures associated with their activation. Too often, these procedures and their implementation get tied up in the red tape of bureaucracy.

The IDEA and Section 504 mandate that the education that children receive must meet their academic, social and psychological needs. The accommodations and remedial services may be broad in range to include an aide in the classroom, occupational, speech or behavior therapy specialists to help staff design relevant interventions, or home tutoring if the child is unable to remain in school. If the public school cannot meet the needs of the child, the school must pay for alternative schooling such as a private school or residential placement.

IDEA and IEP

Qualifying for IDEA services requires a formal process of evaluation by the school. The school's Committee on Special Education (CSE) or equivalent convenes to determine the child's needs. Parental consent is required for initiation of assessment. The evaluation must show that the child has deficits in academic, social or behavioral areas due to the impeding condition. Schools provide free evaluations; however, you have the right to an independent evaluation at your own cost. No one test is a determining factor for services. Matters will proceed more smoothly if your child has an official diagnosis of OCD made by a qualified professional.

When the assessment is completed, the CSE convenes, along with the parent and sometimes the child, to review the results of the assessment and to generate appropriate recommendations. Parents are equal participants in the decision-making process. If the child meets criteria for impairment, the child must be "classified" as having one of the dozen or so disabilities that are designated by the education department. After classification, the team that includes the parent, school personnel such as the teacher, psychologist, special education teacher, guidance counselor and administrator develop an *Individualized Education Plan* (IEP). This written document spells out the accommodations and interventions that will be provided to the child to remedy educational deficits. The IEP must be developed for each child based on his unique needs and signed by the parent to become an official document. IDEA requires updated testing and a new IEP every three years.

Special education classification is confidential and should be withheld from transcripts to colleges. It is against the law for schools to communicate with colleges regarding 504 or IDEA status, so labeling should not follow your child beyond the school. Parents have the right to educational records, and can request that they be amended.

Section 504 Plans

For children whose disability is not as severe, a *504 Plan*, which is less formal than the IDEA and IEP may suffice. The 504 Plan has a broader definition of disability, in contrast to IDEA, for which the criteria are more specific. Having a 504 Plan in place for your child makes it easier to request accommodations or special assistance for your child, as it allows the school to access financial support to meet your child's needs. With a 504 Plan, your child may be able to get a reduced schedule, home instruction, attend classes for a few hours rather than all day, have a classroom aide, resource room help, less homework and other concessions. Many parents prefer to initiate a 504 Plan proactively because OCD problems could emerge at any time. Because these procedures take due time, they choose not to wait until a crisis strikes.

Even though a 504 Plan is less formal than the IDEA, a formal diagnosis is usually necessary to access services. There must be written documentation of an impairment that interferes with your child's learning and socialization. You must initiate a request for a 504 Plan in writing. A 504 Plan can be written by parents and teachers without the involvement of the district administration or CSE. The plan is far simpler and less detailed than an IEP. There are no requirements that testing be conducted. Parental input or consent is not required for implementation of a 504 Plan.

The issue of classification and labeling are emotionally charged issues for many parents. Like most states in the U.S., the state of New York has two categories within which OCD may be classified: *Emotionally Disturbed* (ED) and *Other Health Impaired* (OHI). The ED label has developed a disparaging connotation, and parents cringe at having their child labeled as "disturbed." They are concerned about the label following their child through high school, college and perhaps even into the workplace. Problmes such as stigma, incorrect classification, lack of instructional relevance and exclusion of children from regular education have added to the concerns of parents.

In recent years, children with Tourette Syndrome and OCD have sometimes been classified as OHI because these disorders have been shown to have a neurobiological basis. Those who stand by the ED label argue that exceptions can set an unsustainable precedent because every psychiatric disorder potentially has a neurobiological component; therefore, a child with any psychiatric condition could potentially be classified as OHI. There are larger political, policy and funding ramifications to these labels that are beyond the scope of this book. It is not a simple matter for schools to assign the OHI label for psychiatric conditions.

Parents who have concerns about labeling may want to learn more about the *Rights without Labels* movement (see *Resources*). The concept of Rights Without Labels grew out of the need to remedy problems related to labeling children as "emotionally disturbed" or "handicapped." The thrust of the movement is to meet the special needs of children without labeling them or removing them from mainstream classes. Educational programs are tailored to instructional deficits and strengths that are pertinent to the child's unique needs. Thorough coverage of these provisions is beyond the scope of this book. Parents who wish to learn more can find excellent books and online sources of information in the *Resources* section.

ADVOCATING FOR YOUR CHILD

The parents of children with OCD or Tourette Syndrome have to become vocal advocates for their child. Unless there are pronounced motor tics and crippling obsessions, the child looks no different than all the other kids and most others don't tolerate the behaviors of these disorders. We have spent hours talking to teachers and school administrators; some has paid off handsomely and some for naught. Teachers can intellectually accept Danny's disorder but emotionally not deal with his behavior. His kindergarten and first grade teachers really were not good at accepting the unending questions or outburst, no matter how many times we tried to explain. I once asked the teacher if it would be okay for me to discipline her for blinking, because Danny's questions were as unstoppable as her blinking.

David, grandfather of Danny, age 8

Remember, you are your child's best advocate. You know your child best. Don't be afraid to persevere for what your child needs. When you are ready to approach the school, start with your child's teacher or school counselor, as you see fit. Seek to work in *collaboration,* as equal partners in your child's care. Ask for their help in meeting your child's needs. It is important to have teachers understand that you want to work together with them, not against them. It does not help anyone if you or the teachers take adversarial positions—no one wins, and your child loses badly. Although your child's needs come first to you, the teacher has other children in his class whose parents want their child's need to come first too.

Set up regular communication with your child's teacher or counselor. Communicate both when things are going well and when there are problems. Work directly with the teacher if you have one that understands and is willing to work with you. Use the *Parent-Teacher Log* (Figure 11) to exchange daily notes about your child. Encourage your child to share school experiences with you. Suggest that he let the teacher know when he is having trouble and needs help. Discuss how your child can help himself in school, in the cafeteria and on the playground. Give school and teachers positive feedback when they are responding to child's needs.

Make a written list of your child's difficulties. Try to be as specific as possible. Get a formal diagnosis in writing from your child's pediatrician or mental health professional. Bring facts and information on OCD for the teacher to read. Give the teachers a list of your child's obsessions and compulsions, so that they are aware when a roadblock arises. Knowing can help them understand and work around it rather than enforcing a discipline issue. Be organized and attend every meeting with school personnel with pen and paper in hand. Make copies of all communications and document all phone calls. Keep a binder with everything documented.

If school personnel try to dissuade you from seeking special services for your child, don't take a first "No" as the final "No." Be persistent and determined and take your request to a higher school official. When you attend meetings, take another person who can be cool-headed and can keep perspective if you are likely to get upset. Ask for a parent advocate who can help you navigate through the rules, regulations and other complex issues that arise. Try to find and talk to parents of other children with OCD—they can often help you navigate through the system, and access services faster while avoiding some of the pitfalls they have encountered. You can benefit from their efforts.

All said and done, if you believe that your child's school is not responding to your child's needs despite your best efforts, you may seek *due process*. The law guarantees your right to appeal the school's decision and gives you the right to have an impartial hearing. You also have similar rights if you believe that your child's IEP or 504 Plan is not being followed. Information on due process may be found in the *Resources* section.

Figure 11: Parent-Teacher Log

Child's Name: Haley   Parent/Teacher:Mrs. Francis   Date: Nov 13

0	1	2	3	4	5	6	7	8	9	10
No problems			Mild		Moderate		Strong			Extreme

What went well for the child today? In what situations did he/she experience success? Math homework on time, 100% accuracy

Overall mood/anxiety for the day (0-10): 7

Were there any situations in which the child was upset? If yes, please describe: Second period, Haley wanted to call her mother

Child's mood and distress in this situation (0-10): 9

Describe child's specific behaviors: Crying, pleading to call

Describe child's feelings: Sad, upset, worried about mother

What was happening prior to the occurrence of this situation? Class was reading a book about a family trip to the zoo.

What was the impact of the child's behavior? Not able to finish story, class disrupted

How did your child handle this situation? Said she didn't want to hear the story

How did you handle this situation? Asked her to stop, so that class could complete the rest of the story

How did the child react to your handling? Stopped momentarily, but resumed soon

How long did the episode last? 45 minutes

STRATEGIES AND SOLUTIONS AT SCHOOL

The following are common OCD-related problems that children experience in school. Several potential accommodations and CBT interventions are suggested for each. Parents, school personnel and the child's therapist must work collaboratively to select and apply the suggested interventions as fitting to the child's unique circumstances.

The 3 R's: Reading, wRiting and aRithmetic

☐ Allow oral work, tape-recording or books-on-tape.

☐ Allow typing or use of the computer.

☐ Provide teacher outlines and shorter or fewer assignments.

☐ Allow printing if cursive is difficult.

☐ Allow a peer to be a "helping buddy," providing notes and extra help.

☐ Grade on effort or content rather than appearance.

☐ Allow multiple-choice format for tests, rather than essay format.

☐ Identify triggers or reasons for reading/writing difficulties.

☐ Use *Parent-Teacher Log* to communicate between home and school.

☐ Be consistent in the child management approach at home and school.

☐ Use the *Worry Hill* to explain exposure, habituation and anticipatory anxiety.

☐ Use the *Feeling Thermometer* to describe and rate emotions.

☐ Begin gradual exposure to triggers for writing/reading problems.

☐ Provide a *Worry Hill Memory Card* for easy recall of exposures.

☐ Develop a signal to communicate with the teacher when the child needs a break.

☐ Make a copy of the assignment, then have the child cross out text to prevent re-reading.

☐ Reward for effort; don't punish failure.

☐ Designate a place to "take space" periodically or as needed.

☐ Convey confidence, hope and optimism about recovery.

☐ Set a positive example; role model the desirable behavior for the child.

School refusal

☐ Determine the root cause for school refusal. Don't make assumptions.

☐ Address and remedy legitimate concerns, if possible.

☐ Keep the child in school as long as possible; avoid sending him home.

☐ Encourage the child to talk to the school psychologist or counselor.

☐ Avoid lengthy arguments or explanations about need to be in school.

☐ Use *Parent-Teacher Log* to communicate between home and school.

☐ Use a consistent child management approach at home and at school.

☐ Remove inadvertent bonuses of staying home such as TV or sleeping.

☐ If the child stays home, simulate school environment at home as closely as possible (follow school schedule, sit at desk, do schoolwork)

☐ Use the *Worry Hill* to explain exposure, habituation and anticipatory anxiety.

☐ Use the *Feeling Thermometer* to describe and rate emotions.

☐ Begin exposure with driving to school, entering in low anxiety area or staying for a short while. Increase time to one class, half day, and eventually full day.

☐ Provide a *Worry Hill Memory Card* for easy recall of exposures.

☐ Develop a signal to communicate with the teacher when the child needs a break.

☐ Designate a place to "take space" periodically or as needed.

☐ Rehearse and role-play appropriate behaviors.

☐ Set a positive example; role model the desirable behavior for the child.

☐ Minimize attention to negative behaviors, maximize attention to desirable behaviors.

☐ Reward efforts towards attendance and being on time.

Homebound instruction should not be considered the first choice accommodation for the child who refuses school. Rather, it should be considered as an intervention of last resort, and as a means to an end rather than an end in itself. Plans for homebound instruction should include steps to ensure a gradual return to the school or an alternative environment, and should have a time frame for implementation.

Reassurance questions

☐ Don't dismiss or belittle the child's questions, e.g., "*That's silly, stop it.*"

☐ Don't stop reassurance abruptly or completely.

☐ Use *Parent-Teacher Log* to communicate between home and school.

☐ Use a consistent child management approach at home and at school.

☐ Plan a gradual reduction in the number of reassurances.

☐ Prepare the child for the change in intervention; elicit willingness and participation.

☐ Use *Feeling Thermometer* to describe and rate change in emotions.

☐ Dispel myths and misconceptions about the feared situation; provide accurate facts.

☐ Explain anticipatory anxiety: "*The feeling will pass.*"

☐ Use the *Worry Hill* to explain exposure, habituation and anticipatory anxiety.

☐ Redirect the child, "*Who's asking, you or OCD?*"

☐ Set limits on questions by giving "coupons" that can be redeemed for answers.

☐ Remain kind but firm, "*One answer is good enough.*"

☐ Write the answer on an index card for the child to reference, instead of asking.

☐ Encourage the child to answer his questions for himself.

☐ Provide a *Worry Hill Memory Card* for easy recall of exposures.

☐ Refrain from giving unlimited reassurance, "*We'll have to see what happens.*"

☐ Teach the child to make realistic estimates of danger.

☐ Teach calming self-talk and how to "take space" when upset.

☐ Provide *Corrective Learning Experiences* (see Chapter 12).

☐ Set a positive example; role model the desirable behavior for the child.

☐ Reward the child when he refrains from questions or answers them for himself.

Separation anxiety

☐ Remain calm, matter of fact and firm during routine separations.

☐ Don't hover, question or reassure excessively.

❑ Limit reassurance to one or two times.

❑ Use *Parent-Teacher Log* to communicate between home and school.

❑ Use a consistent child management approach at home and at school.

❑ Limit check-in visits or phone calls when the child is in school.

❑ Allow a transitional object for comfort until the child masters anxiety.

❑ Limit the child's ability to leave school and return home.

❑ Use the *Worry Hill* to explain exposure, habituation and anticipatory anxiety.

❑ Remove the comforts of staying home or returning home from school.

❑ Use *Feeling Thermometer* to describe and rate emotions.

❑ Teach calming self-talk and how to take space when upset.

❑ Provide a *Worry Hill Memory Card* for easy recall of exposures.

❑ Plan gradual re-entry for the child who has been out of school.

❑ Seek opportunities to separate from the child for increasing periods.

❑ Create opportunities for repetition and practice.

❑ Encourage independent activities and self-reliance.

❑ Set a positive example; role model the desirable behavior for the child.

❑ Reward and praise efforts in the direction of separation, independence and initiative.

Perfectionism

❑ Normalize and model imperfection—*"It's good enough."*

❑ Help the child re-label the thoughts, "*Is this me or is this my anxiety?*"

❑ Use *Parent-Teacher Log* to communicate between home and school.

❑ Use a consistent child management approach at home and at school.

❑ Set limits on checking, erasures and revisions by giving a fixed number of coupons.

❑ Set time limits for completion of assignments.

❑ Use the *Feeling Thermometer* to describe and rate emotions.

❑ Teach self-calming and taking space.

❑ Teach the child to make realistic estimates of danger.

❑ Teach the child to examine the worst consequences of imperfection.

❑ Teach the child to examine the evidence for his worst fears.

❑ Use the *Worry Hill* to explain exposure, habituation and anticipatory anxiety.

☐ Generate exposure exercises that involve making mistakes or having less-than-perfect work on purpose, e.g., being late to class, handing in work with obvious errors.

☐ Teach coping skills to manage feared consequences.

☐ Provide a *Worry Hill Memory Card* for easy recall of exposures.

☐ Set a positive example; role model the desirable behavior for the child.

☐ Reward efforts at imperfection.

☐ Schedule planned relaxing activities with no goal to be achieved other than fun.

Contamination

☐ Allow the child to arrive 15 minutes late or leave early, or be last in line in the cafeteria to minimize triggers for fears.

☐ Allow easy and discreet exit from a triggering situation.

☐ Reduce expectations that add pressure.

☐ Use the *Feeling Thermometer* to describe and rate emotions.

☐ Use *Parent-Teacher Log* to communicate between home and school.

☐ Use a consistent child management approach at home and at school.

☐ Use the *Worry Hill* to explain exposure, habituation and anticipatory anxiety.

☐ Identify triggers for obsessions and rituals.

☐ Begin gradual exposure to triggers for contamination.

☐ Provide a *Worry Hill Memory Card* for easy recall of exposures.

☐ Provide specific guidelines regarding when it's okay to wash, e.g., after using bathroom and before eating.

☐ Set a positive example; role model the desirable behavior for the child.

☐ Make You and Me Alone (YAMA) time to increase positive interactions.

☐ Reward effort; don't punish failure.

Inability to complete assignments and homework

☐ Give additional time to complete the work.

☐ Assign shorter or fewer assignments.

☐ Insist that the child has an assignment book.

❏ Carefully structure assignment and homework time.

❏ Reduce the homework load.

❏ Do not send incomplete assignments home for completion.

❏ Limit open-ended choices.

❏ Allow the child to complete every other problem.

❏ Break down assignments into 10 or 15 minute segments

❏ Allow breaks to take space.

❏ Use the *Feeling Thermometer* to describe and rate emotions.

❏ Use *Parent-Teacher Log* to communicate between home and school.

❏ Use a consistent child management approach at home and at school.

❏ Use the *Worry Hill* to explain exposure, habituation and anticipatory anxiety.

❏ Identify triggers for obsessions and rituals.

❏ Begin gradual exposure to triggers.

❏ Provide a *Worry Hill Memory Card* for easy recall of exposures.

❏ Grade and reward for effort, don't penalize for failure.

❏ Allow short breaks between segments to rest or refresh.

❏ Set a maximum time limit for each assignment or segment.

❏ Grade on content rather than appearance.

Trips to the bathroom

❏ Limit trips to the bathroom with prearranged bathroom times.

❏ Gradually reduce frequency and length of trips to the bathroom.

❏ Arrange for a fixed number of bathroom visits per day.

❏ Schedule hourly or half-hourly trips to the bathroom to eliminate the need to sk for permission.

❏ Give the child a fixed number of "bathroom passes" per day that the child can use at his discretion.

❏ Offer rewards for each time the child decides that he doesn't need to go to the bathroom.

❏ Gradually lengthen the interval and reduce the frequency of bathroom trips.

❏ Identify reasons for frequent bathroom visits.

❏ Use the *Feeling Thermometer* to describe and rate emotions.

❑ Generate exposures to triggers.

❑ Use *Parent-Teacher Log* to communicate between home and school.

❑ Use a consistent child management approach at home and at school.

❑ Avoid power struggles.

❑ Use the *Worry Hill* to explain exposure, habituation and anticipatory anxiety.

❑ Identify triggers for obsessions and rituals.

❑ Begin gradual exposure to triggers.

❑ Provide a *Worry Hill Memory Card* for easy recall of exposures.

Panic

❑ Teach proper labels for panic and anxiety.

❑ Teach the child to distinguish between normal anxiety and panic.

❑ Use the *Feeling Thermometer* to describe and rate emotions.

❑ Use *Parent-Teacher Log* to communicate between home and school.

❑ Use a consistent child management approach at home and at school.

❑ Provide a safe place to take space and calm down.

❑ Teach the child to breathe into a paper bag to stop hyperventilation.

❑ Develop a signal system to communicate an impending panic attack.

❑ Place the child's desk near the door for easy and discreet exit.

❑ Provide reasonable reassurance.

❑ Provide *Corrective Learning Experiences* (CLE's) for meltdowns.

❑ Be kind but firm in setting limits.

❑ Teach calming self-talk.

❑ Use the *Worry Hill* to explain exposure, habituation and anticipatory anxiety.

❑ Identify triggers for obsessions and rituals.

❑ Generate gradual exposure exercises.

❑ Provide a *Worry Hill Memory Card* for easy recall of exposures.

❑ Set a positive example; role model the desirable behavior for the child.

❑ Reward efforts at self-calming.

Difficulty shifting gears

❑ Try to understand reasons for the child's behavior.

❑ Accept the child's limitations in flexibility.

❑ Plan, anticipate and ease transitions.

❑ Provide early warning of impending transition.

❑ Provide extra time, visual and concrete cues to aid in transitions.

❑ Keep the routine predictable; avoid abrupt changes.

❑ Use the *Feeling Thermometer* to describe and rate emotions.

❑ Give the child face-saving choices if he is upset.

❑ Make You and Me Alone (YAMA) time to increase positive interactions.

❑ Set a positive example; role model the desirable behavior for the child.

❑ Reward successful transitions.

❑ Use *Parent-Teacher Log* to communicate between home and school.

❑ Use a consistent child management approach at home and at school.

Performance/Test anxiety

❑ Allow untimed tests or shorter tasks to reduce pressure.

❑ Permit writing on the test booklet or checking off answers.

❑ Allow ungraded assignments.

❑ Focus on correct answers, not errors.

❑ Provide a quiet area, without distractions

❑ Permit test-taking orally, on the computer, or in multiple choice format if writing is difficult.

❑ Allow breaks during tests.

❑ Teach time management skills and effective test-taking strategies.

❑ Use the *Feeling Thermometer* to describe and rate emotions.

❑ Teach the child to answer the easiest questions first to build success.

❑ Teach the child to review the test before beginning to answer.

❑ Use the *Worry Hill* to explain exposure, habituation and anticipatory anxiety.

❑ Provide a *Worry Hill Memory Card* for easy recall of exposures.

❑ Use *Parent-Teacher Log* to communicate between home and school.

❑ Use a consistent child management approach at home and at school.

Tics

☐ Don't ask the child to stop tics.

☐ Don't punish or shame the child for uncontrollable behaviors.

☐ Ignore and downplay minor tics and misbehaviors.

☐ Divert peer attention away from the child's tics.

☐ Allow a discrete exit to another space until tics subside.

☐ Place the child's desk near the door for easy exit when tics are severe.

☐ Educate peers to increase sensitivity and acceptance.

☐ Excuse the child from routine expectations when tics are severe.

☐ Use *Parent-Teacher Log* to communicate between home and school.

☐ Use a consistent child management approach at home and at school.

☐ Make *You and Me Alone (YAMA)* time to increase positive interactions.

Meltdowns and explosiveness

☐ Use *Parent-Teacher Log* to communicate between home and school.

☐ Use a consistent child management approach at home and at school.

☐ Provide *Corrective Learning Experiences* (CLE's).

☐ Anticipate and intervene early; use warning cues to communicate.

☐ Use the *Feeling Thermometer* to describe and rate emotions.

☐ Give the child face-saving choices.

☐ Recognize the point of no return.

☐ Provide a safe place to take space when the child is upset.

☐ Refocus peers to reduce disruption to the class.

☐ Don't argue and debate; pick battles and avoid power struggles.

☐ Insist that child make amends for damage done.

☐ Allow a graceful exit to prevent escalation.

☐ Set a positive example; role model the desirable behavior for the child.

FREQUENTLY ASKED QUESTIONS

My son's teacher says that my son cannot move on to the next problem until he has done it perfectly. I'm like that too and I think that's a healthy behavior, but the teacher is concerned he is too obsessive. I don't agree because he's fine at home.

Perhaps you could ask the teacher for specific instances that are cause for his concern and how they affect your child's ability to get work done in school. The primary issue to focus on is whether your child's need to complete things "perfectly" is helping or hampering his progress. Perfectionism is on a continuum and can be both very healthy and productive in right measure. If it begins to interfere with functioning, is out of your son's control, and causes him great distress when interrupted from completing things to perfection, then it is certainly reason to be concerned.

I am concerned about my child's sliding grades. It's hard to see him fail.

When your child is sick, it's most important to take care of the illness. It's less important to have the best grades. Your child's health and happiness are the top priority. After all, the longer your child suffers from OCD, the less his chances of making good grades again. Depending on how severe your child's condition, you may have to let go of those standards until he is well. Remember, the crisis is temporary—once your child and your family have OCD under control, he can get right back on track.

My daughter has not gone to school for a week now. I keep trying to get her back in, but she refuses. What should I do?

Although it is generally best if your child stays in school rather than at home, that's not going to happen overnight. If your daughter is absolutely paralyzed or panic-stricken at the thought of going to school, it won't help either you or her to drag her to school, kicking and screaming. She needs to go back, but right now may not be the time. She may be just too sick— you can't send her in terror, it will make her even more terrified, and she will lose her trust in you. It is best to plan her return to school in conjunction with a therapist. Eventually, she must return to school and she will. This may seem hard to believe in the moment of crisis, but treatment can turn things around completely.

Chapter 14

"Where do we go from here?"

In the midst of a difficulty lies opportunity.

Albert Einstein

Bob is doing very well. His OCD symptoms have not returned in such a dramatic fashion as last year. Oh, it has been one year now! He has had some minor "episodes" but he has been able to overcome them quickly using the methods you have taught him. What he has learned has made him feel so much stronger than the OCD that he is able to self-talk his way out of situations that may have spiraled out of control last year. He is still on Luvox, but on a very low dose now.

Nina, mother of Bob

It's good that I have doctors' notes and my journal to look back on to help me remember. To be honest, I'd just as soon forget those early years. But remembering will help others living with OCD to know that they are not alone and that life can be much, much better.

Sharon, mother of Robert

Leo's doing great. His fourth grade teacher was wonderful and understanding and she helped him help himself. There are ups and downs, but missing spelling words, pencils out of order, mistakes on a video game—they're like water off a duck's back! The things that made him fall apart before are mere annoyances now.

Rita, mother of Leo

Bob, Robert, Leo and the other children in this book have been through the journey of treatment and recovery I have described in this book. Their families have been with them through it all, their experiences mirroring those of their child through the process. Not everyone has reached the same point in their journey, nor has the journey been the same for all. Yet, they have all derived something positive out of it. All credit goes to them for the courage they mustered to take the risks of treatment, the faith they retained in a life above and beyond OCD and the persistence to weather the ups and downs of the course. They refused to let OCD rule their lives. They accepted and used the power of choice to overcome the adversity that had come their way.

RECOVERY IS A JOURNEY, NOT AN EVENT

The process of recovery is not a "once and done" experience. Because OCD is known to be a life long disorder with no cure at the current time, recovery is a journey that spans one's life. As one parent summed it up, "You don't just get well. You have to fight to get well and fight to stay well." For some children, there is little OCD to contend with after treatment. For others, there are some symptoms, perhaps mild in nature, perhaps still severe. But recovery can happen *in spite of* OCD. That's because recovery means that you and your child have found a more effective way of handling life with OCD. OCD will not be in charge of your lives now. You and your child can choose which way to go and what to do with your lives. OCD may never fully go away, but as Sharon reflects, "life can be much, much better." You can have realistic optimism about the future.

Recovery is the process of healing. Healing takes time and tender care. Continue to take good care of yourself, your child and the rest of your family. Nurture yourselves and time will do the rest. When you start to heal, you become whole again. You may not have had the time to think much in the days of discovery and treatment, but now that things may have settled down, you may be free to contemplate your thoughts on many occasions. Even as you reach this stage in the journey, there are many forks in the road. *"Why me? Why my child?"* is one path you can choose as you try to make meaning of it all. That path usually leads you to a dead end. It is a stumbling block to recovery. There are no real answers to these questions, only ones you can create for yourself. Families who are spiritually inclined may find that "turning it over" to a higher power helps them break free of the burden of finding answers to these questions.

FROM ADVERSITY TO OPPORTUNITY

When you turn in the direction of the path labeled, *"What do I do now? Where do I go from here?"* you choose the path on which adversity can be changed into opportunity. You now divert your energy to looking forward to the future, not always glancing back at the past.

Adversity has a profound influence on people. It is generally a sobering experience. It makes you stop and think about yourself, the people around you and life in general. It makes you realize that time is short and cannot be taken back. It makes you so much more appreciative of the gifts you and your family are given. If you can find the good things in adversity, you can turn it from difficulty to opportunity. You can now find a new purpose and recreate a new life for yourselves.

Great people are born of adversity. Great people face difficulty by reaching deep down into the recesses of their character and finding in themselves strength and wisdom they didn't know they had. Like Thomas Merton, they discover, "Perhaps I am stronger than I think." Survivors turn misfortune into good fortune. When they fall, they pick themselves up, dust themselves off and keep going. They are not easily deterred. They don't give up. Everyone is given challenges; they are given to teach us the lessons that strengthen us for the journey ahead. Your attitude and beliefs about life are more important to your happiness than the actual circumstances that you encounter.

You can either choose to dwell in a past that cannot be changed or choose to move forwards into a future that *you* can change. You cannot control the events that come your way, but you can control how you handle them. It's not that difficulty won't visit you again; it's that difficulty will now meet a different person than it did in the past.

OCD, although by no means a desirable illness, will now present you and your child with a terrific opportunity to cope with life's other challenges. The lessons and skills your child learns during CBT treatment include training his mind to think differently, to take charge of his will, to seek and find the courage to face his worst fears. In fact, dealing with life's challenges is *no different* than dealing with OCD: To overcome adversity, you must confront it head on. Escape and avoidance won't make it go away. What powerful lessons to learn! Your child can now put these lessons to use in all walks of life, with any adversity or challenge that comes his way. In many ways, he is better equipped for the challenges of the future than most of us adults are.

Finding hope and opportunity in misfortune means that you must make peace with yourself, your child and the illness. You must find an inner quietude that gives you the strength and the courage to move above and beyond the adversity. The world is neither fair nor easy. If you believe you are a victim, you will see yourself as helpless. If you are helpless, you cannot take charge. Taking charge of your life is essential to recovery.

When you are inclined to feel sorry for yourself or your child, think about someone who is worse off than you. It will not be hard to do. The fact is that misfortune, like good fortune, comes to all. There are just different types of misfortune. Some are easier than OCD, some are worse; be thankful that yours is not worse. When you feel victimized, think of someone with a worse condition than yours—the child with a terminal illness, with his days numbered, with no chance to live out his childhood. Think of what his parents must face, with no way to recover their future. At least with OCD, your child has an 80% chance of recovery. He *can* regain a normal life; the possibility is always there. OCD author Dr. Herb Gravitz suggests that when you feel sorry for yourself, "go and volunteer at a burn unit." It will shock you into a fresh perspective on your misfortunes.

There will be rough spots along the way. For some families, this path of recovery has curves and rocky surfaces, unexpected twists and turns. For some families, it is an unforgiving series of hairpin bends. Visibility is not always the best. But now there's a difference. When adversity comes your way, you can have the confidence to take it on with a new strength that is born of knowledge and experience. You are not a novice anymore. There is no magic on this road, except that which comes from within you and your child as you discover yourselves as above the influence of OCD.

SLIPS AND SLIP RECOVERY

At the end of therapy, my son stopped his extensive bedtime ritual, his constant complaining and worrying about his health, and stopped most of his rituals. He still had some water fears, but they didn't stop him from anything. We had a happy, active child. Things were very good for about two years.

This year, he started middle school. He initially adjusted well to his new schedule and dove into various school activities. In retrospect, I think he did too much. About a month of so after school began, his health obsessions returned. It took a while to realize that he was having a "slip" and we've been working hard to get him back on track. He's getting there. To his credit, even during this difficult time, he's remained active in many school activities and refuses to give them up! This is a far cry from the retreating child of a few years ago. I know that OCD is going to be a problem for my son throughout his life. Because of the work he did in therapy, he now has the skills to manage it. This had made all the difference in the world to my family.

Sharon, mother of Robert

We know there will be bumps along the way and that we will have to get through them using what we have learned.

Diane, mother of Nancy

You know by now that OCD can wax and wane in severity. The times when OCD resurfaces are known as "slips." When slips are severe, they are called relapses. Be prepared for slips and relapses—they are a part of recovery. People with OCD are more prone to slips and relapses during times of stress or transition. Now that you and your child know how to handle OCD, slips and relapses may never be as difficult as the time before your child's OCD was treated. Here's a plan for slip recovery:

Table 16: Steps for Slip Recovery

✓ Expect it and plan for it
✓ Put it in perspective
✓ Don't quit
✓ Pick yourself up
✓ RIDE the Worry Hill again
✓ Scale back
✓ Celebrate successes
✓ Plan for future slips

❖ *Expect it and plan for it*

When you expect it, you are not surprised. When you are not surprised, you are not caught off guard. You can then take control of it.

❖ *Put it in perspective*

It's just a slip, not a failure. It's normal to have slips and relapses. It does not mean that therapy did not work for your child or that he will never overcome OCD. If you don't put it in perspective, you will get demoralized. When you're demoralized, you don't have resolve or energy and your self-talk turns into a self-fulfilling prophecy.

❖ *Don't quit*

It is the only way you can really fail. Have optimism and the resolve to overcome OCD.

❖ *Pick yourself up*

What would you do if you fell off the bicycle? If you could, you would try to get up, dust yourself and get going. If you found that you couldn't move or that your ankle was hurt, you would ask for help. If necessary, you might have to get medical help of varying degrees, depending on the nature of the injury. Eventually, you would be back on your bicycle again, although, depending on the nature of your injury, it might take time. However, if you stayed down and did nothing about it, you'd be there forever.

❖ RIDE *the Worry Hill again*

This is the time for your child to face his fears, more than ever. Exposure should be used with greater vigor than ever to confront the fears that are creeping back in. The idea is to take charge and not let the fears take charge. Be systematic about identifying which fears are an issue, making a hierarchy and going after them with a vengeance.

❖ *Scale back*

Deal with only the necessary things in life during times of stress and waxing. Cut back on everything but essential responsibilities until things settle down; then let your child gradually work his way back up.

❖ *Celebrate successes*

There will more hills in the future, but for every one your child climbs, the thrill of the coast is awaiting him on the other side. Celebrate your child's successes, even if they are small.

❖ *Plan for future slips*

When things have settled, do "preventive" ERP exercises—like preventive dental care. Identify tough areas and intentionally seek out exposures to toughen oneself for future relapses.

A NEW VISION

It is time to find a new vision for your child and yourself. There's no perfect world, no perfect parent and no perfect child. This you know well. Now it's time to find the beauty in your child, to seek all that he or she is and will continue to be in spite of OCD. Reclaim your lives from OCD. Rediscover life beyond OCD.

Now is the time to get back to all the things you put on the back burner when you first developed your battle plan for OCD. Take your time and add them back slowly. Don't rush into it. This is not a sprint, it's a marathon, so pace yourself. Perhaps you will find that some of them don't need to be returned to their place at all. You will find more time on your hands, now that OCD isn't taking up all of it. Your child has to make up for lost time socializing, learning and having fun. Get back to the regular beat of life; encourage your child to be a child again. Let your new vision for your child include a better relationship and a stronger bond with you. Perhaps it will include better communication and deeper compassion between you. Most of all, may it always include hope.

Let your child approach life at her own pace. Don't push too hard. Remember that your child does not enjoy OCD any more than you do, so be patient and supportive as he works his own way through the challenges of recovery. Be patient as he is catching up with his schoolwork. Much of the school year may turn out to be a less than ideal experience academically. Remember that your child is ill. Give him time to recover.

It's also time for a new vision for yourself. Take care of yourself and nurture yourself—make this an expectation rather than a luxury. You never know when the next crisis will arise; you will be better equipped to handle it when you are well cared for. Get the rest you need, the sleep you have lost. Do something fun for yourself. Get back on track with your relationships with your spouse, family and friends. See a therapist if you need help negotiating the rough starts to these relationships. Remember, it's okay to get help.

GIVING BACK

Many families find that reaching out and helping someone else who is just beginning the journey of life with OCD is an immensely healing and redeeming experience. It allows them to make good come out of the bad. It helps them make peace with the illness when they take the "high road."

How can you give back? Perhaps you could join an OCD support group. If you can't find one, perhaps *you* could start one. After all, if there isn't a support group, someone has to start one. That someone could be you. You will not have any trouble finding members for your group, I assure you. Ask your therapist to spread the word among the families she treats and be prepared to answer the phone.

I've witnessed the power of "giving back" first hand on the *ocdandparenting* online support group for parents of children with OCD, to which I am a professional advisor. The group started with a handful of members in 1999 and exceeds 450 members as of this writing. There are parents from all over the US and all over the world—from Australia, Canada, Great Britain and Lebanon. There are newcomers and veterans of OCD in this group and they give tirelessly to each other, sharing their fears, worries, moments of despair and their triumphs. They care and they share, with the compassion and understanding that only comes with walking the same path. There are many parents whose children and families are now doing well. Yet, they spend many hours sharing experiences, giving support and encouraging parents who are struggling to find their way through the maze of OCD. Why do they do it? Where do they find the time and energy? Many parents say that it comes from the healing power of giving back what you have received.

THE WINGS TO FLY

Finally, you must give your child the wings to fly. Allowing your child to develop self-reliance in handling OCD and life is a gift that will last forever. Encourage your child to take risks because not all dangers are bad. Teach your child to "stick it out to the top of the Worry Hill," because he has the power and the courage to do it. Seek and provide your child with opportunities to overcome fear. Encourage independent activities. Such experiences will build your child's self-confidence and belief in his own capabilities. When challenged and hesitant, remind your child of his skills, resources and previous successes. No matter how small they are, they are still successes.

And finally, some words of wisdom from the brave warriors:

Robert, now 14 years old, came to treatment for OCD four years ago, when he was 10.

In my experience, the 10 rules listed below can help you deal with OCD. However, they will not rid you of OCD completely. They will only help you get through it in your everyday life.

1. Know always that you CAN get through it.

2. If you feel like someone doesn't understand what you are going through, try talking it over with them calmly.

3. Don't expect to get rid of OCD overnight, just do your best not to let it wear you down.

4. Try and remind yourself that everyone worries about things.

5. If you are being overwhelmed, take deep breaths.

6. Try to focus on the good things in life if you are having a problem.

7. Sometimes, it is better not to fight it, just face it.

8. Don't forget that there are people who can help you.

9. It is very hard sometimes but try not to ask people to reassure you that you are ok, and that your fear isn't true.

10. It will not be an easy road, but if you try, you will usually succeed in dealing with a fear.

Robert, age 12, CBT "graduate"

Robert's wisdom is so valuable because it is hard-earned wisdom. He discovered each of these "truths" for himself, from his own journey towards mastery of OCD.

And some insights from David and Helen, Danny's grandparents. Danny was four when he was diagnosed with OCD and started treatment. He is now nine years old:

We recognized Danny as having OCD and Tourettes the early summer of his fourth year. He turned four in May and over the Fathers Day weekend had a serious OCD event. Helen was with Danny; I was away on a trip. He could not stop washing his hands. Helen felt terror and fear at the beginning but was able to control those feelings by researching the disorders. I reacted the same way as Helen, controlling my upset by researching and gathering as much information as possible. Through Danny's pediatrician we were referred to a physician but it didn't work. He recognized Danny's behavior as OCD but his first recommendation was medication. Helen and I did research but nowhere in the medical literature could we find anything about medicating a child as young as Danny. His mother Sarah and we felt his brain was still developing and there just wasn't evidence to show injury would not occur. We were just not ready to take that chance. We were able to get another referral and we knew then that we were on the right track.

What was really scary was that once the diagnosis was made we could think back to obsessive behaviors much earlier with Danny. He had to be covered just right even way back when he was in his crib! It continued when he moved to a regular bed. Of course the covers were never right. Hindsight let us realize these were beginning OCD behaviors.

We have had many triumphs with Danny. Following your directions we all helped him get over a near-crippling obsession with blood. We got control of bugs. We found the patience to accept uncontrollable behavior. We had to learn there are things he can't control and maybe we can help him learn to harness. One important technique we utilize is redirecting the situation or behavior. It just isn't any good to butt heads with Danny. It is like two trains crashing together; nobody survives. Better to switch the tracks and go in another direction.

As he has gotten older we can address behavior as OCD or Tourettes. In Danny's case the OCD is primary and there isn't much evidence of Tourettes. At least not to us. There are still some rituals that we find a problem but to Danny they are not and we try to let him control them. His ability to exercise self-control is evident this year with his teacher. She exercises an iron control in her classroom. Danny has exercised great self-control in this room. He verbalizes how hard it is for him and we praise him for doing such a *good job. Anyone who tries to impose their will upon Danny might win the immediate battle but they loose his respect. He is very smart and forms very insightful opinions. We think how hard it must have been years ago for children with OCD or Tourettes. They were just called bad kids; out of control.*

When he was four and five we found that walking and swinging helped him relax and spent hours walking the neighborhood and swinging on our swing set. The neighbors commented on Danny and me out in a snow-covered yard, swinging away. His kindergarten and first grade teachers used the walking therapy as a way to calm him but he soon learned if the classroom situation didn't suit him then a few moves could get him out walking the halls. He admitted using this to get out of doing something he disliked.

There have been times when OCD caused me to laugh inside while others looked on questioningly. Like the time at the zoo when one of the zoo workers was doing a show-and-tell with the five-year-olds. He showed the skulls of two different animals and asked, "Do you know why their teeth are different?" One skull was a cat and the other a reptile of some sort. I'm not sure why, but the answer he was looking for was that the cat was warm-blooded. Well, the kids kept saying things like "Is it real?" and "Did you kill it?" The man was mildly frustrated so he said, "The cat is warm blooded and the snake isn't." Well, Danny jumped up and started saying, in an alarmed voice, "Don't say blood, I don't like blood." I was able to calm him quickly with redirection but others were looking like "What just happened?"

Our advice to parents is get some very good doctors, be very involved and vocal in school as an advocate for your child. Danny has a very hard time doing things that come very easily to other children. He has learned to raise his hand and wait his turn at school, but he often talks non-stop when he gets home. We always give him some space and wiggle room unless what he's doing is dangerous. Danny is very sweet almost to a fault. There isn't a mean bone in his body. He can't understand why kids are mean to each other. When we fall into bed at night exhausted if Danny had a good day, we've all had a good day.

Like so many others, Danny's grandparents David and Helen and his mother Sarah have found their new vision for Danny and themselves. My wish for you is that you find a new vision for your child, yourself and your family.

Resources

Baer, L. (2000). *Getting control*. New York: Plume.

Baer, L. (2000). *The Imp of the Mind*. New York: Dutton.

Chansky. T. E. (2000). *Freeing your child from Obsessive-Compulsive Disorder*. New York: Crown.

Dornbush, M.P., & Pruitt, S.K. (1995). *Teaching the tiger*. Duarte, CA: Hope Press.

Gravitz, H. L. (1998). *Obsessive-Compulsive Disorder: New Help for the family*. Santa Barbara, CA: Healing Visions Press.

Greene, R.W. (1998). *The explosive child*. New York: Harper Collins.

Greist, J.H., Jefferson, J.W., Marks, I.M. (1986). *Anxiety and its treatment: Help is available*. Washington, DC: American Psychiatric Press.

Johnston H.F., Fruehling, J.J. (2002). *Obsessive-Compulsive Disorder in children and adolescents: A Guide*. Madison, WI: Obsessive Compulsive Information Center, Madison Institute of Medicine.

March, J.S., & Mulle, K. (1998). *OCD in children and adolescents*. New York: Guilford.

Moritz, E. K. & Jablonsky, J. (1998). *Blink, Blink, Clop, Clop, Why do we do things we can't stop*. Secaucus, NJ: Child's Work/Child's Play.

Penzel, F. (2000). *Obsessive-Compulsive Disorders: A complete guide to getting well and staying well*. New York: Oxford.

Rapoport, J.L. (1989). *The boy who couldn't stop washing*. New York: Penguin Books.

Swedo, S.A. & Leonard, H.L. (1998). *Is it just a phase?* New York: Golden Books.

Wagner, A. P. (2000). *Up and Down the Worry Hill: A children's book about Obsessive-Compulsive Disorder*. Available at Lighthouse Press (888)-749-8768 (toll free US) www.Lighthouse-Press.com

Wagner, A. P. (2002). *Worried No More: Help and Hope for Anxious Children*. Available at Lighthouse Press (888)-749-8768 (toll free US) www.Lighthouse-Press.com

Wagner, A. P. (2007). *Treatment of OCD in Children and Adolescents: Professional's Kit.* Available exclusively at Lighthouse Press www.Lighthouse-Press.com

Waltz, M. (2000). *Obsessive Compulsive Disorder: Help for Children and Adolescents.* Sebastopol, CA: O'Reilly.

Wilens, T.E. (1999). *Straight talk about psychiatric medications for kids.* New York: Guilford Press.

Support Organizations

Association for Advancement of Behavior Therapy (AABT)
305 Seventh Avenue, 16th Floor
New York, NY 10001-6008
212-647-1890
www.aabt.org

Anxiety Disorders Association of America (ADAA)
8730 Georgia Avenue Suite 600
Silver Spring, MD 20910
(240) 485-1001
www.adaa.org

National Alliance for the Mentally Ill (NAMI)
200 N. Glebe Road, Suite 1015
Arlington, VA 22203-3754
703-524-7600
www.nami.org

Obsessive-Compulsive Foundation (OCF)
P.O. Box 9573
New Haven, CT 06535
203-315-2190
www.ocfoundation.org

Obsessive Compulsive Information Center (OCIC)
Madison Institute of Medicine
7617 Mineral Point Road
Madison, WI 53717
608-827-2470
www.miminc.org
www.factsforhealth.org

Tourette Syndrome Association (TSA)
42-40 Bell Boulevard
New York, NY 11361
718-224-2999
www.tsa-usa.org

Web-based Resources

Online support group for parents of children with OCD

    http://groups.yahoo.com/group/ocdandparenting

Online Teen OCD support group—moderated by an adult

    www.angelfire.com/il/TeenOCD

Online Children's OCD support group—moderated by an adult

    http://groups.yahoo.com/group/OCDKidsSupportGroup

National Association of School Psychologists

    www.naspweb.org

The PACER Center

    www.pacer.org

Special Education Resources

    www.seriweb.com

Peter Wright, an attorney and expert in special education issues

    www.wrightslaw.com

Index

Numerics

5-hydroxytryptamine (5-HT)

   See serotonin.

A

abrupt changes in enabling behaviors, 278

abuse it, lose it, 351

acceptance, 184–185, 212, 224, 403

accommodations for OCD, 378–381

adult vs. child OCD, 44

adversity to opportunity, 403–405

advocating for your child in school, 388–389

age of onset, 43

allying with your child, 267–269, 291

Anafranil (clomipramine)

   See antidepressants *and* medications for OCD.

anorexia nervosa, 71

anticipate and dissipate triggers, 347

anticipatory anxiety, 126, 131, 233, 256

antidepressants

   citalopram, 155, 162

   clomipramine, 103, 154, 164, 168, 169, 175, 179

   fluoxetine, 155, 159, 162, 167

   fluvoxamine, 155, 162, 170

   medications for OCD, 153–155

   paroxetine, 155, 159, 162

   selective serotonin reuptake inhibitors, 155

   sertraline, 155, 162, 167

   trazadone, 167

   tricyclic, 154

   See also medications for OCD.

anxiety

   and habituation, 122

   effect on treatment success, 142

   parental, 80, 111, 195, 216

anxiety disorders

   and OCD, 59–65

   generalized anxiety, 59, 61

   panic disorder, 64

   phobias, 63

   post-traumatic stress disorder, 61

   separation anxiety, 59

   social phobia, 64

Anxiety Disorders Association of America (ADAA), 84, 187, 193

apologizing rituals, 38

arranging rituals, 38, 370

Asperger's Syndrome

   description, 68

Anxiety and OCD Workshops

Aureen Wagner, Ph.D., offers a variety of Workshops on anxiety and its treatment for Parents, Schools and Health care Professionals.

Testimonials from recent workshops

"This was one of the best presentations I have ever been to. Wonderful style, great handouts, clear, useful information. Thank you!"

"Dr. Wagner's workshop was far beyond excellent. Well organized, clear, thoughtful speaker, very insightful answers to our questions."

"It was fabulous to learn 'child friendly' ways to talk to children."

"Very helpful and down to earth in concrete, effective strategies for children, families and schools."

"The creative strategies are very relevant and useful to our work in schools. The detailed handouts will be a great reference."

"Dr. Wagner's metaphors and conceptualizations were unique, very appealing and made perfect sense!"

"Excellent presentation! Very helpful - warm, articulate and positive. Nice balance of lecture, question/answer and large/small group."

"Great presentation—interesting, informative, well prepared, organized. Wonderful overview, clear messages and facts."

"Very articulate, a great "coach", and wonderful use of humor."

Dr. Wagner is so articulate; the presentation was effectively and efficiently packed with useful information. Thank you."

"Usually, conferences like this bore you to tears. This was a super surprise and excellent!"

Please visit **www.Lighthouse-Press.com**
for a complete description of workshops

Up and Down the Worry Hill: A Children's Book about Obsessive-Compulsive Disorder and its Treatment

Self-Help Book Recommendation
www.abct.org **ASSOCIATION for BEHAVIORAL**
2011 **and COGNITIVE THERAPIES**

"The **best** book available for children with Obsessive-Compulsive Disorder!"

Charles Mansueto, Ph.D.,
Member, Scientific Advisory Board,
Obsessive Compulsive Foundation

For children ages 4-16 with OCD, siblings and their classmates

This uniquely creative and heart warming book uses a powerful real-life metaphor to help parents and professionals explain OCD clearly and simply through the eyes of a child. Children and adults will identify with Casey's initial struggle with OCD, his sense of hope when he learns about treatment, his relief that neither he nor his parents are to blame, and eventually, his victory over OCD.

"It's a **masterpiece!** It captures and conveys the essence of effective behavior therapy for OCD...the metaphors are perfect...Parents, teachers and, most importantly, children will benefit enormously from reading it."
   John Greist, M.D., Distinguished Senior Scientist, Madison Institute of Medicine

"A **most helpful** book... carefully motivates the child for treatment."
   Michael Jenike, M.D. Professor of Psychiatry, Harvard Medical School

---

The <u>only</u> Integrated Set of Resources for Children with OCD, their Parents and their Therapists!
Children: *Up and Down the Worry Hill: A Children's Book about OCD*
Parents: *What to do when your Child has OCD: Strategies and Solutions*
Therapists: *Treatment of OCD in Children and Adolescents: Professional's Kit*

Putting the Groundbreaking
Worry Hill Treatment Approach for OCD
into action!

For clinicians

Treatment of OCD in Children and Adolescents: Professional's Kit

This newly revised and expanded popular resource for professionals includes second editions of both the Therapy Manual and Teaching Tools. Dr. Wagner shares her internationally acclaimed Worry Hill protocol for OCD, along with clinical pearls from her many years of experience. She provides expert guidance on special topics including:

- Developing treatment readiness
- Collaborating with parents
- Working with reluctant children
- Overcoming treatment challenges

The Professional's Kit includes:
1. Cognitive-Behavioral Therapy Manual (Expanded Second Edition)
2. Complete set of thirty 8.5" x 11" Teaching Tools (Comb bound, Second Edition)
3. Over 35 ready-to-print-and-use forms on CD (*PC only*)
4. Worry Hill Memory Cards and Feeling Thermometers for use in working with children and families

Benefits:
- User-friendly and appealing
- Step-by-step protocols
- Easy application and record-keeping

- Clear and self-explanatory
- Detailed case examples

"This manual is the **best available resource for clinicians**...clear, concise and accurate... with a rich supply of clinical insights and practical tips. I highly recommend it to all practitioners, from beginners to seasoned clinicians."

Charles Mansueto, Ph.D., Scientific Advisory Board, Obsessive Compulsive Foundation

"This is a **valuable** treatment manual for youngsters with OCD. I **recommend it with enthusiasm!**"

Judith Rapoport, M.D., Chief, Child Psychiatry, National Institute of Mental Health

Worried No More: Help and Hope for Anxious Children

For parents, school professionals
and clinicians

Serious anxiety is the most common emotional problem in youngsters: however, success rates with early recognition and proper treatment are excellent. In this second edition of her landmark book, Dr. Wagner brings scientifically proven and time-tested Cognitive-Behavioral Therapy (CBT) strategies to parents, school professionals and healthcare professionals who care for children.

- How to tell normal from problem anxiety
- Types of anxiety disorders
- Red flags for anxiety
- Expressions of anxiety in school
- Valuable strategies at home and school
- How to find the right professional help
- Effective treatments
- Dos and don'ts of parenting
- Step-by-step plans with examples

This highly acclaimed book is packed with easily readable information, highly effective practical strategies and step-by-step action plans to help youngsters with:

- Separation anxiety
- School refusal
- Excessive shyness
- Worry

- Phobias
- Panic
- Disasters and tragedies
- Obsessions and compulsions

Self-Help Book Recommendation
www.abct.org ASSOCIATION for BEHAVIORAL
2011 and COGNITIVE THERAPIES

"A **masterpiece**...so clear and so practical, that this is the book every school must have and every parent of a child with anxiety should read and reread... provides priceless understanding of the process of excessive anxiety and how to control it."
John Greist, M.D., Distinguished Senior Scientist, Madison Institute of Medicine

"A **very helpful and practical book** that will be immensely helpful to parents and teachers. I highly recommend it!"
Michael Jenike, M.D., Professor of Psychiatry, Harvard Medical School
Chairman, Scientific Advisory Board, Obsessive-Compulsive Foundation

Worried No More: Teaching Tools and Forms on CD

Software for use with PC's only.

The companion kit for school professionals and therapists

This toolkit helps professionals put Worried No More into action with anxious children and their families. It includes 33 colorful *Teaching Tools* (easy-to-use, 8.5 x 11" flip cards), ready-to-use Microsoft® Powerpoint® slides (Viewer software included), ready-to-print-and-use *Forms on CD* and *Feeling Thermometers* to convey key treatment concepts.

Benefits:

- Powerful visual tools for teaching
- Appealing to children and families
- Increases motivation and compliance
- Improves Communication and Learning
- Convenient, Easy-to-use
- Enhances record-keeping

Forms:

- Corrective Learning Experiences
- Parent-Teacher Log
- Home Behavior Observations
- School Behavior Observations
- My Thoughts and Feelings
- The Feeling Thermometer
- My Fear Ladder
- Exposure Progress Record
- Facing My Fears
- The Worry Hill Memory Card

Teaching Tools (sample):

- The Anxiety Triad
- The Noise at the Window
- Physical Signs of Worry
- The Vicious Cycle of Avoidance
- Lessons to be Learned
- Calm Thinking
- Exposure
- Habituation
- Anticipatory Anxiety
- Up and Down the Worry Hill
- The 3 P's of Parenting
- Appropriate Attending
- The *Fearmometer*
- Self-Reliance

www.Lighthouse-Press.com

Anxiety and OCD at School:
Live Workshop for School Professionals

For use with personal computers (PC) with a CD-ROM drive.
Printable 22 page handout.
Running time approximately 1 hour, 50 minutes.

This workshop is ideal for a broad range of school staff, including:

- Mainstream and Special Education Teachers

- Teacher's Aides

- Counselors

- Social Workers

- Speech and Occupational Therapists

- Administrators

- School Psychologists

An audio and slide presentation recorded during one of Dr. Wagner's most popular workshops for School Professionals. Just like a real workshop, you'll listen to Dr. Wagner as you view the slides that accompany the presentation, and follow along with the handout. Packed with practical advice, you'll want to listen to this presentation repeatedly. This CD is ideal for staff development trainings or inservices. Dr. Wagner is a highly engaging and sought-after speaker whose workshops consistently receive outstanding reviews. You'll benefit from her many years of working with anxious children, her user-friendly conceptualizations and her practical Worry Hill innovations.

Comments from Recent Participants

"On a scale of 1 to 10, this **was a definite 10!** Most helpful were the practical strategies for anxiety."

"**Great, great speaker!** Best workshop I have attended in many years (in 28 years as a professional)."

Special Offers

The Worry Hill Master Set for the Treatment of OCD

Order this set and save!

Includes:

1. Up and Down the Worry Hill
2. What to do when your Child has OCD
3. Treatment of OCD in Children and Adolescents: Professional's Kit

. . . .

The Anxiety Treatment Master Set for the Treatment of Anxiety Problems

Order this set and save!

Includes:

1. Worried No More:
   Help and Hope for Anxious Children
2. Worried No More:
   Teaching Tools and Forms on CD

Special Offers

The School Professional's Master Set

Order this set
and save!

Includes:

1. Up and Down the Worry Hill
2. Worried No More: Help and Hope for Anxious Children
3. Worried No More: Teaching Tools and Forms on CD (PC)
4. Anxiety and OCD at School: Live Workshop for School Professionals (PC)

FREE!

Watch videos on anxiety and OCD-related topics
from www.Lighthouse-Press.com

Or visit us to learn about new products, updates,
conferences and workshops

FREE!

A printed color card of the *Feeling Thermometer*
for easy use with your child.

To customers in the USA only, while supplies last.

To receive one, please send an email to
CustomerService@Lighthouse-Press.com with
"Send Feeling Thermometer" in the subject line
and your name and mailing address in the body of the message.

The Essential One-Hour Crash Course for Parents

Worried No More: The One-Hour Workshop for Parents

Topics Include:
- The Many Faces of Anxiety
- Red flags and early warning signs
- The vicious cycle of avoidance
- Parenting traps
- Scientifically-proven techniques
- The Worry Hill that helps kids conquer anxiety
- Parenting that works

- For use with personal computers (PC) with a CD-ROM drive.
- Audio presentation with slides. Running time approximately 1 hr., 15 minutes.

Comments from Parents:
- *"Fantastic! Absolutely superior."*
- *"One of the most valuable workshops ever. I wish I learned this years ago."*

Expert Clinician Consultation

Dr. Aureen Wagner provides consultation to health care professionals and school professionals on the assessment and treatment of anxiety disorders in children and adolescents. Consultation is tailored to suit your individual or group needs.

Topics may include but are not limited to:

- Assessment
- Differential diagnosis
- Treatment plans
- Exposure hierarchies

- Cognitive strategies
- Socratic technique
- Treatment reluctance
- Challenges in treatment

Telephone sessions are scheduled at mutually agreeable times.
For information on fees and scheduling, please visit
www.anxietywellness.com.

For ordering information on these and other resources by

Dr. Wagner, please visit www.Lighthouse-Press.com